Euratlantica

Changing Perspectives of the European Elites

M.I.T. Studies in Comparative Politics

Under the general editorship of Harold D. Lasswell, Daniel Lerner, and Ithiel de Sola Pool.

The Emerging Elite: A Study of Political Leadership in Ceylon, Marshall Singer, 1964.

The Turkish Political Elite, Frederick W. Frey, 1965.

World Revolutionary Elites: Studies in Coercive Ideological Movements, Harold D. Lasswell and Daniel Lerner, editors, 1965.

Language of Politics: Studies in Quantitative Semantics, Harold D. Lasswell, Nathan Leites, and Associates, 1965 (reissue).

The General Inquirer: A Computer Approach to Content Analysis, Philip J. Stone, Dexter C. Dunphy, Marshall S. Smith, Daniel M. Ogilvie, 1967.

Political Elites: A Select Computerized Bibliography, Carl Beck and J. Thomas McKechnie, 1968.

Force and Folly: Essays on Foreign Affairs and the History of Ideas, Hans Speier, 1969.

Quantitative Ecological Analysis in the Social Sciences, Mattei Dogan and Stein Rokkan, editors, 1969.

Euratlantica: Changing Perspectives of the European Elites, Daniel Lerner and Morton Gorden, 1969.

A Study of the
Center for International Studies
Massachusetts Institute of Technology

Published Jointly with the
M.I.T. Studies in Comparative Politics

Euratlantica

Changing Perspectives of the European Elites

Daniel Lerner
and
Morton Gorden

The M.I.T. Press

Cambridge, Massachusetts, and London, England

For Harold Dwight Lasswell
Policy Scientist

Acknowledgments

WE ACKNOWLEDGE first our obligations to the thousands of persons who contributed to TEEPS. Most of these are our panelists, who gave many hours of their valuable time to answer our questions. Taking this as a civic obligation, many of our panelists responded over several years. To all of the TEEPS people who told us what they thought, we are deeply obliged.

TEEPS was born and raised in the M.I.T. Center for International Studies, the most remarkable company of scholars it has been our good fortune to be associated with in academic life. Special thanks go to its Director, Max F. Millikan, who exemplifies for all of us the American ideal of "scholar, gentleman, democrat." Professor Donald L. M. Blackmer guided us wisely and patiently at many critical points. To name the CENIS colleagues who have both stimulated and restrained us, by applying their superior knowledge and judgment to our problems, would be to call a well-known honor roll of American social scientists. We simply thank them, for they know as well as we do how much we owe each and all of them.

What made TEEPS possible, as an exploration of contemporary history, was the intellectual and operational guidance of key people in each country. From start to end, these people were our counselors: Professors Raymond Aron and Jean Stoetzel in France, Professors René König and Erwin K. Scheuch in Germany, Dr. Mark Abrams in Britain. For their faithful and lasting interest over these long years of hard work, we are grateful.

Others who helped over the years in the complex tasks of data collection were Jacqueline Bissery in Brussels; Professor Jean Labbens in Lyons; Professor Dr. Renate Mayntz in Berlin; Professor R. T. McKenzie in London; Dr. Max Ralis in Munich; Helène Riffault in Paris; Dr. Peter Schmidt in Frankfurt. Memorable over our data-collecting years was the brilliant team of French interviewers, which included notably Henri d'Armagnac, Geneviève Auclair, J. J. Marchand, Napoléon Murat, Jacqueline Palmade, Josette Zarka, and Mariza Zavalloni. They labored long and well in a new and difficult vineyard.

In the data-processing phase, we learned much from the early interoffice memos by Lotte Bailyn, Judith Bergson, Judith Davison, Ingrid Hoffmann, and Suzanne Keller. Valuable contributions were made by undergraduates who wrote senior theses at M.I.T.: Judson H. Benjamin, John Child, Jr., Peter Dietrich, John Golden, Bruce Jacobs, and Marc Shulman; *licence* (master's) theses at the Sorbonne, notably by those who had been TEEPS interviewers such as Auclair, Palmade, Zarka, Zavalloni; and the M.I.T. doctoral theses by Morton Gorden, Catherine McArdle Kelleher, Marguerite Nüsslé Kramer, Howard Rosenthal, and Albert H. Teich. Most of these persons, as well as Shridhar Shrimali, were employed at various times as research assistants on the TEEPS project.

Help in the management of the complex TEEPS data base was given throughout the last period of analysis by the inventors of ADMINS, Stuart D. McIntosh and David M. Griffel. The management of man-machine interactions so critical to the final phase of writing was mainly in the hands of Judith C. Spicer, Carolyn R. Teich, and Albert H. Teich, whose special contributions are referenced throughout. The primary editing of the manuscript was done by Nancy C. Poling.

For their reading and valuable criticism of various drafts we are grateful to Carroll G. Bowen, Director of the M.I.T. Press; to Emile Noël of the EEC; and to Professors Hayward Alker, Karl Deutsch, Carl Friedrich, Everett E. Hagen, Paul Kecskemeti, Harold D. Lasswell, Herbert McClosky, and Robert Strausz-Hupé. J.-R. Rabier made possible the studies of the Eurocrats on which Chapter Eleven is based and was a wise counselor. There can be no question of guilt by association, for most of these esteemed colleagues saw only portions of the earlier drafts and none has seen the final version here presented.

Any enterprise that endures as long as TEEPS becomes a family affair. As the demands of field work increasingly affected where they lived and where they went to school, how they dressed and what they ate, the Lerner family became deeply involved in the progress of TEEPS. Amy was born in Paris during the 1955 survey;

Tom became a firm supporter of the "yes-no-don't know" work during the 1961 survey; Louise checked tables and typed pages in the final rush to the printer. Mrs. Jean Lerner nourished TEEPS, along with her other children, throughout the long gestation. When the demands of TEEPS entered the Gorden family, their response was "yes" rather than "no" with very few "don't knows." Family resources were allocated to facilitative efforts with good cheer. And for the many moments which brought the Lerners and Gordens together to share their common burdens, we can only offer thanks and admire the good will which made the difficult tasks seem easier.

We thank, finally, those institutions which provided indispensable financial resources throughout the TEEPS decade. The series of studies on which this book is based has been supported by funds received from several sources, most particularly from the Ford Foundation; without the Foundation's generous grants to M.I.T. since 1954, the Center's research on European attitudes would not have been possible. Additional support for portions of the research has been received from the Center for Space Research at M.I.T., the Carnegie Corporation, and the Department of the Navy. Their funding of the research does not imply endorsement by these organizations of any of the views and findings expressed herein. At every point in its long history, TEEPS was a completely public investigation and its data are freely available in each host country as well as in the United States.

DANIEL LERNER
MORTON GORDEN

Cambridge, Massachusetts
Philadelphia, Pennsylvania
July 1968

Contents

Euratlantica

Changing Perspectives
of the European Elites

General Introduction

THIS BOOK seeks to write contemporary history in a new way. It uses methods of social research that were not available to historians of more remote times and that generally are not used to study our own time as "history." What we mean by history is the perspective that looks at the present as a temporal sequence from the past to the future. The study looks at Europe over the decade 1955–1965 in this perspective.

To write contemporary history in this way, we have adapted that remarkable instrument of social research called the sample survey. In some of its varied uses, such as predicting the behavior of voters and shoppers, the sample survey has become a precision instrument unmatched in the annals of social observation. In the study of attitudes, where there is no specific "payoff" item such as a vote or a purchase to test inferences, no such degree of precision is expected or claimed. Indeed, our claims for the particular adaptation of sample survey method used in this book must be very modest. Only the value our findings may add to the observations of contemporary Europe made by many astute scholars and journalists will justify the time, money, and labor entailed in using the sample survey for this purpose. This will take some years to evaluate. In launching the ship, we are aware that only the sea can decide.

Our aim was to learn how the elites of postwar Europe would face the reality of their diminished postwar power — as elites, as nations, as a continent — and how they would go about the tasks of positive construction. This obliged us to document current history as it happened by recording the attitudes of people who were shaping its course. As the complexity of this task became clearer, our conceptual and methodological perspectives broadened. What had originally been planned as a two-year survey became the ten-

year survey called TEEPS (The European Elite Panel Survey*),
extended in five interviewing waves: 1955, 1956, 1959, 1961, and
1965. It became not only longitudinal but comparative, thus exem-
plifying in a sustained project of empirical research the Lasswellian
conception of social science as comparative history.

The TEEPS project recorded over 4,000 long personal interviews
with leaders in the principal sectors of public life (government,
politics, business, labor, communications, pressure groups, the
church, the military) in Britain, France, and Germany. These were
the three great powers of prewar Europe. How their leaders faced
their diminished postwar potency would deeply affect the future
of the European continent, the Atlantic region, and the world arena.
These considerations, which we discuss in Chapters One and Two,
shaped our procedure as detailed in Chapter Three. The 4,000 personal interviews are our essential data base. We went beyond this
limit in the quest for a clear and comprehensive picture of Europe's
historical situation — all the while seeking, not always successfully,
to correct our errors of omission and commission in the TEEPS
data base as we detected them.

When we were done, we had added another 4,000 self-administered questionnaires and several hundreds of "special interviews."
These studies, most of which are reported only briefly in the present
book, were done as the need to amplify our data base became
persuasive and the occasion became opportune (which is to say,
additional research funds were received). Thus, it early became
clear that French business leaders were not as hidebound (*fermé*)
as our reading of earlier social commentators had led us to believe.
To check this, we distributed among French business leaders a
questionnaire which received a huge response. This showed a degree of support for European integration in general, and the European Defense Community in particular, previously unsuspected
by any commentators. This productive test of conventional beliefs
about French business leaders became the first TEEPS publication.[1]

In like fashion, we became convinced that *gauchisme* (leftism) in
an increasingly prosperous France was a phenomenon that had to
be re-examined at the roots. Convinced by our French consultants

---

* The acronym for our study is TEEPS — The European Elite Panel Survey.
While one of the authors has been in Europe every year since 1944 and
while we rely on this quarter century of European experience for background,
our evidence is adduced mainly from the strictly comparable survey data which,
as explained in Chapter Three, cover the British, French, and German elites
during the years 1955, 1956, 1959, 1961, 1965.

and by our own observations that the school system was a taproot, we sent out a mail questionnaire to the *corps enseignant* represented by a sample of the heads of *lycées* throughout France. We also detailed a wise and skilled French ex-Communist to obtain over seventy interviews with leaders of the Communist Party and its controlled labor union, the CGT (Confédération Général du Travail). To check any bias produced by these sources in our interpretation of leftism and rightism — which is among the important findings of this study — we had a Catholic professor and a team of his best students interview over a hundred leftist Catholic participants in a "*Semaine Sociale*" at Nancy devoted to discussion of social problems and policies. Our understanding of *gauchisme* was confirmed by the prevailing attitudes among these leaders of the "Christian Left." (These are not detailed separately in this book, but they suggest that the Christian Left in postwar Europe merits close empirical study by future scholars.)

Our interpretation of postwar nationalism and socialism was confirmed as well by the findings of a questionnaire distributed to students at the *grandes écoles*, those special graduate schools of France designed to produce the *next* generation of elites. Readers interested in the world-wide phenomenon of "student protest" will find in these records striking illustrations and substantial confirmations of the hypothesis that conventional ideology (Marxism) and classic nationalism are passing from the European scene. These students, a few years older than the Sorbonne rioters of 1968, did not know (DK) whether many of the key issues posed by our questionnaire came from Left or Right — and could not have cared less. Nor did they evaluate these issues in terms of what was "good for France." They reconfirmed strongly our conclusion that the European elites have turned from ideology to pragmatism, from nationalism to transnationalism, from parochialism to pluralism. These are the themes of this book.*

Other "bits" of data have been collected, such as our personal interviews with virtually all *présidents du conseil* of the Fourth Re-

---

* Our conclusions differ markedly, in some of these respects, from those reported in the excellent studies by Herbert Luethy, *A l'Heure de son Clocher,* and by Laurence W. Wylie, *Village in the Vaucluse.* The reader should bear in mind that these earlier studies dealt with villagers and "average" people; TEEPS deals with the elites over a decade of critical change in their thinking. The TEEPS interpretations receive some striking, and wholly independent, confirmation in the later study of French regional and rural life by Henri Mendras, *Las Fin des Paysans,* scheduled for publication by The M.I.T. Press.

public in France, many of the cabinet ministers in postwar Britain, and some of the newly reactivated generals in postwar Germany. These increments of data have been processed, along with the central data base of the TEEPS surveys, by a variety of computerized techniques. These techniques are reported in the annexes, for the information of those readers who are interested in more detailed accounts of our procedures in data collecting, data collating, data comparing, and data computerizing. Suffice it here to say that we began the TEEPS survey at a time when most social scientists used a counter-sorter and only a few adventurous persons used an IBM 101; we completed this book after many experiments with the M.I.T. CTSS system of console-based, on-line, time-sharing, high-speed computation using IBM 7094 "hardware" and the affiliated "software" developed by the ADMINS system.

Since we are not afflicted by "gadget-love," we have tried to use these advances in data management without losing sight of our original objectives. We have maintained our interest in the comparative history of European elite attitudes as the focus of all our experiments. This is why our book is organized mainly as a data-based report of inferences and conclusions. Our conclusions are drawn directly from comparison, by countries and by years, of the attitudes that evolved as the European elites faced their diminished power in the dynamic decade 1955–1965. Where we have gone beyond the stricter canons of inference, we have made it clear that we are in the interpretive mode.

This cautionary note may help the reader differentiate between our findings and the commentaries of the daily press. As we are dealing with contemporary history, our study deals with topics that are often at the top of the news. Some of our conclusions coincide with opinions expressed by editorialists and commentators on events of the day or week; other of our conclusions differ markedly from the general run of press opinion. We claim no superiority for our judgment, but we remind the reader that our data reflect a full decade of comparative studies in the three major nations of Europe. Our conclusion that nationalism and socialism are obsolescent, for example, is not based on the latest Common Market success or non-Communist-Left failure. Nor is our evaluation of Gaullism as a transient phase in Euratlantic relations based on the general's latest *coup de théâtre*. While we have kept an eye on current events, our focus has been on the two surveys that preceded as well as the three surveys that followed De Gaulle's return to power.

Hence, while one need not be a social scientist or a European specialist to read this book, the latter may find some of its content more useful than the general reader. Conversely, the general reader with an interest in the comparative history of contemporary societies may find enlightenment in many pages that leave the specialist cold. This is not a bedside book, but the reader need not take it too hard. Most of the technical material has been placed in the annexes for the use of interested specialists. To make the going easier for the general reader, we spent many months in condensing, reducing, and eliminating much of this material from the main text, with the result that the final version is half its original length. Yet, there remain enough tables in the text to trouble people who do not like numbers — or expect too much from them. Those who do not like numbers are advised to stick to the prose; those who expect more than our numbers give are urged to take up the problems of writing comparative history from longitudinal surveys and improve our work.

Part A is historical and contextual. As we move to Part B, the chapters on the three P's (protection, prosperity, prestige) become more descriptive and data based. In Part C the mode of the three chapters is expository and analytical. Part D, which concludes the main text, tends toward interpretive and evaluative analysis of the findings. The annexes elaborate some of the analytical problems raised in the text itself. We have organized our book in this way to reward the specialized reader without punishing the general reader. We hope that we have shared with both some of the enlightenment and excitement that we gained from this intellectual adventure.

POSTSCRIPT (MAY 1969)

As we were proofreading these pages, General De Gaulle resigned after defeat in the popular referendum. Our evaluation of Gaullism "as a transient phase in Euratlantic relations" therefore becomes current history at least three years ahead of schedule. In reminding the reader that our data were collected and analyzed while De Gaulle was at the height of his power, we also alert him to the opportunity of testing our indicators for the post-Gaullist period by carefully observing French and European policies in the months and years ahead.

Part A: Contexts

Introduction

IN THIS FIRST SET of three chapters, we seek to delineate the historical "contexts" in which we have worked and written. The TEEPS decade 1955–1965 was rich in events bearing on the efforts to shape a viable Europa and Atlantica. It began with a setback to both ideas by the rejection of EDC (European Defense Community) in 1954; it ended with another setback to both by the rejection of Britain's application for membership in EEC (European Economic Community) in 1965 and the subsequent transfer of NATO (North Atlantic Treaty Organization) from Paris to Brussels. These were perceived as serious setbacks by those European elites committed, as most of them are, to the building of Euratlantic institutions.

In mid-decade, with the signing and implementation of the Treaties of Rome in 1958–1959, a very significant success had occurred. This was the creation of Euratom, the first agreement to "Europeanize" the major new field of atomic energy for peaceful purposes, and of the Common Market, which by general elite consensus has become the "motor of modernization" for the European economies and their "transnationalization" by common economic policy. So powerful was the impact of Common Market success upon the thinking of the TEEPS panels that by 1965, despite the constraints imposed mainly by French policy and the opposition expressed mainly by De Gaulle, most of our respondents believed that European integration had reached a "point of no return." As expressed by Walter Hallstein, then President of the EEC Commission: "The Six have invested so much in the Common Market that none of them could leave it without irreparable damage to their own economies."

While the economic side of Europa in this sense appeared to be implanted firmly in the expectations of the TEEPS elites, the military side of Atlantica appeared to be more problematic for many. The Gaullists had decided to have their national *force de frappe*; the transnationalists, as Hallstein told us in his interview, had not yet taken up serious consideration of "the military dossier." It became clear in the latter half of the TEEPS decade that so long as De Gaulle remained in charge of French national policy, no serious effort would be made to "save" the

11

existing institutions of Atlantica (mainly NATO) that might entail real trouble for the existing institutions of Europa (mainly EEC).

The trouble was real. The European elites were deeply committed to their goal of prosperity via EEC. They were also deeply committed to their goal of protection, although less convinced that this could be done only via NATO. They were ready to give De Gaulle a long lead on the issues of prestige (De Gaulle's own word being *grandeur*) so long as he did not attempt to replace American "hegemony" (De Gaulle's own word) with that of France. Out of these troubled attitudes have come our deepest conclusions, such as the need of European elites for an "American nexus" to build the institutions of Europa and Atlantica conjointly. This is why the first two chapters of Part A are written as "contexts" for the design of our TEEPS surveys and for the results they produced. The third chapter seeks to give a realistic and accurate account of how we faced these "contexts" in writing the comparative history of the three major nations of Europe over a dramatic decade for Euratlantica.

CHAPTER ONE

Europa and Atlantica: The American Nexus

"AMERICANIZATION" is an epithet that evokes strong feelings in the contemporary world. It indicates a widespread anxiety among peoples living in societies that have not achieved the unique adaptive capacity of the United States, the capacity to absorb innovation routinely and to maintain dynamic equilibrium. These peoples are concerned about their own society's absorptive capacity: Can it really incorporate the bewildering diversity of American perspectives and practices? They also are worried about the American impact on personal and conventional morality: Are American ways feasible ways, or even proper ways, for themselves — and especially for their children? Despite their anxieties, however, people everywhere perceive that American lifeways are penetrating and pervading their traditional ways of thinking and acting.

Nowhere has the concern over "Americanization" been more acute than in the relatively diminished nations of postwar Europe. And nowhere in Europe has the anxiety about America's "cultural imperialism" been more poignantly articulated, or more transparently fearful, than in France. There is a long tradition of French ambivalence — of admiration transfused with anxiety, of awesome envy — going back over a century to Tocqueville's classic analysis of the American democracy.

Its modern French expression was formulated in the aftermath of World War I by André Siegfried, revered scholar of the *Académie Française,* who wrote: "The United States is presiding at a general reorganization of the ways of living throughout the entire world."[1] This prescient perception of "Americanization" as a global

13

process was shared by other European intellectuals observing the collapse of their dynastic monarchies at home and the disruption of their colonial empires around the world. Everywhere the impact of the American Model — its lifeways as well as its ideas of the Good Life — was great and growing. But it was in the highly developed countries of Europe, with their larger capacity for absorption and adaptation, that "Americanization" proceeded fastest and furthest. While the smart set of Cairo were learning to smoke Lucky Strikes, the Europeans of London–Paris–Berlin were teaching their provincial compatriots to absorb and adapt jazz, to experiment with mass production, and to demand direct universal suffrage.

By the same token, European observers of the "Americanization" process were the first to interpret its inexorable impact upon their familiar world — often admiring its promise for their democracy, often deploring its vulgarization of their culture, only occasionally (since Tocqueville) penetrating to the source of America's special potency for promoting multifarious goods and ills. This deeper source was thematized in the peculiarly American commitment to the "pursuit of happiness" — the right of Everyman to the richest and fullest life he could win for himself. When wedded to the political ideas of respect for "life, liberty, equality, fraternity" (which America shared with France and other democratizing Western societies over the past two centuries), the "pursuit of happiness" augured a social revolution of unprecedented dimensions. Its myth became known in more recent decades as The American Dream — an inspiring dream for some Europeans and for others a nightmare.*

It remained for an American sociologist, Daniel Bell, to identify the psychosocial source of Europe's acute postwar *malaise* about "Americanization" in the *equalization* of Everyman's expectations and demands from the pursuit of happiness. With modesty and delicious irony, Bell formulated a "Tocqueville's Law" capable of universal application in postwar Europe as earlier in prewar America: "In a society pledged to the idea of equality, what the few have today, the many will demand tomorrow."[2] Perceptive Europeans have, as we shall see in the last section of this chapter, formed a just — if often reluctant — appreciation of this aphorism. "Ameri-

---

* For an exposition of how The American Dream has been routinized over the past two centuries, see Daniel Lerner, "Comfort and Fun: Morality in a Nice Society," *The American Scholar*, Vol. 27, No. 2 (Spring 1958), pp. 153–165.

canization," now conjoined with the existential superpower of America, is recognized as the common condition for the two major options through which postwar Europeans seek to build the good life. These options, which are the central subject of this book, we designate as Europa and Atlantica. We postulate that recognition of America's crucial role in the achievement of either or both of these presumably compatible goals — European integration and Atlantic partnership — has permeated the thinking of enlightened Europeans.

To gauge the psychic distance many Europeans have traveled to reach this perspective, and to appreciate the continuing appeal of such political counterformations as Poujadism, Gaullism, Little Englandism, it is useful to sort out the attitudinal components of European ambivalence toward "Americanization." We examine first the sources of fearfulness among the European elites, both in their perception of American lifeways and their projection of these lifeways in their own countries. We then conclude with a summary evaluation of European-American relations in the present phase of acceptance.

A. THE PHASE OF ANXIETY

Traditional ambivalence about America has been heightened in postwar Europe by its dependence upon American superpower. The acute and utter dependence of the first postwar decade, when Europe lay devastated and distraught in a world bipolarized between the dictates of Moscow and Washington, has lessened considerably. By the second postwar decade, which is the historical period covered by this study, most of the West European nations (in the "American camp") had recovered a fair measure of economic prosperity and political equanimity. Relaxation of the Cold War between Russia and America also had loosened the bipolar vise. But Europe's dependence on American power and purpose, though now less extreme and obvious, was no less fundamental to its well-being. It was certain that Europe could not guarantee its own military security and likely that it could not promote its own long-term economic prosperity. Under these conditions, what assurance could there be for political autonomy and stability?

These conditions are defined by the key issues of protection, prosperity, and prestige, which we shall later examine in empirical detail. They represented national needs which, in the majority opinion of European leaders, could no longer be satisfied by national means. Needed were transnational modes of collective action — Europa and Atlantica — that could be achieved only with the active cooperation of America. This became postwar America's "vocation in Europe" and its reciprocal form was postwar Europe's "American vocation."[3]

The interpenetration of collective action required a massive "American presence" in every country of Europe — military and diplomatic establishments, Marshall men and businessmen, supplemented by task forces of technical advisers and research specialists. American people brought with them American ways along with American films, radio, picture magazines, and news media. Fearful Europeans began to speak of the "American invasion"; hostile ones derided America's "Coca-Cola culture" and "bathroom civilization." Among the graffiti on European walls, "Kilroy was here" was replaced by "Yankee go home!"

These were the vocalisms of the politically organized and emotionally overwrought "protesters" of postwar Europe. There was much occasion for anxiety and hostility in their lot, and rich America was a convenient object-symbol for its displacement. But what motivated the more sophisticated and responsible European leaders who are the subject of our study? We trace their anxiety and ambivalence to the fear of three trends that were widely identified in Europe as "Americanization": (1) mass culture; (2) mass consumption; and (3) mass politics.

Each of these, which we describe in this chapter, derives from the common concern of the European elites that their own inherited emblem of equality, activated by the new American "pursuit of happiness," would undermine the foundations upon which European civilization had been built: ". . . what the few have today, the many will demand tomorrow." Considering the scarcity of material resources in postwar Europe, responsible leaders could infer that such an acceleration of popular demand would rapidly outrun the available supply of satisfactions. Unsatisfied demands, spiritual as well as material, would magnify existing frustrations, undermine social equilibrium, and subvert political stability. In general, they feared the disruption caused by an intolerable gap between what people want and what they get. The stimulus of "Americanization," they feared, would produce the scourge of every traditional social order: an excessively imbalanced Want:Get Ratio.[4] As Whitehead put it: "The major advances in civilization are processes that all but wreck the societies in which they occur."[5]

1. Fear of Mass Culture

The association of mass culture with American society has been sufficiently publicized, in this country and abroad, to need no elaboration here.[6] Our interest is not to argue the pros and cons of mass culture as an American phenomenon but rather to diagnose its alleged role in the "Americanization" of Europe. It is well to note that this discussion has concerned mainly the intelligentsia of the two continents, and to note further that intellectuals historically have occupied a more prestigious and influential place in European than in American society. European intellectuals have had a more important set of vested interests to defend — and for many of them the attack on mass culture has been, at least in part, a defense of those "class interests."

This is not to imply that there has been no genuine issue of intellectual standards and aesthetic judgment. On the contrary, mass culture has produced definite and often deliberate depredations upon the high standards of traditional elite culture. As custodians and beneficiaries of this tradition, European intellectuals have felt themselves threatened by these depredations and increasingly powerless to prevent or remedy them. It was indeed the set of constraints imposed by their tradition of high culture that inhibited European intellectuals from absorbing and adapting the new skills needed to shape and share the great potential of mass culture.

The rapid rise of the mass media, particularly the audiovisual media operated by electronic instruments, is a case in point. Quite a different order and organization of skills is required to produce a television show than a play, opera, or ballet, as television often requires elements of all three traditional forms plus some others. An oral newscast needs different talents than does a printed *feuilleton*. Commercial art, industrial design, and broadcast commercials are simply a different world of cultural experience than the *beaux arts*.[7]

The routinized artists and intellectuals who served and conserved the traditional high culture of Europe had neither the skills nor the talents required by the new media of mass culture. In defense of their own interests, they counterattacked with fine contempt and resonant phrases. As the historically anointed and ego-involved curators of high culture, they proclaimed that mass culture was the beachhead through which would march the menacing armies of mass consumption and mass politics. Their fears were justified, but their warnings fell on deaf ears. For mass consumption and mass politics, it soon became clear, were exactly what the peoples of Europe — just as peoples everywhere in the world — wanted.[8]

2. *Fear of Mass Consumption*

In sounding the alarm against mass consumption, European intellectuals were appealing to the bourgeoisie of their own society, the relatively small (by American standards) middle class from which they mainly derived and by whose implicit values they mainly operated. The concern was that the standards and amenities of bourgeois society would be degraded and cheapened by "vulgarization" (the symbolically appropriate term which Europeans use instead of the Americanism "popularization"). Just as mass culture threatened the intelligentsia as intellectual and aesthetic arbiters, so ran the argument, mass consumption threatened the bourgeoisie as arbiters of manners and morals. But the counterattack on mass consumption — as so much else in Europe during the first half of the twentieth century — was too little and too late.

The inexorability of mass consumption and its linkage to the spreading mass media were more quickly and clearly perceived by the elites of the ex-colonial, newly independent "emerging nations" seeking development.[9] While these elites often had acquired their higher education in Europe, it was much easier for them to slough off the routinized habits of European ideas and tastes as they faced the accelerating imbalance in the Want:Get Ratio among the peoples they were to lead into new ways of life. To them Bell's formulation — "what the few have today, the many will demand tomorrow" — was readily apparent and acceptable as a guide to public policy. Thus Sukarno, a charismatic leader of the *tiers monde*, made the essential connection between the spread of mass culture and its sequel in mass consumption and even mass politics:

The motion picture industry has provided a window on the world, and the colonized nations have looked through that window and have seen the things of which they have been deprived. It is perhaps not generally realized that a refrigerator can be a revolutionary symbol — to a people who have no refrigerators. A motor car owned by a worker in one country can be a symbol of revolt to a people deprived of even the necessities of life. . . . [Hollywood] helped to build up the sense of deprivation of man's birthright, and that sense of deprivation has played a large part in the national revolutions of postwar Asia.[10]

Readers who reflect on Sukarno's words will perceive their relevance to the peoples of postwar Europe. While Lerner's 1950 lectures at the University of Paris were picketed with student placards reading "Coca-Cola Professor, go back to your refrigerator!" villagers in Lorraine were still piling dung heaps at their doors to provide winter fuel and spring fertilizer, and peasant women in Alsace were still pitching hay onto horse-drawn wagons where their husbands sat in the driver's seat. But this centuries-old social order was to change abruptly as Europeans recognized among themselves the Want:Get dictum pronounced by Sukarno: "a refrigerator can be a revolutionary symbol — to a people who have no refrigerators. A motor car owned by a worker in one country can be a symbol of revolt to a people deprived of even the necessities of life. . . ."

3. Fear of Mass Politics

Just as mass culture stimulated the demand for mass consumption, so both together accelerated the expectation of mass politics. Clearly, when the refrigerators and motor cars portrayed by motion pictures become "revolutionary symbols," then the political life of a society must be deeply involved. The postwar return to "politics as usual" in the great nations of Europe was only a routinized reaction to the pronouncement of international peace. But it soon became apparent to Europe's leaders that republican "politics as usual" was as surely a casualty of World War II as dynastic monarchies had been a casualty of World War I. Willy-nilly, and in one way or another, they had to face the immanence of mass politics.

Recognition was forced upon them in the immediate postwar years by the demand for self-determination among the subject peoples in their colonies and dominions around the world. In 1947, a full year before the Marshall Plan focused attention upon its own domestic growth, Britain symbolized the new political order by declaring the independence of India. Once again, it was among the elites of these emerging nations that perception of a mass political process was most acute. Nasser, among the most durable of the postwar generation of charismatic leaders, stated the case in these terms:

It is true that most of our people are still illiterate. But politically that counts far less than it did twenty years ago. . . . Radio has changed everything. . . . Today people in the most remote villages hear of what is happening everywhere and form their opinions. Leaders cannot govern as they once did. We live in a new world.[11]

Fear of mass politics was a long-established tradition among European leaders, whom successive generations of Jacobins, *communards*, and anarchosyndicalists kept in a state of chronic anxiety throughout the nineteenth century. The anxiety became acute between the two world wars, even among the democratic intelligentsia of Europe, as they watched mass politics sweep their countries under the direction of totalitarian ideologues. These totalitarians used the mass media to promise mass consumption in order to enlist mass participation in their political campaigns. None who lived through the 1930's can readily forget the radio oratory of a Hitler, who promised the German people oranges for their children and *Volkswagen* ("Peoples' Autos") for themselves. Intellectuals from every European land sounded the alarm against this version of mass politics. A Russian, Serge Chakotin, exposed its dependence upon mass media propaganda in *The Rape of the Masses* (1940). José Ortega y Gasset, the Spanish republican exiled in France, foresaw the rising demand for mass culture and mass consumption in *The Revolt of the Masses* (1932). Emil Lederer, the German professor exiled from Hitler's Reich, gloomily appraised the future of mass politics in *The State of the Masses* (1967). The interwar era of "coercive ideological movements" — the Bolsheviks, Fascists, Nazis, Falangists who took power; the Vichy, Quisling, and other puppets who were dominated by them — left a strong distaste and distrust of mass politics among the postwar elites of Europe.[12]

Small wonder, then, that even as late as 1956 the European elites we interviewed pronounced a resoundingly negative judgment on the idea of mass participation in the formation of public policy — and especially foreign policy. We asked each of our panels some variant of the question whether "the public should have more influence on foreign policy," prefaced by the rather leading preamble: "Since war and peace concern ordinary people as well as their leaders, would you say that . . . ?" Nevertheless, the elite panels remained firmly opposed — negative responses amounting to about half in France, two thirds in Britain, and three fourths in Germany.

Mass politics, like mass culture and mass consumption, remained intellectually *non grata* to the elites — but behaviorally they were already reshaping the ways of living among the peoples of Europe. "Americanization," upon which the fearful elites projected their anxieties and hostilities, was accelerating at an unprecedented tempo. We turn next to a cursory review of these accelerated changes in the structure of European societies. We consider these changes "structural" in the sense that they modified the behavior of many or most individuals, that they codified new interpersonal modes in institutions which routinize and regulate behavior, and that they altered the international relations of Europeans — elite and mass — *across* as well as *within* countries.

B. THE PHASE OF ACCELERATION

The "acceleration of history" has preoccupied scholars since the Industrial Revolution initiated in England during the seventeenth century. Public interest in this process has grown with the highly visible transformation of techniques and lifeways in our own time — the Technological Revolution, sometimes called the second industrial revolution. So rapidly have our ways of living altered that sensitive observers have been able to write social history as autobiography, simply by recounting the changes they have witnessed in their own lifetime. A popular exposition of this type was Frederick Lewis Allen's *Only Yesterday* (1931), followed some years later by *Big Change: America Transforms Itself 1900–1950* (1952), perhaps a unique record of two "accelerations of history" in a single lifetime.

1. American Challenge and European Response

The speed and cumulation of social changes activated by new technology, which Allen regarded as characteristically American, have now become the way of the world. Everywhere technological innovation and human adaptation is in progress, as shown by Karl Polanyi in *The Great Transformation* (1944). It is this rapid integration of new human resources with new technological resources — of men with their machines — that sparks the contemporary acceleration of history and animates the "Americanization" of the world. For America is only leading the way in a direction which societies everywhere are taking. The "American Model" is a challenge to which other peoples respond in the manner and measure of their desire for the good things of life represented by mass culture, mass consumption, mass politics — which, as desire accelerates, are transformed from symbols of ambivalence to symbols of aspiration.

In this sense, European interaction with the American Model has been the most intimate and its acceleration the most intense. For no other region of the postwar world was so well equipped with an existing stock of developed technological and human resources to promote the rapid integration of men and machines in new ways. The statistical evidence is available in the voluminous reports of the OEEC and OECD as well as the *Statistical Yearbook* of the United Nations. Here we wish to evoke the "human side" of the acceleration of history in postwar Europe. Our study concerns the people-problems of European society, the problems generated by the abrupt transformation of ideals, ideas, attitudes, and opinions. While our focus will be on their leaders, it is important to understand the behavioral mechanisms at work among the people they have led. Europeans today — leaders as well as led — are no longer quite the same as they were only twenty years ago. They have accelerated history; and history, in its turn, has transformed them.

2. The Case of France: From Static to Dynamic

France is our case in point. For France, as World War II ended, though physically less damaged than Britain and Germany, was considerably less advanced in the technological revolution that antedated the war. It fell further behind on the technological route during the war, which accelerated nuclear development in Britain and aerospace development in Germany while the Nazis used Vichy France as an agricultural supplier and industrial service station. As the war ended, France was by its own epithet *le pays arriéré*, the "backward nation" of Western Europe.

But postwar France was soon to discover that a political liability had become a societal asset. A substantial proportion of the French population had become the displaced persons of wartime Europe — some dragooned into the Nazi labor camps, others refuged in the open zone under Vichy stewardship, still others enlisted in the Free French forces in London and North Africa. With the end of hostilities, Frenchmen — traditionally the most "settled" of European peoples, the least prone to emigration or even internal migration (except to Paris) — had become a mobile population. And mobility, as has been demonstrated in one region of the world after another, is a necessary condition of modernization. It is only when people are free to move — and in fact move in large numbers — that the new men with new ideas emerge who absorb and adapt the resource potential of their new environment.*

The new mobility of postwar Frenchmen knelled the passing of romantic, and retarded, regional France. No longer did the stereotypes of the easygoing *méridional* (southerner) or bluff *normand* (northwesterner) serve any useful purposes of analysis or action, when a very large fraction of the more active people in the South and Northwest had not been born or raised there. The South, no longer the traditional *midi* of wealthy English vacationers seeking the sun, erupted into a postwar phase of economic and demographic expansion that is still accelerating from Toulouse to Nice. Even tourism followed Bell's dictum, "what the few have today, the many will demand tomorrow." The *midi* is no longer a preserve of overprivileged Britons but a playground for the salariat and even proletariat of France, from *cheminots* to *midinettes*. The meridional sentiment of yesteryear is revived only when Marcel Pagnol's film *Fanny*, its classic eulogy, is rerun in local cinemas.

Perhaps the most perceptive study of the transformation of southern France is *Village in the Vaucluse* by Laurence Wylie. Already changing in the early postwar years, Wylie's village (despite its relative isolation in the hill country of Provence) was in full acceleration when Wylie restudied it ten years later. He observed all the factors of modernization in operation there:

Mass Culture: At the two cafés where, ten years earlier, the villagers had foregathered each Sunday afternoon to compete in their own tournament of *boules* (outdoor bowling), they now congregated to watch the matches telecast from Paris or Le Mans.

Mass Consumption: The courtship pattern which had, only a decade earlier, ritualized the Sunday afternoon *promenade* in the nearby woods had vanished. Now the attached couple jumped onto their motorbike (or jalopy among the more affluent) and sped off to Marseille or other urban center.

---

* The functions of mobility — physical, social, psychic — are a central theme in Daniel Lerner, *The Passing of Traditional Society: Modernizing the Middle East* (paperback edition, New York: The Free Press, 1964).

Mass Politics: The heritage of party loyalty, from generation to generation, had also been swept into history's dustbin by the Vaucluse villagers. With it, the traditional pattern of provincial politics — whereby the father voted for the local *notable* of his ideological persuasion and the son voted as his father — was rendered obsolete. The younger generation, only a decade later, looked beyond the village scene to the television screen, chose national rather than local *notables,* and voted as they pleased.[13]

Underlying these rapid changes, as Wylie's restudy makes clear, was the new mobility of Frenchmen. In his Vaucluse village, the total population had remained stable over the decade, but many of the individuals had *not* lived there ten years earlier. These were the mobile new men with new ideas for whom *boules, promenades,* and local *notables* meant little. Whether by coercive or voluntary displacement during wartime, whether by internal migration in the postwar years, mobility was the motor of modernization. Its guides were the media (movies and television) of mass culture; its means (motor vehicles and cheap public transport) as well as its ends were mass consumption; its outcome was the rising demand for political participation on the national level. Wylie's findings in the Vaucluse were confirmed by his own and other studies in the diverse regions of France.[14] It was soon clear that to label provincial France "the French desert," as Gravier had done in a brilliant but belated portrait of prewar France, was an early anachronism of the postwar period.[15]

The obsolescence of traditional French categories of discourse was revealed in detail by studies ancillary, but indispensable, to the main research on which this book is based. One such study showed that all major theses advanced by French observers to explain the defeat of EDC were in error — by reason of their adherence to the regional stereotypes of prewar France.[16] The regions simply did not behave, in 1954, as the stereotypes said they should. This finding led to a more complete and systematic analysis of the relationships between regions and modernization postulated by leading French scholars in the great debate over "static *versus* dynamic France." Statistical analysis of growth rates on all major indices, by *départements,* showed no significant correlation with traditional regions. On the contrary, growth rates accelerated *only* in regions where urbanization rates accelerated, regardless of regional location and stereotyped "characteristics." The growth of "urban regions" (what the French since have learned to call *conurbanisation*), produced by the mobility of individuals, was the great accelerator. Upon the rural regions of France it produced two major modernizing effects: It brought villagers to the city, and it brought the city to villagers.[17]

The current generation of French social scientists has studied carefully the epochal transformation of France from a rural society (plus Paris) to an urban society. This deep change from the ecological structure of France since medieval times is described in a book by Henri Mendras appropriately entitled *La Fin des Paysans*.[18] The phase of acceleration signaled by this ecological shift was documented in an impressive series of surveys in 1961 by the Institut National d'Etudes Démographiques, under the direction of Alain Girard, entitled *La Réussite Sociale en France* (Social Success in France).

3. Accelerating Europe: New Questions and Answers

What has happened in France is visible as well in Britain and Germany, and indeed throughout Western Europe. Everywhere the new mobility has unbound European peasants from their native soil (though it comes as a shock to many Americans when they learn that there were many, and still are some, real peasants in postwar Europe). Urbanization has mobilized the regions and urban regions have incorporated the parishes. Men have been liberated from ancient bonds by every form of mobility — notably *job mobility*, an aspect of "Americanization" that has impressed Europeans ever since the perspicacious Karl Marx, a century ago, publicized a letter written home by a young Frenchman who had emigrated to San Francisco in the wake of the gold rush:

> I was firmly convinced that I was fit for nothing but letterpress printing. . . . Once in the midst of this world of adventurers who change their occupation as often as they do their shirt, egad, I did as the others. As mining did not turn out remunerative enough, I left for the town where in succession I became a typographer, slater, plumber, etc. In consequence of thus finding out that I am fit for any sort of work I feel less of a mollusk and more of a man."[19]

Mobility has liberated the women of postwar Europe as well. In traditional European society, woman's primordial role as a sex-object was supplemented mainly by her function as a work-horse (if poor) or a clothes-horse (if rich). Postwar women have acquired a great number of new roles in the professional, clerical, and industrial sectors of the economy. When the women of provincial France "go to town" nowadays, they are garbed in multicolored frocks rather than the black shrouds which over long centuries certified their custodianship of the dead (*culte des morts*).

The mobilization of youth in postwar Europe was sped by the newly available, cheap technology of motorization — whose early seed, the Vespa of Italy, has fertilized multiple progeny of motor-bikes and motor scooters in every European land. The moderniza-tion of postwar youth is a dazzling exhibition of this phase of acceleration.* Although the process was labeled "Americanization" in the early postwar years, when the "zoot-suiters" of this country were paralleled by the "zasus" of France and the "teddy-boys" of Britain, its indigenous sources have since become evident. It was in Britain that the "mods" invented long-haired boys and mini-skirted girls — along with the innovative music so brilliantly exem-plified by the Beatles. And it is among French youth, despite De Gaulle's parochial judgment that Britain is not sufficiently European, that these "mod" ways have come to represent *le stand-ing* (a nice example of the *franglais* that Gaullism rejects as anti-liturgical).† A Berlin student, recently on trial for throwing a rock at the visiting Shah of Iran, declared himself in terms that would by now sound familiar in virtually every major city of the Western world:

Teufel, who is pleased that his name means "Devil," eagerly pleads guilty to despising contemporary German society and to practicing nonviolent rebellion against it, particularly with active ridicule.[20]

Although this was reported in a front-page survey by *The New York Times* under the headline "European Youth Is Found Muti-nous Against The Establishment," it is noteworthy that The Estab-lishment takes a relatively tolerant, and even sympathetic, view of its mobilized youth — especially in a country where parental authority and disciplined children were long regarded as the cor-nerstone of the social order.‡

For it is likely that such exhibitionistic behavior is perceived by the European elites as only a transitory symptom of an accelerated process of social change that is transforming the lifeways of all

* The leadership of European youth in accelerating social change is now being seriously studied by Roy Macridis and others.
† The Sorbonne "happening" of May 1968 bears witness.
‡ That the youth mobilization has spread beyond the three "great powers" of Europe is illustrated by the Dutch "Provos" (from the word provocation) and their comparable numbers in Belgium and Sweden. Even in Franco's Spain the youth today engage in psychocultural exhibitions and sociopolitical demonstrations. The process is operative as well in the Communist countries of East Europe, notably the "tamed" regimes of Poland and Czechoslovakia.

their peoples. Tolerance by the elites is expressed in active programs to absorb the accelerating changes among youth by adapting traditional institutions to meet their demands. The *Times* survey concludes: "However amorphous younger Europeans may be as a group, they are now regarded by the Governments in power as an important element on the national scene."[21] An instance of the process at work is the accelerated growth of public education in every country of postwar Europe. None has moved more vigorously in this direction than France, where the population of university students has multiplied manyfold in the postwar years. Yet the 1968 winter semester at the Sorbonne began with a massive and violent demonstration because even its greatly expanded (and overcrowded) facilities could accommodate only 130,000 students — whereas 160,000 applicants demanded admission.*

This is a deeper and more serious matter for the European elites than the length of boys' hair and girls' skirts. For this phase of acceleration has brought the European economies to a level of unprecedented prosperity and continuing growth. As each country passed through its own "economic miracle," beginning with the German *Wirtschaftswunder* in 1950, its psychocultural traditions and sociopolitical institutions became obsolescent. By the start of the second postwar decade, when our study was initiated, it was apparent to many European leaders that a "cultural gap" of major proportions was already in being. Projected growth rates showed that a comprehensive program of social change had to be activated promptly and accelerated rapidly. For guidance in shaping public policy that would provide new answers to these new questions, European leaders turned from their inherited ideologies to the American Model.[22]

C. THE PHASE OF ACCEPTANCE

We have seen that Europe moved from a phase of anxiety in the first postwar decade, under the impact of "Americanization," into a phase of accelerated growth. Our survey shows that by 1961, as the visible benefits became apparent midway through the second decade, the European elites entered a phase of acceptance. Amer-

---

* Note that this passage was written in January 1968. The Sorbonne eruption, which brought a reported ten million Frenchmen out on strike, occurred in May 1968.

ican tutelage was sought and welcomed. An appreciation of American practices was consolidated which led to an unprecedented acceptance of American policies among the opinion leaders and decision makers of postwar Europe. This entailed a reversal of inherited roles which, as we shall see in the next section, appears to have become a permanent feature of Euratlantic relations. This we call the "American Nexus."

It is essential to observe that while acceptance of the Euratlantic relationship is durable, it is also partial. The reversal of roles, given the postwar acceleration of social change on both sides of the Atlantic, means that Europe and America have bypassed each other in the historical process. The American Model has been only partially incorporated by Europeans — and partial incorporation, as Harold D. Lasswell has shown, is one way of restricting external influence.* That part of the American Model which has been most fully absorbed and adapted is its allegedly technological component. Not so the psychocultural and sociopolitical components — nor even, fully, the economic component. The fear of mass consumption, we have seen, interacts among anxious Europeans with the fears of mass culture and mass politics. They have incorporated only slowly and partially the lessons taught by the American Model on the shaping and sharing of all values in a social system that is continuously expanding its scope while accelerating its tempo. This is not surprising when one considers that America has been developing its lifeways for nearly two centuries, while the living generation of European leaders has confronted the contemporary configuration (as represented by the American Model) only over the past two decades.

Rather more surprising to Americans is the reversal of world perspectives entailed by the reversal of world roles in the postwar period. While America has been enlarging its new commitments to every continent of the world, Europe has been retrenching its old imperial commitments by decolonizing its global domains. These role reversals, to which the European elites have been more acutely sensitive than most Americans, have altered traditional American notions of European "sophistication." The matter is well

---

* The concept of "restriction by partial incorporation" was developed by H. D. Lasswell in *World Politics and Personal Insecurity* (New York: Free Press, 1935; 2nd ed., 1965), a truly seminal work which built theoretical foundations for this and many other subsequent studies.

summarized by a scholar who studied the responses of American management personnel to sustained working experience in Europe:

> . . . thoughtful Americans discussing life in Europe sooner or later mention their shock at discovering how provincial in outlook many Europeans are. This is a reversal of old roles. Moved to Europe, where their businesses and outlook tend to be as wide as the Western world, these Americans find well-educated men and women in many capitals who are influential members of an elite, who speak several languages, but who hardly think in terms beyond those of their own social group, much less the continent on which they live or the world beyond. Such Europeans confuse social sophistication with knowledge of the world.[23]

The parochialization of European perspectives was manifest in the attitudes of Europeans not only toward the wider world but even with regard to their own country and continent. This has been apparent, even among the Europeanizers, since the defeat of EDC in the French National Assembly. It was a French parliamentarian who, in that Great Debate, warned his colleagues against merely "raising parochialism to the European scale."[24] The subsequent analysis of this major setback of postwar Europe's effort to enlarge its national perspectives concluded:

> One type of oversimplification that strikes a foreign observer is the French tendency toward explanations that are wholly contained in the universe of internal events.[25]

That strong traces of parochialism still exist in Europe, and not only among the French, is reported by a researcher among scientists of different nationalities at CERN — Europe's international center for nuclear research — and several other transnational science centers. They often complained to him of "a characteristically American tendency to speak of Europe as an entity in places where a European probably would not have done so.[26] If Americans sometimes lose nuance by gazing at the whole forest, Europeans often lose perspective by staring at a few trees. The difference helps to clarify the process of "partial incorporation" whereby postwar Europeans have sought to absorb and adapt the American Model to their own perceived needs.

1. The American Model: Apprenticeship and Achievement

The perceived needs of postwar Europe may be ranged under three broad heads: protection, prosperity, and prestige. The three P's are a shorthand expression, used for expository convenience,

which subsume the major values operative in every modern society
organized as a polity. It was to satisfy these needs that postwar
Europe, receding from world power, turned for help to the acced-
ing superpower of America. There was great poignancy, of course,
in this historic reversal of roles. While America was long decolo-
nized from Europe, Americans in large numbers retained, at the
level of popular culture as of high society, a sense of filiopietism
toward the European lands of their origin.[27] Such sentiments did
not inhibit the even stronger sense that America was superior in
every form of power — certainly material and probably moral — to
the folks who had been left behind on the Old Continent.[28]

It was with the conviction of beneficent power and purpose,
having twice accomplished the rescue of Europe from self-immola-
tion in flames ignited by the incendiary Huns, that America now
turned its "know-how" to accomplish the recovery of Europe. These
were the men of the Marshall Plan. The success of the Marshall
Plan and its sequence of agencies — ECA, OEEC, OECD — are writ
large in the conspicuous achievement of European Recovery. Be
it noted as well that rarely, if ever, in the annals of proconsulship
has role-reversal between great nations been accomplished as
rapidly, effectively, and even graciously as by the men of the
Marshall Plan.

From Paul Hoffman down, the Marshall Men diffused among
Europeans from their headquarters in the Palais Talleyrand a
new image of contemporary Americans in action. They supplanted
the older stereotypes associated with bohemians self-exiled on the
Left Bank or tourists dressed in loud neckties and expensive cam-
eras or the hurly-burly G.I.'s of an improvised civilian army. They
provided Europeans of diverse social standing, but particularly
those elites and subelites with managerial and operational responsibilities, a vivid example of "know-how" as a behavioral mode
rather than a self-congratulatory slogan. The great psychological
lesson taught by their example was the reality of goal-oriented
effort. The Marshall Men knew what they wanted to do, how to
try to find the best available way of doing it, and when to go on
to the next task. Europeans absorbed this lesson fast. When the
Americans mounted their amazing Berlin Airlift a year or so after
the Marshall Men went to work, awed and admiring Europeans
readily recognized this as another instance of the "know-how syndrome" in operation.

A second major lesson taught by the Marshall Men was the efficacy of *pluralist task-force institutions*. The Marshall Men included industrialists and bankers, officials and academicians, professional specialists and labor leaders, administrators and publicists. Moreover, these teams from the society where "private enterprise" was alleged to be the official religion were exercising their combined know-how under the blessing of American public policy in behalf of European public welfare. To the compartmentalized sectors of European society, the very existence of such a "multidisciplinary task-force" appeared miraculous. As these radiated out from the Palais Talleyrand to the cities and towns of Europe in task-oriented "productivity teams," their message was writ plain for all to see by their behavior. It was by rapidly absorbing and adapting this message that Europeans recovered and, as productivity took command, prospered.

Europe was "ready" to receive the message and to act on it. Wartime devastation had deprived many millions of the basic needs of life: food, clothing, shelter. Such needs had to be satisfied without delay. Europe was also relatively well-advanced in the techniques of mass production and distribution. In Britain such firms as "The Fifty Shilling Tailors" were experienced in the large-scale merchandising of clothes. Even the finicky French had been prepared by such gastronomic "chain stores" as *Cercle Bleu* and *Nicolas* for the second postwar decade's explosion of *supermarchés* (supermarkets) in the American style and very nearly on the American scale. The German prewar effort to produce motor cars for mass consumption, Hitler's publicized *Volkswagen*, rapidly became a postwar reality. With such breakthroughs into heavy industrial production for mass consumption, the dikes of traditional European economy were rapidly flooded. Not only the fundamental human needs of food and clothing but also the mass production of amenities expected in developed societies were accelerated by Europeans apprenticed to the American modes of industrial production.[29]

Before long Americans conveying advanced technologies to their opposite numbers in Europe noted that their apt apprentices had passed to the stage of independent achievement. Indeed, before much longer, they further noted that the European apprentices had begun to overtake and surpass their American tutors in some advanced sectors of modern technology. The same observer who reported the shockingly "provincial outlook" of many Europeans also evaluated their accelerated technological progress in these terms:

Before and after World War II, America was known as the land of mass production, the Mecca of advanced tooling and design. This is no longer the case — at least not to the same degree. The Renault assembly line in France is the envy of the industry. Germany's Volkswagen trundles out over one million cars per year from an effective and continuously improving plant. Ignis, the Italian refrigerator manufacturer, has conveyerized production equipment that is modeled from, and an improvement upon, older U.S. systems. An American industrial consultant, recently back from a trip through a number of Italian plants, was dazed to discover that investment-happy engineers were writing off and replacing major items of equipment in three years. There have been changes. The best equipment in Europe today is as good as, or better than, much of the best U.S. equipment.[30]

2. Partial Incorporation: A Psychosocial Note

This, then, is the current state of the "great leap forward" that China has dreamed of but Europe has accomplished. It was an accelerated leap into the world of modern technology based on a willing acceptance of the American Model. Given the widespread aspiration for prosperity and aptitude for technological change among Europeans, they were able to pass rapidly from apprenticeship to achievement. "Takeoff" has led Europeans, in apparent accord with the Rostovian model, toward the stage of "high mass consumption."[31] As Europeans moved from poverty to recovery, their demands for the good things of life accelerated, thus illustrating the wisdom of the old French aphorism that *"l'appétit vient en mangeant"* (appetite comes with eating).

But "partial incorporation" has its limits. To absorb and adapt the technological component of the American Model was a giant step forward in the direction Europeans wished to take. The promotion of mass consumption was another important, if as yet insufficient, step in the same direction. These forward strides stirred among the peoples of Europe new demands that are generally associated with rising mass consumption — namely, demands for the media of mass culture. These, as Nasser and Sukarno have reported from underdeveloped societies where mass consumption is still but a gleam in some eyes, incorporate deeper demands for mass participation in public affairs and political life. As the European elites confronted these new popular aspirations in the prospering societies of the second postwar decade covered by our study, their need shifted. Having passed through the phase of anxiety about "Americanization" into a phase of acceptance of the American Model, they now faced the consequences of their own accelerated success. Partial incorporation, we recall, signifies *restriction* by partial incorporation. The Europeans had traveled a considerable distance along the American route to modernization. Could they, should they, now seek to go all the way? As they pondered the pros and cons of this profound issue for their own future, the European leaders entered a new phase of ambivalence.

D. THE PHASE OF AMBIVALENCE

Ambivalence differs qualitatively from either anxiety or acceptance, although it combines properties of both in a kind of anxious acceptance with reservations. For the ambivalent person, full acceptance is not possible; the object of desire has some competitor and full rejection of the competitor is not possible. While the object of desire is highly valued, so is its competitor. Ambivalence results. This is the most difficult situation in the theory of decision-making; it is much harder, for example, than the classic political choice of the "lesser evil," for it faces its victim with two "almost-equal goods." Where the goods appear to be truly equal, the ambivalent person suffers from paralysis of will and immobilization of action; where the valued goals are "almost equal," he usually exhibits vacillation in choice and oscillation in decision. On many key issues that now confront the European elites, as we shall see in the findings of this study, vacillation and oscillation are fairly characteristic responses in the present period.

1. Reach and Grasp: New Aspirations and Old Constraints

The issues that evoke European ambivalence are both internal and external: They concern the evolution of their domestic society and the place of that society in the new world environment. Precisely this interaction between what one is at home and what one is abroad remains difficult for European leaders to grasp. This may be a residue of their traditional imperial perspective, now obsolete, which allowed Great Britain to develop a political democracy in its home islands while managing the world's largest empire by political fiat. It may account for the posturing of De Gaulle, in a world of continental superpowers, *as if* his now relatively prosperous "hexagon" of fifty million Frenchmen were an adequate base for world leadership.

We are dealing here with an extension of the French tendency, noted above, "toward explanations that are wholly contained in the universe of internal events." This is the tendency that led some Frenchmen to misinterpret the real options available to them in rejecting EDC and as a consequence to beat a hasty and humiliating retreat, four months later, when they were obliged by American insistence to ratify WEU (West European Union), which included Britain. Since WEU did what the French rejection of EDC tried to prevent (Germany's accession to NATO), but without the measure of French control that EDC had conferred, this was a costly error of perspective. It was an error committed after four arduous years of vacillation and oscillation.

De Gaulle has simply reversed this erroneous perspective by his effort to act in the world arena as if external policy today could operate without any reference to "the universe of internal events." His severe setback in the French elections of 1967 has shown that the lessons of EDC still apply — even to De Gaulle. The most poignant lesson is that one cannot be "great" outside, in the postimperial age, without being "great" inside. As our post-mortem on EDC put it:

The effort to comprehend foreign policy decisions in *any* country requires a context in which "internal" and "international" events endlessly interact and reciprocally influence each other. It is no less true in France than elsewhere that national sovereignty has been compromised by the facts of life in a bipolar arena of world politics. The current arena of world politics requires many "international decisions" to activate policies that exceed the independent capacity of any single nation.[32]

The interaction of internal and external policy is operative today in all nations that bear any responsibility for world order, including *a fortiori* the United States and Russia. As this book will deal mainly with the external relations of the great European nations, we focus on internal issues in the concluding section of this chapter on the domestic evolution of European society. In particular, we are concerned with the efforts to bring mass culture and politics into an equilibrium ratio with the accelerated growth of mass consumption.

We have seen that France has been not only highly ambivalent but laggard in the postwar acceleration of mass culture. Its per capita growth of television, for example, is among the lowest in Europe. As compared with Britain and Germany, radio as well as television remain under exclusive and rather rigid government control — a source of severe and growing complaint among Frenchmen who seek to promote the mass media as the vehicle for mass politics. Again turning to the American Model for guidance, opposition candidates in the 1967 elections accused the Gaullists of government monopoly over information and opinion — and demanded the American rule of "equal time."*

A rather different picture is presented by postwar Germany, where the mass media developed rapidly during the past decade. As a result, current German debates about mass culture are well in advance of those in France. Be it noted that the postwar German media were initiated and shaped largely by Americans who manned the Information Control Division of the military government. If the press and radio have been "tame" on some issues — fewer and farther between with the passing years as the affair of *Der Spiegel* and the resignation of Strauss dramatically demonstrate — they have generally honored their commitment to be "free and responsible." Television, which developed after Allied Information Control lapsed, has followed suit. Postwar Germans have been well served by their mass media. This was shown, as early as 1956 in our surveys, by the elite responses to our question: "Is it possible for people who are interested to keep well informed on international politics?" The great majority of German panelists saying yes (77 per cent) was only slightly smaller than in Britain (81 per cent), where the long and rich history of media development had not been deformed by a Goebbels ministry under a Nazi regime. The German panel, moreover, was more than half again as positive as the French panel (50 per cent).

This appears to account for the relatively high level of discussion among German opinion leaders about the future development of their mass media, which they see as the dynamic component in the further evolution of mass participation in culture and politics. The point is illustrated by a thoughtful feature article in the prestigious *Frankfurter Allgemeine,* November 11, 1967, which started from the thesis "that in small and medium-sized towns there is a growing demand for things cultural." It cites a series of cases where specific towns have "rejuvenated the traditional and the modern" by creating

---

* The ironic outcome was that telecast time was divided "equally" — half to the Gaullist Party (UNR) and half to all other parties combined. (To this we add the May 1968 nationwide strike demand for liberation of radio–TV.)

new institutions of enlightenment: Regensburg by a university (due to which "the decline that set in during the nineteenth century has been reversed"); Ulm by a secondary school; Wolfenbüttel by a library; Ingelheim by new industry; Höchst by a theater; Oberhausen by a film club. The concern with extending the perspectives and participation of the hinterland illustrates what Karl Deutsch and Stein Rokkan have aptly called "the mobilization of the periphery."[33]

For, says the *Allgemeine,* "any one of these can widen the horizons of the people in a town by making them aware of current movements in 20th century life." And this development of mass culture among provincial Germans is required not only by its interactive function with mass consumption and mass politics but as the psychological condition for a satisfying life in a modern, democratic, participant society. The *Allgemeine* concludes:

> The cliché that small town life is quiet and restful no longer applies. Mass media such as the cinema and television have introduced into medium-sized towns a noticeable tendency to imitate large towns and cities, outstripping them in modernity. Nowadays the large town or city is often quieter, more serious and generally less hectic than many a market town. In outward appearances and in the general pace of life in a small town it would seem that the community was suffering from nervous strain. There would be reasons to deduce that inner development in the small town was not keeping up with the outside tempo of life.[34]

German concern to follow social diagnosis with therapeutic action stimulated the formation of the Michel Commission on the mass media. Modeled on the American and British Commissions of a decade earlier, its 242-page report is a document worth reading for its judicious and detailed concern with "free and responsible" institutions of public enlightenment. Issued in October 1967, the report "concluded that press and radio, in contrast with various sectors of the film [and television] industry, have developed favorably."[35] Within a month, on November 6, 1967, the Munich Film and Television College was opened. Press commentary was enthusiastic: "This special college will combine scientific, technical, and artistic studies. Plans for a college of this kind were made ten years ago, and actual preparations have taken three years. At last the Federal Republic has its 'directors' factory'!"[36] Within days thereafter, the appropriate Bundestag committee unanimously approved a Film Promotion Bill designed to give financial help to film makers who help themselves — on condition that they reinvest earnings in new films, particularly films for young people and documentaries (which are eligible for special grants). The stated objectives include "raising the standard of films, encouraging cooperation between film and television corporations, and an equitable market-oriented evaluation of the films promoted."[37]

This rapid and reasoned policy response to felt social needs demonstrates that Europeans have achieved an absorptive and adaptive capacity appropriate to highly developed societies. The mobilization of mass participation in culture, consumption, and political life is no easy matter for any country, however developed it may be, but Europeans have been moving in this direction rapidly and, by and large, effectively. The management of societal equilibrium within the present structure of world politics appears to be feasible.

But other new aspirations are appearing among some European leaders whose reach is likely to exceed their grasp. These are aspirations which assume a transformation of the present world arena by European power for European purposes. Such aspirations greatly exceed the capabilities of any one European nation or any presently conceivable combination of them. This takes us into the question of Europe's place in the world community, which this book is mainly about. As the data to be reported will amply demonstrate, most European leaders are aware that their role in world politics is constrained by their own weakness, severally and jointly, relative to the bipolarized superpowers. Most of them are aware, at least since Suez, that it is dangerous for them to initiate major international actions without consultation and consent in Washington. Indeed, most of them have come to accept, more rather than less willingly over the second postwar decade, American leadership in world affairs, at least in the measure that America's responsibilities as their guarantor bespeak America's rights as their leader. These propositions will be documented in the body of this book.

Since some aspirations have recently been voiced and echoed among Europeans of a "Gaullist" persuasion, and since these appear to challenge the axiomatics of American leadership, it is well to conclude this discussion of the "Americanization" of domestic societies in Europe with a brief consideration of the "American Nexus" in Europe's world position. This will complete the picture of Euramerican interaction and outline the framework within which the empirical studies in this book are to be understood.

2. The American Nexus and Europe's Options

That acceptance of American leadership continues strong among the European elites is evidenced by many current expressions of public attitudes in the three countries. Among the British elite, an editor of the Conservative *Daily Telegraph* assures us that "Anti-Americanism is Non-U" — rather a dramatic change among Britons whose traditional adherence has been to Crown and Empire.[38] Continuance of the new pro-Americanism into the next generation is augured by the strong preference of German, as of virtually all European, students for advanced study in American universities — a significant reversal of traditional roles that has occurred only among the generation that will supply the future elites of Europe. Among the more noteworthy expressions of long-term commitment to the American Nexus is the book by J. J. Servan-Schreiber, editor of the leftist *L'Express* and formerly a leading anti-American, which has become a sensational best-seller in France and throughout Europe. Entitled *The American Challenge,* the book is a detailed explication of the psychocultural and sociopolitical dynamics that animate America's technological supremacy and a sustained sermon to the effect that Europeans can do no better, in the visible future, than to absorb and adapt the continually evolving American Model.

The argument central to such essays, which are now common coin in the public exchange of European opinion, is that American superpower is not the product of a single historical factor (e.g., continental space) or of a single psychological factor (e.g., profit motive). Rather, it is the outcome of manifold processes which include historical opportunities, geophysical advantages, human resources, social institutions, personality developments, political perspectives, and even philosophies of living. Among such Europeans, in short, America is now perceived not as a mutation of technological evolution but as the model of a new society — one whose power in the world derives from, and continually interacts with, the great strength of its domestic social order. These Europeans now believe that American society has developed a capability to absorb and adapt even the most serious of its internal social problems that is special, and perhaps unique, among the highly advanced and rapidly accelerating countries of the world. It was in this sense that *L'Express,* while editor Servan-Schreiber was still a leftist anti-American, headlined a feature story: "L'Amérique accroit d'un demi-France par an" (America increases by half-of-all-France each year).

As antipathetic anxiety yielded to awed admiration, Europeans began to perceive that to be a postwar world power on the American scale required a different social order than that which had sustained their global empires over preceding centuries. The American Model, now understood in the full pluralism of its multidimensional power, presented a goal to emulate rather than a rival to compete with. On the economic side, this led from the early enthusiasm for "productivity" to the broader current concerns (including the psycho-social components) with "management." On the cultural side, it activated such programs as we have noted to accelerate the growth of mass media, of public education to the highest levels, of all the institutions of public enlightenment. On the political side, it led to a clearer appreciation of American problems and to a readier acceptance of American policies.

So far had this "change of heart" about American leadership gone, by the time of our 1961 survey, that the European elites acquiesced in American policies even on issues that earlier had seemed most controversial. By substantial majorities in every country (slightly lower in France, where the "Don't Know" response to most questions is generally higher) the elite panels stated that American U-2 overflights of Soviet territory were justified, that America was right to insist on "mutual inspection" as an indispensable condition for any disarmament agreement with the Russians. The European elites also preferred that American conduct of such disarmament negotiations be done bilaterally with the Russians rather than multilaterally (including Europe) or through the UN. They even supported the American policy of "step-by-step arms control" as against the Soviet campaign for "complete and general disarmament" launched by Khrushchev.

On the recurrent trouble spot of Berlin, where Europeans had feared that bipolar conflict might lead to a war that would destroy their continent, huge majorities (three of every four among our panelists) now supported the American policy of a "firm stand." On the traumatic experience at Suez, where Europe's leaders proved their impotence without American support, the panels agreed that the Americans were right to abjure the Anglo-French military action by 88 per cent in Germany, 56 per cent in Britain, and 41 per cent in France (where "nationalist" responses usually are stronger on matters touching French patriotism).[39]

These strongly pro-American attitudes of 1961 reposed upon a solid basis of confidence in America's power and purpose in world affairs. When asked whether the United States, despite the vulnerability of its own continent to direct attack by the new weapons (Soviet nuclear missiles), "will be prepared to continue its guarantee of the military security of Western Europe," the affirmative response was given by 92 per cent in Germany, 89 per cent in Britain, and 68 per cent in France. All things considered, as De Gaulle was later to emphasize after the Cuban "missile crisis," this was a striking vote of confidence in American leadership, including two out of every three among the reticent French panel.

But the statements of De Gaulle had, as early as 1961 when his attention was still riveted on Algeria, begun to cause concern among the other European elites. We asked: "Which of the main Western Allies is most likely, by its own policies, to hamper the fullest development of a sound Western policy in world affairs?" While virtually no panelists named the US, substantial majorities of Germans (68 per cent) and Britons (58 per cent) named France. The French elite were especially troubled by this question. Reflecting their characteristic tendency to take a more nationalist position than the others, only 18 per cent of the French panel named France as most likely to hamper "a sound Western policy." The largest number, a very substantial plurality of 40 per cent, fell into the "Don't Know" category. They either would not, or could not, say.

By 1965, with the Algerian crisis behind him, De Gaulle had turned his oratory against the *"anglosaxonnes"* (an archaism referring to earlier centuries when Britain and America were alleged to consist mainly of ethnic Anglo-Saxons). Univocally, he had withdrawn French military units from NATO, had refused Britain admission to the Common Market, had declared his intention to undermine American "hegemony" (his personal term for what others generally called "leadership") in the Old Continent. De Gaulle's unremitting efforts in these directions had, by 1965, accentuated existing ambivalence and fostered new uncertainty — especially in France, but in the two other countries as well.

Despite their troubled reaction to the shock treatment administered by De Gaulle — perhaps, indeed, because of it — the European elites rapidly closed ranks with each other and behind

American leadership. As we shall see in the detailed analyses of the 1965 surveys (Chapters Four through Six), some modifications of American leadership in the direction of Euramerican "partnership" suggested by President Kennedy appeared more often among elite responses. But the basic commitment to the American Nexus exhibited in 1961 remained firm in 1965. Since that time, following De Gaulle's ejection of NATO from France, the commitment appears to be reconsolidating preparatory to its strengthening. In October 1967, a conference including fourteen of the fifteen NATO members, in which only France did not participate, agreed on a plan to extend NATO's transnational prerogatives — "to convert what has been essentially a military alliance into a political unit capable of arriving at an Atlantic consensus on policies to be pursued in other parts of the world."[40]

Thus, the ambivalence produced by new aspirations confronted by old constraints moved toward a reasonable resolution. New visions of national *grandeur* were transmuted by the durable verities of transnational necessity. For the nations of Europe, the great transnational options were Europa and Atlantica. In the evaluation and activation of both these options, the American Nexus has remained the common condition. We have seen why this was necessary for the recovery and modernization of domestic European society. We turn now to consider why the American Nexus was equally indispensable to Europe's external place in the world.

CHAPTER TWO

Europe in the World Community

THE PEOPLES of Europe are relatively free by world standards because over long centuries they developed high personal capacities which include the potential for continuing personal growth. They have acquired an appropriate set of incentives which were amplified and accelerated by postwar "Americanization." So rapidly have their capacities and incentives grown in the postwar period that Europeans today feel relatively deprived of opportunities. In the sense, and only in the sense, that their opportunities may be less ample than those open to Americans — although substantially greater than personal opportunities open to the rest of the world — postwar Europeans *are* relatively deprived of freedom.

A. WORLD CONTEXT: EUROPE'S RELATIVE DEPRIVATION

"Relative deprivation," as we have learned from recent studies in social psychology, is a function of "reference group," those other persons with whom one compares one's own lot.[1] Where the comparison produces a positive sense of what one may become, the outcome is empathy and emulation.[2] Where the reference group produces values (objects of desire) that lie beyond one's grasp, the more likely outcome is frustration and fear. Where the two reactions are entangled, their product is anxiety and ambivalence.

This, as we have seen, has been a characteristic sequence of postwar European reactions to the American Model. In the early years, when a prostrate Europe looked upon prosperous America as upon a planet beyond reach, the model produced fears of the mass society — its culture and its consumption, its production and its politics. In the second postwar decade, as the Marshall Men and other overseas Americans helped Europeans to absorb and adapt the technology of "productivity," the mood changed to a positive sense of acceptance. Prospering Europe, its reach now considerably extended, could react to America's world leadership with empathy and to its domestic society with emulation. As Paul Samuelson quipped in London's *Punch*, the Europeans perceived that "what one fool can learn to like, so can another." He continued:

Speaking seriously as an economist, I wonder whether much in culture that is thought to be peculiarly American is not rather a simple reflection of what characterizes any economy whose per capita income has risen above $3,000 a year.[3]

As European prosperity transformed European culture in the American direction of mass consumption, the satisfaction of some appetites whetted others — again the case of *"l'appétit vient en mangeant."* As Europe came abreast of American mass culture, some Europeans began to think in terms of American world power. For reference group theory teaches us that the valued object tends to be perceived as a whole. As Karl Marx put it long ago in his Introduction to *Das Kapital*: "The more developed society presents to the less developed society a picture of its own future." A "picture" in this sense is a diffuse but selective image which includes all the desired facets of the valued object.

But, in turning their gaze upon American world power, desirous Europeans extended their reach beyond their grasp. By simple extension of Samuelson's hypothesis, if it takes about $3,000 per capita income to emulate American culture, it probably takes at least $6,000 to emulate American power. In 1965, when our last survey of European elite attitudes was made, America's "real per capita income" was more than double that of Britain, France, Germany — and increasing at a similar rate.[4] Hence, by the time these countries reach present American levels, American growth is likely to have maintained the present "gap." And while the transformation of culture is often more costly in human terms, the augmentation of power through technology is always more costly in money. This is the source of current European ambivalence, which we will consider in detail, about the notorious "technological gap."

A significant product of this particular imbalance in the Want: Get Ratio, where national reach exceeds societal grasp, is the tendency to displace frustration onto public objects, in particular the political authorities. An interesting indicator of this process is the "Gallup International Satisfaction Index," which asks national samples of Europeans whether they are satisfied with their personal situation and with their country's performance. The results shown in Table 2.1 were reported for the 1963 survey:

TABLE 2.1. INTERNATIONAL SATISFACTION INDEX*

	Britain	France	Germany
Satisfied with Personal Situation†	61%	58%	67%
Satisfied with Country's Performance	41%	34%	28%

* Adapted from Gallup International Releases, September 1963.
† Mean of per cent satisfied on seven criteria: your housing situation, your children's education, your family income, future facing you and your family, standard of living of yourself and your family, amount of leisure and free time you get to yourself, the work you do.

Most striking is the "satisfaction gap" in all three countries. Very substantial majorities are satisfied with their personal situation — about two of every three in Britain and Germany; somewhat less, but still well over half, in France. The picture is reversed when the same respondents are asked to judge the performance of their own country as a whole. On this, about two of every three express dissatisfaction. While the surplus positive valuation in Britain is extremely interesting, the general consensus is clear: the peoples are far more satisfied with their personal situation than with their country's performance. Of the countries reported, only Norway showed a perfect equilibrium (or anything near it): 67 per cent expressed personal and public satisfaction.

Such findings doubtless provided food for thought among the elites and governments of these countries. We note indeed that, since this 1963 survey was reported, the governing Conservatives have been turned out by Labour in Britain and the two major parties in Germany (CDU and SPD) have formed their unprecedented Grand Coalition. While De Gaulle personally was reelected President by a narrow margin in 1965, his prestige and his party (UNR) suffered a severe setback in the legislative elections of 1967.

In the absence of qualitative and explanatory data from the Gallup poll of 1963, any inference must be speculative. Reflection on subsequent events and our own elite survey in these three countries suggest that popular estimates of government capacity for sweeping action may be excessive. In Europe today, national policy is constrained by the web of transnational interactions and institutions that has been spun in the postwar decades. Such constraints operate as well upon the United States and Russia as upon others, but the constraints upon the weaker nations of Europe cut wider and deeper — according to the old saw that the weaker must hang together or hang separately. An acute British observer has referred to this as "the logic imposed upon all Europeans in an age which leaves no middle ground between the superpower and the confederation of free peoples."[5]

The idea of a "confederation of free peoples" has stimulated many European intellectuals for generations.[6] But it was only after World War II that the political leaders of Europe — Churchill, Adenauer, Schuman, Spaak — began to consider seriously the embodiment of this idea in operative institutions of decision and execution. At this point, the idea proliferated into many forms: Big Europe and Little Europe, the Atlantic Community, the Free World, the United Nations. All of these represented, in one way or another, a "confederation of free peoples" (the Soviet Bloc had not yet been formed when the United Nations was created).

As the first postwar decade ran its course, debates were heard and decisions were made. The Cold War erupted and most of the world was bipolarized, in some measure, between the superpowers. The United Nations' potential role as institution builder for a world community — the "one world" that Wendell Willkie expounded to eager readers everywhere — was rapidly constrained as its major agency for decision making, the Security Council, became a divisive rather than a unifying force. The idea of a Free World was transformed into a non-Communist world. The Atlantic Community was activated mainly through the military institution of NATO. The European Community was riven first by the East-West partition ("Iron Curtain"), then further subdivided in the western region by two rivalrous combinations (EEC and EFTA) mainly concerned with their own economic well-being.

Hopes for a postwar world commonwealth of human dignity were rapidly constrained and parochialized. "Regional associations" became the order of business at the United Nations. The regionalism that became operative in various parts of the world was principally concerned with goals that had previously been the business of nationalism: protection, prosperity, prestige. Globalism was demoted, and parochialism was raised to a higher level. Even the grand ideas of Europa and Atlantica which animated the second postwar decade were regionalized in this sense. Europa was mainly identified with The Six; Atlantica included Britain, Canada, and the United States. How did this restrictive regionalization of ideas that originated with a larger scope come about?

B. EUROPEAN POSTWAR SEQUENCES

1. Europe in 1945: The Psychohistorical Aftermath

Europe, as World War II ended in 1945, was a neighborhood of diminished lands inhabited by debilitated peoples. They had known neither peace nor prosperity in their lifetime. The earlier bloodletting of 1914–1918 had drained Europe's human resources; the inflation of the twenties had wasted its economic resources; the Nazism of the thirties had subverted its political resources. World War II was the manifest symptom and active agent of Europe's material and spiritual decline. Its central tendency was irrational — a war no European could "win" — and its outcome was fratricidal. Hitler's war did not bring oranges to German children, as he had promised, but it did deprive other European children of their oranges.

The leveling effect of World War II was *down*. Victors were in no better state than vanquished. For every Hamburg there was a Rotterdam, for every Düsseldorf a Coventry. For every Nazi who heiled Hitler, there was a Quisling elsewhere in Europe. Just as military operations damaged its material state, so psychological operations weakened its spiritual condition. As the war ended, the lands and peoples of Europe were ravaged. If the outcome was not quite Wagner's *Götterdämmerung*, it did move Europe a long step toward Spengler's *Untergang des Abendlandes*. The decline of Europe was palpable and, it appeared, permanent.

For Europe's peoples had been touched in those deep and vital parts that animate a high civilization and activate its social system — namely, their identifications and expectations, their self-confidence and self-reliance. The damage to European property could be repaired in relatively short order by a society with modern resources. It was not at all evident, however, that the damage to the European psyche could be so readily repaired. What resources could be used to heal the deep wounds of guilt among Germans, of shame among Frenchmen, of weariness among Britons?

Everywhere in Europe hatred rankled, spite flared, vengeance acted: the French *maquis* (including many whose "resistance" had signified only concealment) showed their righteous wrath by shaving the heads of female collaborators and hanging the necks of male collaborators; the Czech "patriots" slapped people overheard speaking German in the streets; the Italian avengers went from their manhandling of Mussolini to bigger and bolder feats of castration and concupiscence. Europe, in 1945–1946, was a living laboratory of political psychopathology.

Where the long years of prewar and wartime frustration did not eventuate in projection of self-hatred and violent aggression, they produced the less overt but equally pathological symptoms of regression. These were especially marked among the multimillions of Europeans classified by postwar relief agencies as "victims of Nazism" — in the concentration camps, forced labor camps, and the Displaced Persons (DP) camps. Outside of the camps, there were other multimillions of ethnic and ideological DP's. The physical displacement of Europeans had begun with World War I, notably with the emigration of Russians after the Bolshevik Revolution and its aftermath in Eastern Europe. It had continued during the early interwar years with the crumbling of empires and the eruption of pent-up antagonisms between their previously constrained ethnic formations, notably in the former Austro-Hungarian and Ottoman empires.[7]

During the later interwar years, displacement of unwanted persons became the deliberate policy of the coercive ideological movements — Fascism in Italy, Falangism in Spain, Nazism in Germany.[8] By World War II, especially after the occupation of the Low Countries, the fall of France, and the invasion of Russia, DP's from every part of Europe had been pushed to and beyond the water's edge of their old continent. Physical displacement became a normal way of life among postwar Europeans.

Even among those other millions of Europeans who had remained physically in place, a process of psychic displacement occurred. There were the widespread symptoms of fatigue and apathy that might be expected after the anxieties and privations of a long war. These were deepened, among generations that had known neither peace nor prosperity in their lifetime, by the sense of an aimless past and purposeless future. No exhilaration was diffused by a victory that left winners in the same boat as losers, particularly when the boat was swamped and seemed ready to sink. The peoples of Europe, having lost the spiritual guidance of their traditional nationalisms and ideologies, found no ready replacement to orient their future prospects. Nor, at first, did their leaders.

Yet the European boat, waterlogged and apparently rudderless, did not founder. Today, twenty years later, Europe sails a tide of prosperity higher than any known to past or present generations. How did this happen? What resources enabled Europe to rise from postwar depression to the heights of prosperity? These are the questions we ask today.

When our study began in September 1954, a fortnight after the defeat of EDC, other questions figured more appropriately on the European agenda. These were the questions arising as the nations of Europe moved out of the first postwar decade into the second. The decade 1945–1955 had made it clear that the European nations were capable of managing their own recovery — from the celebrated *Wirtschaftswünder* of Germany to the economic "miracles" in Benelux, Italy, and France. The recovery decade in turn raised questions for thoughtful leaders, aware that their recovery clearly had been achieved under rather special conditions (Marshall Plan and NATO). Were these conditions of past success reliable and adequate for future needs? Were new conditions necessary or desirable to promote their prospects?

As Europe moved into its second postwar decade, these were the questions that preoccupied European leaders. Less grandiose and universalistic than the terms of the traditional ideologies that flourished in imperial Europe, they were more appropriate to the narrower scope and shorter range of policy concerns in postwar Europe. They were, indeed, a relatively candid acknowledgment that the global reach of former European empires exceeded the grasp of present European nations; that the nations were more likely to prosper in the years ahead by cooperation rather than competition; that Western Europe as a whole in the postwar world arena was dependent in some critical matters of national interest upon the United States.

Recognition of these new conditions of life launched the nations in their second postwar decade upon the course of European and Atlantic interdependence. The years 1955–1965, which are covered by our surveys, thus became the first decade of Europa and Atlantica convergence. It was in this decade that European leaders, confident that the worst of their postwar crisis was over, began to think of their short-term problems in the context of their long-term existence, to seek a more precise and palatable definition of their national and regional role in the world. If they did not always "look shining at new styles of architecture," surely "a change of heart" was clear in the attitudes that shaped such events as WEU (1955), Suez (1956), *la relance européenne* (1957), Treaty of Rome (1958), Fifth Republic (later 1958), Algeria (1956–1962), rejection of Britain (1963), EEC agricultural fund (1964), ejection of NATO (1965–1966).[9]

The evolution of European attitudes over this distinctive historical period will be reported nation by nation and year by year. Here we turn to an overview of fundamental factors that have conditioned European attitudes throughout the decade; we then review the contextual situation in each country and in the European environment during each year of our study. Our question is: As the leaders of Europe faced the relative deprivation of their historic world power, what factors conditioned the fundamental "set" of their postwar attitudes and actions?

2. The 1955–1965 Decade: Fundamental Factors

The framework of postwar politics for Europe, as for the rest of the world, was the bipolarization of global power between America and Russia.[10] The impact of bipolarity, however, was greater in Europe than elsewhere. For it was Europe itself, over the long centuries since the Holy Roman Empire, that had always exercised world dominion. No intruder — Mongol, Arab, or Ottoman — had been able to impose its will upon the Old Continent. On the contrary, Europe had spread its own rule throughout the navigable globe. Disputes over particular parcels of the world's real estate were conducted almost exclusively among the European nations on European terms. Now, abruptly and abysmally, the long era of European dominion was over. Global decisions passed from Europe to the two non-European superpowers.[11]

This provides the framework of postwar politics for Europe because each of the fundamental factors identified below derives, more or less directly, from bipolarity: (1) displacement of the world power center from Europe; (2) dismantling of the European empires; (3) European incapacity to guarantee their own national security; (4) European incapacity to promote their own national prosperity; (5) the European "crisis of confidence." We consider each of these briefly as background for closer examination of European elite attitudes toward protection, prosperity, and prestige in the drastically altered postwar world (see Chapters Four through Six).

a. Displacement of World Power Center. The displacement of the world power center from Europe entailed two painful consequences for the continental nations. No longer could they, singly or in concert, make controlling decisions over those large areas of Asia, Africa, and the Middle East that only yesterday had been their exclusive domain. Nor, even more painful, could they make some decisions about their own national policies without the concurrence, and sometimes the initiative, of the United States as a major supplier of resources needed to make such decisions operational. Our data on Euramerican relations show how the European elites responded to the displacement of the world power center.

b. Dismantling of Empires. The dismantling of European empires began in earnest during World War II, passed its floodtide during the decade of our study, and nears completion today. The British, either wiser or wearier than the continental colonizers, early in the postwar years made a clear commitment to peaceful decolonization by mutual consent and cooperation. The model case was India, in 1947, with Pakistan, Burma, and Ceylon also granted independence. As British rule over the huge subcontinent was terminated, the French Empire, less graciously and more violently, was being ejected from its former strongholds — from Syria in the Middle East, from Indochina in Southeast Asia, from Algeria in North Africa. One after another, more or less forcibly, the European nations were removed from their former dominions — the Dutch from Indonesia, the Belgians from the Congo, the Portuguese from Goa. Efforts to salvage remains of the collapsed empires, as in the British Commonwealth and the French *Communauté*, produced limited or negligible results.

Wherever the European imperium withdrew, there the United

States, whether by invitation or by its own initiative, usually filled the "power vacuum." The clearest cases involved a formal declaration of American involvement. These have occurred not only in the ex-colonial continents but in Europe itself. Indeed, the first such postwar declaration occurred when Britain, no longer able to maintain its traditional "sphere of influence" in the Balkans, invited the United States to take over — as it did by enunciating the Truman Doctrine, which guaranteed the security of Greece and Turkey. This was followed a few years later, during the great Suez crisis, by American replacement of traditional British responsibility in the Middle East via the Eisenhower Doctrine.

The Suez crisis of 1956, as the decade we are studying got under way, was the great watershed of Europe's diminishing powers in the postwar world. The point was not so much that it certified the end of European empire, for the end of empire was already quite clear. Moreover, Anglo-French objectives at Suez were certainly not imperialist, despite the blatant Soviet propaganda, in the sense that they included the recolonization of Egypt. The Suez attack aimed rather at recovering national property rights of which they had been illegally deprived, in the judgment of the British and French governments, by the hostile unilateral act of another sovereign power.

The real point of Suez was that, even on so narrow an issue of national interest, the two greatest former empires of Europe were unable to act effectively in their former domains without the policy concurrence of the United States. When the Soviets threatened (Suez was the first major instance of Soviet propaganda tactics that came to be called "nuclear blackmail") and the Americans withheld their guarantee, the Anglo-French leadership felt obliged to abandon their objectives at Suez. The salient results were the resignation of Anthony Eden as prime minister, the further disarray of the Fourth Republic, and the transfer of Middle East responsibility to America under the Eisenhower Doctrine.

Suez was a humiliating failure for two great European powers and it taught a humbling twofold lesson to all the nations of Europe. One lesson was that the American guarantee of European security carried a price tag that could be marked up as Washington judged the occasion to require. At Suez it was made clear that the American guarantee would not extend anywhere in the world arena where European policy initiatives were taken without American approval.

This taught the hard lesson of Europe's place in America's picture of world security. The second and related lesson, which in 1956 seemed even harder to Europeans uncertain that their economic recovery was durable, was that their national prosperity, as well as their national security, was subject to constraints imposed by their own relative weakness and by American world policy. The Anglo-French action had been justified as a response to an illegal deprivation of their property rights which threatened vital national economic interests. They learned, however, that this argument was unconvincing when it ran against the mainstream of vital American political interests. It is worth elaborating briefly the sense of these lessons, which are respectively the third and fourth "fundamental factors" just listed, for postwar Europeans.

c. Incapacity to Guarantee National Security. European incapacity to guarantee their own military security followed directly from two factors: (1) the inability of these war-weary, prosperity-loving nations (with sophisticated urban-industrial populations) to reconstruct conventional defenses with their high human costs; (2) their inability to reproduce the high-cost nuclear technology created during World War II.

There is an interesting question, which we shall leave moot, why these European nations rich in fiscal and human resources did not develop a real nuclear capability while so poor a country as Russia was doing this. The important point is that Europe, faced with a strong conventional threat from the Soviet Union which it felt unable to meet conventionally, eagerly turned for protection to the American nuclear monopoly — an absolute monopoly at the time NATO was created (1949). This situation was short-lived. For the very first postwar decade was marked by the successful Soviet challenge to the American nuclear monopoly. By the second postwar decade, to which this report is oriented, the superpowers had achieved nuclear parity, in the sense of a nuclear sufficiency that made "mutual deterrence" seem a plausible strategy for both. But the continental nations had not even begun to catch up, despite the highly publicized notion of a French *force de frappe*, and Britain had even lost its marginal advantage relative to the continent with the decision to limit development of its Blue Streak missile.[12]

The plain fact was that no postwar European nation, nor any coalition of them, could afford to mount an adequate defense against

Soviet attack. And expansionist Soviet strategy in the first postwar decade, the Cold War years when Stalin ruled Russia, gave Europeans ample justification for anxiety on this point. This was a fundamental factor indeed in the evolution of postwar Europe. For whatever subtle differences have been stressed by theorists of nationhood, they are agreed on the primacy of national security from foreign conquest. An indispensable requirement of nationhood, in the language of the American Constitution, is "to provide for the common defense." Without this, no nation can long endure.[13]

Accordingly, the felt need for a viable security system animated the search for transnational institutions and processes which will be reported in detail. On the strictly military side, Europe's utter dependence on the American guarantee required a new transatlantic organization of the type represented by NATO. However dissident some voices may sound today, particularly in Gaullist France, NATO was the welcome and effective institutional guarantee of European security during the first fifteen years of its twenty-year treaty term (which expires in 1969). In the debates over NATO organization that will resonate on both sides of the Atlantic over the years immediately ahead, it will be useful to take heed of this report's findings on NATO as the bedrock of Atlantica during the postwar decades.

d. Incapacity to Promote National Prosperity. Alongside the classic requirement of adequate military security, nationhood entails the ancient responsibility of maintaining at least minimum conditions of well-being for its people — the obligation, again as formulated by the American Constitution, "to promote the general welfare." Until quite recent times, governments took a relatively relaxed attitude toward this obligation: The religious preachments which sanctified poverty were matched by the political practices which sustained it.[14]

With the spread of an urban industrial class in the nineteenth century, among all the modernizing societies of the West, a sharply rising set of demands for well-being became audible in the public forum and an expanding set of responses became visible in the political arena. By the twentieth century, rising demands for public welfare and social security had been clearly articulated and powerfully aggregated. In the postwar period that concerns us here, the responsibility of government for maximizing the satisfaction of such demands had been incorporated into Western political mores. The nation-state had acquired a fundamental commitment to promote national prosperity, a commitment binding upon conservative, liberal, and radical governments alike. The new era of Participant Society foreseen by earlier prophets, based on the concepts of social welfare prescribed by socialists and instrumented by the techniques of fiscal management prescribed by Keynesians, was suddenly upon us.[15]

In this new situation, however, the leaders of postwar Europe suffered from severe frustrations. The underlying ideas of social welfare had originated in the European intellectual tradition and were familiar to all who had been schooled in that tradition. When they were transformed from ideas into mores by their articulation as political expectations and popular demands, however, they required a deep reshaping of the traditional resources and techniques of government. For this purpose, the nation-states of postwar Europe found themselves suddenly inadequate. They did not have the resources, and without them could not operationalize the techniques, needed to promote national prosperity on the scale expected and demanded by their peoples.

Their only recourse was to find an effective transnational alternative. Two basic organizing ideas were at hand — Europa and Atlantica — and both were tried. The Atlantic idea, which promised to guarantee military security effectively through NATO, was applied to the problem of economic well-being through OEEC (later OECD). Despite its considerable contributions to European recovery and reconstruction in the immediate postwar years, the OEEC appeared inadequate to promote European prosperity on a scale and tempo that would meet popular expectations and demands. Accordingly, a pioneering effort to apply the European Idea was made with the Schuman Plan which created, in 1950, the European Coal and Steel Community (ECSC).

Both of these experiments produced some successes promptly and gave promise of larger benefits in the long run. Yet, their constitutional structure and operational mode — perhaps, paradoxically, because of their rapid results — provoked resentments and regenerated doubts among some European leaders. This is the process of "restriction by partial incorporation" which is a fundamental mechanism in the psychohistorical sequence, the vacillations and oscillations, of postwar Europe. The crux of the issue was deeply psychic, involving nothing less than one's personal and collective self-image. The troubling questions were: Could one gain a new identity as a European without losing one's old identity as a Frenchman (Italian, German)? Could the elites reshape nationalism without renouncing nationhood, the sense of psychocultural community cultivated over long centuries of political collectivity? Could one entrust the "national interest" to a transnational decision-making agency which regarded any nation as only one among six or more?

Such questions, once lodged in the psyche, tend to produce anxiety and ambivalence even among those overtly hospitable to transnational experimentation. Among those deeply ego-involved with national imagery, transnational initiatives evoke violent resistance. Such reactions underlay the "crisis of confidence" which Europe, having undergone many similar crises in the long course of its historical transformations, faced as it weighed the alternatives of Europa and Atlantica in the second postwar decade.

e. Incapacity to Maintain National Prestige. Public issues that touch private persons in vital places are not readily or rapidly resolved. The idea of European unity has been heard in the public forum for centuries. From the Holy Roman Empire to Hitler's Reich, any transitory measure of unification was achieved only by subjugation, occupation, and forced pacification. Where achieved by negotiation, it was enforced by superior power outside the continent, as the Congress of Vienna was policed throughout the nineteenth century by the Pax Britannica.

Only after the mutual destruction of World War II, which left the Old Continent with several Carthages rather than one Rome, did the idea of transnational integration acquire compelling force in the minds of European leaders. That the idea has not yet received full institutional expression only two decades later scarcely constitutes evidence for or against its long-term viability. Rather more remarkable is the wide scope of the integrative institutions that have been made operational in recent years.

These integrative institutions have weathered severe storms, exemplified in the polar oppositions that often divide France and Holland within the EEC;[16] the flotsam of continuously heavy seas is visible in such epithets as "Eurocracy" and "Euromania." They have not, however, laid the ghosts of Europe's national past. As the continent which invented modern nationalism and brought nations to the highest peaks of political power, Europe naturally finds it hard to be the first to disown its progeny. The contemporary crisis of confidence thus involves ambivalence for the many Europeans who would like to have both the familiar comforts of nationhood and the expected benefits of transnational integration.

The crisis also involves anxiety for those Europeans who, wanting both national comforts and transnational benefits, fear that in seeking both they may end by having neither. That ambivalence and anxiety have racked the living generation of Europeans is natural, as we have seen, for choosing between two desired objects is the hardest test in the theory of value. One tends, by some intuitive minimax process, to clutch the "lesser evil" but without relinquishing hope of the "greater good." The effect on policymaking is vacillation and oscillation.

The long-run prospects for eventual European integration are relatively optimistic. Youngsters growing up in the euphoric environment of integration today — enjoying the benefits it brings in easier tourism, more scholarships, better jobs — will probably find it less painful than their parents to say "I am a European" without thinking "I am *really* a Frenchman (Belgian, Hollander)." If they do not make the integrative institutions more fully operative, then their children are likely to do so.

While the passage of time will ease the present crisis of conscience and confidence, however, the living generation of Europeans must continue to face hard decisions between stark choices in the short run. In the struggle between nationalism and transnationalism, despite the intervention of Gaullism, our data indicate strongly that transnationalism is winning — at least attitudinally, if not always politically. The apparent contest between the organizational forms of transnationalism designated as Europa and Atlantica, a contest largely initiated and sustained in its present form by Gaullism, remains to be clarified before its outcome can be determined.

The contest between Europa and Atlantica, which arose in the second postwar decade and is likely to persist over the years ahead, is interwoven with all the central concerns of this study. Our data chapters will report on those key issues in the contest which we have briefly reviewed — the quest for transnational protection, prosperity, and prestige; the reshaping of personal identifications, expectations, and demands among the living peoples of Europe. We have seen that one key term is crucial in the Europa-Atlantica contest;

however, for it shapes the definition and conditions affecting the operation of virtually every other term. This is the role of America. As the data will show, many among the European elites we have surveyed tend to formulate their options on nationalism, internationalism, or supranationalism mainly in terms of their attitudes toward European dependence, interdependence, or independence of America. It may therefore be useful, at this point, to outline the three principal scenarios that have structured European elite attitudes toward the world arena over the past decade, with special attention to the Euramerican component.

C. THREE EURATLANTIC SCENARIOS*

Postwar Europe began with the traumatic recognition that its historic role as the world's power center was lost, that it must chart a new course bounded by the bipolar centers now located in Washington and Moscow. Eastern Europe's choice was made for it by Soviet policy and the Red Army; for the past two decades it has remained Sovietized. Western Europe, politically free to choose its own course, was compelled by the force of its circumstances — military, economic, sociological — to seek the protection and patronage of the United States.

American acceptance of responsibility for West European security and welfare in the face of Soviet expansionism was rapid and radical. In 1947 at Stuttgart, Secretary Byrnes accepted the challenge of Cold War, and the Truman Doctrine was established. In 1948, the European Recovery Program proposed at Harvard by Secretary Marshall was embodied in the OEEC. In 1949 at Washington, the NATO Treaty put the military security of twelve (later fifteen) European nations under American guarantee. Thus, in the three short years following V-E Day, American responsibility for European safety and recovery was mutually acknowledged, institutionally formulated, and operationally activated. Europe's readiness for self-help within this framework was activated a year later, when the Schuman Plan placed the coal and steel of six continental nations under the supranational High Authority of the ECSC.

---

* This section can be usefully read in conjunction with the paper by our colleague, L. P. Bloomfield, "Western Europe to the Mid-Seventies: Five Scenarios," M.I.T. Center for International Studies, No. A/68–3. We have focused on the three scenarios justified by the empirical findings of the TEEPS study. These are readily compatible with the Bloomfield scenarios.

Hence, by 1950 Euratlantica was off to a strong start. It represented a degree of cooperation between the best political minds and wills on two continents that is probably unique in the historical record. On the American side, the manifold policies of Euratlantic cooperation were initiated by the Marshall Plan. On the European side, the Monnet Model laid out a long-term blueprint for building a United States of Europe. The two scenarios, conceived on two different continents, produced a coherent drama that appeared to inspire the principal actors and induce a healthy catharsis in their audience.

But in the wings skulked an Achillean hero frustrated by the plot, by the story line, and especially by the bit part that had been assigned to him. De Gaulle had wanted a plot about Euronationalism, in which the story line would elevate France, with himself in the starring role of Marianne. So, in the isolated message center of Colombey-les-deux-églises, served by a devoted cast of supporting players, he wrote out his own scenario of Euronationalism — which he called *l'Europe des patries* — and waited his turn upstage center. This came in 1958, with the Algerian crisis, as a relatively minor walk-on part in the world drama, but De Gaulle recast it in the heroic mold. By 1960, the Euratlantic scenario was in doubt; by 1965, it was in difficulties; by 1970, when the treaties which created the institutions of Atlantica and Europa come up for reconsideration, the Euratlantic drama will surely have to be rewritten in terms that accommodate the Gaullist scenario.

That De Gaulle as political actor has played a starring role in the third scenario of the Euratlantic drama is beyond doubt, as is the effect of his role upon the story line of the next act. That De Gaulle has altered the basic plot, or the outcome of the Euratlantic drama as a whole, is highly doubtful. To see why this is so — one major conclusion we draw from our decade of TEEPS research — we sketch the three scenarios in turn.

1. The Marshall Plan: Atlantica

The American conceptualization of the postwar world was comprehensive and global. Though formulated with a keen eye for American interests, the American image of world politics was not parochial and the self-serving facets of its policies were interfaced with benevolence toward others who were cooperative. If anything, the postwar policies initiated during President Truman's momentous years of decision[17] were assailed as excessively global and comprehensive, rather vulgarly as "globaloney" by the Luce press and in more considered terms by Walter Lippmann's critique of "containment" as excessively comprehensive.[18]

American policy for the postwar world was also responsible in its "respect for the opinions of mankind" and restrained in its mindfulness of long-term consequences. Thus, as the Soviets (not yet — lacking nuclear weapons — officially a superpower) steadily annexed one after another country of Eastern Europe, America made no move to annex any part of Western Europe. Such an objective, well within the capacity of American power, lay outside the scenario of American purpose. Nor, as it became clear that without external impediment the Soviets soon would possess their own nuclear arsenal, did American policy — despite the Great Debate of the late 1940's — ever incorporate the notion of a "pre-emptive strike" designed to ensure America of a nuclear monopoly and with it world hegemony.

World hegemony, with its short-term panaceas that eventuate in long-term malignancies, never entered into the conception of American policy. Nor, at the other end of the scale, did America use its great power to promote mankind's dream of a world commonwealth. Despite the urging of World Federalists and other proponents of "one world," American policy followed its more restricted scenario, perhaps because its role in world leadership was too new to incorporate so vast a vision. If postwar American leadership eschewed both world hegemony and world commonwealth, it did rapidly become the foremost protagonist of innovative institutions to promote world cooperation. The creation of the United Nations at San Francisco in 1945 remains a monumental tribute to the benevolent purposes which restrained its awesome power and shaped its global policies in the postwar world.

As the machinery created at San Francisco grew creaky, with the bipolar conflicts between Russia and America that generated the Cold War, the United Nations turned toward regional cooperation as a substitute for global cooperation. American policy adapted to this new situation by augmenting and accelerating its programs for the protection and prosperity of the world's regions. Under the "bold new program" announced as Point IV in 1949, American aid spread from Europe to developing countries on every continent. The NATO model for European security was extended in a globe-circling system of alliances with areas threatened by Soviet expansionism — MEDO (later CENTO) in the Middle East, SEATO in Southeast Asia, ANZUS in the Australia–New Zealand region of the Pacific. The century-long "Americanization" of Alaska and Hawaii was acknowledged, at long last, by their full incorporation into the United States.

It would be naive to disregard the importance of American self-interest in these basic policies, but it would be cynical to see only this in the programs whereby these policies were activated. Enlightened self-interest led responsible Americans to perceive each such regional arrangement as a *quid pro quo* conferring substantial benefits upon all participants. Whereas military aid conferred *mutual* security (usually presumed to be more beneficial for America), economic aid often was a *unilateral* benefit to the receiving country — the gift a prosperous America conferred upon poorer lands to help them help themselves.

The precedent for such regional arrangements was the Euramerican model initiated by the Marshall Plan and consolidated by NATO. And throughout the postwar decades — despite the often anguished attacks by "Asia Firsters," not to mention "America Firsters" — mutual cooperation with Europe has remained a top priority in American world policy. The Euramerican foundations underlying the Atlantic scenario had been built over centuries. They reposed upon the solid ground of mutual interest and reciprocal need, common perspectives and shared aspirations. The strong chain of these Euramerican links was perhaps most apparent in their unspoken assumptions. Just as Americans could not realistically conceive of annexing Europe (or fragmenting it) under American hegemony, so Europe could not realistically conceive of joining the Soviet side in the Cold War that bipolarized the postwar world (despite extremist calls for a *"renversement des alliances"* during the EDC controversy).

These psychopolitical foundations were made explicit in the wartime meeting of Churchill and Roosevelt on the Atlantic seas which produced the Atlantic Charter, with its ringing declaration of the "Four Freedoms" for all peoples. What was needed, for the postwar world, was the construction of a durable superstructure of new Euramerican institutions that would transmute common attitudes into collective actions. This was done and Atlantica came into being.

The Atlantic structure, with American power as its backbone, promptly produced visible benefits for Europe. With the creation of NATO, Soviet expansionism toward the West was immediately checked. The satellization of Europe, which had continued steadily through the Czech coup of 1948, was arrested in 1949. Since then, despite intense pressure at Berlin and elsewhere, no further area of Europe has been brought under Soviet control. (Query to future historians: Would Turkey, Greece, West Germany, Austria, Yugoslavia, Italy, Finland, and Denmark, even France and Benelux be independent nations today if some functional equivalent of NATO had not been activated promptly after 1945?)

The success of NATO was matched by the Marshall Plan institutions. Economic recovery was not so immediate as the military arrest of Soviet expansion, but it too occurred with unprecedented rapidity. By 1950, only two years later, the "economic miracle" (*Wirtschaftswünder*) was apparent in Germany and soon thereafter became visible elsewhere. American "productivity teams" guided by Marshall Men were active throughout Europe; reconversion and rationalization became the slogans of Europe's new technological thrust into industry and even agriculture; the European Payments Union (EPU) eased the traditional burdens of multilateral exchanges among the diverse hard and soft currencies as well as the acute postwar problem of dollar shortages.

Atlantica in 1950 was off to a good start, with a bright course ahead, in the critical sectors of military protection and economic prosperity. In that same year, largely as a result of Atlantic successes, occurred the first major move toward Europa — a new European scenario which, paradoxically, was later to be turned by some against the concept of Atlantica that nurtured it. This was the Monnet model.

2. The Monnet Model: Europa

We recall that the Schuman Plan, which created the ECSC, institutionalized a supranational High Authority over the coal and steel of six continental nations including France, Germany, Italy, and the three Benelux countries. ECSC was the first stage in the grand design of Europa proposed by Jean Monnet and informally endorsed by the United States. A series of "communities" — economic, military, political — was to bring transnational integration by successive stages to a point where the desirable and feasible outcome would be a United States of Europe. Monnet's publication of his model opened with the sentence: "The United States of America was the world's first common market." The initial stage was to integrate the European economy so that recovery would lead to self-sustaining growth and increasing prosperity. The second stage would integrate Europe's military capacities to provide fuller participation in the American protection of their own continent. The crowning stage of political integration would create a Europa truly capable of sharing with America the destiny of Euratlantica.

The economic stage was successfully launched with ECSC, but the Monnet model was arrested and very nearly destroyed by the struggles over the second stage of military integration. Promptly after the institution of ECSC, the creation of a European Defense Community (EDC) was proposed for the same six nations. Monnet resigned his leadership of ECSC to direct the campaign for EDC, which was soon ratified by all member-nations but France (which had put forward the EDC proposal as the Pléven Plan). The proposal divided French leaders deeply, the most bitter schism since Henry IV surrendered at Troyes according to one French historian and since the Dreyfus Case according to another. After four years of polemic and controversy, the French Assembly, having undergone an accession of Gaullist and Poujadist anti-EDC deputies in the legislative election of 1951, rejected the treaty in 1954.[19]

The EDC outcome was a setback to the Europa of the integrationists, to the Atlantica of the Americans, and a clear warning that both of these transnational ideas would have to cope, in the long hard years ahead, with sentiments prevailing among some French decision makers. It was here foreshadowed that Europa and Atlantica were contesting ideas among leading Frenchmen — and that, in this contest, the role of America would be a crucial term. The stage was set for the entry of De Gaulle.

But the Europeanists had a few years of grace; and, under the vigorous leadership of Monnet, they made the most of it. Regrouping their forces after the shock of EDC's defeat, they had by 1956 undertaken the new initiative (*la relance européenne*) that led to the Treaty of Rome in early 1958. Their timing was essential to their cause, for within months De Gaulle was in power at the head of the Fifth Republic. Thereafter, European integration as envisioned by the Monnet model remained at the economic stage authorized by the Treaty of Rome. No movement toward the military or political stages of integration in Monnet's Europa has been discernible during the Gaullist decade. Instead, Europe and America with the rest of the world were confronted with an alternate scenario for their political future, the Gaullist design.

3. The Gaullist Design: Euronationalism

A full appraisal of De Gaulle is beyond the scope of this study. However the future may judge his stature as a statesman, it is now clear that he has been a vigorous publicist, effective among some of his contemporaries. We confine ourselves to his design for a *Europe des patries*, which we call "Euronationalism," and we are less concerned with the *mystique* that has suffused Gaullism than we are with the plain intent toward Euratlantica expressed in many of his declarations and some of his actions.

This plain intent has one supreme objective: that France shall lead continental Europe in the formation and execution of any and all common policies, thereby raising the influence of France in Europe and *a fortiori*, through the continent's aggregated resources, in the world. The pursuit of this supreme objective has entailed one set of ancillary policies within the EEC and another with respect to France's great-power allies.

Within the EEC, a major policy has been to constrain all forms of transnationalism that do not bring a net economic advantage to France at little or no cost to its national political sovereignty. This has been exhibited in the consistent French focus upon the Council of Ministers (in which each of the six members is represented *qua* nation) as against the EEC Commission (which is charged by the Treaty of Rome with the initiation of transnational programs binding upon all member-nations after acceptance by the Council of Ministers). France has carried this so far as to insist upon, and obtain, the retirement of Walter Hallstein upon expiration of his term as President of the EEC Commission — because he was "too transnational." Among the early acts of De Gaulle in power, indeed, was to remove from the presidency of Euratom his compatriot Etienne Hirsch — because he was "too European" in the field of nuclear energy development, a field in which Gaullism sought for France a pre-emptive or at least pre-eminent place on the continent.

A second policy that France has pursued vigorously within the EEC is the structural paralysis, or at least functional impairment, of the European Parliament. Gaullist delegates at Strasbourg, where the European Parliament convenes, have blocked every initiative to create direct Community-wide election of representatives by the peoples of the member-states (rather than their delegation by national parliaments as at present). This issue became acute during our 1965 survey, which included Eurocrat as well as national elite panels, owing to the creation of a common agricultural fund to be administered by the EEC Commission. It was argued that, according to the theory of popular sovereignty over public funds shared by all member-countries, such substantial sums of money could not properly be administered by appointive officials without surveillance and control by directly elected representatives of the EEC constituency. In killing this idea, the French threw a bone to its adherents by allowing the formation of "party fractions" across national lines among majority delegates from the Christian and Socialist parties. The condition was that there should be a third party fraction representing the Euronationalist position, a fraction composed almost entirely of French Gaullists and rather an anomaly in a European Parliament created to legislate in the transnational interest of the Community electorate.

A third policy designed to maintain and enhance French leadership within the European Economic Community has been the exclusion of new members. Such lesser European powers as Greece and Turkey have been allowed to attain "associate status," which gives them consultation *but not voting* rights. What is shared with associate members is information and some access through the corridors of transnational negotiation, but not participation in the decision-making power. Such status has also been conferred, through the initiative of France, upon its former colonial dominions in Africa. But no major power, notably Britain, has been admitted to the closed EEC circle of the original Six.

By its policy of exclusion, Gaullism (we call it thus because many French officials at EEC are vigorously opposed) has gained some important side-benefits. Its support of associate status for Austria has provided a counterpoint (transparent but used) to the charge that Gaullism seeks to make EEC an exclusive club under French leadership — a charge often expressed at Brussels in the quip that EEC has become a "mafia of Frenchmen plus Mansholt."* Of more

---

* Sicco Mansholt, a Vice-President of the EEC Commission from the Netherlands, has won his great personal prestige and influence by the breadth of his knowledge of European affairs and the force of his personality. He led the successful agricultural campaign.

substantial value has been the French championship of associate status for its African ex-colonies. This gained France not only good will as their spokesman in high places but favorable arrangements for their tropical products; this compared favorably with Britain's ex-colonies in Africa, which have sought associate status for themselves without the help of a Britain itself deprived of EEC membership. That other French leaders share the Gaullist penchant for "scoring points" against their allies is shown in one condition laid down by the Mollet government for its ratification of the Treaty of Rome after its signature by the other five partners. Mollet, the Socialist head of a pre-Gaullist administration in early 1958, stipulated that there be created an Overseas Development Fund to which Germany and France would contribute equal shares (40 per cent each). As postwar Germany had no overseas dependencies and the money was spent almost entirely on the French territories in Africa, this stipulation in effect represented a transfer of German funds to the French aid budget.[20]

Scoring points, however useful for sustaining French pre-eminence within EEC and among former colonies, is not an adequate policy for dealing with major allies. Toward America, Britain, and Germany, the Gaullist regime has adopted postures that look global and sound comprehensive. Although formulated and articulated with the nuance that is a characteristic French talent, Gaullist policies all serve the same supreme objective: the pre-eminence of France in Europe and thereby its role as a world leader. The policies which instrument this objective can be stated in simple terms that are barely blunter than the public utterances of De Gaulle himself: (1) keep Germany in and under; (2) keep Britain out and supplicant; (3) keep America in-and-out on terms that are manageable by France.

The policy toward Germany was expressed most fully in the Franco-German Treaty of Cooperation (1963) initiated by De Gaulle and signed by Adenauer. From the start, German elites were restive under this Treaty. Immediately upon its presentation to the Bundestag for ratification, a preamble was inserted that nullified its latent anti-American and anti-British features as well as its anti-Atlantica and even anti-Europa potential. While virtually all Germans agreed, as did people everywhere in Europe and America, that Franco-German amity was a desirable and even essential condition, few thought that this required so high a French price tag.

The German elite, in particular, were predisposed to stay in Europa and Atlantica, but not under French direction. While Adenauer remained Chancellor, the Treaty was tolerated. Under the subsequent regimes of Erhard and the Grand Coalition, the Treaty became a dead letter in the Gaullist design of Euronationalism.[21]

French policy toward Britain has served its supreme objective in several ways. It has maintained good bilateral cooperation on such aeronautical projects as the *Concorde* and even some multilateral cooperation in such aerospace projects as ESRO and ELDO — projects that bring British technological superiority in some key fields, as for example the only indigenous computer industry in Western Europe, into direct working arrangements with French specialists.* But this has involved no compromise of the Gaullist design for Euronationalism under French leadership. On two occasions now De Gaulle has personally and publicly rejected British applications, by Conservative and by Labour governments, for admission to the EEC. This has served the Gaullist policy of keeping Britain out and supplicant. It has also served the deeper purpose, and more complex policy, of dividing the Anglo-Americans, so that American ins-and-outs of Europa and Atlantica become more amenable to French management.

Gaullist policy toward the United States is a subject that requires many specialized studies and volumes of exegesis. In general, it may be said that De Gaulle's bark has been worse than his bite, for he has more voice than teeth. But he is not completely toothless. While his personal tour of Latin America was theatrical, French concessions on a bilateral basis may cut into American trade with those countries. While the French gift of bicycles to Hanoi organized by the "Billion-For-Vietnam" movement may only irritate the American administration, the Gaullist role in Cambodia may affect the course and outcome of military action there.[22] Even the persistent Gaullist policy of weakening American leadership in NATO so that the alliance can be restructured in closer conformity to his supreme objective is not entirely without consequence. It may well be that the ejection of the NATO headquarters from France, and its relocation near Brussels, will produce a long-term boomerang

---

* For a look at some of the ways in which French technologists react to working in an international situation, see Daniel Lerner and Albert H. Teich, "International Scientists Face World Politics: A Survey at CERN," M.I.T. Center for International Studies, 1968, No. C/68-1. Also a doctoral dissertation, M.I.T. 1969, by Mr. Teich.

effect upon France akin to that produced by the French rejection of EDC in 1954. While we conclude that the Gaullist effort to reshape Europa and Atlantica in terms of Euronationalism cannot succeed, it has accentuated anxiety and increased ambivalence in the short run. What, then, are its proximate prospects?

D. A DEVELOPMENTAL CONSTRUCT: FROM EURONATIONALISM TO EURATLANTICA

The proximate prospects for Europe as its elites face the options of Euronationalism *versus* Euratlantica lie in the future and so cannot be known with certainty. The methods of scientific knowledge apply only to events that have already occurred. About future events we can only form working hypotheses to which attach a greater rather than lesser degree of probability. The "policy sciences" seek to formulate such hypotheses about the probable configuration, or context, in which particular events are likely to occur. We call such contextual hypotheses developmental constructs. These constructs are not prophecies derived from simple extrapolation of current events. They are rather more complex projections of alternative futures — deductively derived from theoretical reasoning and inductively tested by empirical data — among which the most probable course of future events can be inferred.

1. Europa and Atlantica

We have sketched in the preceding pages the reasoning that has shaped our appraisal of past and present events in Europe and the world community. The chapters that follow will present the empirical data on European elite attitudes we have collected over the second postwar decade, concluding with detailed evaluations of the findings. Here, before turning to the data base, we offer a synoptic view of the developmental construct to which our evaluation of the data has led us. Stated simply: Europe and America are moving *from* nationalism *to* regionalism.

On the American side, the regionalist trend coexists with partial and incomplete trends toward globalism in the sense of World Commonwealth.* On the European side, globalism in the sense of

---

* The State Department's official justification for its partial measures is that a more comprehensive policy is "impractical" now: "To move to some form of Atlantic union with our Atlantic allies could only diminish the prospect for eventual attainment of such an objective." *The New York Times,* March 25, 1967.

national empires around the world has diminished to the vanishing point — symbolized, as we write these lines, by Britain's abandonment of her traditional role "east of Suez."[23]

With the disappearance of empire has coincided the decline of national *grandeur* as the supreme objective of public policy. The trend has been *from* the idea of "national honor" — the supreme rationale of European political life before World War I, but dead as a dodo after World War II despite the revivalist rhetoric of De Gaulle — *to* the idea of "national interest."* In postwar Europe, the national interest of virtually every nation has come to be identified with regionalism that includes both European integration *and* Atlantic cooperation.

Our construct, then, postulates that the most probable trend of European policy — the general configuration of future events — will be from Euronationalism through further integration of the continent to Euratlantica. The continuing integration of ECSC, Euratom, and the Common Market is indicated by their recent merger of executives into a single Commission for the whole EC. The conviction that European integration is durable is evidenced, as our evidence will show in detail, by the near-universal agreement in all of our 1965 surveys that EC has reached the "point of no return." (See Chapters Five and Eleven.)

The durability of existing institutions of economic integration is likely to lead, as a major next step, to their expansion. This means primarily the inclusion of Britain and some of its present partners in EFTA — probably with associate status in EEC for those other members of EFTA who desire it. This projection is documented by the elite expectations revealed in our own data base, with the frequent caveat that this step must await the retirement of De Gaulle. But we note with interest the spread of similar expectations among the people of France. A recent cross-section poll of two thousand Frenchmen twenty years or older on the year 2000, conducted by the French Institute of Public Opinion, was reported as follows:

> Despite President de Gaulle's veto of Britain's entry into the European Common Market, the average Frenchman is far more optimistic about eventual European unity than any of his neighbors — especially the British.

---

* For the important transition from "honor" to "interest" as the basis of national policy early in this century, see Charles A. Beard, *The Idea of National Interest* (New York: The Macmillan Company, 1934).

These and other attitudes were indicated today in a survey of how the French see the world in the year 2000.

Asked whether they thought Europe would be "one country" by the turn of the century, 43 per cent of those polled replied yes.*

The elite and public of France appear agreed that they want not only a larger but also a more integrated Europe than the Euronational scenario associated with De Gaulle. Apparent from the early years of our study, elite sentiment on this point was visible as well in the 1959 and 1961 surveys that followed De Gaulle's return to power. (See Chapter Five.) So strong was the rift that a year later, in May 1962, five ministers resigned from De Gaulle's cabinet in protest against his "attacks on the concept of an integrated, supranational Europe." The press comment added:

> The sudden political crisis brought before the country in a most acute way the issue of what kind of Europe France wishes — the loose cooperation of sovereign nations advocated by General de Gaulle or the supranational form involving surrender of some national sovereignty.[24]

An enlarged and durable Europa would then, on the evidence of our surveys, be ready to face seriously the common problems that bind Euramerican relations into a solid community of interests. These are the common problems of protection, prosperity, and prestige that have constituted "America's vocation in Europe" and are rapidly shaping "Europe's American vocation.[25] Our data do not justify the projection of political integration between Europe and the United States. There appears to be no common interest that

---

* Lloyd Garrison, "Many French See Unity for Europe," *The New York Times,* December 26, 1967. See also Howard Rosenthal, "The Popularity of Charles De Gaulle: Findings from Archive-Based Research," *Public Opinion Quarterly,* Vol. 31, No. 3 (Fall 1967), pp. 381–398, and Karl W. Deutsch *et al., France, Germany, and the Western Alliance* (New York: Charles Scribner's Sons, 1967). The findings of this elite survey done in 1964 are similar to our own in many respects. The authors of both studies have worked cooperatively and have found considerable cross-validation, with minor exceptions. One major difference, however, arises in the interpretation of the future of nationalism in Europe. While the strength of nationalism is asserted to be strong by Deutsch *et al.*, we find it to be diminishing. This difference is explicable in part by the longitudinal nature of our study; the differences in semantic usage (national differences are not to be equated with nationalism); and the time frame which sets the expectations underlying future projections. Deutsch and his colleagues project the future against the "heyday" of integration. We believe that to compare the present against the point of greatest acceleration, deriving projections of the future from some linear assumption, may create false expectations. Consequently, regardless of the pace of institutional developments, elites will increasingly consent to internationalize their behavior.

would be served by such political integration in the visible future; it might indeed impair the American capability ultimately to move toward the larger goal of world commonwealth. (Only the scenario which projects a persistently aggressive and much more powerful China also projects an Atlantic federation; the outlines of such a configuration are too remote to support a realistic developmental construct, but one can just as aptly speculate that this scenario would call for a military alliance, rather than a political federation, which would extend beyond the regional confines of the North Atlantic area.)

What common interests are now visibly operative, and what our data readily support, is the projection of a Euratlantica that is more closely integrated economically and militarily on the continent, and also more closely coordinated across the Atlantic in the Euramerican system. The skeleton of this developmental construct we now outline in a paradigm followed by a brief expository rationale.

2. The Paradigm

What we seek to represent in this paradigm is the *relative emphasis* given by each of the three main scenarios to the regional extension and policy scope of its interests. The factor of regional extension is important because it indexes the range of inclusiveness, in terms of the putative ultimate goal of a world commonwealth that would be all-inclusive, which each scenario in fact projects for itself. The factor of policy scope indexes the degree of integrativeness — the formation of a common polity in theory and in practice — projected by each scenario for the basic issues of protection, prosperity, and prestige. The factor of relative emphasis indexes the priority of values in each scenario on a short time-scale. For in the brief postwar period that has elapsed since these scenarios were activated (the Treaty of Rome, for example, has just passed its tenth birthday), each scenario has yet to move beyond its own *top* priority; its secondary priorities have remained partially or totally inanimate.

To epitomize the complex events of these postwar years we present a simple visual aid in tabular form. In this table, American initiatives for intercontinental cooperation, such as the Marshall Plan and NATO, we designate as *Euratlantic*. European initiatives to "match" American efforts within the Atlantic framework, such as the institutions created (or aborted) under the Monnet model, we call *Euramerican*. The third sort of initiatives which have sought to restrict the Atlantic framework by partial incorporation, represented notably by the Gaullist design, are labeled *Euronational*. The regional extension of each scenario is indicated by the following brief descriptions:

Euratlantic: Perspective that *includes all* the developed nations of the Atlantic Basin (Western Europe and North America); outward-looking to other developed nations of the British Commonwealth (Australia, New Zealand) as well as Japan in such institutions as GATT and the Club of Ten; outward-looking to the developing nations that may become "partners" in some significant sense proposed by the Atlantic Charter. Essentially, the largest operational perspective of European and American leaders.

Euramerican: Perspective that *includes most* of the developed nations of the Atlantic Basin, but focuses on the relations of continental Europe with the United States regarding the key issues of prosperity, protection, and prestige. Outward-looking when it favors the integration of Britain and the EFTA countries, or when it favors the association of less-developed countries in Europe and Africa, the Euramerican perspective becomes inward-looking when it puts the short-run welfare of The Six before the long-run benefits of the larger Euratlantic system.

Euronational: Perspective that *includes some* nations, European mainly, by the test of their utility to one's own nation as perceived by the persons in charge of national policy at any given moment. Inward-looking in the sense that even its outward-looking aspects are governed by national self-interest. The clear case is Gaullism in France; the less clear cases are British and German "Gaullism." In every case, these people put national prestige above and beyond the requirements of national (hence transnational) protection and prosperity.

In Table 2.2, the policy priorities of each scenario are rank-ordered in terms of protection, prosperity, and prestige. These rank-orders are "arbitrary" in that they are based only on our assessment of the net judgment appropriate to each scenario. The association between regional and policy priorities is shown in each cell of Table 2.2.

TABLE 2.2. PARADIGM OF GRAND SCENARIOS*

	Euratlantic	Euramerican	Euronational
Protection	1	2	2
Prosperity	2	1	3
Prestige	3	3	1

* Scale: 1 = higher priority; 2 = middle priority; 3 = lower priority.

The four major propositions represented by this paradigm can be stated in summary fashion: (1) each scenario differs in some respect from the others; (2) the Euramerican scenario shares at least one element with each of the others; (3) the Euramerican scenario is closer to the Euratlantic in its relative emphasis on the association between each regional base and each policy goal; (4) the Euronational scenario differs most from the other two.

The first three propositions are readily evident from inspection of the table. Proposition (1): Since none of the numerical patterns is identical with any other, by rows or columns, each scenario differs in some respect from the others. Proposition (2): Since the Euramerican scenario shares with the Euratlantic a 3 on Prestige and with the Euronational a 2 on Protection, clearly the Euramerican scenario shares at least one element with the others. Propositions (3) and (4) can be demonstrated most readily by summing the differences between each pair of scenarios. Thus, if we add the differences between each pair of numbers in the first two columns, the sum is *two* $(1-2=1; 2-1=1; 3-3=0; 1+1+0=2)$. But, when we perform the same operation on the differences between the Euronational and each of the other two columns, the sum is *four*. This is the "proof," given our postulated rank orderings, that the Euratlantic and Euramerican scenarios are closest to each other as in Proposition (3) and that the Euronational scenario differs most from the other two as in Proposition (4).

That the sum of differences is doubled between the Euronational and the other two scenarios is a formal demonstration that nationalism, even in its revivalist form of Euronationalism under De Gaulle, is relatively isolated from the main currents of postwar thinking among the European elites. While the numbers used are arbitrary, we note that the same patterned differences would be produced by any other set of ordered numbers. A brief explication of the historical meaning of the paradigm in the light of postwar events will conclude this chapter on Europe's role in the world community as reshaped by the movement *from* nationalism to regionalism (Euramerican *and* Euratlantic) in the second postwar decade.

3. The Rationale

The Euratlantic scenario, designed mainly in Washington, focused primarily on economic and military cooperation. It began with the Marshall Plan (1948) for European recovery, followed promptly by the NATO Treaty (1949) for Atlantic security. As Europe recovered and prospered, in the second postwar decade, the economic institutions were transformed from assistance (OEEC) to advisory (OECD) and negotiating (GATT) purposes. Top priority was focused on protection under the American guarantee.

The Euramerican scenario, designed mainly in pre-Gaullist Paris, began with a more ambitious policy scope that included political as well as economic and military integration. In the Monnet model, the European economic community (EEC) was to be followed by a defense community (EDC) and crowned by an integrative political community (EPC). When EDC (Pléven Plan) was rejected at the close of the first postwar decade (1954), the creation of EPC was aborted. Attention returned to the need for strengthening the successful conception of the economic community (ECSC) under the Schumann Plan (1950). In the second postwar decade, with ratification of the Treaty of Rome (1958), the EEC was created. Top priority among Euramerican scenarists—taking the American guarantee as given — was on prosperity.

The Euronationalist scenario, designed mainly by De Gaulle, required no new conceptions or institutions. Each nation already possessed economic, military, and political institutions. What was needed, in the Euronationalist perspective, was to enhance their power and status. Since economic prosperity was already in progress in France as throughout Europe, when De Gaulle returned to power (1958), his scenario focused on elevating national institutions of political autonomy (via the constitution of the Fifth Republic) and military autonomy (via the national *force de frappe*). The Gaullist vocabulary of *grandeur* thus bespoke the top priority allocated by Euronationalism to prestige.

These indications of the rationale underlying the three major scenarios account, in a general way, for the different priorities al-

located by our paradigm — in particular the distance of Euronationalism, with its focus on prestige, from the two other scenarios
which value prestige only as it grows out of their enhancement of
prosperity and protection. While the differences are significant,
however, we underscore the many points of interaction and interpenetration among the three scenarios. Even the Euronational design has been affected by the visible successes of EEC representing
Euramerica and NATO representing Euratlantica. Gaullism itself
is best appreciated as the most extreme current instance of "restriction by partial incorporation."

This appreciation of residual nationalism is central to our own
perspective on Europe today. It produces the interpenetration of
ideologies which we shall document in Chapter Eight. This, in
turn, is exhibited in the "oscillation effect," which we have already
explained. It is beautifully documented in our data base by the
remarkable finding that, however much individual respondents have
changed their opinions on specific issues over the years, the configuration of total response patterns has remained relatively stable.

We shall soon show this in more technical form as our data demonstrate the proposition that "marginals dominate partials" (i.e.,
subgroups within elite panels reflect the same tendency as total
panels). Here we conclude with the reminder that partial incorporation produces a short-run oscillation effect among individuals which
does not reverse the amplitude or direction of the larger long-term
movement of basic attitudes. It only obscures the degree of emerging consensus at any particular point in time. Our data will show
that there *is* an emerging consensus within, and a convergent consensus between, the elites of the European nations. Further, that
this convergence goes in the direction postulated by our developmental construct: *from* nationalism *to* regionalism. The convergence
is based on the shared long-run expectations that personal and
public values (protection, prosperity, prestige) will be enhanced by
the larger community of interest embodied in the Euramerican and
Euratlantic scenarios.*

* We thank H. D. Lasswell for help in formulating the ideas expressed in
these concluding paragraphs.

CHAPTER THREE

The Story of This Book

OUR concern is with living history, history being made by the present generation that will continue in the making by future generations. We have inserted ourselves into this flow of history to focus, under systematic observation, only a short, narrow span in its long, broad course. TEEPS has studied systematically only the opinions expressed by the elites of three European countries (Britain, France, Germany) over a single decade (1955–1965). This is something of a record for length and breadth in the contemporary annals of empirical, comparative, quantitative, and policy-related social research.[1] But, in historical perspective, it is a relatively thin "slice of life." Only by locating our data in this perspective — by historically orienting their central tendencies and variant distributions — can we relate our findings to the comprehensive configuration of events whereby the past becomes the future.[2]

We designed the TEEPS surveys with the historical perspective in view. This is why, in seeking to learn about the broad course of European events from our thin slice of its living history, we have focused our study so sharply upon the most salient factors of decision making in Europe: asking the most influential people within the most powerful nations the most important questions on their agenda for decision. From the responses to these questions given by the British, French, and German elites over the past decade — responses which it is the primary purpose of this book to describe and evaluate — we seek to illumine the historical process whereby Europe is passing from its recent past to its proximate future.

The questions that initiated our inquiry arose from the straitened conditions of postwar Europe: How were its leaders going to face the reduced power of their own nations, and of the continent as a whole, in the postwar world arena? What decisions, given the narrowed options available to them, would they make regarding the future of their nations and their continent? By what means, given the shrinking resources of which they disposed, would they make their decisions operational? In what measure would their decisions be consensual, tending toward an integrative future, or dissensual and probably disintegrative?

These are large questions, which are not answered once and for all by any elite in any nation. On the contrary, it has taken a decade of seriatim surveys, involving many questions asked of many people in many countries over many years, to provide even the partial and provisional answers that are reported in this book. It is important to bear in mind the perspective outlined in preceding chapters as we turn to a detailed account of how the TEEPS surveys were made and what results they yielded. By way of transition to these empirical matters, we seek in the next section to convey some sense of postwar Europe as a "field" for American researchers. It is one thing that anthropologists speak of "going into the field" when their environment is a Pacific archipelago or an African tribe. It is quite another matter when the "field" is Western Europe, a region in most ways as advanced as America and in some ways more so. Hence, "the feel of the field" to American researchers studying the second postwar decade of European society is worth conveying.

A. THE FEEL OF THE FIELD

The TEEPS survey started at Paris in September 1954, a fortnight after the French defeat of EDC. Many problems of sheer feasibility confronted us: Would we be able to gain access to the French elite? Would they answer our questions? Would their answers be responsive or evasive, candid or covert? The positive findings on feasibility were so clear and comprehensive that the French experiment of 1954 became the pretest on which we based the next ten years of comparative surveys, including Britain and Germany, that began in 1955. Since the French pretest experience was basic to the research design and field procedure of subsequent TEEPS surveys, particularly during the early years, we present some notes on the interviewing of Frenchmen that were written in 1956 as the second comparative survey was completed.

1. The Early Years: Interviewing Frenchmen and Others[3]

When a Frenchman answers the telephone, he says: "*Je vous écoute*" (I am listening to you). In this way he takes up a position of defense against the unknown interlocutor at the other end of the line. To the greeting on the street *Comment va?* (How goes it?), one is likely to receive the ironic reply *On se défend* (One defends oneself). In this slightly mocking fashion, with their special gift for self-conscious clarity, the French take note of a profound trait in their national character. The defensiveness of this posture startles an American used to the open style of saying "hello!" to every anonymous telephone ring and "fine!" to every casual "Hi! How are you?"

Defensive remarks greeted us when we arrived in September 1954 to start interviewing elite Frenchmen of the *milieux dirigeants* (ruling circles). What could one learn from such interviews? Besides, how could it be done? There was widespread doubt about the value and the feasibility of the enterprise. The French, we were told, would never talk to a stranger with no other claim to their confidence than that of being an interviewer. Two years later, we had in fact managed to complete over 1,500 long interviews with Frenchmen of very high standing. To these questions had responded (in round figures): 500 top businessmen; 300 leading intellectuals; 300 political leaders; 100 high civil servants (representing *le grand corps de l'Etat*, the major ministries); 100 senior military men; 100 clerical and lay leaders of the church; and 100 officials of labor, farmer, and other pressure groups.

The trick was to get them started; but, once started, how they talked! The average length of the interviews was over two hours, and a fair number of them ran on toward eight hours. (The same interview schedule, in Britain and Germany, averaged a bit over one hour and was fully answered.) Rather often the interviewer was requested to return, after a single session lasting two or three hours, by respondents eager to have their full say in an interview that took rather the form of an interior dialogue uttered aloud. The essential is that, once engaged, the Frenchman talked volubly. But, to engage him, one had to scale the defensive wall, as the French put it, *franchir le mur*.

Once the entry to privacy has been made, the interviewer must still deal with the special French conventions of cognition. Their metaphysics, which tends to endow the external world with active attributes of its own, also creates new problems of question formulation for an American habituated to more pragmatic ways of thought. In our earliest interviews we were baffled by the recurrent request from respondents to state "precisely" various questions that seemed to us already precise. It required much conversation and reflection before we realized that, for the French, precision has a quite different and special meaning, a literally Cartesian meaning. What makes a question "precise" for Frenchmen is its capacity to frame the object of reference in a specific context (*bien délimité, dans un cadre qui lui est propre*). The object of reference, to be clear, must be perceived as discrete (*discret*); and its external boundaries must be sharply defined (*circonscrire l'objet* in the conventional vocabulary of French philosophy).

French insistence upon a discrete, disengaged object of reference underscores their revulsion against relationships without clearly perceived boundaries. The language abounds in pejorative phrases to express this horror of inadequate distantiation — *dans le jus, dans le sirop, dans la soupe* (in the juice, the syrup, the soup). These images convey vividly the sense that fluidity (*des idées floues*) is the enemy of clarity. Other expressions of distaste for "fuzziness" are *dans le cirage, dans le coton,* and *dans la vaseline* (in the wax, cotton wadding, vaseline) — where the soft and shapeless mass without defined margins provides the antonym of clarity and precision.

The limits which such a posture imposes upon the interview are illustrated by a respondent who served as "consultant." The director of an important national research organization, with long experience in survey work, this man seemed perfect for our purpose. Indeed, he gave us many practical suggestions for question wording that helped us to avoid the vague and achieve the "precise." At five different questions scattered through our interview schedule, however, this man threw up his hands in utter contempt and despair. "You will never get any Frenchman to answer questions like these," he declared, without explaining why. These were our questions:

1. If you were *président du conseil* (prime minister), what would be the main lines of your policy?
2. If you had to live in another country, which one would you choose?

3. If you had your life to live over again, what sort of life would
you want?
4. Who are the most enviable people in the world? Why?
5. What would you do in a Communist France?

What these questions have in common is that they ask the interviewee to imagine himself in a situation other than his real one
(i.e., they are "role-playing" questions). Such an idea is regarded
as frivolous, not worth the attention of Frenchmen, who are, after
all, *des gens sérieux* (serious people). These questions, we were
told, would provoke resistance among people who consider as their
strongest traits realism, skepticism, and mistrust. And indeed
they did, many interviewees regarding them as merely silly: *De la
blague! De la fantaisie pure!* (A gag! Pure fantasy!).

An instructive study could be made of the diverse ways in which
people of different nations respond to role-playing questions of this
sort. Our British and German interviewees, for instance, responded
to precisely these questions with only minor incident. In general,
such questions are handled with greater facility by people habituated to ready ego involvement with the new and strange. These are
people who, having a less rigid conception of themselves and their
proper conduct in the world, show a more supple capacity for rearranging their self-image upon short notice. A clear difference in
the capacity to empathize, to "play roles," emerged from interviews
conducted in the Middle East several years ago. There it was possible to identify the Traditionals by their total incapacity to answer
such questions as "What would you do if you were president of
Syria?" By contrast, the Moderns seemed to experience no difficulty
whatsoever when asked what they would do as editor of a news-
paper, or as leader of their country, or if they had to live in another
country.[4]

There is a vast psychic difference between the illiterate and un-
tutored traditionalism of the Middle Eastern peasant and the cognitive traditionalism which prevails among the contemporary elite of
France. The Frenchman has acquired his traditionalism as an intellectual discipline and as part of an explicit psychic code. He is
taught from childhood an articulate conception of *le bonheur* (happiness or well-being) and a system of appropriate behavior designed to maximize his satisfactions. Whereas the Arab peasant
usually has no sense of possible alternatives to his traditional ways

but simply "does what comes naturally," the Frenchman has a very sophisticated rationale for his conduct. Not only is he quite aware of other ways of behaving but he can (and usually does) tell you with great clarity why his way is better than any other.

The personality associated with traditionalism takes a quite different turn, then, among the French. It explains why Frenchmen often accuse Americans, who think of themselves as great individualists, of lacking just this trait (*manque d'individualisme*). For contemporary Americans, individualism implies nonconformity; expressing one's self means doing something just a little differently from the other fellow. For Frenchmen, individualism lives quite comfortably with a massive conformism. Their underlying principle is not to do some things a little differently but rather not to do very many things at all. In the eyes of Frenchmen, the American loses individuality by identifying himself too readily with other persons, by associating himself too intensely with public causes, and by joining too many organizations. The Frenchman guards his individualism by maintaining his self (*le soi*) inviolate from the impingements of the public arena.

The heritage of French *méfiance* (mistrust) has been fortified by their recent political history. The crushing humiliation of defeat in 1940 led to a vast upheaval in traditional family life. Millions were locked into military prisoner-of-war camps, forced-labor camps, or concentration camps. Others joined the active resistants of the *maquis* or went into hiding in southern France, and still others left metropolitan France altogether for London or Algiers. Displaced from their normal routines of home, family, work, and leisure, two common elements of current history pervaded the conscience of Frenchmen who lived through these years: national degradation by German military might and, perhaps more profound, the Vichy spectacle of Frenchmen turning against Frenchmen.

The mark left by these events was still visible in the course of our interviewing pretest a decade later. There was, particularly in the early months, a great mistrust of unknown interviewers asking questions, even though all our interviewers were French. Several interviewees mentioned that the last time they had been approached in such a manner was under Vichy, and some told of the dire consequences that befell persons who had been so indiscreet as to answer questions truthfully.

To cope with political *méfiance* of this explicit sort, we were obliged to take reassuring measures. We constituted a *comité de patronage* (committee of sponsors), composed of Frenchmen of high national reputation. Each interviewer was equipped with a personal letter signed by the president of our committee, the revered André Siegfried of *L'Académie française*, introducing him to the interviewee and reassuring the latter that his answers to our questions would be held in the strictest confidence. The anonymous system of filing and coding our interviews was explained so that the interviewee should suffer no anxiety as a result of having spoken candidly. On very many occasions this presidential letter was preceded or followed by a telephone call from a member of our *comité de patronage* or another person of high standing who had confidence in our project.

These measures were productive. Persons who earlier had been unwilling to receive our interviewers, or reticent about answering their questions, now began to talk more freely. As our engaging of respondents gathered momentum, we resumed asking "indiscreet" questions which earlier had seemed wholly impossible, for example, "What would you do in a Communist France?" Our successes increased, but remained incomplete. We had opened doors leading to spokesmen of those social formations which constitute the political Center and Right — businessmen, high civil servants, military leaders — even chiefs of the non-Communist trade unions and other spokesmen of the Moderate Left. But we made less headway on the Extreme Left, a sector of the political continuum which is inadequately interpreted even in France and which reaches far beyond the Communist Party and its fellow travelers. A few words on this problem and how we dealt with it are in order.

There exists in France a pervasive political sentiment called *gauchisme* (leftism). It is a sentiment because it is not defined by specific judgments on specific issues, but expresses rather a diffuse general hostility to the powers-that-be and things-as-they-are. One approximation of a psychological definition of this sentiment was sketched by Albert Camus in *L'homme révolté*, with reference to "the alienated intellectual." But the special importance of *gauchisme* in France is rather its sociological diffusion beyond the intelligentsia. Types of Frenchmen have been affected by the chronic oppositionism of *gauchisme* who, in other countries, are conservative or have no clearly defined political sentiment at all — such as army officers, civil servants, rich businessmen. A systematic sociology of the diffusion of *gauchisme* in France would do much to explain the French incapacity to act decisively on critical public issues during the last two decades.

It was among these *gauchisants* that our inquiry encountered the most widespread suspicion and resistance. We had decided, early in the game, that complete candor on the sponsorship of our study was essential. Our interviewers had been instructed to respond, when questioned, that the inquiry was jointly sponsored by French and American universities and that an American professor was a member of the scientific committee directing the study. The impact of this disclosure upon French *gauchisants* was strong enough to draw caustic remarks, to limit responsiveness, and, in some cases, to distort substance. Some *gauchisants* who did respond evidently designed their remarks primarily to cause anguish to the American professor — although such performances were more frequent among those who took their *gauchisme* rather lightly.

More committed leftists not only refused to answer at all but in some cases went further. We were reported to the weekly journal *L'Express,* then a leading mouthpiece of *gauchisme,* and for some time thereafter were haunted by a young reporter determined to denounce and expose our enterprise. Several hours of explaining carefully our interview schedule, our sampling procedure, and our modes of analysis failed to persuade her that it would be impossible for us to derive information useful to the police, French or American. It was perfectly clear to the reporter that there must be some hidden trick; once an American was involved, the enterprise was necessarily a maneuver of the Right and, *ipso facto,* despicable.

The extreme *gauchisant* went even further. In two regions we were denounced to the departmental *préfet.* Our interviewers there reported that, unless we could clear matters with the *préfet,* their usefulness would be at an end. In Paris we were subjected to two visits by agents of the DST (*Défense de la Sécurité du Territoire,* the French FBI). These persons scrutinized very carefully our intentions, procedures, and, most particularly, our affiliations in France. We were able to surmount these inquiries, as those of the regional *préfets,* only because our *comité de patronage* was composed of Frenchmen of impeccable standing.

Interviewing Frenchmen thus involves a number of special problems derived from the national character, reinforced by behavioral codes and social institutions, and made acute by current political conditions. Making initial contact is complicated by the distance-maintaining mechanisms embedded in the French code of courtesy. The *formules de politesse* serve as index and agent of French mistrust of the strange, their identification of security with privacy. Most refusals were based squarely upon the feeling that such an interview was an unwarranted intrusion into their personal affairs. Few said simply "No!" Rather more evaded a flat refusal by having their secretaries phone to postpone the rendezvous indefinitely as a less rude rejection. But, of those who explained instead of evading their refusal, many said: "This is not my concern!" "I do not know your Institute!" "Could you have Monsieur X (a member of our committee known to him) phone me to explain your purpose and introduce you?" To scale the defensive wall was not at all, among Frenchmen, a routine matter.

Once received, however, the interviewer figured as a person rather than a faceless machine for recording a one-way flow of short answers. Quite often, before granting a rendezvous, the interviewee specified that, if this was merely "*un Gallup*" (i.e., Yes-No contact poll), he was not interested. He would, however, be willing to *discuss* some of the important questions that concerned us. In such discussions the interviewer figured as a respected specialist. His own opinions on the questions, and on the respondent's expressed views, were often solicited. This was partly a gesture of courtesy but mainly an expression of the profound preference for dialogue in French discourse.

The impact of the interviewer as a person was especially dramatic among leftists, who are perhaps more richly endowed with the manipulative inclinations of the propagandist. Quite often a *gauchisant* who began by refusing an interview sponsored by "The Americans," and berating the French interviewer for using his talents under such auspices, would then be drawn into heated discussions of the specific questions. After several hours of such dialogue, which furnished some extremely rich data, he might conclude by inviting the interviewer to have a drink — over which, if a relentless ideologue, he might advise the interviewer to quit his job and take more respectable employment.

The insistence upon a highly participant interviewer, one who relieved the respondent's anxieties about "exposing" himself to a strange person, gradually reshaped the basic format of our interview. In the early phase, a particularly gifted and versatile member of the interviewing team had tried out a variety of roles, ranging, as he put it, from the *lampiste* (poor slob) to the *gavroche* (dead-end kid). His experiments indicated that the preferred role was that of the competent specialist, who, maintaining a posture of self-respect, exhibited the expectation that he would accord and receive respect in relationship to the respondent. It was less effective to say, "Please answer my questions or I will lose my job," for example, than to say, "I am obliged to ask you a number of questions, but you are obliged to answer only those that interest you." The latter formula seemed to define the relationship between subject and object, the distance between interviewer and interviewee, in a manner liberating to respondents worried about "engaging" themselves in a strange situation that might lead to *déception*.

As we moved into the main phase of pretesting the interview, the highly structured questionnaire with which we began became a minimally directive dialogue in the format of a free-flowing conversation. This transformation of the schedule augmented the need for precoding and other technical devices for assuring uniform reporting. We also used more personal procedures for testing interviewer reliability — mainly brief daily meetings between the research director and each interviewer and a weekly three-hour meeting attended by all interviewers. At each session detailed discussion of the day's and week's interviews maintained clarity and consensus among interviewers on the permissible range of variation in wording questions and precoding responses.

The consistency developed thereby was demonstrated in the subsequent coding phase, when high rates of speed and reliability were obtained by the former interviewers acting as coders. While lacking the simplicity of objective procedures, the method of continuous personal consultation among interviewers solved empirically some thorny problems of open-ended interviewing in a sample survey. These problems are threefold: (1) Since respondents are not obliged to choose one precisely worded answer (precoded) to a precisely worded question, strict comparability of responses is reduced; (2) as comparability is reduced, so the analytic code must be expanded to take account of more numerous variations in the responses; (3) as the code is expanded, so reliability among coders tends to be reduced (since increase of choices normally increases chances of errors). All these factors put greater responsibility upon the individual interviewers.

Daily review of each interview between the interviewer and re-search director, supplemented by weekly reviews of the full week's work among all interviewers, enabled us to solve problems of comparability as they arose. The interviewers presented every significant variation of question and response that occurred in their conversations. Each variation was thrashed out until a clear agreement on its interpretation (coding) was understood and accepted by all interviewers. Naturally, such a procedure depends greatly upon the quality and quantity of the personnel. It is the research director's taxing job to review each interview, detect significant variations, mediate and arbitrate differences of interpretation among interviewers. The interviewers must be few in number, high in quality, and reliable in performance.

Our team consisted of six "hard-core" interviewers, who stayed with the project from start to end. Only a few others were taken on, at peak periods or for special purposes, and each of these worked directly alongside a member of the "hard core." In a larger team, the demands of continuous intercommunication might easily become excessive. Each interviewer must be intelligent enough to recognize the essential content in each of his responses, to detect the significant variations among them, to discriminate the comparable and non-comparable components exhibited by the verbal variations. Finally, the interviewers must be reliable, since the method hinges on establishing very high consensus (virtual unanimity) among the team. Comparability can be steadily increased only as the interviewers reach clear and common understanding on how to deal with varied responses. Hence, any deviation from the "hard core" increases the time and cost of obtaining comparable responses and reliable codes — since the whole team marks time while any new member is brought into the consensus.

Even under favorable circumstances, as in the present study, the method lacks some of the satisfying certifications conferred by stricter procedures. It is impossible to determine precisely how many significant variations of response have been undetected or misinterpreted (consensus can be formed on an erroneous interpretation). Yet the "hard core" of this team was able to obtain reliability scores averaging around 90 per cent in coding each other's interview records at high speed during the final stages of the pretest. This indicates that the method *can* gain the richer data obtained in open-ended interviews without paying the excessive costs of ambiguity, noncomparability, and unreliability in their analysis.

The initial conditions of our study imposed the method upon us by the unassailable argument of *faute de mieux*. Our exploratory pretest showed that highly structured, fully precoded interviews would get us nowhere — or, at least, nowhere we wanted to go. They would save us time, money, and uncertainty, but they would not produce the data we wanted. Since these initial conditions involved nothing less than French culture and personality, as characterized in the preceding pages, they were not amenable to rapid rearrangement for the purposes of our study. Having to do the best we could, we did. The method evolved merits consideration by scholars concerned with studying personality cross-culturally.

A postscript on the sequel may be worth noting. Our cross-national interviewing program, begun in 1955, was executed in five "waves" over the next ten years. By the spring of 1959, when we reinterviewed a panel of 100 French respondents many of whom had been interrogated one or more times in preceding years, we were able to use a structured, precoded questionnaire in a contact-poll type of interview. In this 1959 survey we encountered less rejection or evasion of our questions, fewer "don't knows" and "no opinions," than in any preceding year. This fact raises important questions. Had these particular respondents become habituated to interviews by their previous experience with us — either accepting more readily invasion of their privacy by interviewers or ceasing to regard our interviewers as strangers? Or had some transformation of French behavioral conventions, expressive of traditional French culture and personality, become manifest in this short spate of years? Neither hunch carries *prima facie* conviction with it. Our analysis, at present, indicates that a satisfactory account of the data will have to contain elements of both explanations. Whatever the new psychocultural mixture in France, it was by 1959 clearly not the same mixture as before. But this is a different story that unfolds as we present our data.

The transformation noted in France between the 1954 pretest and the 1959 survey did not appear in any such dramatic form among the British and German respondents. There was no parallel need for transformation in these countries, since psychic resistance to our interviews had been relatively low from the start. In both countries, rejection and evasion of our questions (the "don't know" responses we tabulated as DK rate) were consistently lower than in France throughout the decade and most markedly during the early years. Both countries also showed a much lower refusal rate (unwillingness to receive our interviewer) and break-off rate (unwillingness to complete the interview once begun).

There are several factors that appear to explain these national differences. The Germans, including their elites, had been continuously interviewed by Americans since the end of World War II. Most Germans who applied for work under control of the Allied military government had been obliged to complete the enormously long and complicated *Fragebogen* (questionnaire) — a document later satirized in a novel of this title by Ernst von Salomon. Thereafter the flow of questionnaires and interviews from the occupation authorities, and from such home agencies as BBC and VOA, was steadily widened by the rapid growth of indigenous survey agencies (DIVO, EMNID, Demoskopie, etc.). By the time our first TEEPS survey started in 1955, the German elites were habituated to receiving interviewers; if anything, the complaint was often heard that the frequency of interviews left them little time for anything else. They cooperated with TEEPS because its academic sponsorship by the University of Cologne (under Professors René König and Erwin K. Scheuch) was serious, because American participation was generally regarded as a positive attribute, because the cross-national features of the survey and the questions engaged the personal interest of many Germans.

In Britain, the TEEPS survey encountered no psychic resistance of any consequence. The survey tradition was as long and well established in Britain as in America. The government's Social Survey and such private agencies as Mass Observation, British Institute of Public Opinion (Gallup affiliate), Research Services Ltd. (Roper-Wilson affiliate), along with a strong tradition of market research, had accustomed Britons to deal with the full range of sample surveys. Largely for this reason, and thanks to the personal participation of Dr. Mark Abrams (Director of Research Services, Ltd.) from start to end, the TEEPS surveys in Britain were executed with the minimum of administrative difficulty and the maximum of technical efficiency.

Indeed, the British survey was generally used as the paradigm for the comparative surveys in France and Germany. The sampling design to be matched elsewhere was established there each year.

So, too, was the schedule of questions to be translated in the other countries. The pretest of the schedule, the field instructions to interviewers, the codebook, and the coding were done in Britain before the parallel survey machinery was established in France and Germany.

As the TEEPS survey progressed from year to year, both the psychological and technical problems of the work were significantly simplified. Other problems arose as we faced the increasing complexities of comparing nations over time. Some of these arose from the changing environment of Europe during these years. To these matters we now turn.

2. The Later Years: Comparing Nations

A sharp divide separates the early years (1955–1956) from the later years (1959–1961–1965). Between 1956 and 1959, great events had occurred in the world. In France, the Fourth Republic had passed into history and the Fifth Republic had newly emerged with De Gaulle at its helm. European integration had passed from the doldrums of the EDC defeat, through the agonizing reappraisals of the *relance européenne,* to the Treaties of Rome instituting Euratom (the European Atomic Community) and the European Common Market. The post-Stalin Russia led by Khrushchev was moving from Cold War in the direction of Peaceful Coexistence. A new postwar "era of good feeling" appeared to be in the making.

Of these events, and their reflection in our surveys, this book will have much to report. Our present concern is to indicate the major alterations of research design and field procedure that were made during the years between 1955–1956 and 1959–1965. The interim period was devoted mainly to collating, processing, and interpreting the TEEPS data gathered during the early years. The substantive findings, which are presented in detail later, merged with methodological considerations to effect major alterations in sampling and questioning. In the later years, samples were substantially reduced both in sectors and size, while questions were restricted both in substantive scope and mode of response.

To appreciate the significance of these alterations, recall that the 1954 pretest in France had used an instrument that was largely open-ended. Respondents answered each question entirely in their own words, which were recorded verbatim (as nearly as possible) by the interviewers and subsequently collated (according to an empirically generated codebook) by the coders. These open procedures, which have fidelity and fullness of the resultant interview protocols to recommend them, could hardly be justified once the analytical task of collation was complicated by the requirement of comparison across years and countries. Their greater amplitude, obtainable only at considerably greater cost, loses its value when responses must be reduced to comparable categories according to a common codebook.

Accordingly, all subsequent surveys in the later years became increasingly closed. Interviewees in all countries were obliged to formulate most of their answers in terms presented to them by the interviewers. While the interviewees retained their freedom to choose among the precoded alternatives offered them, their situation increasingly became what survey jargon calls a "forced choice." Instead of recording verbatim the full flow of their discourse, our interviewers reduced their responses to a preclassified phrase.

Why did European leaders of such eminence submit their complex and refined thoughts on great current issues to the presumed "indignity" of such forced choices? Many European specialists of social research in fact forecast (with the same confidence as their peers in the early years had announced that the elites would not agree to be interviewed at all) that no version of a closed questionnaire would be answered by these elites. Yet, the verifiable fact is that they did answer fulsomely and in large numbers. Throughout the later years of the survey, the refusal rate was relatively low and the break-off rate was miniscule among old as well as new respondents in all countries. That the European elites did submit to forced choices, despite the grave doubts of scholars experienced mainly in other fields than panel surveys, is itself a finding of interest to those concerned with European society as well as specialists in survey research.

The transition in TEEPS survey procedure in the later years appears as a manifestation of the more general reshaping of attitudes that has accompanied the modernization of postwar Europe. If we locate survey research among the new and varied symptoms of modernity, then it is clear why the leaders of modernizing Europe have increasingly accepted personal interviews along with such other symptoms of the rise of Public Opinion as press conferences, television appearances, public relations, political campaigns, universal military service, and progressive taxation. In this context, having accepted the "invasion of privacy" with which survey research once seemed to threaten traditional Europeans, for whom the ideas of *lèse-majesté* and *Majestätsbeleidigung* symbolized the hierarchical and inviolate privileges of rank, the postwar elites were readier to accept forced choices as a communication mode. This predisposition was reinforced, in the later TEEPS years, by some special characteristics of the three principal components of the survey: (1) interviewers, (2) interviewees, and (3) interest of the questions.

The special characteristic of the interviewers is that they were selected, trained, and seasoned by the same survey institution in each country throughout the full decade of the TEEPS survey. The same survey agencies and many individual interviewers, all of them nationals of the respective countries, worked on the successive surveys from 1955 through 1965. Hence, there were numerous occasions when the same interviewer was repeating the same questions to the same interviewee. This facilitated giving short answers in precoded terms.

The special characteristic of the interviewees is that they constituted a modified "panel" — a technical term for persons who are interviewed repeatedly on the same questions. That is, according to the TEEPS research design we shall describe, a substantial proportion of the interviewees in each country each year were a panel in this sense. For most of them, the giving of short answers apparently became easier as the years went by. That new interviewees also exhibited readiness to take forced choices was partly due to the status achieved by TEEPS among elite circles in the three countries, which made selection into the panel honorific for many prospective interviewees (hence the low refusal rate). Partly, too, the high responsiveness of new interviewees was due to their interest in the questions asked (hence the low break-off rate).

The special characteristic of the questions — the third principal component of the survey — was their topicality in high politics. These questions were, or should have been, high among the preoccupations of all persons with elite standing. Many interviewees, indeed, thanked the TEEPS interviewers for giving them the opportunity to perform their "civic duty" — to think through, and bring to a forced choice, their opinions on crucial issues confronting their nation and their continent in the wider world.

Given these three factors — the durability of the survey personnel, the familiarity of the respondent panels, the intrinsic interest of the questions — even the closed procedure by forced choices achieved notable results in data collection. We attribute this, in large part, to the careful "pretests" which preceded the survey in each country each year. These pretests enabled us to screen out some questions, screen in others, and improve the formulation of those that remained substantively intact. Naturally, some questions were retained for purposes of comparability even though they were criticized as outdated or otherwise inappropriate (the French respondents being particularly vocal on this point). But, by and large, a reasonable balance between interviewee interest and analytical requirements was maintained.

Other procedural alterations were made to encourage responsiveness. Often the wording of a question was changed, even though this meant sacrificing item-comparability by strict standards in order to present the issue in more topical and interesting terms. Wherever possible, the questions were phrased in such a way as to avoid inhibiting the interviewee by forcing his choice too brusquely. Instead, the respondent was allowed to speak his mind freely. If this response did not fit clearly into one of the precoded categories, the interviewer would then ask: "Do I correctly understand you as saying . . . ?" (and supply the exact precoded phrase to be accepted or rejected). In every case, the gist of the respondent's *obiter dicta* was recorded as well as his "short answer" to the forced choice.

These alterations of the data-collecting procedures — and such others as the increasing use of "filter" questions (to avoid unnecessary questioning of respondents on irrelevant points) or of "split ballots" (to maximize the value of fewer responses by quasi-simulation techniques) — required appropriate adjustments in the data-processing and data-analysis procedures. For example, respondents who did not make a clear choice between the forced choices (yes or no, for or against) were classified as a separate category of "don't knows" (DK), signifying only that they were unwilling or unable to respond in our terms, as compared with "no answers" (NA), who did not respond in any terms.

So strict an interpretation of our data placed considerable constraints on subsequent analysis, particularly in those years where sample size (n) had been reduced to 100 respondents in each country. We first experimented with this small n of 100 in Britain and France during the 1956 survey. Earlier marginal distributions had revealed that reliable inferences could be drawn from so small a sample size over a wide range of issues — in particular, on issues where the marginals showed a strong central tendency with small random dispersion. Encouraged by this finding (and pressured by our dwindling research funds) we set n at 100 in all three countries during the 1959 and 1961 surveys.

Analysis of these later surveys indicated that the reliability of marginal and especially cross-tabulational distributions obtained from small n might be more limited than suggested by the 1956 results. Accordingly, in the terminal 1965 survey, n was raised above 300 in Britain and Germany. This enabled us to perform a series of computer experiments which determined the exact limits of statistical reliability for different panel sizes on different types of questions.* The central idea was that marginals are reliable in the measure that they do not reflect changes in the panel sizes over the years of the surveys. To test the sensitivity of marginal distribution to n, we simulated different size panels from our own data. Respondents in the 1965 survey from Britain were random ordered. The first fifty respondents were listed as a simulated panel, and marginals were produced for this subgroup on fifty questions. The next fifty respondents were then selected, and their marginal distribution on the same fifty questions was produced in the same fashion. Following this, simulated "sets" of 75, 100, and 125 were randomly drawn and marginals were produced for each of these. The marginal distributions were then compared within each randomly drawn set. If the variations from one to another randomly drawn "set" were statistically significant, we would have to conclude that marginals are sensitive to n and therefore unreliable for comparative analysis. This would have cast serious doubt on the value of comparing TEEPS surveys with different n over successive years. If the panels showed insensitivity to n, then we could report the marginals with more confidence, asserting that these distributions would not have changed significantly if we had increased the size by another 25, 50, or 100 respondents. The results of the test are presented in Table 3.1.

The statistical law of large numbers applies: the larger the n, the less sensitive to n are the marginal distributions. Since our minimum-

---

* These experiments were carried out by our students at M.I.T., notably John Golden, Judson H. Benjamin, and Bruce Jacobs (with the aid of Dick Barnes of Barss, Reitzel, and Associates). See Annex Six.

TABLE 3.1. SENSITIVITY TO n

	Number of Questions with Differences above 5 Per Cent and Below 10 Per Cent	Number of Questions with Differences above 10 Per Cent
Test 1: 50-member panels	12	14
Test 2: 75-member panels	15	10
Test 3: 100-member panels	23	5
Test 4: 125-member panels	24	3
Test 5: 150-member panels*	23	0

* In this case, compared with the full panel of 313 members.

size panel in all surveys was 100 (in 1959 and 1961), we adopted a conservative criterion for evaluating attitude change as reflected in the marginals of those years. At our minimum level, we cannot and have not drawn inferences from marginal changes less than 10 per cent, since this is the level at which such marginal changes may be due to sensitivity to n. However, we feel secure in reporting changes greater than 10 per cent, for our panel sizes have always exceeded the minimum threshold at that level. The majority of our panels were well above the minimum n, even at the 5 per cent level. In these cases, the insensitivity to n argues for the reliability of the marginals.

An additional inference may be drawn from these TEEPS tests of reliability. Except for the special requirements of cross-tabulation, elite surveys require many fewer respondents than previously considered necessary to achieve a reliable measure of elite opinion. Our rule-of-thumb n of 100 panelists (over the TEEPS middle years) is close to insensitivity. The addition of a very few respondents would achieve a high degree of reliability.

Another major question about reliability is whether variations between occupational sectors produce significant effects upon the marginal distributions in any country. In the early years of our surveys, sectoral variations often were quite marked on certain issues. For example, the first published TEEPS report showed that business leaders were significantly more pro-EDC than other elite sectors in France; moreover, that those substantially involved in export were more pro-EDC than other business leaders in France.[5]

Table 3.1 shows why sectoral variations by occupation and their possible influence upon the marginal distribution of any n have been attenuated. A growing consensus on many key issues has been exhibited in all countries over the years of our TEEPS surveys — a convergent consensus that is discussed more fully in all our later chapters. Whatever the reason, however, the *fact* of reduced sectoral variation is critical. For in reducing total n, we were obliged to reduce the number of sector samples as well. At the start of our study, there were eight principal sectors: government (high civil service), politics (elected officials), communications (mass media and intellectuals), business (heads of firms), church (hierarchy of bishops and above), military (hierarchy of generals with a few strategic colonels), labor unions (heads of national federations and their major components), and pressure groups (heads of farmer, wholesaler, and retailer federations and their major components).

In the later years, we dropped the church and military sectors, merged labor unions with other pressure groups, and focused on the first four sectors: government, politics, business, and communications. Whatever loss of information this might entail, and whatever its effects might be on issues other than those we studied, our computer experiments demonstrate that the cost has been minimal relative to the benefit for TEEPS.

Underlying these statistical tests of reliability is the excellence of the elite panels chosen by our "boards of experts" in each country. For the initial selection of the French panel, TEEPS relied upon the judgment of such expert witnesses as André Siegfried, Raymond Aron, and Jean Stoetzel, buttressed in special fields by Jacques Fauvet (politics), Bertrand Hommey (business), Generals Gallois and Stehlin (military), and Georges Rotvand (communications). In Britain, additionally, Dr. Mark Abrams and his associated experts made it possible to "objectify" the sampling of certain sectors — in the sector of "communications," for example, by selecting every person reproduced at least twice over the past five years in *The Listener*. The German board, led by Professors König and Scheuch, was buttressed by Professors Eugen Kogon, Max Stammer, Morris Janowitz, as well as by Drs. Max Ralis and Renate Mayntz. It would be excessively tedious to report here the details of the procedure whereby these "boards of experts" produced name lists that enabled us to reach comparable and stable elites in all three countries. The proof that they did so is shown by the statistical tests just reported.

The next question of consequence is how we moved from research design to research product. To this question we now turn.

B. FROM DESIGN TO PRODUCT: COLLECTION, PROCESSING, ANALYSIS

We have conveyed some sense of the human interactions involved in the successive years of our survey. The feel of the field is always important in data collection that depends upon voluntary responses given by those under study. It is the empirical filter through which the theoretical research design one starts with becomes the available research product one ends with. It is to the end product that we now give our attention, reviewing the size and shape of the data collected, the processing through which these data passed, and the analysis that turned them into the findings reported in this book.

1. Data Collection

The total n of each survey varied widely by year and by country, usually by design and occasionally by circumstances. Beyond the elite sample surveys subjected to comparative statistical analysis, data were collected as well from other sources and by other procedures. To keep these various end products distinct, Table 3.2 presents only the number of interviews obtained by the elite sample survey in each country and year. The number shown in each cell is

TABLE 3.2.   DATA BASE n BY COUNTRY AND YEAR*

	Britain	France	Germany	Total
1955	100†	800	150	1,050
1956	350	400	600	1,350
1959	100	100	200	400
1961	100	100	100	300
1965	350	200	350	900
Total	1,000	1,600	1,400	4,000

* The round numbers are usually somewhat smaller than the total n of interviews recorded, since a few interviews were dropped in each survey owing to incompleteness, unresponsiveness, and related reasons.

the net n that was actually collected, processed, and analyzed in the final operations.

2. *Data Processing*

The processing of the data has a history of development no less diverse than the collection of the materials. The initial processing was done with models of attitude formation that assumed the presence of branching tree structures in the respondents' minds. These branches could be identified by finding one main trunk (or idea) which subsumed the existence of branches (dependent ideas). Thus, we postulated one central response which would include some dependent choices and exclude others. The choice of key ideas (trunks) was based on our field encounters and on concepts current in the literature — classic paradigms according to such factors as age, political party, media exposure. We hoped to classify respondents on scales that would indicate to which attitudinal types they belonged by assuming one or two key attitudes and then finding the sociological determinants.

The hardware for data processing appropriate to this model of attitudes was a simple counter and sorter. This hardware was simple because it merely counted responses and sorted them into different labeled bins. These labels should then have identified our coded respondents. While we get ahead of our story here by reporting limited success with that attitude model, it was its failure which forced us to develop improvements in hardware and software that would better implement the original model, and eventually to seek other models.

To improve our capacity to test the initial model, we moved to significantly larger machines — first the IBM 7040 and then the IBM 7090. These computers could readily produce more tests of hypotheses than we could generate. As the size of our data base grew and as the failure of simple sociological and ideological branches of logic trees continually failed to account for the increasing data, we were obliged to deal with our more complex phenomena by improving our data-processing machinery.

Size and diversity made the data base difficult to access into the new machinery. Accordingly, we had to recode several years of the surveys in common terms in order to make comparable inputs and outputs possible. We made questions which were strictly comparable easy for the computer to find by locating them in common files.

Where the comparability was not so strict, as was often the case in a study which took the need to be contemporary in respondent interest as seriously as the need to be rigorous in research design, we recoded in more general categories. With the data base thus prepared for more advanced computer technology, we resumed our search through the materials for patterns of significance, both statistical and political.

Even this "clean" data base, however, was complicated anew by the addition of another survey in 1965, when the European area was showing significant signs of change. This survey, to be "contemporary" in 1965, had to be less strictly comparable on a number of dimensions. In order to make cross-comparisons between 1965 and preceding years, we were obliged to improve our computer capacity once again. This was the ADMINS system, which gave us simultaneous access to several data files, over all years and countries of the TEEPS survey, regardless of their state of item comparability. The details reported in Annex Seven give an account of the ADMINS system. With this new data-management capacity at our disposal, comparative analysis was much facilitated. We now could begin with the assumptions of key attitudes and search for their impact through all years and countries with relative ease, while sitting at an on-line, time-sharing console and receiving rapid replies to our queries from the high-speed computer.

However, even this ultimate step in improving our data access hinged on our capacity to search out and find determinate patterns. While our machinery had improved, our model of attitudinal research had not. We still sought those key ideas which would subsume others and account for relatively few groups in our data base; and we only had easier and faster means to disprove our original ideas. It was at this point that we redefined the effort to give a parsimonious account of European attitudes by a small set of isms, ists, and types. The new ADMINS system could enrich our typology by searching out which respondents, in which countries, in which years could be identified as one type or another — and even show us which variations and deviations we would have to take account of in our typology if we wanted to include these particular respondents.

We moved to still more elaborate hardware, in the IBM 360-67, the most advanced machinery operating in the country; and we exposed our data to a free-search technique through both factor analysis and numerical taxonomy. Both techniques are described in Annexes Six and Seven. One outcome was that we determined that some of our early hypotheses — complicated beyond clarity by the intervening modes of data processing — could now be reformulated more simply, more richly, and more accurately. One principal finding: The European elites had transformed themselves.

3. Data Analysis

The Europeans have transformed themselves so that they are no longer responsive to the dominance of patterned ideological formulations. This finding has the most profound implications for the analysis presented in this book. As we have indicated, our data on the total distributions of responses, the marginals, tend to set the pattern for the various subgroups within the elite. This signifies that all elite sectors have been permeated in significant degree by the convergent consensus that has developed in postwar Europe. If the subgroups, opposition and establishment alike, share a basic set of dominant attitudes, then sectoral analysis becomes less important. For this reason, our book most frequently reports only marginals, i.e., total distributions.

We have examined a myriad of particular relations and partial explanations. The central finding they produce is that the European elites have been transformed from ideologues to pragmatists. This has fundamental implications for their attitudinal biographers. We thus take the general view in this book that the constant which underlies the many particular findings we report is this: The elites tend to unite rather than divide on the key issues facing Europe today. In the next three chapters, we report the relevant data under the headings of protection, prosperity, and prestige. Since the findings are general, we have also sought general explanations. These are set forth in the chapters in Part C. We now turn to the detailed findings that have led us to the conclusion that the European elites have transformed themselves by taking on the attitudinal pragmatism appropriate to the pluralistic society created in Europe during the postwar era.

Part B: Issues

Introduction

PART A dealt with the contexts that have framed historical events and political decisions in postwar Europe. The drive to integrate Europe — to create Europa — was activated by the push of fear and the pull of hope. Hope for a better life through cooperation with each other, even if this required pooling their resources in a single community, pulled the nations toward Europa. Fear of the consequences of national weakness, particularly in confrontation with the expansionist power of Stalin's Russia, pushed Europeans toward close cooperation with the Anglo-Americans in Atlantica. The ideas of Europa and Atlantica were seen as compatible and their respective institutions — OEEC and NATO (Marshall model), ECSC and EDC (Monnet model) — were designed to coexist constructively.

As the "European miracle" took shape and the fear of Soviet power receded, the focus of elite attention shifted slightly from protection to prosperity. The European Community, animated by its Common Market, achieved levels of economic growth and well-being previously unknown on the Old Continent. Its mood was optimistic and its confidence in the new transnational institutions relatively high. The solid support of the European elites and their growing participation in the management of transnational affairs augured well for the constructive evolution of the Euramerican and Euratlantic ideas. Central to this evolution was widespread elite acceptance of the "American nexus." In this perspective, which took cognizance of American superpower, continuous interaction between Europe and America was seen as indispensable and beneficent. Upon this "Euramerican" base reposed the "Euratlantic" structure, which included all of Western Europe and North America. The maintenance of NATO, the transformation of OEEC into OECD, the creation of GATT and the Club of Ten — all these gave institutional expression to the importance of Euratlantica on the key issues of protection and especially prosperity. Prestige, it was assumed, would accrue to each partner from the common growth of military strength (mainly American) and economic well-being (mainly European).

Some dissident voices were heard among the European elites represented in our TEEPS panels. But these dissident voices were relatively

101

few in number, relatively unfocused in perspective, and relatively weak in influence until the later years of the TEEPS decade. It was not until De Gaulle freed himself of the Algerian problem and focused his attention upon the position of France (and Europe) in the new world arena that European dissidence acquired a single strong voice explicitly opposed to the Euramerican idea and the Euratlantic institutions that had been built upon this foundation.

In retrospect, it appears that much of Gaullist oratory has been "sound and fury, signifying nothing." However, Gaullism did produce one important attitudinal modification in France and elsewhere that our TEEPS survey felt obliged to take account of after the 1959 round of interviews (conducted within the year of De Gaulle's return to power at the head of the Fifth Republic). This was the "nationalist" reaction-formation to the transnational commitments made attitudinally by the European elites, and politically by their governments, during the postwar years. We had been careful, from the start of TEEPS, to watch for "nationalist" protest; after 1959 this was as central to our inquiry as the evolution of transnational ideas and institutions. In consequence, we are now able to present empirical data on the interaction between the new postwar ideas of Euramerica and Euratlantica and those counterformations we have called Euronational.

That we adopted the label Euronational signalizes our judgment that Gaullism has been a severely contained perspective on Europe's present and future. While beating the drums of national *grandeur*, De Gaulle has not been able to free himself of the attitudinal commitment to Europa with which he has been surrounded by his own elite and people — as well as the elites and peoples of his principal neighbors. Each time he has identified France and Europe, as any experienced content analyst can demonstrate, he has willy-nilly strengthened his own bondage: While his tongue spoke France, the ears of his listeners heard Europe. A seasoned French official, aware of this boomerang effect in much of Gaullist oratory, told us: "The paradox is that the inscription most likely to be carved on De Gaulle's tomb is FATHER OF EUROPA."

Be that as it may, the outcome for TEEPS was the partitioning of our elite panels into the Euronationalist as well as the earlier Euramerican and Euratlantic categories. The added category was called Euronationalist because there are virtually no true-blue nationalists visible among our TEEPS panelists. Those who exhibit nationalist preferences typically do not oppose them to European commitments. Indeed, there is virtual unanimity, by all our tests, that Europa is desirable as well as feasible: in short, that Europa is here to stay. This convergent consensus in favor of Europa carries with it some measure of commitment to Euramerica — what would Europa be without it? — and thereby also some commitment to Euratlantica, if only because European participation in Atlantica has been so important to the American sponsors of the Euratlantic idea.

These are the considerations that have shaped our presentation of the data in Part B. An enormous amount of data were collected, processed, and analyzed by the TEEPS project. Many of these data have been made available in earlier publications, student theses in several countries, public "research reports" to the Center for International Studies at M.I.T. Here we have sought to present "the issues" emerging from our analysis of this huge data base as they are likely to matter to most readers interested in the shaping of elite attitudes in Europe during the second postwar decade — which is the TEEPS decade.

We offered the European elites a wide selection of topics from political and economic issues to such items of table-talk as how to raise children, what one could learn from the mass media, whether modern art was likely to "overtake and surpass" the classic arts, what could be learned by travel and/or reading foreign languages, how much influence public opinion should have on national and foreign policy. To the latter, more social, questions the European elites responded only diffidently and diffusely. (We will report these responses as we proceed, notably in Part C.) The real attention and interest among the TEEPS panelists was on the key issues of national and transnational policy that we have ordered under the rubrics protection, prosperity, prestige. To these we turn in the three chapters of Part B.

CHAPTER FOUR

Protection: Military Issues

BY THE time our interviewing began in 1954, the nations of Western Europe had ceased to rely on wars and to build armies against each other. They had not yet agreed to build one continental army for the common defense. A fortnight after the fall of EDC, we began to probe European elite attitudes about the modalities of protection for Europe in the face of the threat from Russia. EDC had been designed as a "community" vehicle for rearming West Germany as part of an integrated military machine designed to protect Europe. The rejection of this option by the French parliament resulted in bringing West Germany into the Atlantic security system (NATO) through the Western European Union (WEU). In taking the Atlantic route to European security, the die was cast for the foreseeable future. These were to be the Atlantic years.

The Atlantic-based system of protection was firmly established in 1954 as the primary bulwark against possible hostile action by the Soviet Union. When our interviewing ended a decade later, the Atlantic-based defense system and the nature of the threat it was designed to defend against had been laid open to question on some major dimensions. The story of these Atlantic years may well be told in the movement of European elite opinion on these issues. The attitudinal base for the Atlantic system of protection was constructed over a decade dominated by the Cold War. We turn now to focus on the events of that decade and the attitudinal responses of the European elite.[1]

We took soundings of the perceived general level of international tensions throughout the decade in order to help characterize the environment of attitude formation. Figure 4.1 illustrates the national responses in each of the surveys. The questions used to elicit

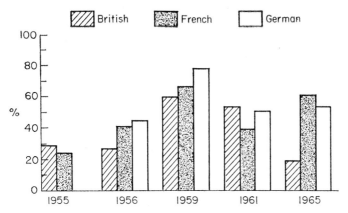

Figure 4.1. Those choosing harshest alternative to characterize East-West relations.

general measures of tension varied from year to year, for we had early decided to be "contemporary" rather than "rigorous" in our formulation of issues. While this procedure limited strict comparability across the years, the questions in each survey were the same for each country. This enabled us to make cross-year comparisons with respect to the key issues even though the test items varied. Thus, we can present the per cent of each panel choosing the harshest alternative offered in each year to describe the East-West conflict. In the early years, we asked respondents to characterize the international situation as "Cold War" or "Coexistence"; in later years (1959 and after) we changed the wording to the then-current terms "continued conflict" or "peaceful accommodation." In spite of these variations, Figure 4.1 reveals comparable patterns.

As Figure 4.1 shows, the national panels have tended to share roughly the same pattern of response in any given year. With a few noteworthy deviations over the years, estimates of the international situation are fairly stable in each country. While there are occasionally differences as high as 18 per cent, they are usually attributable to the British underevaluation of the harshest alternative relative to her continental neighbors. Thus, the first finding is that by and large the elites of Europe share a common perception of international tension; the second finding identifies the British as least likely to choose the harsh alternative.

Yet while the peaking of tension occurred in 1959 in all panels, probably reflecting the Berlin Crisis, the national and yearly variations in tension levels did not produce directly comparable variations in institutional commitments to deal with the tensions. This third finding will be documented more fully later, when institutional commitments are examined. At this point, however, we note that the variations in Figure 4.1 fail to support a proposition that has often been postulated: namely, that the lessening of Soviet pressure on Europe has led to the loosening of NATO ties. Generally, we found this statement too limited to explain the course of attitudinal development during our decade of interviewing.

Before we explore the approaches and institutions favored for dealing with the international situation, it should be noted that throughout the years the Soviet danger to Europe was perceived to be primarily political by a plurality or majority of all panels. In the early years, when we asked if the respondents expected a Third World War, the positive response included about one fifth of the panel in each country. By the later years, less than 5 per cent of any panel thought a Third World War would break out. Consistently throughout the decade, the fear that the Soviet challenge was primarily military was discounted in favor of a predominantly political evaluation. Thus, while the challenge was perceived throughout the decade, falling off only in Britain, it was never evaluated primarily in military terms by any panel.

With the dynamics of the elites' attitudes toward the East-West challenge in mind, we turn next to the forms of protection that were favored among the many possible options open to them. We explore, in turn, the elite responses to various plans for military security: disarmament agreements, the American guarantee, NATO, European defense, and national defense.

A. THE DISARMAMENT RESPONSE

One solution to threat is to alter the environment in such a manner that the danger is eliminated. The decade began with many such proposals, notably those from the British and Polish governments, which sought various forms of disengagement in Central Europe. The hope was to remove fighting capability from the zone where fighting was most likely to occur — and most likely to involve Western Europe. The decade ended with only limited agreements between the big powers, including a number of small nations, seeking to restrain further development of nuclear capacities for destruction. However, these limited agreements did not play the major role that was hoped for in earlier years by advocates of disarmament plans. The events of the decade are interpretable in many different ways; our object in this chapter is to trace the response of the elites as they examined the disarmament alternative for the protection of Europe.

The disarmament response in this particular case shares a more general characteristic of all responses under examination which may be viewed either as competing or compatible with other alternatives. One trait characteristic of all panels, which will be noted in later chapters, is to pronounce favorably on many alternatives, apparently on the view that inclusiveness is better than exclusiveness. They are, therefore, in a position to accept opportunities as they appear — attitudinally prepared to exploit situations. While all panels contain minorities of idealists who exclude all but the most desired vision, the majorities are highly pragmatic. These conclusions are presented prematurely, for they are important to keep in mind while examining the decade's attitudinal history. The history of choice among the European elites is characterized by an inclusive mode of thought. Under these conditions, we sometimes find that evaluations are formed by expectations about feasibility and acceptance of alternatives rather than by private preferences.

The disarmament response shares these general elite characteristics. Disarmament had a serious following in the middle years of the surveys. The public questioning of deterrence as the dominant posture for the West reached sufficient proportions that we pursued a line of questioning which would reveal how profound was the interest and what specific forms it took. We asked, "For the next few years, would you give major attention to strengthening the Western deterrent or pursuing general disarmament, as a matter of relative priority?" To 1959, in Britain and Germany, general disarmament took priority over improving the Western deterrent. In France, priority was given to deterrence, but a substantial minority favored disarmament; and by 1961, the desire for general disarmament had increased since the earlier surveys. The French as well as the British panels substantially increased their priority for disarmament. The Germans, despite a decline, still favored disarmament by a substantial majority of two to one. The trend was toward convergence of panels with majorities everywhere for the disarmament priority.

This interest in disarmament applied to its most extensive forms, not merely to arms control aimed at damage limitation. In both the 1961 and 1965 surveys in almost every panel, 80 per cent or more of the respondents gave priority to the objective of reducing the probability of war over measures to reduce the destructiveness of war. However, they expected that the desirable larger measures would most usefully be negotiated on a stage-by-stage basis rather than in a big package proposal of general and complete disarmament.

As one measure of the seriousness of disarmament interests, we asked if one of the desired steps might include nuclear control. In 1965 we asked, "As a major objective of future negotiations, would you approve depriving all nations of major nuclear weapons in order to create a nuclear monopoly by a supranational force designed to maintain peace?" While this produced a split British panel (40 per cent yes, 46 per cent no), majorities in the French (65 per cent) and German (59 per cent) panels were for so strong a supranational measure as a nuclear monopoly.

Returning to more general measures, we asked the respondents in both the 1961 and 1965 surveys if they expected more useful results would be obtained from bilateral or multilateral or generalized (UN) negotiations. A dispersion of opinion among the choices marked most panels, but bilateral negotiations between the Americans and Russians attracted most panelists. There were, however, two small changes to note as of 1965: a plurality of French panelists favorably assessed multilateral negotiations; the German panelists lost their consensus of 1961 and dispersed their responses. Thus, while the superpowers were still held most responsible for disarmament, the panels increasingly wanted other countries (mainly their own) to play a role in negotiations as well.

The convergence of response in all countries on questions about disarmament shows that a consensus is apparently developing in Europe on the desirability of finding an alternative to the deterrent posture. This is apparently related to our previous finding that the elites have not defined the Russian threat primarily in a military fashion. Further, under questioning explored in Chapter Seven, the elites reported that the present posture does not offer an attractive long-run political position for the West. As a result, many panelists turned to disarmament as the posture more appropriate to the present character and prospective balance of East-West political forces.

It should be emphasized, however, that discussion of Europe's desire for disarmament is complex. The deterrent posture and the disarmament posture do not necessarily call for critically different judgments of the short-range elements of deterrent policy. In the short term, one may prefer to enforce deterrence in order to create the conditions for *détente* and disarmament in the long term. Furthermore, recalling the hypothesized role of expectations in European pragmatism, one may value a response and give it priority, all the while saying yes to the opposite alternative because the expectations lie in the direction of the alternative. That is why we now turn to an examination of the elite's expectations about the future of the disarmament response to the tensions of the Cold War.

Figure 4.2 illustrates a growing disbelief that there will be a gen-

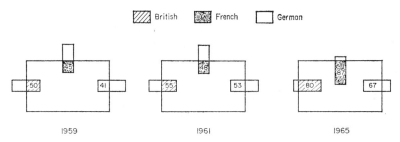

Figure 4.2.   Those believing general disarmament treaty is unlikely.

eral agreement on international disarmament in conventional and nuclear weapons. The convergence among panels is portrayed as the bars move into the rectangular box which symbolizes "agreement space." The amount of the bar in the box denotes the per cent believing a general disarmament treaty is not likely. The amount of the bar out of the box denotes the contrary.

It was clear by 1965 that general disarmament agreements were not part of elite expectations. In fact, when asked about probable developments in the next five years, a majority of all panels thought that other nations would develop nuclear weapons. Each panel included some small fraction, at least 10 per cent, who could name four or five countries likely to be nuclearized. One fifth of the French panel expected Germany would develop nuclear weapons in the next five years (although only 2 per cent of the Germans had that expectation).

Perhaps it is this very pessimism about the likely success of disarmament measures that finally puts restraints on the acceptance of the disarmament response. In the last two surveys, large majorities of the British and French panels did not seriously consider unilateral nuclear disarmament for themselves. In 1965, the French were even sharply divided about signing the Test Ban Treaty, 48 per cent for and 44 per cent against. Nor could a majority be found by 1961 for a disengaged, demilitarized zone on the continent. Only the British were interested in such a disarming measure.

However, when the panels were asked to evaluate specific measures affecting their immediate security or their national capacities, the desirability of disarmament gave way to a pragmatic concern for protection. They felt, almost unanimously, that mutual inspection systems were essential. Also, majorities condoned American insistence on safeguards against surprise attack at a time when Americans were being accused of exaggerating the danger (1961). Majorities of the panels even went so far as to agree that U-2 flights over Soviet territory were necessary safeguards, although the British thought the flights "aggressive" even if necessary.

As a further test of the immediacy and pragmatism of the elite's concern for protection, we divided the 1961 French and British panels into two groups, the one giving priority to deterrence and the other to disarmament. While we did find some persistent differences, these were not on key attitudes relating to a preparedness military posture. In Britain and France, both the deterrer and disarmer positions included majorities who wanted to keep West Germany in NATO rather than neutralize her. A similar failure to discriminate according to disarmament priorities applied to the evaluation of the credibility of the American guarantee and the deterrence capacity of NATO. Among the disarmer group, there were even more respondents for national nuclear forces than against, though not as many supporters for national systems as we found among the deterrers.

Such lack of discriminatory results suggests that the disarmament priority is desired but that long-run desirability does not inhibit different responses to the presently available alternatives. This is just one example of the many to be presented in which the elite defines options as compatible and inclusive rather than competitive and exclusive. The disarmament priority, then, does not indicate a firm choice of present policies but a desire to capitalize on opportunities should they arise. Support for the disarmament priority is apparently a passive act since it is limited to acceptance of disarmament were it likely to occur. Rejection of alternatives in order to create the disarmament situation is not part of the attitude set. (This type of passivity contrasts sharply with pacifist minorities, especially in Britain, who preferred unilateral disarmament. The implication of the unilateral priority was much more active in terms of its rejection of the deterrence system for Europe and the espousal of alternative schemes of world order.)

From the results just given, it is clear that the elites were not prepared to seek disarmament for Europe if it meant reduction of their own — or American — power. The more attractive alternative was the efficient organization of power. There were, of course, a number of different options open to Europe's leaders as they sought an appropriate organization of power for their own protection. The alternatives will be examined in the order of their apparent importance for most of the elite over the decade. We therefore begin with the American guarantee as a response to the Communist challenge.

B. THE AMERICAN GUARANTEE AND THE EURAMERICAN SCENARIO

While the chief form of American interaction with European security affairs is through NATO, there remains a visibly independent position for the leader of the alliance. America is the protector of Europe, for her arsenal is designed to guarantee European security. But America has other military commitments.

There has been much public discussion in the last half of the TEEPS decade, most of it initiated by French justification of the *force de frappe*, which alleges a weakening of the guarantee in the face of American vulnerability to Soviet missiles. We probed for the European results of this French discussion, beginning in an early form with the 1959 survey in Germany and France. The Sputnik demonstration of Soviet achievements in rocketry had impressed a majority of the French elites and evenly divided the German panel. However, both panels in 1959 thought America *would match the Soviets in time*. The image of Soviet power was established, but confidence in America's long-term superiority remained.

In 1961 and again in 1965, we asked the elites to evaluate the significance of Soviet rocketry directly in the context of the American guarantee. We asked, "As the North American continent becomes more vulnerable to direct attack by the new weapons, do you think the United States will be prepared to continue its guarantee of the military security of Western Europe?" The responses to the repeated questions showed a high degree of stability among highly consensual panel: Germany in the range of 90 per cent, Britain in 80 per cent, and France in 70 per cent. There were few doubters, even in France, where public discussion had highlighted the uncertainty of an American protector whose own homeland was threatened by nuclear destruction. This discussion had no apparent effect on the European elites, who remained strong in their belief that the American guarantee was good, even under conditions of American vulnerability to Soviet missiles.

We can, however, report small minorities, less than 20 per cent in each country, who thought the guarantee was subject to political change. The change from a Kennedy to a Johnson administration made the guarantee less credible for these marginal minorities. Even though the numbers are small, we report them by way of contrast with the pronouncements by some commentators who amplify these minorities into a prevailing new "European" position. Clearly, the majority of the elites considered America still to be a reliable ally when faced with the tests of military vulnerability and political change, even after the shift from Kennedy to Johnson.

We asked them both about the credibility of the American guarantee and how much they valued it. We used different measures, but in each case only very small minorities, again under 20 per cent, said that a Fortress America idea (1961) or a weakening of the American guarantee (1965) was *not at all dangerous to Europe*. Majorities in both years and all panels thought the loss would be *very* dangerous. Although the German choice of *very* dangerous declined from 91 per cent to 68 per cent, most of the loss went into the *fairly* dangerous category. Thus, the American guarantee is both credible and necessary to the protection of Europe. The Euramerican scenario is a key element in the elites' thinking.

We were then prepared to ask, if the American protection is so valuable to the Europeans, what are they willing to give America in return? Concretely, one real contribution that Europe can make is to help with the American "dollar problem." We pursued this area in some detail, with markedly different results from 1961 to 1965.

When asked if they considered the American "dollar problem" to be a matter of long-term concern to Europe, the elites responded affirmatively and with slightly increasing majorities. But the response changed sharply when the elites were asked if their countries should help with the dollar problem by sharing the cost of Western defense. Table 4.1 illustrates the changed response.

TABLE 4.1. LARGER EUROPEAN SHARE IN WESTERN DEFENSE COSTS

	Britain		France		Germany	
	1961	1965	1961	1965	1961	1965
Approve	71%	46%	53%	28%	71%	32%
Disapprove	23	37	23	47	21	41
DK	6	17	24	25	8	27

Table 4.1 identifies the first serious sign of an important change in alliance relations. In Britain and Germany, earlier approval changed into either disapproval or uncertainty. In France, it became a clear reversal of position. On this important issue of Euramerican relations, therefore, one tide had turned. In 1961, the elites were prepared to pay for what they valued. In 1965, their estimate of value received had not changed as markedly as their willingness to pay for it. In terms of helping America out of a Euramerican problem, treated in part by the extension of American resources for the protection of Europe, the elites showed a new reluctance to commit a larger share of the new European prosperity to the abiding requirement of European protection.

We recall that the Erhardt government turned recalcitrant on the key issue of paying a larger share of the costs of Western defense. The German elite's affirmative response declined between 1961 and 1965 from nearly unanimous agreement to less than majority agreement. This shift represents the only discernible crack in the positive attitudes of the German elites toward the Euramerican scenario — and thereby the first important signal of the new complexities of the European response to their own perceived need for protection. It will become clear that the decade has witnessed some important variations of position among each of the TEEPS panels. These we will explore later in greater detail (Chapter Nine). Meanwhile, we continue with our data on the European response to the American guarantee, which indicate that these variations ring

changes upon a stable theme: i.e., the merit of the Western defense system built around the American guarantee. What these
variations suggest is a changing elite perception of the role some
Europeans want to play in the Euratlantic format for security.

There are other, more general, measures that are indicative of alliance solidarity in each country. In the case of Britain, we examined
the special "Anglo-American connection" to find out how it had
fared in the last several years of Anglo-American relations. As Figure 4.3 indicates, in the tug of war between the "very" and the

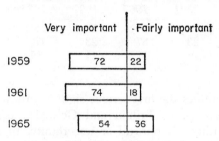

Figure 4.3.   British panel's evaluations of Anglo-American connection.

"fairly" important categories, a majority of the elite continued to
choose "very important," but there has also been a decided shift
to the "fairly important" evaluation. This decline was characteristic
of all British evaluations of overseas connections: Commonwealth,
United Nations, and the Atlantic Alliance as well. The increased
approval of a European Community was a strong exception to this
general trend. We shall explore this phenomenon in more detail
in Chapter Nine.

The German panelists were also asked in 1965 to evaluate the
importance of their special connections to America. At that time,
86 per cent thought German-American relations to be "very important." When the question was posed more specifically in terms of
military security, 61 per cent rated the German-American connection
as most essential for German protection, 73 per cent giving priority
to NATO. Thus the alliance has a few more adherents than the
bilateral connection, but both draw substantial majorities of panelists.

Although we have no trend data, for only in 1965 did any serious
thought arise about bilateral relations other than through NATO,
it is clear that the alliance connection has not suffered the same

degree of weakening in Germany as in France and possibly Britain. The German situation is complex and will be explored in a broader context in Chapter Nine, where we will be able to see the pressures under which German evaluations must be made.

The French have not had a special connection to America in recent years. To preview the 1965 results, 90 per cent of the French panel thought that De Gaulle had weakened American leadership, as contrasted with 61 per cent of the German elite and 58 per cent of the British. Furthermore, only the French panel made a distinction between the two questions of America's leadership and the weakening of the Alliance itself: 37 per cent saw De Gaulle's policies as disrupting America's role, but not the security system itself.

The picture that emerges from the elite evaluation of the American guarantee of European protection is reasonably clear. In all countries, the elite panels have evaluated the American guarantee as credible and important. But European willingness to pay the American bill for services rendered has declined sharply. Few question the need for American participation in the protection of Europe and therefore the need for a Euramerican format. However, signs of weakness appear in the Europeans' willingness to pay their way in terms of American conceptions of their commitment to the Euramerican equation.

This mixed picture must be tied to other elite attitudes regarding the need for the protection of Europe. While the American guarantee reposes upon American military power, it is mainly manifested in the broader context of NATO. It is this aspect of the Western security system that we then asked the TEEPS panels to evaluate.

C. NATO AND THE EURATLANTIC SCENARIO

Throughout the decade, NATO has provided the framework for deterring the East and defending the West. In the period before our interviewing began, NATO was a controversial issue, especially among French leftists who rallied behind the anti-American and anti-NATO "Yankee Go Home" slogan. After our interviewing finished, NATO was once again a controversial treaty in France — but this time especially among Gaullists who rallied behind the idea of a national *force de frappe*. The latent motives for these manifestly similar attitudes were very different. The former epitomized postwar malaise in which antimilitarism and social reform were the prevailing sentiments. The latter, in the context of a "recovered" and more self-confident Europe, speaks with accents of national autonomy and power. While the NATO controversy thus had come full circle in public discussion, it is noteworthy that the TEEPS elite panels exhibited a far more stable position over the decade of our surveys.

In 1956, we asked the elites if they were for or against a number of existing transnational organizations, among them NATO. The favorable response was strong in each panel: Britain 82 per cent, France 71 per cent, and Germany 77 per cent. In 1959 and 1961, we posed the question differently, asking if there were any existing European organizations more important than NATO. While a number of panelists did not choose between them because they felt the organizations were not comparable, a substantial proportion of NATO supporters explicitly avowed that no European organization (including the universally acclaimed Common Market) was more important than NATO. The percentages are given in Table 4.2. Except in France, pro-NATO sentiment even showed a marked increase by 1961 on this most difficult of the tests used in our survey.

TABLE 4.2. NO EUROPEAN ORGANIZATIONS MORE IMPORTANT
THAN NATO

	Britain	France	Germany
1959	28%	28%	45%
1961	49	24	67

We also asked specific questions designed to reveal the content of the elite's high evaluation of NATO. In 1961 and 1965, we asked them about NATO's capacity to fulfill its major functions: deterring the Soviet Union and defending the West. There is stability and even growth in French elite confidence in NATO's deterrent capacity. By 1965, the French even joined the other panels, in which two thirds or better of the respondents affirmed their confidence in NATO. This strong positive evaluation in 1965 included substantial numbers of respondents expressing confidence that NATO could accomplish its defensive mission, whereas in earlier surveys deterrence was stressed but defense was not taken seriously as a NATO function. By 1965, almost half of the British and French panels and 57 per cent of the German panel affirmed confidence in NATO's defensive capacity, and even higher percentages affirmed its deterrent capability.

Still further support for the alliance was found in a continued series of responses to questions asking if the panels approved of integrating a major part of their armed forces into European, NATO, or UN commands. In the present context, we report only the NATO choices in Figure 4.4. But we note that, except among the Europe-oriented French, they are the highest of all desired commitments.

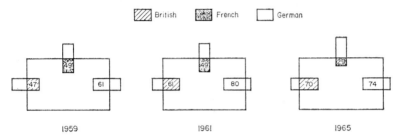

Figure 4.4.   Those approving NATO command for an integrated army. In 1965, in Britain and Germany, the question was changed from previous years, making comparison difficult. A filter question, asking about integration in principle, preceded the question for an evaluation of NATO. Thus the approval of NATO is only by those who approve integration in principle: 58% in Britain and 38% in Germany. (In Germany, the question asked for more interpretation than elsewhere. Since the Bundeswehr is already closely integrated into NATO, the low number is understandable.)

We also looked for indications of NATO support in the context of specific technological alternatives. The Polaris weapon system was looked upon with great favor by the elites in 1961. They judged it to be the most important weapon system available as compared to ground forces or space vehicles. To pursue further the political import of this technological evaluation, we explored the attitude of panelists regarding control of Polaris. In a battery of questions about Polaris, one raised explicitly the principle of collective defense as possibly in conflict with the principle of national sovereignty. We deliberately framed this question as a forced choice:

The key problem of Polaris control appears to force a choice between adopting the most effective system of collective defence now available, or maintaining intact the historic institutions of national sovereignty. Should Britain [France, Germany], in this situation, give priority to collective defence or national sovereignty?

The elites responded positively and consensually in favor of collective defense over national sovereignty. Every panel showed a clear majority in favor of adopting the Polaris system whatever the cost to "historic institutions." Variations reflected the usual national patterning that we have noted. Thus, as compared with the huge majorities in Germany (95 per cent) and Britain (84 per cent), the French majority was smaller (55 per cent). Considering the characteristic reticence of the French panel, especially on military matters, this is an impressive majority. Across the board and beyond the apparent faith in Polaris, we take this response as significant evidence that by 1961 the TEEPS elites had reached a convergent consensus that the protection of Europe could best be entrusted to the Euratlantic system as represented by NATO.

After 1961, a number of important events occurred in the field of Euratlantic security. We mention only the British retrenchment on Blue Streak and the French expansion of their *force de frappe*, the cancellation of Skybolt and the subsequent Nassau agreements, the failure of multilateral force (MLF) and Atlantic nuclear force (ANF) proposals to bring Polaris under Euratlantic controls. As an outcome of these events, the choices open to the elites in 1965 varied according to country, and we had to adapt our questions accordingly. Table 4.3 reports the results of questioning adapted

TABLE 4.3. NATIONAL OR MULTINATIONAL FORCE (1965)

Britain		France		Germany	
National Force	27%	Force de frappe	20%	National Force	4%
Multinational (Atlantic)	41	Atlantic Force	19	Multinational (Atlantic)	55
Other	14	European Force	39	More Integration	38
DK	18	DK	22	DK	3

to national options in 1965. In spite of the different national forms of our questions, it is clear that all countries still showed a preference for some form of collective as opposed to national security. We can also detect the convergence of British and German orientation to Euratlantica (via NATO) in contrast to the French orientation to Europa — although the French panel endorses Atlantic about as much as national options for their protection. There is thus a common adherence to the Euratlantic security framework, with a French preference for the Euronational framework when it is offered as a forced choice.

A picture begins to emerge which shows stable and solid support for NATO throughout the decade, although the French gave more support to the Euronational scenario (but not a nationalist scenario) in 1965. We explored these national differences still further by measuring NATO support against the options which are posed most acutely for each national elite. De Gaulle's challenge to NATO takes different forms in different countries. In Britain, the NATO choice is forced to compete with a European orientation. In the French case, NATO membership itself is at stake. In the German case, reunification is held up as the alternate prize. We now report on each national context in its turn.

In Britain, we asked questions in different years designed to elicit the results of forcing a choice between the Euratlantic versus the Euronationalist scenarios. We asked which European organization was more important for Britain than NATO. In 1959, 57 per cent of the panelists were able to select a European organization more important than NATO, although by 1965 this had declined to 47 per cent. As a clue, we note that in the intervening survey of 1961, most of the British who chose any alternative opted for the OEEC, an Atlantic economic organization, as NATO's chief rival. In 1965, the Common Market, a European economic organization, was the major contender.

The 1965 shift probably reflects the beginning of a European orientation as well as the primacy of economic over security considerations. In 1959, the British chose the most Atlantic of the economic options. In 1961, security pressures were still greatest and the Atlantic military form, NATO, was predominant. By 1965, economic pressures had taken priority, but there was no Atlantic economic organization with sufficient strength to compete with the Common Market in the new British search for a solution to economic problems.

Whatever the reasons, there has been an increase of interest in Europe relative to the NATO choice. We need not overinterpret these measures here. At this point, we underline the continued support for NATO over the decade in the positive evaluation of its functions and as a vehicle for integrating armies and weapon systems. That this evaluation was under strain when put to a forced choice suggests the existence of cross-currents in the British elite. They have not, as yet, played a role destructive of the British commitment to a Euratlantic security system.

The French choice has been direct and immediate. De Gaulle has repeatedly withdrawn forces from NATO, and by the time of the 1965 interviews was playing the role of recalcitrant ally. We asked the French panels:

When the NATO treaty expires in 1969, should France leave the alliance, should France stay only if NATO is completely reorganized, or should France remain a member of the NATO even if the organization is only little changed?

Table 4.4 reports the results.

TABLE 4.4.   FRENCH RELATIONSHIP TO NATO (1965)

Withdraw in 1969	5%
Remain if Reorganized	50
Continue with Small Changes	34
DK	11

It is clear that the elite in France did not favor withdrawal and that there was still a sizable minority that accepted only small changes. The majority wanted a reorganization. We did not test for what forms of reorganization were desired, but we can estimate their sentiments from their opinions on a larger national and European voice in the NATO structure.

The response to this question also shows where the opposition to NATO has tapered off. The French panel wanted reform, not rejection, of the Euratlantic alliance which they have relied upon as their primary source of protection throughout the decade. It has sought a more European orientation that does not, however, exclude NATO.

The German dilemma has been less immediate and less manipulable. NATO has been championed by opposing sides as a block and, conversely, as the only route to unification. In three surveys, we asked the German panelists for their responses to the question, "What would you prefer: a divided Germany whereby West Germany is a member of NATO or a reunified Germany?" Figure 4.5 demonstrates the tug of war between the competing options.

The don't know response has been fixed at 12 per cent every year, but, except for 1961, when all pro-NATO sentiments were highest in all panels, a reunified neutral Germany has received a slightly higher number of supporters. While the German panels have ac-

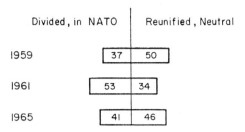

Figure 4.5. The German dilemma.

cepted every opportunity to say yes to NATO, there also was a substantial portion of them who would say yes to neutrality and reunification if it became a real opportunity.

Thus, all three countries have expressed qualifications to their general overwhelming favorable support of NATO over the decade. Substantial groups of NATO supporters would no doubt like to have their profound NATO commitment made harmonious with a British need for European cooperation, a French desire for reform, and a German requirement for reunification. It must be emphasized, however, that these cross-currents have not washed away the abiding interest expressed in Euratlantic cooperation. The cross-currents need further examination, for NATO's survival is not only a question of how much favor it generates but also the viability of alternative responses. Most notable among the contenders for the NATO job as protector of Europe is a European-based organization.

D. THE EUROPEAN RESPONSE

Throughout the decade 1955–1965, few, if any, respondents felt that Europe alone could ensure its own protection. Rather they considered a European force as an outgrowth of their American attachment. More recently, European-minded Frenchmen have seen the French national force as the basis of a European force. While the European response has thus been considered the end goal of either a growth from national forces or a growth from Atlantic forces, it has never itself been evaluated as a sufficient framework for the defense of Europe.

During the course of this study, which was begun shortly after the failure of the first major attempt to integrate European forces in the EDC, we gave our respondents repeated opportunities to reevaluate the French parliament's refusal to pass on the European option. Britain showed an increased negative feeling, France an increased positive feeling, and Germany a high, stable degree of support.

Here we did not compare the European option to any other. By itself, and in an inclusive framework that does not force a choice, there remained a significant interest in a European Defense Community. However, when the European option was compared to a NATO option, important national variations emerged. We asked for an expression of willingness to integrate a major part of national armed forces into a supranational army under various commands. Table 4.5 reports the countries' responses to an integrated European army independent of NATO and one based within the NATO command.

TABLE 4.5. APPROVE INTEGRATION IN TRANSNATIONAL COMMAND

	Britain		France		Germany	
	European Choice	NATO	European Choice	NATO	European Choice	NATO
1959	26%	47%	42%	49%	48%	61%
1961	32	61	49	49	43	80
1965*	11	70	54	29	14	74

* There are important variations in coding in 1965. In that year, the British and Germans, but not the French, were given a forced choice separately, as had been the previous pattern in all countries. Also, in Britain and Germany, only those approving integration were asked regional preferences.

Table 4.5 clearly indicates substantial British support for NATO, as well as an increasing reluctance to back an integrated European army. While the German panels also showed substantially more interest in a NATO than a European option, a large group said yes to both, except when the 1965 questioning forced a choice. The French differed from the other panels in their strong and increasing support for a strictly European security system.

E. THE NATIONAL RESPONSE

No matter how nationalism is defined, we can no longer insist that it be based on a nation's capacity to defend itself. Whatever year, panel, or fashion we posed the question, the national option for defense was subordinated to a collective security framework.

Thus the first goal of the elite in modern Europe has been protection, but not by national means. Whether we asked a limited question such as whether arms production should be done in an international pool or by home production (international pool chosen by two thirds of the British and three fourths of the French and Germans in 1959), or a more general one about the priority for force structures (international chosen by majorities of all panels in 1965, as in Table 4.3), or a sweeping question such as collective defense versus national sovereignty (collective defense chosen by a majority in France and with near unanimity in Britain and Germany in 1965), the national option has been subordinate to collective security.

In sum, the national response was desired within the context of alliance relations, either in the Euronational context for the French or the Euratlantic context for the British. No panels wanted to stand alone. There were minorities, sometimes sizable, who sought independence but not isolation.

In the arena of modern weaponry, the national unit does not have the capacity for self-defense, and the survey of responses shows that the national response, like the others, is deeply enmeshed in the collective security system the West has devised as its protection against the tensions and pressures of Cold War and coexistence. Only in the area of national nuclear weapons did the majorities appear to favor the right and capacity of a nation to defend itself. However, it was generally agreed that the defense was not against a military threat but against a weak political position. We shall discuss this in more detail in Chapter Six.

We have examined each of the major centers for the organization of power to protect Europe. We first noted that disarmament alternatives were desired but not expected. We did not examine the role of the UN in the security of Europe, for while the UN gathered favorable support in all panels to play a significant role in preventing the spread of conflicts, the UN has not been conceived as playing a security role in the European theater. Protection would have to come from within the West, and the primary protector was the American guarantee. We noted that all panels felt the guarantee was credible and valuable; however, by the end of the decade, there was some rethinking of the price to be paid for the guarantee. The majority of all panels refused to help America out of her dollar problem by paying more for European defense. Thus, the

Euramerican scenario became subject to the first major strain in the 1965 survey.

The North Atlantic Treaty Organization received the most stable and consistent support from all panels throughout the decade. While we found challenges to NATO taking different forms in each country, the essential primacy of the alliance was not questioned by the elites. Regardless of panel nationality, America is seen as essential to the protection of Europe. On a great variety of measures, NATO remained the most attractive alternative to Europeans in search of protection. The Euratlantic scenario is certainly the dominant choice.

We also examined the European response, and once again national variations were visible. While all panels showed considerable support for a European defense capacity, only the French preferred it over other alternatives. For the British, the idea itself was in decline by the end of the decade. The European response achieved far less consensus than NATO, national variations being marked — but in the European arena, it is just this consensus that is necessary for a European option to succeed. The national differences betray the option in a way that is significant for future attempts; they throw blocks in the path of its creation.

The German panel finds itself with a narrow range of options — not flexible enough to grant freedom of priorities. These differences put strain on some of the national aspirations. The German panel includes a large number of people who want independence; but they feel the need for protection while agreeing not to produce the atomic weapons that give political leverage to the others. Other forms of German independent action are also precluded, for the European option which might allow such freedom is not seen by the Germans as a viable substitute for Atlantic relations. No other competing alternative can attract sufficient support unless it is somehow made compatible with the Euratlantic scenario.

The French panels' desires for alternative protection systems can find no other European supporters, for the French alone pose the European and national options as competitors to Atlantic relations. However, for gratification of French desires, the other neighbors are necessary; and Britain and Germany opt for a Euratlantic security structure when forced to a choice.

Only the British panels find little tension in the Atlantic relations. They seek no conflicting alternatives and are content with their priorities. The only difference of emphasis which might be detected is a British predilection to minimize the threat to the West and to seek nonmilitary solutions to the East-West problem. However, as the decade wore on, even this British position weakened in favor of a strong collective security option.

Thus, we come to the lowest common denominator of the decade's choices. The American-based Atlantic security system, the Euratlantic scenario, receives the greatest support from all panels. It is the only option that is not blocked by virtue of disagreement with neighbors. While the French panel is least in favor of the present arrangements, the panel members recognize the need for its existence. This cannot be said for other options. European, national, or world security systems may be desirable; but there is no consensus about the necessity for their existence. There is a consensus in Europe that these have been the Atlantic years.

CHAPTER FIVE

Prosperity: Economic Issues

In the late sixties, only those of short memory can fail to be impressed with the European movement toward prosperity. At the beginning of the fifties, there was much doubt about Europe's capacity to surmount the next level of postwar economic growth. The economic "miracle," aptly named in the light of earlier expectations, had occurred only in Germany — the defeated but needed country. While the Marshall Plan had been welcome and successful as a restorative device, Western Europe was not without worry over the next steps. Even when success began to show, inflation provided worries which concerned our panelists. In Germany in the 1956 survey, just as many panelists thought the German standard of living would not be raised as thought it would be: 46 per cent each. While the British and French panels were fairly optimistic about their own standard of living, they were not nearly so sure about themselves as they were about the world as a whole.

By the 1959 survey, the picture had changed dramatically.[1] Economic levels were rising. Growth had occurred continuously. Neither inflation nor recession had taken its dreaded course. The Germans clearly made up their minds on the optimistic side regarding their own growth; and the other countries became even more certain of themselves than of the rest of the world.

By 1959, prosperity was recognized everywhere, and the anticipation was that it would be durable. By 1961, our panels were almost unanimous in their opinion that the European community would "effectively develop the economic potential of Western Europe." By 1965, the commitment to and belief in prosperity were so deeply felt by the panelists that we turned exclusively to their views on developing the community of continually prospering European na-

126

tions. This dramatic reordering of elite expectations, as has been indicated in Chapter One, also called for a reordering of the institutional base of Europe. In this chapter, we pursue an examination of the attitudinal response to the requirement of a new institutional base to ensure prosperity for modern Europe.

A. INSTITUTIONS OF PROSPERITY

Jean Monnet believed that the appropriate way to get support for European institutions was to create them first and then let approval grow. The trend data presented in Table 5.1 testify to the correctness of his judgment.

The table illustrates high and growing support for all the institutions of prosperity. Even the Council of Europe benefited from the enthusiasm, though least in Britain where standards of parliamentary performance are highest. The success of the appeal to the elite attitudinal base was so clearly consensual that, by 1961, we stopped asking panelists about the European economic organizations. The consensus that had been built since the early years of the TEEPS surveys became so strong that the idea of collective economic growth had ceased to be a matter of discussion. By 1965, two thirds of all panels even believed that European integration had passed the "point of no return." At worst, they believed that delays might occur. But essentially, time was on the side of European integration.

Thus, from the beginning of our surveys, there was a strong assertion by the elite of their approval for seeking national economic advancement in a community framework. Pro-European sentiment became as common as favorable sentiments for God and Mother. In Europe, the home of nationalism, the elites were making an almost automatic affirmative response to institutions that required transnational commitments. Euronationalism's minimum form, without looking to maximum potential, included support for institutions of European integration. There was special favor shown to one of the European organizations, the Common Market. Quite specifically in 1959 and 1961, we asked the panelists to select the most valuable of the existing European organizations. In all years, the Common Market received the greatest number of mentions from the panels.

There was some national variation. The French panel moved from 39 per cent to 49 per cent naming the Common Market as most

TABLE 5.1.   APPROVAL OF EUROPEAN ORGANIZATIONS

	Britain			France			Germany		
	ECSC	OEEC	Council of Europe	ECSC	OEEC	Council of Europe	ECSC	OEEC	Council of Europe
1955	65%	77%	52%	70%	63%	44%	52%	65%	47%
1956	71	81	55	73	73	62	70	72	86
1959	78	80	56	79	71	66	78	91	84

valuable — far ahead of its nearest rival, the Coal and Steel Community, with 13 per cent. In Germany, a majority selected the Common Market in both years with no near rival. Only in Britain did the Common Market have a rival. In 1959, there was a virtual tie with OEEC at one third each, and again in 1961 at one quarter each. We repeated the question in Britain in 1965 and found a tie once again, only this time the only significant rival was another European grouping, EFTA. One third of the British panel chose each of the two major European groupings (EEC and EFTA), and the more Atlantic option (OEEC–OECD) was named by only 15 per cent of the panel. (This European trend in British thinking will be given more attention in Chapter Nine.)

We are dealing with a success story from the standpoint of the European elites' willingness to participate in transnational institutions of economic integration. The focus of that story is the Common Market. Accordingly, we examined it in some detail, searching not only for levels of approval but for estimates of the tensions and strains that beset the Common Market at the close of our decade of interviewing.

We began by asking what the panels thought were the most significant over-all achievements of the Common Market. The dominant answer — given by 76 per cent of the French, 66 per cent of the Germans, and 54 per cent of the British — was "economic growth of the continent." Political or social gains or increases in European identification were not deemed as important as the Common Market's contribution to the common prosperity.

However, while agreement on this one positive attribute was high, very little else in our investigation of the Common Market showed an equivalent meeting of the minds. For example, the national panels differed in selecting the most significant *failure* of the Common Market. The German panel included a majority who thought that the rejection of Britain was the most significant failure, whereas the French majority cited inadequate political unity. The British panel could not agree on a single focus.

Perhaps even more potentially disruptive of future Common Market accord were the evaluations of the main *purpose* of the Common Market. Table 5.2 portrays a picture of national discrepancies.

The German panel had a clear national consensus that the main purpose of the Common Market was to make a step toward a

TABLE 5.2. MAIN PURPOSES OF THE COMMON MARKET (1965)

	Britain	France	Germany
Defend Europe's Common Interests	28%	34%	7%
Enlarge Sphere of Europe's Interests	46	9	2
Independence and/or Equality	16	38	4
Step toward United Europe	—	—	72
Other	4	9	5
DK	6	10	10

United Europe — an option not offered to other panels. The others were divided among themselves, and not symmetrically. While a minority of both panels saw common interests to be gratified, another French minority saw independence as a goal. Coming at the matter from quite a different perspective, a substantial British group (almost half) found in it an opportunity to enlarge European interests, whereas only a small fraction of the British chose independence. These Franco-British differences, and the German difference from both, will be explored in greater depth, for they manifest themselves in various ways.

Perhaps one of the most important national differences arises in connection with the projected role of the European Community vis-à-vis the United States. For the British, there was a firm and growing rejection of the notion that the European Community might be a "political counterpoise" to the United States. The 1961 majority of 56 per cent which rejected this idea swelled in 1965 to 79 per cent against making Europe competitive with America. The French showed no such restraint: 60 per cent saw Europe as a political counterpoise in 1961. Despite a change in the wording of the question, which biased 1965 answers by stipulating a short term of five years, over 40 per cent of the French panel still perceived the EC as a "counterpoise." The Germans, of whom less than one quarter accepted the counterpoise view in 1961, matched the French judgment by 1965. Clearly, the British view of the European Community is less euphoric — certainly less political — than that expressed by the continental elites. This difference, among many others, indicated the need for detailed information about British-continental relations. We therefore focused the attention of the panels on the thorny issues of British entry into the Common Market.

It is quite certain that the British panel has favored entry into the Common Market. In both of the latest surveys, a positive response for entry came from three quarters of the elite, and explicit opposition reached only 12 per cent. Of the panelists in France and Germany, at least three quarters anticipated positive benefits from Britain's entry. Yet, while British entry was deemed desirable, it was not considered necessary for Common Market growth over the long term. Three quarters of the British and French felt that the Common Market had durable positive prospects without Britain, and 59 per cent of the Germans agreed. Furthermore, roughly three quarters of the French and Germans believed that the stability of the British pound was a matter of long-term concern to Europe. Thus, the welcoming of British membership was not without some reservations. Especially did British entry lose a sense of urgency for those who believed that European prosperity was assured even without her.

The difficulty in the future of a common path to European prosperity, however, lay in the British-French conflict. We probed this in the last two surveys. One question asked: "As the conflict between the Inner Six and the Outer Seven seems to be centered in Britain and France, which country would you say was responsible for the present divided situation?" We found that the French tended to blame the British and the British, especially after 1961, tended to blame the French. While the Germans were divided in 1961, by 1965 they tended to agree with the French, blaming the British.

The situation of mutual recrimination was not aided by the estimate, shared by at least two thirds of all panels, that Britain would suffer more by the continuation of the conflict. This, no doubt, provided less motivation for the French to take the lead toward finding a solution. While 79 per cent of the British were prepared to take the lead in 1961, their willingness fell to 57 per cent by 1965 (still a majority). But a small change of heart occurred in the interim. The fractional loss in favor of British initiative in 1965 tended rather to the option that both should take the lead, an interesting ambiguity in the definition of a leader. The French believed that Britain should take the lead, only a fifth of the French panel choosing the escape option of "both." The Germans divided almost equally for all options. In sum, Britain was clearly regarded as the loser in the conflict; and the largest number agreed that Britain should seek a solution.

We probed to see if the solution lay in forming a larger economic community. In 1961, almost all panelists agreed that it did. However, there was no real agreement on the scope of this preference. Fully 59 per cent of the British thought that merging the Inner Six and Outer Seven would be the solution to the conflict, but only 35 per cent of the French agreed. Moreover, going beyond that merger, only one fifth of the French panel thought a Euratlantic institution was the best solution. The Germans swelled the French minority into a plurality when 40 per cent chose the Euratlantic solution, slightly more than those choosing a merger of Sixes and Sevens. There was no common ground among the elites for solving the problem. The response patterns showed unique national distributions of preferences. Without consensus within countries, it was impossible to expect consensus among countries. While all panels agreed on the desirability of British entry into the Common Market, there was considerable division of opinion within countries on how it might be achieved.

In sum, we can see that a European consensus has been built in favor of the existing institutions of prosperity. Indeed, European integration as an economic matter has been perceived positively by all elites in all years. In whatever form we tested this question, the approval always has outweighed the rejection by far. This being true in all national panels and in all years, it was striking to find the tensions of disagreement over definitions of what panelists were responding to with favor. While all panels said yes to the European Community, they clearly harbored different notions of it. For many of the French, there was a political meaning which the British did not share. For the Germans, caught between shared values with the British for the Atlantic component and shared values with the French for the European component, there was much ambivalence. The British appeared to be in flux, for on some measures they approached the French conception, while on other measures there was a pulling apart.

In 1965, our panels had not yet achieved a consensus among themselves as to the next steps for the European Community, nor even to the direction these steps might take. There was no resolution of the Euratlantic or Euronational scenarios. The elites clearly have not finished the business of resolving their national differences, although they agreed that the European Community was a valued relationship for all members and that all three countries should both contribute to and share its assets.

Perhaps it is this lack of consensus that explains one note of pessimism that characterized all national panels in 1965. When we asked if the Six would form some sort of political union in the next five years, the largest number in all panels said no. The British showed the largest division: yes, 38 per cent; no, 51 per cent. The French were next: yes, 35 per cent; no, 46 per cent. The Germans were most evenly divided in their estimate: yes, 45 per cent; no, 47 per cent. If the partners cannot agree on the political formula but agree on the need to build European economic institutions for prosperity, then prosperity may require the community to evade political issues. These may have to be sidestepped in the interest of economic formulae. We explore this in the conclusion of this book. However, we must first examine the conflicts of political vision.

In search of the sources of disagreement, we asked a number of questions about conflicting commitments. In these questions, we were concerned particularly to see what conflicts might exist between the European Community and other national ties, especially ties overseas.

B. CONFLICTING COMMITMENTS

As our decade began, each of the countries was faced with conflicting commitments between a European focus and other relationships. The French had to be concerned with the effect of a European program on its relations with the former French Empire. The British had to measure the incongruence between European demands and Commonwealth necessities. And the Germans of the West had to decide what relation European unity bore to the Germans of the East.

By the end of the decade, the French had made a successful accommodation, even to the point where European commitments were aiding former African spheres of influence, with European added to French resources. The British still had much to accomplish in order to harmonize their economic ties to the Commonwealth and their European interests, but some Commonwealth nations encouraged Britain to draw closer while others saw a possible solution to the conflict. Only the Germans appeared to have made no "progress" in accommodating European integration with German reunification.

In the 1959 survey, we asked the French to evaluate the importance of the French-African Community for the position of France in the world. When offered different options, the following were chosen: basic, 61 per cent; great but not indispensable, 31 per cent; slight, 2 per cent; and don't know, 6 per cent. We then asked if its value was mainly economic (26 per cent), political (18 per cent), or social (37 per cent).* The dispersion showed a lack of consensus on the main value of the Community, but this did not prevent the panel from agreeing (72 per cent) that the values were lasting.

In the 1965 survey, the priorities were more difficult to discern, for the Community seemed to slip from focus. The largest group (35 per cent) refused to choose a main value, asserting they were all equally important. The economic value slipped from 26 per cent to 9 per cent in 1965. While the social value maintained its relative position as first among the three single choices (made by one quarter of the panel), the political value was close behind, with 22 per cent of the ballots. Only 8 per cent did not fit into these codes. The diffusion of purpose became evident by 1965, but the willingness to assign value indicates continuing significance.

Since the Community represents basic and long-term values for the French respondents, their answer to the following question is even more impressive. Our question asked: "If there had to be a choice, should France sacrifice some of its French Community interests in order to promote European integration?" The panels displayed a stable preference for Europe in the competition between conflicting commitments. In both 1961 and 1965, about 60 per cent of the panels were willing to sacrifice the Community interests to promote European integration. The remainder were almost equally split between a refusal to sacrifice and a don't know response.

The majority gives an impressive measure of the intensity of the French commitment to Europe. A majority of the panel is willing to sacrifice its highly valued Community interests if necessary to promote its even more highly valued European interests.

The British had to make a similar choice in promoting their com-

---

* The remainder chose all three (11 per cent), other (4 per cent), no value (1 per cent), and DK (4 per cent).

mitments to Europe or maintaining Commonwealth preferences. When we asked for a definition of the main value of the Commonwealth, the British did not agree among themselves what its main value is to Britain. In 1961, the economic, political, and social categories were not far apart in popularity.

In a replication of the French loss of focus, by 1965, the dispersion of choice increased and no single category contained a substantial plurality of panelists. However, while there was no consensus identifying a single set of values as the greatest, there was a strong consensus on the belief that the Commonwealth was valuable. Especially in 1961, its value was held to be of long-term duration by 91 per cent of the panel.

Nevertheless, repeating the French pattern, the British panel was willing to "sacrifice" (1961) or "reduce" (1965) its Commonwealth interests in order to promote its European interests. Between 50 and 60 per cent of the British panels in both years were willing to give Europe the priority in the conflict of commitments.

The stable majorities reflect a sharing of priorities with the French that overseas interests should be sacrificed for European considerations. The main difference between French and British panels is that the French have a greater number of don't know responses whereas the British have a somewhat larger committed opposition, roughly one third.

From these data, it appears that the interpretation which sees the French and British at odds about the Common Market because of Commonwealth ties does not apply to the British panel. Since 1961 (and perhaps earlier, though we have no direct test of that), a majority of the British elite panel has expressed normative judgments favoring the reduction of Commonwealth interests in order to promote a European commitment. It is not the former colonial overseas ties that separate the French and British panels from each other or from a commitment to Europe.[2]

The commitments of the German panel are obviously quite different. There is no conflict between Empire and European integration. For West Germans, the potential conflict is between European integration and German reunification. We examined this situation in some detail.

First we asked whether German reunification would strengthen or weaken European unity. In 1959, 70 per cent of the panel thought reunification would strengthen European unity. Then we asked whether German participation in several European organizations would hamper or promote the chances for reunification. In 1959, only 27 per cent thought European obligations would hinder reunification. Roughly one third each thought that such participation would not harm their chances or that it was unrelated. The attitudes were similar in 1965. One third saw a conflict, and two thirds did not. Just as in the French and British cases, other national commitments were not seen as necessarily detrimental to European interests.

Perhaps one reason for German perception of ready compatibility between European integration and national reunification is their expectation that reunification is not likely to be achieved soon. In 1965, 93 per cent of the German panel had the least expectation of reunification. Furthermore, 46 per cent of the German panel thought that the Germans were putting enough stress on reunification already and 13 per cent thought there was too much stress. Thirty-six per cent, a sizable minority, thought there ought to be more stress. The question that elicited this response from the minority was: "Do you think that Germany puts too much or too little or enough stress on its national interests, especially in regard to reunification?" The general context of this question makes it a less pure measure of a conflict of priority between reunification and integration. However, it is a measure of the fact that the majority of Germans, like the French and British, did not find a source for differences over Europe in their other pressing national goals.

C. SHARING EUROPEAN PROSPERITY

We wanted to know the extent to which the European elite now considered that the continent was in a position to share its prosperity with others. In the last two surveys, when no doubt was expressed about the success and durability of European recovery, we asked if the European countries should make a substantial increase in their long-term commitments of economic aid to the underdeveloped countries. In 1961, all panels were nearly unanimous in their desire to increase aid from Europe to other nations. In 1965, each panel lost about one fifth of its aid advocates; but since the starting point was near unanimity, about three quarters were still in favor of an aid program.

In the area of foreign aid, there was a very clear consensus in all countries. There were even symmetrical distributions of agreement on tactical considerations. Preferential terms of trade in both export and import were agreed upon as successful tactics.*

The main disagreements were over bilateral or multilateral forms of organizing aid, and these did not appear until the most recent survey. In 1961, two thirds of all panels favored multilateral administration of aid through a common policy. In 1965, only the French maintained their preference, the other two countries going in opposite directions. The Germans switched completely, with one half now preferring a bilateral aid program. The British panel weakened in its prior preference for multilateral forms: 42 per cent chose multilateral and 31 per cent chose bilateral forms.† One quarter of the British panel took an evasive option outside of the code categories (DK).

By 1965, then, the earlier consensus on aid was shaken. The panels passed from near unanimity to partiality, including partiality for different forms of aid. They also viewed each other's aid programs with more critical eyes. Both the French and British (73 per cent and 70 per cent), but not the Germans, thought the German aid program should be increased. The Germans, in the main, thought that the other two nations had sufficient aid programs or had already extended themselves. But the French disagreed: One half of the panel advocated an increase of British outlays, with only one fifth recommending the same course for themselves. The largest number of British were satisfied with their own performance, only one third recommending an increase; but only one third was satisfied with the French performance. Thus, the large proportion of the 1965 panels which expressed interest in a substantial increase of foreign aid were apparently referring to others, not to themselves. Only in the recommendation that the Germans increase their aid did the large numbers reappear, and here the Germans did not agree.

* The British panel had a slight preference for import over export preferential terms: 61 per cent for import, 52 per cent for export.

† Of those British panelists who wanted multilateral aid in 1965, 80 per cent wanted it administered through the UN. No other panels were so exclusively committed to the UN as the British. The French chose the UN most often of any choice (47 per cent), but also had a large segment of European supporters (31 per cent). The Germans also had a large group for the UN (35 per cent), but rather than electing a European option, 36 per cent preferred an Atlantic agency.

We recall that this European tightening of the purse strings applied to relations with America as well. We had asked the panels if they thought the American dollar problem was of long-term concern for Europe. Two thirds of each panel replied affirmatively. However, in the previous chapter we saw that the 1965 panels were not willing to share their prosperity to lighten the American costs of protection for Europe. A similar decline took place when the panels were asked if they would bear a larger share of foreign aid to help the dollar problem. From 1961 to 1965, there was a dramatic drop in willingness to share the burden, with all except the British panel falling below a majority in their willingness to help the United States. Indeed, there was some sentiment that America should not even share in the source of European prosperity, the Economic Community. Table 5.3 shows an unwillingness, except by the Germans, to bring America into an economic community. We asked: "Should a larger economic community be formed by creating a new Atlantic institution that would include the Common Market, other European countries, and the United States?"

TABLE 5.3. EXPANSION OF COMMON MARKET INTO ATLANTIC INSTITUTION (1965)

	Britain	France	Germany
Yes	41%	34%	66%
No	53	49	28
DK	6	17	6

The French panel's negative response might be expected in the light of other considerations already reported, but the division among the British panel on this issue is a unique contrast to their usual support for Atlantic options. The Germans' positive response was as might be expected. But one may wonder whether this routinely repeats a long-standing preference, which is now undergoing re-examination and has not yet crystallized on economic issues.

This last suspicion is raised by a dramatic change in the German panels' responses to the questions reported in Table 5.4. We asked if the European Community will produce a political counterpoise to Russia and/or the United States.*

* The same question was asked in 1961 and 1965, except that in 1965 a five-year limit was specified for the formation of the counterpoise, whereas there

TABLE 5.4. EUROPE AS A POLITICAL COUNTERPOISE

	Britain		France		Germany	
	1961	1965	1961	1965	1961	1965
Counterpoise to USSR						
Yes	43%	18%	69%	42%	82%	52%
No	51	77	18	50	16	42
DK	6	5	13	8	2	6
Counterpoise to US						
Yes	38	16	60	41	23	42
No	56	79	18	51	65	52
DK	6	5	22	8	12	6

The British were most stable in their view of the European Community as essentially free from the Cold War context and not politically engaged. Such a view was consistent with the other results showing little British political interest in the Common Market. The French, who were reported earlier to have seen political significance in the Common Market, also view the European Community as a prop for European "independence" from both the United States and Russia. The interest in "independence" has waned somewhat, as we reported earlier, perhaps because the panelists reject the extreme definition De Gaulle has given that word. On these issues, French attitudes are in flux.

The Germans offered the most extreme 1961 view of Europe in the Cold War context. The anti-Soviet, pro-American posture was dominant. By 1965, the Cold War context remained, but much attenuated, and the desire for "independence" through the European route was nearly as strong as the French. This posture was consistent with similar German feelings reported in the discussion of protection for Europe. It suggests a re-evaluation of the scope of Euratlantic commitments in 1965.

Consistent national differences in the view of Europe thus

___

was no time limit in 1961. This change will tend to decrease, to some extent, the percentage of positive responses, but may not account for the size of changes that actually occurred. Also, in France and Germany in 1965 the two questions were posed simultaneously, whereas otherwise they were posed as two separate questions. This might account, to some extent, for the convergence of the two questions in Germany in 1965.

emerged from the varied issues covered by the surveys. The British were essentially apolitical; the French saw Europe as politically potent; and the Germans were gradually moving toward the French view.

When we asked predictions instead of preferences, political importance was attributed to the European Community by large groups in all panels. Two thirds of all panels foresaw increased influence for the European Community vis-à-vis Russia in Eastern Europe in the next five years. A French majority, and roughly evenly split German and British panels, thought the West European countries were likely to increase their political influence vis-à-vis the United States in Latin America in the next five years. Thus, the counterpoise role was predicted by a sizable number of panelists in all countries as a matter of expected behavior. Only the British did not have a matching group with an orientation desiring a united Europe to play a world political role. As we have seen in other contexts, the British were more economic in their European orientation, while the French were avowedly political with equivalent expectations and the Germans increasingly so. When we asked the Germans directly in 1961 if Germany was giving priority to political over economic interests in Common Market participation, 61 per cent said the commitment was a political one. In 1965, in response to slightly different wording, the political option was chosen by 45 per cent and the economic option by 27 per cent. Another 25 per cent thought there was no differential emphasis. The political option remained the choice of the largest group.

These diverging national views on the political meaning of European integration were among the most profound differences that appeared. The tensions reported earlier were not traceable to differences in attachments to former overseas territories. While there were differences on aid program priorities, these were not crucial for the formation of Europe. The tensions are most clearly related to the differences in political definitions of Europe. We turn, therefore, to the political implications of European integration in order to discern further national differences. If the nations are to unite because of mutual interest in maintaining European economic growth, it is often argued that political conditions must also be met. Special attention must be given to the way in which European integration affects the sovereignty of each nation involved. We tested for attitudes toward national sovereignty to see if the commitment to prosperity had weakened ties to the nation-state in favor of collective policies, just as the commitment to protection had weakened the role of the sovereign state in favor of collective security. The answer is that there are parallels, but once again the European consensus has some important national variations within it.

D. PROSPERITY AND COLLECTIVITY

One step toward collectivity is a recognition of its necessity. We asked if present trends were making the nation-state obsolete as a political form.

All panels, in a rank order by degree that will soon become familiar — Germany, France, and Britain — had majorities that believed the nation-state is obsolete. The German panel was near unanimous in 1961, dropping to about three quarters by 1965. This set of distributions is indicative of much of the story that our surveying uncovered throughout the decade. We tested for the passing of nationalism, or more appropriately the transformation of nationalism to include transnational relations in many forms. Almost always we received a similar response, dominant groups saying yes to internationalism or supranationalism of every form. National variations showed the Germans to be most willing, the French second, and the British least willing to join institutions that curb national decision powers in favor of collective decisions. For example, in 1959, when we asked panelists to characterize their own stance in international matters, we received the replies given in Table 5.5.

TABLE 5.5.   SELF-DESCRIPTION (1959)

	Britain	France	Germany
Nationalist	13%	28%	4%
Internationalist	65	30	37
Supranationalist	15	35	48
DK	7	7	11

The most intense form of cooperative identity attracted the most Germans and the least British members. The French were the most evenly distributed of the three, but with a plurality of supranationalists. The British clearly made the mid-range choice of internationalists.

When we posed the question differently in the same survey, we obtained the same rank ordering of countries. This time we asked: "Assuming all participating nations would do the same, how far would you be willing to see Germany [France, Britain] limit its sovereignty for the benefit of an international community?" Table 5.6 illustrates the same pattern of response. The British were shy of

TABLE 5.6.   HOW FAR LIMIT SOVEREIGNTY? (1959)

	Britain	France	Germany
Not at All	7%	12%	1%
For Short-Term National Necessities Only	4	8	15
Also for Fundamental Political Issues	45	12	18
As Far as Establishing a Supranational Force	40	58	65
DK	4	10	1

a majority for the most extreme form of cooperation, but the continental panels revealed a majority commitment to collective action.

The same commitment was revealed in an even stronger test of relinquishing national power. We asked: "Up to what point should your country limit its right of independent action in order to promote a common foreign policy among the NATO partners?" As Table 5.7 shows, even this form of national sovereignty was ceded by many panelists. Only the British refused to move in great numbers from the traditional position. Both continental panels, and especially the Germans, give a repeated demonstration of willingness to relinquish national sovereignty.

The pattern was clear even by 1959, when support for specific Europe organizations had reached new heights, as shown in the early tables of this chapter. We now see that general positive sentiments for cooperation are as strong as for specific organizations except in Britain. Since the European regional base was the obvious referent for general sentiments at the time of discussion and in the context of the interviews, support for such transnational cooperation had reached substantial levels by the middle years of our decade.

In 1961, we continued to test for general sentiments, and we

TABLE 5.7. SOVEREIGNTY AND FOREIGN POLICY (1959)

	Britain	France	Germany
Traditional Form of Alliance (no nation is subjected to the majority rule)	41%	24%	6%
Stronger Form of Alliance (consultation obligation)	29	34	37
Common Supranational Council (determines common foreign policy)	19	34	51
DK	11	8	5

tended to find continued high levels of support for the transnational options. The French and German panels came closer to each other in this respect. When given a choice between a United States of Europe and a weaker confederation, 52 per cent of the French and 51 per cent of the Germans chose the stronger option.

We asked for the desired degree of support for international associations in a question worded as follows: "The postwar trend has been towards international associations which limit each participant's national sovereignty to some extent. To what degree would you favor Britain moving in this direction: wholeheartedly, or positively with some reservations, or only cautiously, or not at all?" Table 5.8 reports the results. Once again the French panel took the

TABLE 5.8. FAVORING INTERNATIONAL ASSOCIATIONS (1961)

	Britain	France	Germany
Wholeheartedly	24%	43%	33%
Positively with Reservations	53	34	43
Only Cautiously	20	16	21
Not at All	2	3	—
DK	1	4	3

leading role as advocate of the most extreme sentiment for cooperation. If French nationalism was active in 1961, it was confined to only a few respondents or it had an amazing capacity to include much transnational sentiment in its Euronationalist belief pattern. Once again, the British were least interested in close involvement.

In 1965, we dropped the general questions in favor of more detailed investigation of the specific issues of European integration.

As we have reported, we also found differences of opinion on these questions. Tensions occurred, especially, between the British and the continental panels. The political interpretation of Europe was given by the continental panels alone; we can now see that the politics they desired were those of close European supranational cooperation. The British, if they maintained the priorities of the middle years, did not have such an orientation in mind.

On at least two counts, the British did not resemble the French and German panels. For the British, there remained attachments to America which are still evident in the later questioning. Europe was not seen as a political counterpoise to the US. Second, European integration had more economic than political overtones for the British, and they were least interested in transnational decision making. The British, especially, guarded foreign policy options to themselves. Thus, on these counts, both of which De Gaulle mentioned in his 1963 press conference on British entry into the Common Market, the British panels stand distinctly apart from the continental consensus. The British want collective prosperity, but they have not accepted the same political price tag as the continental elites. The Euronationalist scenario of the French and, increasingly, of the Germans, competed with the Euratlantic scenario of the British. While the British panel too is moving its regional economic priorities toward the continent, it has not yet accepted the same political meaning of this move that its partners intend.

If, today, one follows British governmental pronouncements closely, one finds that the bid to enter Europe is now being made with a special effort to overcome exactly the major political points that previously were blocking British entry. It sometimes appears that the most ideological Europeans today are the British. They insist, using the very rhetoric of our questions in the middle years, that they are "European." They take great pains to illustrate that their Europeanness includes transnational cooperation, and especially cooperation with Europeans in preference to Americans. The sensitivity of the British to De Gaulle's charges and the recurrent patterns in our elite data testify to differences that heretofore have divided our triad of nations. Speculation as to whether or not the British will succeed in convincing the continental powers of their Europeanness is outside the bounds of this empirical history. The 1965 survey showed still a great deal of unwillingness of the British to burn bridges. While prosperity was a desired goal, only a mi-

nority of the British panel had consciously weighed it above protection. Britain, like Germany, is caught between prosperity and
protection. As we will see, both national panels respond similarly
to these common pressures.

Protection and prosperity have one basic characteristic in common. In contemporary Europe, neither can be guaranteed within the
framework of the nation-state. Collective security and economic
integration thus have been accepted by all panels to a great degree,
even at the expense of old political forms. The Europeans have
largely agreed to turn their backs on their own invention — nationalism — in their quest for protection and prosperity that are valid
in contemporary terms. In a world of superpowers, only the nuclear
giants can protect the others. In a world of supereconomies, only
the continental size units can sustain adequate levels of prosperity.
Thus, the attitudinal trend goes well beyond Euronationalism
where the national economies are geared to adapt international
policies. While this level of cooperation may not be expandable to
fit comfortably in the Euratlantic scenario, recent trends favoring
the tighter regional ties have overwhelmed mere national solutions.
There are differences among the nations who must become partners,
but it is agreed that partners are necessary.

There is one last "P," prestige, that is also part of the attitudinal
base of the current European elite. The capacity to reorient prestige aspirations to the demands of the modern world brings out the
last remaining national differences which may make the other P's
difficult to achieve. While there is a will for collective action, there
will only be a way if the prestige that has been associated with
nations in the past can be displaced to the transnational agencies of
collective action in the future.

CHAPTER SIX

Prestige: Ranking the Nations

FROM the earliest years of the TEEPS survey, it was clear that the European panels did not rank their nations among the world's top powers. The center of world politics had moved outside of the European continent for the first time in modern history. The decline of the European nations not only was perceived by their elites; it was even, as it now appears, greatly exaggerated by them.

Such devaluation of their nations was associated with some deep transformations of traditional European attitudes among the postwar elites. It underlay the passing of nationalism, which is fundamental to the choices reported over the decade. Here we note only that in all years of our survey, a substantial majority of every panel has affirmed that the idea of the nation-state is obsolete. What is more, they have avowed with equal frequency that its obsolescence is a good thing. Such avowals, among opinion leaders in that area of Europe which created modern nationalism and spread it around the world, represent a deep-sea change in European political attitudes. Hence, these findings merit consideration.

To determine these underlying evaluations and expectations, we asked several sets of questions that reveal how the European elites perceive the present environment, the proximate future that they will face over the next five years, and the more remote future that will confront the next generation of elites — their own progeny — at the end of this century. How the TEEPS panels rank the nations now, in the next five years, and in the year 2000 is nothing less than their projection of the world environment in which they expect to live.

Questions about the short-run future usually fixed the period as "the next five years," and answers may be understood in terms of

146

this standard point of reference. A variety of reference points was tested to determine long-run perspectives — such as "in your own lifetime" and "in the next generation." Since such differences in question wording might account for an indeterminate amount of variability in the answers, our later surveys tended to use a fixed reference point expressed as "by the end of this century, roughly the year 2000." Given the age distribution of our respondents in all three panels, which averages over fifty throughout the decade, their long-term responses can be understood as projecting a period beyond their own elite activity in public affairs. We look in turn at their short-run and long-run perspectives as we review their projections of the world environment.

In 1956, we asked all panels: "Which nations would you say play a decisive role in world politics today?" Aside from America and Russia, which led all lists, the responses distributed as follows:

TABLE 6.1. DECISIVE NATIONS TODAY (1956)

	Britain	France	Germany
Britain	53%	27%	79%
France	11	14	27
Germany	16	14	25
China	37	10	62
India	27	10	56

Note: Britain and Germany sum to over 100 per cent because some respondents named several countries; France sums under 100 per cent because some respondents named none.

Britain, the continent's offshore island, drew a substantial majority of ballots — but only at home and in Germany, not among the French panel. The two continental powers ranked low in everybody's book, their own as well as their neighbors'. Indeed, China and India were ranked as "decisive" nations by twice (even thrice) as many panelists ranking France and Germany. (Again the exception is France, where the responses were meager and the differences insignificant — nonresponsiveness on this and similar questions reflecting, quite possibly, the depressed and self-critical mood of France in 1956.)

We then asked: "Do you expect this to change? In what way?" There was substantial prevision of change, but little of it augured increasing power in the world for the nations of Europe. The similarity of response in all three panels is striking.

TABLE 6.2. INCREASINGLY POWERFUL NATIONS (1956)

	Britain	France	Germany
China	52%	34%	26%
India	32	13	23
Germany	22	8	21

Note: These sum to more or less than 100 per cent as explained in Table 6.1.

All panels ranked China as the leading contender for increasing power in the world arena. India, while lagging considerably behind China, nevertheless distinctly gained second place in all three panels. Among the European nations, however, only Germany received a significant fraction of 1956 ballots as likely to increase its world power in the future. And Germany was a relatively poor third, especially among the dour panelists of France, who accord their neighbor only a meager 8 per cent as compared with nearly twice as much for India and over four times as much for China.

These 1956 perspectives of the European elites seemed to us so meaningful for their attitudinal structure and so relevant to potential attitude change among them in the future that we devised a more systematic pair of questions for the 1959 survey, which we used virtually unchanged in the 1961 and 1965 surveys.

In the 1959 survey we asked: "Which nations would you rank as the five most powerful in the world today, in order of importance? What changes do you foresee in this ranking by the end of the century?" With the attitude continuum scaled down from "decisive" and specified as "most powerful," the response frame specified as "five" to be "ranked" in "order of importance," and the time dimension specified as "today" and "end of the century," this pair of questions did yeoman's service for our essentially comparative research. On the "ranking" side there were three separable, but linked, factors of response to be described and interpreted: (1) the relative ranking of the superpowers, the United States and Russia, in first and second place; (2) the relative ranking of the three great European nations — Britain, France, and Germany — in the next three places, comparing here, of course, the ranking by themselves and by their neighbors; (3) the relative ranking of the two "sleeping giants" reawakened by postwar decolonization, China and India, with respect to each other, the European nations, and the superpowers.

TABLE 6.3. MOST POWERFUL NATIONS TODAY (1959)

		Britain	France	Germany
US	First	88%	63%	95%
US	Second	7	29	3
US	DK	5	8	2
USSR	First	16	41	4
USSR	Second	73	53	92
USSR	DK	11	6	4

As Table 6.3 shows, the 1959 panels of European opinion leaders responded by ranking the United States clearly as "most powerful in the world today" relative to Russia, its only serious competitor. In the competition for the next three ranks, the most significant response was DK. As compared with the clearly perceived and evaluated superpower of the United States and Russia, revealed by the low DK in Table 6.3, the relative positions of the European nations today (and of the two principal Asian contenders) is shrouded in uncertainty. Table 6.4 reports the distribution in each

TABLE 6.4. NEXT MOST POWERFUL NATIONS TODAY (1959)

		Britain	France	Germany
Third:	Britain	72%	45%	57%
	France	0	10	1
	Germany	4	5	1
	China	27	30	25
	India	1	1	1
Fourth:	Britain	20	41	17
	France	8	57	16
	Germany	30	27	12
	China	28	16	26
	India	4	4	6
Fifth:	Britain	7	6	11
	France	31	23	22
	Germany	37	19	18
	China	18	13	11
	India	10	3	7
DK:	Britain	1	8	15
	France	61	10	61
	Germany	29	49	69
	China	27	41	38
	India	85	92	86

panel ranking the three European and two Asians as third, fourth, and fifth "most powerful in the world today." The prevalence of DK is impressive, with the noteworthy exception that all panels are least uncertain about Britain and most convinced that Britain was the *third* "most powerful nation today" in 1959.

The rest of the story, about the continental nations themselves, is highly deviant. France, least DK about herself, is most convinced that it ranks *fourth* — an appraisal not at all shared by her neighbors. Britain and Germany are equally DK about France, virtually two out of every three panelists not ranking France among the first five powers or not ranking her at all (both responses being combined in their DK of 61 per cent). Among the relatively few Britons and Germans who do rank France, the larger number place her *fifth*.

By contrast, Germany was most uncertain about herself and distributed the few rankings given herself almost equally between fourth and fifth place. If anything, her British and even French neighbors tend to rank Germany higher than does the German panel.

The great contender for top-five listing among the world's powers is China, which received relatively lower DK, and considerably higher ranking from all three panels. The Europeans had a less clear image of the other Asian contender, India, which received the highest DK and lowest ranking as a powerful nation today from all three panels.

The 1959 picture of world power distributions changes in extremely interesting ways as the question shifts from "today" to the future: "What changes do you foresee in this ranking by the end of the century?" Table 6.5 lists the responses to this question.

As might be expected in a question dealing with the remote future, uncertainty increased among all panels as they contemplated the end of the century. But the uncertainty was sufficiently differentiated with respect to particular nations that several estimates of the future power position appear as relatively firm. Thus, while uncertainty grew about the first and second most powerful nations in A.D. 2000, it is clear that in the short-term future the panelists thought: (1) the relative positions of United States and Russia will not change; (2) the United States tends to be first; (3) Russia tends to be second.

The future of the European nations themselves aroused the most doubt among the panelists. In Britain and Germany, about 90 per cent responded DK when asked to rank France, and the percentage was similar in Germany and France with respect to Germany. Even doubt about Britain's future rises sharply, and it is clear that Britain is no longer expected to maintain the *third* rank it holds "today" by the end of the century. Nor is there any substantial conviction,

TABLE 6.5. MOST POWERFUL NATIONS IN 2000 A.D. (1959)

		Britain	France	Germany
First:	US	43%	27%	60%
	USSR	22	22	13
	China	20	18	11
Second:	US	17	15	9
	USSR	41	20	47
	China	8	10	12
Third or Higher:	Britain	23	2	9
	France	0	3	1
	Germany	7	12	2
	India	2	3	2
Third:	China	20	16	27
Third or Lower:	US	15	10	4
	USSR	12	9	13
Fourth:	Britain	19	25	13
	France	1	21	2
	Germany	15	19	5
	China	12	3	15
	India	9	7	9
Fifth:	Britain	15	8	12
	France	10	14	5
	Germany	24	0	4
	China	2	2	4
	India	7	1	7
DK*:	US	25	48	27
	USSR	25	49	27
	Britain	43	65	66
	France	89	62	92
	Germany	54	69	89
	China	38	51	33
	India	82	89	82

* DK here means not mentioned among the first five (includes no ranking at all).

even among the British panel, that by A.D. 2000 Britain will rank even in *fourth* place. The outlook is even cloudier still for the future of the two great continental nations.

As recorded in 1959, the European image of the future world arena was already focused on China. Compared with the other Asian giant, India, the DK was extremely low — lower even than when the panels projected their own national future. Thus the European elites have a firm conviction about the future of China — in a word, that China is clearly on the way up as a world power. A clear majority of British and German panelists and a split panel in France ranked China among the top five powers by A.D. 2000. Moreover, about one fourth of all panelists saw China displacing either the United States or Russia by ranking her as either *first* or *second* in the world arena. The rest see their own nation, or its European neighbors, as displaced from the top five by ranking China third, fourth, or fifth.

This crystallization of European perspectives on the present and future was thus associated in the 1959 survey with other attitudes on key issues of world politics. When the identical question was put to all three panels in 1961 — panels that comprised better than half who had been interviewed before — they ranked "the five most powerful nations in the world today" in the order given in Table 6.6.

The main findings of this table leap to the eye. Methodologically, it is important to note that: (1) All three panels tended to distribute their ballots in the same *direction* — agreeing on *which* nation is first, second, and so on down the line. (2) The British and German panels tended toward consensus in *frequency* — casting a similar *proportion* of their ballots in the same cell of the table. (3) The French panel tended to deviate in *frequency* mainly by reason of its high unresponsiveness as shown in the DK figures.

A fourth observation may be made that is less general. On those rare occasions where France deviated from the other panels in direction — as when she gave China a higher ballot for *third* place than Britain (hence a plurality opposite in direction from that given by the other two panels) — the French panelists may well have been motivated by their nation's traditional rivalry with Britain. This rivalry had already been exacerbated in 1961 by De Gaulle's rejection of the "Atlantic" purpose for Western policy reposing on the axiomatic "Anglo-American special relation." We note its apparent operation only to remind the reader that French "exception-

TABLE 6.6. MOST POWERFUL NATIONS TODAY (1961)

		Britain	France	Germany
First:	US	79%	72%	88%
	USSR	20	26	12
	China	1	2	0
	Other/DK	0	0	0
Second:	US	15	14	10
	USSR	83	59	82
	China	1	2	4
	Other/DK	1	25*	4
Third:	Britain	55	30	63
	China	34	38	31
	Other/DK	11*	32†	6
Fourth:	Britain	30	18	25
	France	14	25	17
	Germany	18	25	13
	China	28	8	31
	Other/DK	10	24*	14*
Fifth:	Britain	6	8	3
	France	36	25	34
	Germany	28	19	26
	India	14	8	5
	China	8	4	10
	Other/DK	8	36*	22*

* We combined Other/DK because it is fractional in most cases. Where it exceeds 10 per cent, as in the cases marked *, the number represents virtually all DK — simple unresponsiveness — notable, as always, among the French panel.

† This is the only significant exception to the rule just stated. The 32 per cent here comprised: 10 DK, 11 Germany, 10 France, and 1 US.

alism" on matters of relations with Britain (and the "Anglo-Saxons," as De Gaulle, defying all of recent history and sociology, persists in labeling us) is capable of reversing the *direction* of European consensus. We shall consider this issue more fully later.

In the 1961 survey, positions of United States and Russia respectively as *first* and *second* world powers, seemed to have been consolidated. Britain still occupied the *third* place, although with an increasing consensus that China is a serious rival for this position.

On this, as in their ranking of *fourth* place, the French panel exhibited two characteristic attitudes. First, they tended to devalue Britain, or at least to rank her lower than do the other panels. Thus, except in France, those who gave China priority for third place tended to assign Britain fourth place. The French panel, on the contrary, gave Britain a low ballot for both places and even allocated to the continental nations a higher ballot for fourth place. Second, they tended to equate France and Germany as "powerful nations today." Both received 10 per cent of the French ballot for third place, and 25 per cent for fourth place. This represents an interesting, if small, difference from the other panels. Britain tended to rank Germany slightly ahead of France. On the other hand, perhaps associated with the self-depreciation that has structured many political attitudes among postwar Germans, Germany tended to rank France slightly ahead of itself. The relative positions are clearest in fourth place, for which France and Germany appear to be the "natural" contenders.

Of particular note in these rankings of the European nations is the modification of their earlier image of China among the 1961 panels. In the 1959 survey, about one fourth of the panelists saw China as displacing either the United States or Russia in the two top places of power. By 1961, this appraisal had been drastically revised, possibly because of the failure of the Great Leap Forward, possibly because of the Soviets' demonstration that they could at that time contain Chinese influence upon world communism fairly effectively, possibly in recognition of the continuing and unprecedented expansion of the American economy and military power. Whatever the reasons, it is clear that the 1961 panels no longer considered China to rank with the superpowers. For first place it drew only a trivial fraction of ballots: 1 per cent Britain, 2 per cent France, 0 per cent Germany. For second place, its showing remained wholly insignificant: 1 per cent Britain, 2 per cent France, 4 per cent Germany.

Rather, China now appeared to dispute pride of place with the Europeans. Both the British and German panels designated China as Britain's principal competitor for third place, and a plurality of the French panel affirmed that China had already displaced Britain. Most important, however, is that China clearly outranked the continental powers in third and fourth place in their own eyes. This finding is reinforced when the 1961 panels rank the nations at the end of the century. China clearly outranks all the European nations, even Britain, for third place in the world by A.D. 2000 — and perhaps most decisively among the British panel.

We retested these relatively crystallized images of the present and future world arena in our final 1965 survey. We asked: "Which nations would you rank as the five most powerful in the world today, and what is the order of their importance? What do you think the position will be by the end of the century?" Table 6.7 shows the distribution of responses for both time periods in the series — the column headed 1965 representing "the world today," the column headed 2000 representing "the end of the century."

For purposes of comparison in 1965, we asked the same question of a panel of 100 top officials of the European Communities (Common Market, Coal-Steel, Euratom), designated as EC. The EC panel members are all high administrative officials and therefore compare most directly, in a formal sense, with the "government sector" in the three nations. They include, however, many who have been active as well in the political, academic, communication, and business sectors of their own nations — and they include "nationals" of the Netherlands, Belgium, Italy, Luxembourg, Britain (relatively few), France, and Germany. It is reasonable to interpret their responses as from a potential "government sector" in a more fully integrated European federal or confederal state. The EC panel is discussed more fully in Chapter Eleven and is included here for its comparative interest.

This is a very remarkable table. For us, given the framework constructed empirically from all previous surveys, this 1965 table stands as a resumé of European attitudes formed and changed over the past decade — and a reminder of unresolved issues that will be important to European (and other) elites over the decade ahead.

Of immediate interest is the rank ordering of nations. By 1959–1961, there was little doubt among European panelists that the top two places belonged to the US and USSR. An even more impressive consensus — considering that a highly leftist Europe still located Russia as Left and the United States as Right — identified the United States as *first* and Russia as *second*. These rankings, in a very unstable world, have remained more constant than any other distributions reported in our tables.

China's position in third place, both in 1965 and 2000, remained stable from the earlier surveys; however, she fell from contention with the superpowers. Fully a third of the British and French, and somewhat more of the Germans, ranked her in the third spot, creating a close competition with Britain which is resolved only at the end of the century to the advantage of China. Thus, substantial groups in all countries admitted that China had firmly won her way into a ranking spot among nations. The position of the Europeans both as subjects and objects was not nearly so clear.

Table 6.8 summarizes how the Europeans see themselves and each other. If prestige is to be acquired in a modern nation, it can be had

TABLE 6.7. MOST POWERFUL NATIONS: 1965 AND 2000 (1965)

	Britain		France		Germany		EC	
	1965	2000	1965	2000	1965	2000	1965	2000
First:								
US	84%	63%	83%	56%	97%	87%	90%	68%
USSR	4	8	4	3	2	5	3	6
China	0	7	0	6	1	6	0	8
Other/DK*	12	22	13	35	0	2	7	18
Second:								
US	4	11	3	3	2	7	4	10
USSR	80	45	81	46	97	72	87	49
China	2	11	1	9	1	19	4	16
Other/DK	14	33	15	42	0	2	5	25
Third:								
USSR	3	16	0	9	2	21	3	22
China	33	31	35	33	45	58	58	35
Britain	39	8	20	0	42	11	20	4
Other/DK	25	45	45†	58	11	10	19	39
Fourth:								
China	12	12	8	9	21	12	13	16
Britain	27	13	22	4	35	39	38	10
France	25	6	31	10	25	15	17	6
Germany	10	8	12	9	15	17	6	8
Other/DK	26	61	27	68	4	17	26	60
Fifth:								
China	18	2	8	0	12	4	7	4
Britain	7	8	15	12	11	26	14	12
France	26	11	27	14	48	43	32	11
Germany	17	8	20	7	21	20	17	4
Other/DK	32	71	30	67	8	7	30′	69‡

* Except where indicated, Other/DK represents mainly DK.

† Eighteen of this 45 per cent is a vote for Germany in third place by 1965. Compare this with the fact that no French panelists believe Britain will be in third place by the year 2000.

‡ Includes 12 per cent saying India and 21 per cent saying Japan will be in fifth place by the year 2000.

only on the grounds of adequately providing the nation with protection and prosperity. Prestige comes both from a strong self-image and a ratifying image of the neighbors who grant the prestige.

This plethora of numbers reflects some striking trends. Britain's rank both in her own and others' estimation declined from a substantial third-place to a minority third-place position and was judged no longer to be in contention for third by the year 2000. The German view of Britain is a strong exception.

The French self-image also declined from 1959 to 1965, and dramatically so in the case of the future. Since this was the period of De Gaulle's call to *grandeur*, the results are most striking, especially when it is recognized that France's neighbors were more impressed by the posture of *grandeur* than France herself. The British increased their evaluation of France slightly, but the Germans' response was dramatically sensitive to De Gaulle's message. The German panel increased its ranking of France among the top five, and a majority held France in that position even by the end of the century. Overall the Germans are the most stable and positive grantors of national position, as they seem to be impressed by French performance. In Chapter Nine, we will discuss how this credibility for national posture reflects German ambivalence about how Germany fits into a collective Western posture. Neither the German panel nor postwar German policy is firm in granting prestige of place to Germany. The British almost discounted the Germans by 1965 and certainly did so by the end of the century. The French are more serious about the German contention for position. Fully one half believed in 1965 that she ranks among the first five, and while they see her rank declining by the end of the century, it is no more serious for Germany than for the others. The German view of Germany is low compared to that of her neighbors, although her self-judgment for the year 2000 is more sanguine than the others are willing to grant.

All of this suggests a credibility gap of no insignificant dimensions. While the French and Germans are closer to a mutual admiration pact than the British are willing to grant, the trend is distinctly downward. Only the Germans are stable in their evaluation of power for Europe's leading two nations, but they do not include themselves in that evaluation. Elsewhere, *grandeur* has been in the eye of the beholder, not in the mind of the country itself.

TABLE 6.8. EUROPEAN RANKINGS OF EUROPEAN NATIONS

	Britain				France				Germany			
	1959	1961	1965	2000*	1959	1961	1965	2000	1959	1961	1965	2000
Third:												
Britain	72%	55%	39%	8%	45%	30%	20%	0%	57%	63%	42%	11%
France	0	0	0	0	10	10	6	0	1	0	4	0
Germany	4	4	0	0	5	11	18	0	1	0	7	7
Fourth:												
Britain	20	30	27	13	41	18	22	4	17	25	35	39
France	8	14	25	6	57	25	31	10	16	17	25	15
Germany	30	18	10	8	27	25	12	9	12	13	15	17
Fifth:												
Britain	7	6	7	8	6	8	15	12	11	3	11	26
France	31	36	26	11	23	25	27	14	22	34	48	43
Germany	37	28	17	8	19	19	20	7	18	26	21	20
Summary of All Three Ranks:												
Britain	99	91	73	29	92	56	57	16	85	91	88	76
France	39	50	51	17	90	60	64	24	39	51	77	58
Germany	71	46	27	16	51	55	50	16	31	39	43	37

* This is the 1965 evaluation of the rankings in the year 2000.

The decline of national status from 1959 can mean only that the last link in the chain for European collaborative action is now prepared.

The uncertainty of European elites about the future position of their own nations helps to explain their desire for collective forms of transnational solutions to the demands of protection and prosperity. Indeed, if a nation cannot alone guarantee her sources of protection and prosperity, then it cannot maintain high prestige. The subordination of the national state, reported in earlier chapters, is now better understood through the admission that all the European nations will find it difficult in the long-term future to maintain high-ranking national stature.

A desire for prestige independent of the two superpowers remains, however, and is most in evidence in the opinions of the elites on national manufacture of nuclear weapons and the desirability of an independent position between Eastern and Western camps.

Demand for a national position has remained strong in the importance attached to nuclear capacity, but even here it is not exclusive of collective considerations. Table 6.9 shows the rather consistent positions of Britain, France, and Germany on this question as indexed by approval of national nuclear capacities.

The propaganda and public argumentation of France have not increased support for national manufacture of weapons. Nor has the apparent French *fait accompli* led to elite approval elsewhere.

TABLE 6.9. APPROVE OF NATIONAL MANUFACTURE OF NUCLEAR WEAPONS

	Britain	*France*	*Germany**
1955	65%	—	—
1956	58	49	24
1959	63	50	9
1961	57	46	9†
1965	54	53	18‡

* The German question was preceded by "Given a suspension of the present prohibition. . . ."

† In 1961, the Germans were also asked if they wanted to possess (not manufacture) nuclear weapons. Thirty-three per cent said yes and another 11 per cent qualified their answer by approving of possession only in the NATO context.

‡ Almost all of those responding affirmatively qualified their response to include only tactical weapons.

The stability testifies to a certain immunity among the elites to the French arguments that have occupied the professional strategists. This same stability also shows the ineffectiveness of the British public debate on the reduction of Britain's nuclear capacity. Indeed, on a separate question asking if ballistic missile systems should also be manufactured, the British support climbed to 77 per cent by 1965.

What is the significance to Europe of *national* nuclear weapon systems in face of the fact that such weapons have required national subordination to a collective security system and a superpower? In the 1965 survey, we asked the British if they thought their nuclear force was militarily and politically advantageous. Fully 60 per cent and 62 per cent responded in the affirmative. When the French were asked this question, their opinions on the military and political roles were not so similar. Only one third thought the *force de frappe* was militarily significant, but 59 per cent thought that it was politically important. Clearly, the national response in France was politically motivated.

Excepting the British belief in the military significance of their force, no elite panel judged the French or British force as militarily significant. Furthermore, when the French panel was asked if their *force de frappe* had political or military significance for their neighbor, Germany, less than one fifth thought it of value in either capacity. The political value for the French elite was clearly limited to defending France's interest in the alliance. In spite of these limits, 76 per cent of the Frenchmen thought France would continue to support a *force de frappe* independent deterrent.*

This sign of French nationalism does not mean its elite thought such weapons a viable defense against the Soviet challenge, for we see here, as elsewhere, that national military capacities were subordinated to collective security measures. Yet such a split in the elites dramatically demonstrates the emotional political power behind nuclear weapons.

There are limits even to the political meaning of national nuclear forces, however, and they can be found in the response to general questions asked in the context of the proper role of each nation in the divided world of East and West camps. As Table 6.10 illustrates,

---

* The Germans concurred in this French prediction. (Forty-seven per cent said France would maintain and 28 per cent said France would improve her force.) Only 45 per cent of the British thought that France would maintain her plans for an independent deterrent. Twenty-four per cent did not know.

TABLE 6.10. LIKELY TO AND SHOULD TAKE A NEUTRAL ROLE
BETWEEN EAST-WEST CAMPS

	Britain		France		Germany	
	Likely	Should	Likely	Should	Likely	Should
1961	10%	16%	5%	14%	—	—
1965	1	7	26	15	11%	19%

the elites think it both unlikely and undesirable for their countries
to take a neutral role.

It is clear that the national response took place within the Western
alliance structure. Even among the French dissidents, there were
more panelists who predicted neutrality than desired it.

While the national response did not include separating from the
alliance, a degree of independence was sought by all panels. Table
6.11 indicates a much larger interest in *independence* than in *neutrality*, especially among the German respondents.

TABLE 6.11. LIKELY TO AND SHOULD TAKE AN INDEPENDENT
POSITION BETWEEN CAMPS

	Britain		France		Germany	
	Likely	Should	Likely	Should	Likely	Should
1959	23%	30%	37%	45%	22%	41%
1965	20	36	64	36	37	48

While some of the differences are small, notably among the
British, the direction of movement is revealing. In Britain, those
saying "likely to" decreased while those saying "should" increased
— quite possibly a reflection of elite skepticism about the new
Labour Government's claim to a new and independent foreign policy. In France, the direction of change reversed by a considerably
larger magnitude. There, those saying "likely to" increased greatly
while those saying "should" decreased substantially — almost certainly an expression of concern over the aggressively independent
course already taken by De Gaulle. Only in Germany, recorded as
the European elite most acquiescent in American leadership throughout the TEEPS decade, did the 1965 panel converge toward the
view that their country both "should" and was "likely to" take a
more independent position in the East-West conflict. Not until after
our survey, with the Kiesinger government in 1967, did indepen-

dence take on any specific meaning. While the German panels were desirous of national independent action, the frequency of its expression was probably greater than its intensity. We will explore this German interest in independence in other contexts later. In the context of national military response to Cold War threats, it is clear that the German panelists did not have in mind any serious independent forces or specific actions which have shown up on our broad array of test questions.

It is against this background of evaluations and expectations that much of the attitudinal history we have reported for the TEEPS decade can be assessed. Any observer must appreciate that it was not easy for the elites in Europe's three great powers of modern history to agree that the world is bipolarized between the American and Russian superpowers. This evaluation was often withheld in the early survey years of 1955–1956, since many European panelists (always, particularly, the French) apparently found it hard to acknowledge that world leadership had passed definitively from their own nation and from their own continent.

The new image of the world environment as bipolarized between the superpowers began to crystallize in the middle years (1959–1961) of the survey. By then, the European elites seemed to be convinced that there was a qualitative difference between the superpowers and themselves — a wide, and widening, series of "gaps" in military force, technological development, and organizational (or management) systems. As it was borne in on them that the superpowers were here to stay, despite any preferences they might have to the contrary, their new images crystallized rapidly. By 1965, the new pragmatism had done its work. Future expectations were based squarely on empirical evaluations rather than ideological preferences. As we have seen, there was no longer any serious doubt among them that the first and second places of top power in the world had been pre-empted, respectively, by America and Russia.

The projection of these new images entailed the consolidation of attitudinal postures that many European elites earlier had accepted only tentatively, partially, or not at all. There was, for example, the consolidation of confidence in the American nexus as guarantor of European protection, prosperity, and even prestige — the image we have called Atlantica. There was, as well, the consolidation of pragmatic judgments that European well-being was to be sought through transnational institutions and even integration — the image we have called Europa. In preceding chapters, we have seen that most protagonists regarded these images as compatible, indeed as mutually reinforcing, throughout the TEEPS decade. In the next section, we explore the psychodynamics of their compatibility with Euratlantica.

Part C: Transformations

Introduction

In Part A, we outlined the historical forces transforming the attitudinal map of Europe's elites. In Part B, we documented this transformation. In Part C, we offer explanations of the conditions that underlie the transformation. Chapter Seven suggests the nature of the evaluations and expectations that accompany the transformation. The passing of traditional ideologies and identities is unfolded in Chapter Eight, and the psychological mechanisms that have freed the Europeans from previous thought patterns are suggested. There it is shown that the European identity is no longer exclusively ideological and national, for the elites have evolved a capacity to appreciate transnational frameworks in carrying out their national responsibilities. Chapter Nine then deals with the attitudinal "postures" and societal "processes" that have led these once-great powers of Europe to become "nations in transition."

Our effort in Part C is explanatory and explicative. We seek to clarify why the European elites, as represented by the TEEPS panels, have been able to converge so rapidly toward a consensual set of attitudes on their key issues. We have seen that there remains considerable uncertainty about some issues and substantial ambivalence about the new "System" of thinking among the European elites. These variant and deviant cases cannot be ignored or even minimized. Yet, the consensus has become strong and stable enough to justify the general inferences that we put forward in Part C.

167

CHAPTER SEVEN

Evaluations and Expectations: Projecting New Images

THE *crise de conscience* that pervaded Europe at war's end differed from previous spiritual crises in its greater scope and intensity. One must go back to the wars of religion, the Reformation and Counter-Reformation that swept over Europe three hundred years ago, to find its equal. Not since then, it appears, had Europeans been so permeated by distaste for themselves and distrust for each other as was the generation between the two world wars. The subversion of Europe's modern social order, a process activated by World War I, was carried beyond imaginable limits by the coercive ideological movements that overran most of Europe during the interwar years. It was possible to overlook the terrorism of Lenin's Bolsheviks because they acted in the name of a humane-sounding ideology — and besides, they were Russians. It was possible to take lightly the castor oil antics of Mussolini's Fascists because they were, after all, Italians. It was rather more difficult to disregard the Falangists who, under Franco, strangulated the Spanish Republic at birth. And it was downright impossible to ignore Hitler's Nazis, who proclaimed and operationalized their radical opposition to the fundamental values on which the modern democratic civilization of Europe had been built.

The course of World War II further undermined the foundations of modern European life. The Nazi-Soviet Pact taught a lesson in cynicism to those who had wanted to believe that socialist principles and Bolshevik practices were compatible. The rapid Nazi conquest of Europe cut through democratic insulation and subjugated

169

its peoples once again to the primitive jungle law of "might makes right." The behavior of many European leaders under Nazi hegemony, as represented by Quisling and Laval (or indeed Pétain), added insult to the injuries that had brought the proud democracies of the Old Continent to their knees. Their liberation by the Anglo-American forces was perceived by the pessimists of European doom as only a reprieve, by the optimists of European recovery as a full pardon. They agreed that Europe was in a state of sin; they differed mainly on whether a new state of grace was attainable. For believers this meant a new growth of faith and works.

The new state of grace required a "transformation" of European lifeways rather than another "restoration" of the type Europe had so often experienced in prior centuries. Transforming lifeways is a secular process; Europeans sought new men with new ideas who could (in Auden's phrase) "look shining at new styles of architecture." Only a hopeful — but realistic — projection of their future could subsume and surpass the bitter events of recent memory and the abundant evidence for present doubts. Needed were secular leaders in the arduous experience of transforming traditional evaluations of the European past and present that would sustain new expectations of Europe's future in the world community.

We have reviewed the salient issues of Europe's involvement in the postwar world — protection, prosperity, prestige — and the three major scenarios wherein Europeans projected alternative modes for dealing with these issues. We have summarized the degrees of transnational cooperation proposed to Europeans — traditional alliance, loose confederation, integrated community (federation leading to a United States of Europe) — and seen that, in general, they preferred the closer and more binding forms of cooperation. Among the institutional forms they have considered — Little Europe, Big Europe, Atlantic Community, Free World, United Nations — there was no predisposition to reject any. It was by the pragmatic test of effectiveness in meeting their new and widely shared purposes that Europa and Atlantica emerged as the principal modalities of policy action leading toward Euratlantica.

A. PROJECTING WORLD ENVIRONMENT

We have already reported in detail the issue-oriented and task-related character of the European options for transnational modes

of action. Each such option represented a choice based on evaluation of the available alternatives in the context of a more or less
conscious set of expectations about the probable world environment
in which they would operate. We bear in mind, as a frame of reference, that the European elites reveal an acute awareness of their
diminished role in the world — both as separate nations and as a
cooperative (if not yet integrated) region. From this awareness derives an equally sharp sense that Europeans have a relatively reduced role to play in shaping the future world environment. The
key to this complex of evaluations and expectations is the variable
we have called protection — issues of war, military security, and
the overwhelming superiority of the superpowers.

Throughout the TEEPS decade, few panelists have questioned
the superior power of the United States and the Soviet Union relative to all other nations of the world. In every country and year of
our survey, the bipolar superpowers pre-empted the two top places
on every list. As a result, no European nation could do better than a
feeble third place — and there was over the decade a diminishing
consensus on which European nation, if any, this might be. The
course of these evaluations and expectations among the TEEPS
panels has been detailed in Chapter Six. Here we observe only
that the superiority ascribed to the superpowers made them appear
as supreme arbiters of the future shape of the world arena — with
Europe's leaders cast in the role of anxious but relatively impotent
bystanders.

Over the years, for example, we asked panelists: "How would a
global war be most likely to break out — by design, by accident, by
extension of a limited conflict?" Throughout the decade, relatively
few thought a global war was likely to break out at all and virtually
none thought it would be by design. Fear of war among Europeans was predicated, rather, upon the unpredictability of the superpowers and upon Europe's incapacity to influence the operation
of their nuclear weapons systems. Through much of the decade
European anxiety was nurtured by fears of a nuclear "accident,"
as epitomized in the sensational American novel *Fail-Safe*.

Then came the Cuban missile crisis. As Europe froze with fear,
President Kennedy obliged Chairman Khrushchev to withdraw Soviet missiles from Cuba — but only after anxiety for all concerned,
leading to an agonizing reappraisal of the European predica-
ment. For the earlier bugaboo of "accident" Europeans now substi-

tuted the vivid horror of "extension" in any local conflict involving direct confrontation between the superpowers. This general movement of opinion in all panels is exhibited in Table 7.1.

TABLE 7.1.   OUTBREAK OF A GLOBAL WAR

	Britain		France		Germany	
	1961	1965	1961	1965	1961	1965
War by Accident	33%	16%	40%	23%	20%	13%
War by Extension	40	63	33	44	56	68

It is reasonable to suppose that the aftermath of the Cuban missile crisis is a substantial component in the widespread European opposition to current American military operations in Vietnam, since the danger of confrontation with Russia (or even China) is among the reasons most frequently cited by opponents. For despite a certain weariness with the Cold War in relation to their own affairs, as has been reported in preceding chapters, many TEEPS panelists are inclined to believe that conflicts between the United States and Russia will continue "in the remaining years of this century." In Table 7.2, we report the proportion of respondents that affirmed that bipolar conflicts would continue during each year of our survey.

TABLE 7.2.   THOSE AFFIRMING THAT BIPOLAR CONFLICTS WILL CONTINUE

	Britain	France	Germany
1955	29%	24%	—*
1956	27	41	45%
1959	60	67	78
1961	53	39†	51
1965	15†	57	48

* Not asked.
† As question wording varied between years and countries, these figures are in some measure artifacts of question variation.

Several characteristics of Table 7.2 are noteworthy. The Germans, given their greater proximity to the Russians and greater dependence on the Americans, more often tend toward the expectation that bipolar conflicts will continue. The British, with their greater insularity from the Soviets and "special connection" to the Americans, less often tend to this view. The French fluctuate a bit more erratically than the others. The feature of particular interest is that the movement of expectations is similarly patterned in all three countries — rising from a low in 1955, peaking in 1959, and declining again by 1965. But the expectation of continued conflict in 1965 is high; when added to the response that bipolar conflict would not only continue but intensify, it is clearly the majority expectation. (The alteration of question wording in Britain in 1965 is particularly unfortunate, as it is clear from other evidence that the original question would have produced a similar patterning.)

The expectation that bipolar conflict will continue, whether they like it or not, puts the European elites in a position of continuing dependence upon initiatives taken by the superpowers — again, the awkward posture of the anxious but impotent bystander. Although concern among Europeans over the Soviet threat has diminished considerably since 1959 and they no longer regard the threat as primarily military in character, the TEEPS panelists are aware that a danger to their own security and stability remains as long as bipolar conflict continues. As late as 1961, nearly nine out of ten respondents in each panel considered the Soviet threat to be "still a major factor in international life."

Even in 1961, and again in 1965, substantial pluralities of the panelists saw the threat as primarily political rather than military. But they saw it also "as a long-term issue that we must be prepared to live with for a long time to come" (rather than "as a short-term issue likely to diminish in the years ahead"). A long-term political contest between two superpowers is likely, at any time, to erupt into a military confrontation. Accordingly, the key strategies are: (1) mutual deterrence to constrain conflict at least over the short-term future, and (2) reciprocal disarmament to constrain conflict over the long-term future.

We have seen that European projections do not include a high expectation of disarmament. Indeed, this expectation has declined steadily since 1959. We asked the TEEPS panels: "Do you consider it likely that a general agreement on international disarmament, covering both conventional and nuclear weapons, will be reached in the next few years?" Table 7.3 shows the proportion of respondents saying no to this question.

The sense of impotency that accompanies this dour projection is shown by the response to another question, that the best way to conduct disarmament negotiations is "bilaterally between America

TABLE 7.3. THOSE AFFIRMING THAT GENERAL DISARMAMENT
IS UNLIKELY

	Britain	France	Germany
1959	50%	45%	41%
1961	55	48	53
1965	80	87	67

and Russia." Their preference for this option over generalized negotiations within the UN or multilateral negotiations in which their
own nations might participate attests their evaluation that the superpowers are supreme, at least in matters nuclear, and their derived expectation that things will go better if bystanders remain in
watchful waiting as the protagonists act.

This same reliance on the superpowers characterized responses
concerning the short-term strategy of mutual deterrence. We have
seen earlier that better than two of every three 1965 panelists, a
stronger consensus than in previous years, believe that "NATO, as
now constituted, is strong enough to deter the Russians over the
next five years." We have seen that similar proportions believe that
NATO reposes upon the American guarantee and will continue to
do so in the future. We have seen — as, for example, in the judgments on the Polaris system — the widespread conviction that the
future of American deterrent power is the future of European protection.

These evaluations have reshaped elite images of Europe's place
in the world arena, indeed have reshaped European images of the
future world environment. During the early years of the survey,
the feeling was widespread among TEEPS panelists that history
was on the side of Russia and world communism. Since 1959, that
feeling has diminished steadily. We asked, "Do you think that, by
the end of this century, the world balance of power will favor the
Communist or the Western side?" Table 7.4 gives the distribution
of those saying Communist side.

In similar vein, the earlier feeling that American (and with it
Western) "power and influence in world affairs" was likely to decline under conditions of mutual deterrence, which was perceived
as favoring the political initiative and skill of the Communists, had
dwindled by 1965. In that final survey, well over half of all TEEPS

TABLE 7.4. THOSE AFFIRMING THAT WORLD POWER WILL FAVOR
COMMUNIST SIDE AT END OF CENTURY

	Britain	France	Germany
1959	47%	38%	20%
1961	42	33	15
1965	27	26	20

respondents positively affirmed that "the West as a whole is likely
to maintain or improve its position relative to the Communist countries under these conditions [of mutual deterrence]."

These great expectations — the brightest image of the future
world environment recorded during the TEEPS decade — came into
view in the 1965 survey along with some other projections that
appear at first to be incompatible. There was, for example, the increased number of respondents that sensed trouble brewing *in* the
West *for* the West. We asked: "Are the most important problems
facing the Western world in the years ahead likely to come from
within the Western system of alliances, from the Communist bloc,
or from the uncommitted areas?" While many respondents expressed
primary concern for the uncommitted and Communist areas (particularly China), the proportion mainly concerned with problems
coming from *within* the Western alliance more than doubled in
Britain and France — while remaining stable in Germany at about
20 per cent — from 1961 to 1965.

This increasing expectation of trouble within the Western Alliance is borne out in the growing disinclination, newly manifest in
the prosperous Europe of 1965, to "foot America's bills." We recall
from Chapter Four that those approving a larger European share
in Western defense declined by about half between 1961 and 1965.
(See Table 4.1.) Where there had been solid majorities of supporters in 1961, there were by 1965 only dwindling minorities. With
respect to economic aid to underdeveloped countries, the decline
of European support, while somewhat less dramatic, was very substantial and in the same direction. As Western defense and economic aid were principal components of the proposals made by
the United States, clearly these results represented a serious defec-
tion of the European elites from American policy initiative — and
possibly, although this remained to be seen, from American political
leadership.

B. PROJECTING THE ISSUES

1. The Euramerican System

Our review of the issues was designed to explain why an increasing number of TEEPS panelists had come to believe, by 1965, that the "most important problems in the years ahead" were likely to come from *within* Atlantica. While more panelists still foresaw that the main problems of the future would arise from the Communist Bloc and Uncommitted Areas, those projecting intra-Atlantic problems had increased to a substantial minority by 1965: óne out of every five in Britain and Germany, one out of every three in France. The importance of these projections was not their size so much as their apparent reversal of earlier trends toward a converging consensus among the European elites.

As the image of Europa and Atlantica was fundamental to these projections of future problems, we undertook to reanalyze our data on these images. The findings are complex and nuanced. In sum, there are two principal findings: (1) commitment to *both* Europa and Atlantica has increased over the years; (2) commitment to Europa increased *more* than to Atlantica — indeed, for the first time in the 1965 survey, the Atlantic commitment showed a relative decline in Britain and France (the question was omitted from the German survey). We asked panelists to rank the importance to their country of the European and Atlantic communities, the options being very important, fairly important, not so important. The distribution of those saying very important is given in Table 7.5.

TABLE 7.5. THOSE RANKING EUROPA AND ATLANTICA AS VERY
IMPORTANT COMMUNITIES

	Britain		France	
	1961	*1965*	*1961*	*1965*
European Community	58%	57%	69%	71%
Atlantic Community	67	57	56	31

The shift is somewhat less dramatic than may appear because most who dropped out of the "very important" category after 1961 simply changed their ballot to "fairly important" in 1965. The shift is also less dramatic in Britain, where there was no increase in ballots rating Atlantica as "not so important" — as compared with

France, where this rating increased by 10 per cent between 1961 and 1965.

A further nuance was revealed when we put the panelists to the forced choice of naming "the single most important" of their country's key relationships. Table 7.6 shows the results of choices between the European and Atlantic communities in 1961 and 1965.

TABLE 7.6.   THOSE RANKING EUROPA OR ATLANTICA AS SINGLE MOST IMPORTANT COMMUNITY

	Britain		France		Germany	
	1961	1965	1961	1965	1961*	1965
Europa	9%	27%	31%	57%	—	25%
Atlantica	10	21	11	10	—	25

* Question not asked.

Among the Germans, where we have no 1961 data, the 1965 results reveal the accustomed ambivalence between Europa and Atlantica that this panel exhibits throughout the TEEPS decade. The British show a substantial increase of priority to both communities, though rather more to Europa. An important source of this increase is the sharp decline of British priority to the Commonwealth as the single most important key relationship — a decline from 33 per cent in 1961 to 10 per cent in 1965. It would appear that the decline of the Commonwealth priority occurred from the moment when Britain submitted its first application for Common Market membership in 1961. The very significant increase of French priority to Europa, particularly as represented by the Common Market, derived largely from a substantial decrease of DK (which had always been highest in France during preceding years).

Indeed, the low DK on this forced choice is itself an important nuance in the 1965 results. The significant increase of priority to Europa was due not to the decline of Atlantica but rather to the decrease of uncertainty. The sharp reduction of DK signified the crystallization of elite opinion. This crystallization involved an important new version of the familiar imagery: Commitment to Atlantica was to be maintained and even increased, but not at the expense of Europa. Where choices were forced between these and other key relations, *both* gained priority. But where choices were forced between these two top-priority commitments, by 1965 Europa had gained the edge.

The critical shift in 1965, given the continued German ambivalence, was between Britain and France. Britain, without weakening its Atlantic commitment, moved in the direction of strengthening its priority toward Europa — mainly at the expense of earlier Commonwealth preferences. France, without abandoning its Atlantic commitment, moved even further toward top priority for Europa — at the expense of earlier uncertainties expressed as DK. The solid majority of 57 per cent designating European Community as "the single most important" of France's key relationships documents the powerful consensus that had crystallized in France by 1965. Despite the vigorous Euronationalist leadership of De Gaulle, all this new pro-Europa sentiment became predominant among the French elite by 1965. This pro-Europa sentiment also became "available," whether individual French panelists intended it so or not, to bolster the Gaullist projection of "independence" (of the US) as the key issue for the future of Europe.

The Gaullist issue, so formulated, clearly underlay European concern that the main problems facing the West were likely to come from *within* Atlantica. The issue was posed in two ways: (1) France *versus* Britain within Europa as its minor term, and (2) France *versus* America within Atlantica as its major term. Because Anglo-American solidarity was of primary concern to De Gaulle, the terms occasionally were merged to project the contest of political aspirations as France against the "Anglo-Saxons."

In every case, it was Gaullist France that seemed to many panelists likely to provoke the main problems facing the West in the years ahead. This is shown by their responses, over the Gaullist period, to the question: "Which of the main Western allies is most likely, by its own policies, to hamper the fullest development of a sound Western policy in world affairs?" These responses are given in Table 7.7.

Let us recall that the 1959 survey was conducted during De Gaulle's first year in office. He was then preoccupied mainly with the Algerian conflict and had not yet projected publicly his own grand design for Europa and Atlantica. During this early period (1959), only one out of four French panelists affirmed that De Gaulle would find a satisfactory long-run solution to the Algerian problem — and majorities of British and German panelists affirmed

TABLE 7.7. ALLIES HAMPERING WESTERN POLICY

	Britain		France		Germany	
	1959	1965	1959	1965	1959	1965
America	11%	19%	3%	35%	1%	3%
Britain	—*	—*	61	12	36	6
France	52	61	8	23	50	66

* Option not given.

that De Gaulle should "end hostilities promptly." Although pre-occupied elsewhere and not yet the architect of a counterconsensual Grand Design, Gaullist France even in 1959 already was perceived as the most likely source of trouble *within* Atlantica by a majority of British and German panelists. This rose to two thirds in both countries by 1965, a rather formidable expression of concern among the principal allies of any nation.

To the French elite panel, naturally, the picture looked rather different. In 1959, they identified the most troublesome ally as Britain. This was the year when Britain, having refused to sign the Treaty of Rome, created its own free trading bloc (EFTA) that was widely construed as a rival to the continental Common Market (EEC). In that year, Britain, having burned its fingers in a joint venture with France at Suez, refused to support Gaullist efforts to pacify Algeria. That was a year, too, when the continuing development of Blue Streak seemed destined to maintain Britain's place in the nuclear club, while France seemed to be indefinitely excluded. By 1965, this picture had undergone radical revision. The Algerian problem had been resolved without British support. The British Blue Streak had died with a whimper, while the French nuclear *force de frappe* had been born with a bang. As a final irony of accelerated history, Britain's bid to transfer its affiliation from EFTA to EEC had been rejected — by France. By 1965, Britain no longer seemed capable of being "troublesome" to most French panelists, witness the spectacular decline from 61 per cent to 12 per cent over this brief but eventful six-year period.

To the resurgent France of 1965, with its high evaluation of itself and its great expectations of the future, the main ally whose policy was most likely to "hamper" had become the US — witness the increase from 3 per cent to 35 per cent over the same six-year period. The Gaullist grand design by now appeared to require the diminution of American power in order for French power to expand. De Gaulle's personal interventions around the world — in Latin America, in Canada, in the Middle East, in Vietnam — seemed designed to disrupt, where it could not hope to replace, American preponderance. The main arena of Gaullist conflict with the United States remained, of course, Europe. The Franco-German Treaty was a major effort to wean Germany from American dependency; the rejection of Britain from EEC was intended to weaken the Anglo-American "special relationship"; the ejection of NATO from France was designed to divide America from all of its European allies by undermining the cornerstone of Atlantica.

While history has yet to render its verdict, it was not apparent by 1965 that Gaullist policy had achieved any conspicuous successes against the "hampering" policies of the United States. The Franco-German Treaty was generally regarded as a dead letter; the Gaullist rejection of Britain had stimulated the other EEC members to organize efforts to ensure her ultimate entry into the Common Market; the Gaullist ejection of NATO had provoked the other alliance members to propose an extension of NATO's scope to the political, as well as military, requirements of Atlantica. Throughout Europe, there was widespread concern that the Gaullist grand design might prove to be counterproductive by subverting the existing arrangements of Atlantica under American management without substituting a viable — not to mention superior — set of arrangements under French management.

This concern is clearly exhibited in the TEEPS data for 1965, when two out of every three British and German panelists designated France as the most troublesome ally — the one most likely, by its own policies, to "hamper the fullest development of a sound Western policy in world affairs." The same concern was apparent as well among a significant fraction of the French panel. Those designating France as the most troublesome ally increased from 8 per cent in 1959, De Gaulle's first year as head of the Fifth Republic, to 23 per cent in 1965 — a tripling of French panelists seriously concerned about the direction of Gaullist policy. We recall in this connection the findings recorded in Table 6.11 on the question of an "independent position" for France. In 1959, some 45 per cent of the panel thought France "should" take a more independent position, while only 37 per cent thought she was likely to. By 1965, after six years of Gaullist "independence," the situation was clearly reversed: 64 per cent thought France was "likely to," but only 36 per cent thought she "should."

2. Protection

These concerns arose mainly in connection with the projection of the issues — protection, prosperity, and even prestige — that we have already reported. Clearest was concern over Europe's protection. We have seen that relatively few panelists, including Frenchmen, assigned military significance to the *force de frappe* (mockingly referred to by many as the *farce de frappe*). While many believed that its national nuclear force was likely to gain political advantages for France, even these respondents considered the force insignificant for the protection of Europe. Virtually none, even among the Gaullists, took the view that the French forces could replace the American guarantee over the short or long run.

The optimistic expectations that appeared so strongly in the 1965 survey were based mainly upon the consensual evaluation that the Euratlantic security system was both efficacious and durable. The principal components of this evaluation were the beliefs that: (1) NATO, as constituted, was sufficient to deter the Russians over the short run ("next five years"); (2) American power would remain superior to Russian power over the long run ("end of the century — year 2000"); (3) the American guarantee via NATO would remain the foundation of European and Atlantic security. Gaullist attacks on NATO therefore produced a boomerang effect among the elite panels, including a substantial number of Frenchmen, by provoking them to re-ensure their assets in Atlantica.

3. Prosperity

The picture was somewhat different with respect to the issue of prosperity. The TEEPS decade was the period of the "European miracle." For the first time in economic history, nations achieved annual growth rates exceeding 5 per cent over a sustained period. Indeed, European growth rates were higher than American during the period 1955–1960 and about equal during the period 1960–1965. By 1965, Europe had achieved levels of prosperity and "self-sustaining growth" unknown to any previous epoch on the Old Continent. The "European miracle" was due, in very large measure, to American aid during the Marshall Plan period and beyond. And many Europeans took cognizance of this — despite Edmund Burke's dictum that "gratitude is not a political emotion."

Indeed, European recognition of their economic interdependence with America was less a matter of gratitude than a sober evaluation of the economic facts of life as recorded in the analyses of OECD and the policies of EEC. The principal fact was that Euramerican economic linkage had evolved historically to become a parameter of prosperity for both sides, and for the Europeans perhaps even more than for the Americans. So deeply and widely was this evaluation diffused among the European elites that even the vaunted nationalism of Gaullist France apparently felt obliged to take cognizance of it. This was symbolized by French consent to authorize the EEC Commission to negotiate transnationally, for all six member-nations, in the "Kennedy Round" of negotiations at GATT.

The very notion of Euramerican partnership-in-prosperity is what made some new issues salient for the European elites. In such a partnership, they wanted to be "equal partners." This meant that they had to "catch up" and then "keep up" with the Americans. As they perceived the extreme difficulty — the virtual impossibility in any foreseeable future, according to many Europeans — of achieving this aspiration, the elites became deeply involved in such concerns as the "technological gap." This concern, expressed also as the "management gap" and a half-dozen other "gaps" that we shall examine in Chapter Ten, arose mainly from the desire to make Euramerican economic interdependence mean something more than European dependence.

Excessive aspiration is always frustrating; and a good many European leaders were, between 1961 and 1965, suffering from frustration. During these years, the super-American growth rates they had achieved in 1955–1960 declined to American levels or below. In the same period, while Britain abandoned its Blue Streak and France alone on the continent initiated a modest missile program, the US took a commanding lead in the world's missile systems — and in its aerospace programs as well. Europe's most ambitious effort to "catch up" even in commercial aviation, via the joint Anglo-French *Concorde*, was foredoomed, according to many Europeans, the moment America decided to launch a competitive enterprise. And all the while, American private investment in Europe was growing at an unprecedented rate. One large European firm after another, particularly in the "glamour industries," was coming under American ownership and management. The spectacular take-over of Machines Bull by General Electric, leaving the continent without an indigenous computer industry of any consequence, brought European anxieties to a neurotic level. Some excited Europeans, as represented by the influential shaper of elite opinion *Le Monde*, took to prophesying the decline of Europe to a condition of "industrial helotry."

It is within this framework that we understand the 1965 reversal of European attitudes toward the "American dollar problem." We have noted the very sharp decline between 1961 and 1965 in the willingness of most panelists to approve a larger European contribution to the costs of either Western defense or economic aid to underdeveloped countries. As these were the two main fields in which American initiatives had sought larger European contributions, this reversal of attitude represented a sharp rebuff to American leadership in shaping Euramerican economic policy, perhaps the sharpest since World War II.

This rebuff was accentuated when panelists were equally disinclined to approve other suggestions for solving the "dollar problem" that would be relatively painless for the Americans, such as "revaluation of the dollar vis-à-vis European currencies" or "use of the international monetary system as a stabilizer." The number of respondents approving either measure declined substantially from 1961 to 1965, particularly on the question of dollar revaluation: from 30 per cent to 4 per cent in Britain, from 19 per cent to 11 per cent in France, from 23 per cent to 7 per cent in Germany. In fact, the only suggestion on our scheduled list that drew increasing approval from the TEEPS panels was the one likely to prove most painful for American businessmen and travelers in Europe: namely, "restriction of American purchases and investments in Europe." On this item, approval increased as follows between 1961 and 1965: from 11 per cent to 25 per cent in Britain, from 3 per cent to 38 per cent in France, from 16 per cent to 38 per cent in Germany.

Clearly, the alarm that American "takeovers" through private investment would lead Europe into "industrial helotry" had spread among the elites. Nor were the elites as indulgent as before toward the annual "invasions" of American tourists, students, and other visitors in a Europe no longer in acute need of dollars. The 1965 survey recorded a new and impressive display of anxiety, ambivalence, and even animosity toward the idea that Europeans should contribute to the improvement of the American fiscal or economic position.

It is easy to understand this reaction at a time when all of Europe was undergoing deep frustration that America was already so far ahead in the technological and other gaps that Europe could not soon, or ever, catch up. But frustration is a poor guide to policy. Itself the progeny of excessive aspirations, frustration tends to spawn false evaluations and expectations. These in turn distort, at least while the frustration is intense, one's image of the future. We turn, then, to the issue of prestige. How Europeans projected this issue, over the TEEPS decade, weighed heavily in the shaping of their new images of the future world environment and their own place in it.

4. Prestige

During most of the TEEPS decade, the European elites were gradually adjusting to the recognition that Euramerican cooperation implied at least enough acceptance of American leadership to keep the new system of relationships stable. America was recognized to be incomparably stronger and richer. Upon American strength Europe depended for its protection, upon American riches for its prosperity. It was the American guarantee of its protection and American cooperation in the maintenance of its prosperity, in turn, that Europe depended upon for its prestige. The firm commitment of US high policy to these objectives under the banner of "Europe First" had helped to regain European prestige in the early postwar years. The policy was "proved" by the allocation of American riches to Europe under the Marshall Plan and of American strength to Europe during the building of NATO and the successive Berlin crises.

The accelerated movement of postwar history seemed, for most of the elites, to be carrying Europe toward a new and epoch-making system of transnationalism. Under this system the symbols of prestige were no longer to be identified with national but rather with transnational power and wealth. The new transnational symbols that captured aspiration and allegiance were Europa and Atlantica. These stood for the new system of Euramerican relations within which American leadership and European pride could coexist comfortably. It was expected that there would be differences, even conflicts, among the West European and North American partners. It was even foreseen that, as the Europeans regained (indeed surpassed) their former wealth and some of their former strength, they would rightfully claim a larger share in the decision-making councils of the new transnational system. This was clearly acknowledged in the organizational structure of OEEC and NATO. Its operational expressions, during the TEEPS decade, were the successful transformation of OEEC into OECD and the unsuccessful American initiative to create a multilateral nuclear force (MLF) followed by the equally unsuccessful British substitute proposal to create an Atlantic Nuclear Force (ANF).

That some proposals to adapt the new system to changing situations would succeed and others would fail was also foreseen. The Euratlantic institutions provided amply for discussion and negotiation to meet such contingencies. What was not foreseen, however, was that any member-nation would adopt as its supreme policy the objective of subjugating the Euratlantic institutions to its own national prestige. To accept such a reversal of priorities, any transnational institution would have to provide for its own subversion — hardly a rational procedure!

It is for this reason that the Gaullist policy of national *grandeur* was perceived as an attack upon the foundations of the Euratlantic system of relationships. Europa was to be reconstrued as a coalition of sovereign nations (*Europe des patries*) rather than an integrated community (*Europe sans rivages* or more grandly *Etats-Unis d'Europe*); and this Europa was to operate more rather than less explicitly under French leadership. Atlantica was to be disassembled into two parts: America under US leadership and Europe under French leadership. During the early Gaullist years, the rhetoric of *grandeur* was widely regarded among the European elites as ridiculous and the initiatives designed to activate it (such as the Franco-German Treaty, the rejection of Britain, the "negotiations" with the Russians) were regarded as at best fanciful and at worst destructive of the Euratlantic system.

As the 1960's got under way, however, a combination of factors appeared to give the Gaullist rhetoric a ring of credibility. European leaders perceived that their extraordinary growth rates were higher than America's. The young new President Kennedy began to speak, in tones of great sincerity, about the Euramerican system as based upon "two pillars" and went on from there to develop the rhetoric of "equal partnership." To a growing number of Europeans it now appeared that prestige was being reassigned from the transnational to the national level and that the way to enhance one's share was by building national rather than cooperative power and wealth. This was a confused interpretation of what Kennedy meant — since the clearest expression of his intention was the "Kennedy Round" of negotiations at GATT, whereby Europe collectively was to deal with America. Somehow, some European nationalists took this to mean that *each* European nation was to be an "equal partner" of the US. It was through this confusion of attitudes and images that Gaullism, with an unintended assist from Washington, produced the remarkable ambivalence and inconsistency among the European elites recorded in our 1965 survey.

Ambivalence and apparent inconsistency with respect to NATO, cornerstone of Atlantica, were exhibited in responses to questions scattered through different parts of the 1965 interview schedule. Table 7.8 gives the responses to one pair of questions: "Do you feel that De Gaulle's policies have weakened American leadership of the Western alliance? Has the alliance itself been weakened?"

TABLE 7.8. DE GAULLE AND THE WESTERN ALLIANCE (1965)

	Britain	France	Germany
American Leadership	58%	90%	61%
Alliance Itself	58	53	73

On this showing, the outlook for NATO is very bad indeed. A majority of all panelists affirm that De Gaulle's policies have weakened both American leadership and the alliance itself. Yet, on another pair of questions, the panels appear to project a much brighter future for NATO. One question asked: "Do you approve of the integration of a major part of the nation's armed forces into a permanent supranational force?" The affirmative responses ran as follows: Britain 58 per cent, France 67 per cent, Germany 93 per cent. The follow-up question then asked: "Under which auspices would you prefer this — European, NATO, or some other?" A preference for NATO was expressed by 70 per cent in Britain, 74 per cent in Germany, and 30 per cent in France. The French panel showed an even more spectacular reversal of form when asked whether France should leave or stay in the alliance "when the NATO treaty expires in 1969." Only 5 per cent thought France should withdraw; 84 per cent thought that France should stay in. If most panelists believe that De Gaulle has weakened the alliance, apparently few of them believe he has weakened it enough to be seriously damaging!

Nor, apparently, do they think that De Gaulle's policies have weakened the Common Market, cornerstone of Europa, enough to be seriously damaging. In another pair of questions, the first asked: "With the decision on a common agricultural price policy and the entry into Kennedy Round negotiations, officials of the Common Market believe that European integration has reached a 'point of no return.' Do you agree?" Those agreeing that a "point of no return" in European integration had been reached ran as follows: Britain 66 per cent, France 67 per cent, Germany 67 per cent. This is among the most consensual responses on a controversial question recorded over the whole TEEPS decade: two out of every three panelists in all countries affirmed, in effect, that history had — whether De Gaulle liked it or not — already rendered its verdict in favor of European integration. Our follow-up question, designed to test whether respondents fully understood the initial question and the meaning of their answer, asked: "Do you think that further European integration can still be stopped . . . ?" Those thinking it can still be stopped were: Britain 16 per cent, France 15 per cent, Germany 4 per cent. In the new image projected by these elites, the future of Europa was indeed secure!

What, then, of the relationship between Europa and Atlantica? Was the Common Market going to replace the American leadership believed to have been weakened by De Gaulle? Our interview question asked: "In the next five years, is the Common Market likely to produce a political counterpoise to the U.S.A.?" Those saying yes were: Britain 16 per cent, France 2 per cent, Germany 2 per cent. If Gaullist leadership could no longer impede the integration of Europa and if integrated Europa could not produce a political counterpoise to the US, then apparently Europa — and with it the Euratlantic system of relations — was going to have to continue with American leadership, however weakened. We take it that this is why the panels, despite the weakening they perceive in American leadership and the Alliance itself, continue to project and prefer an integrated system of collective security under the Euratlantic auspices of NATO.

We have highlighted the ambivalence and ambiguity of elite responses in 1965 as a guide to the future, for we do not believe that history has yet closed the book on issues facing Europa, Atlantica, and the Euramerican system of relations. While 1965 closed the TEEPS decade, it was only another year in the shaping of European evaluations and expectations. Projecting new images of their own future is bound to evoke ambiguity and ambivalence among Europeans, for it involves the reshaping of their deepest ideas of themselves and their place in the world. To this reshaping of identities and ideologies in Euratlantic terms we now turn.

CHAPTER EIGHT

Ideology and Identity:
Reshaping Old Values

EUROPE created the ideologies of modern political life and taught them to the world. From Magna Carta to the Four Freedoms, ideas codified by Europeans were absorbed and adopted into the most diverse cultures on every continent. Sometimes they were implanted directly by European colonizers, who occupied much of the world's real estate in the name of their country and its ideological code. In other times and places, Europeanization was accomplished by indoctrination of the colonial elites in the colleges and governing institutions of the home country. Each imperial power of Europe became a locus and focus of modern ideology. Just as postwar Europe accelerated its modernity by "Americanization," so the imperial domains of prior centuries initiated their modernization under the aegis of their respective colonizers — India was "anglicized" and Indochina was "Gallicized."[1]

A. EUROPE: LOCUS AND FOCUS OF MODERN IDEOLOGY

With the postwar dismantling of empires, the nations of Europe turned to their own deep problems at home. They soon perceived that the end of global expansiveness had left behind a residue of ideology that was obsolescent. In the new bipolarizing world of the Cold War, they were no longer the protectors but the protected. This unaccustomed role put upon them pressures for new ideas that could be codified and activated in new institutions. American guarantees of their military security and economic prosperity, under OEEC and NATO, called for close and durable *transnational* in-

189

stitutions that had never before existed in peacetime among the
prestigious, powerful, and competitive nations of Europe. The new
ideas projected by the Monnet model required an even deeper
transformation of conventional ideology, for they pushed the European nations beyond transnational cooperation in the direction of
supranational integration.

What these ideas involve, if you say them fast, may not seem
particularly painful. But the word "regionalism," which we have
used to subsume these ideas, undermined the key symbols — and
collapsed the traditional codes articulating these symbols — upon
which European political life had been built over the centuries of
national greatness. These were the symbols of NATION, which had
evolved from the beginnings of exploration and colonization in the
fifteenth century, and of CLASS, which had developed as its principal competitor in more recent times. As the reshaping of values
among the postwar elites (and peoples) of Europe has involved
the contest between these two symbolisms — and their ultimate
replacement — we consider briefly what they have represented as
Europe moves from the past to the future.

1. The Key Symbols: NATION and CLASS

A key symbol is one which provides the rationale and morale of
a polity — the words by which its deeds are explained and justified.
It is "key" in the sense that, whatever variants it may produce and
whatever other words may cluster around it at different times and
places, this symbol epitomizes the idea underlying all the variants
and clusters that contain it. The key symbol may be mentioned explicitly, as in the shift from "national honor" to "national interest"
that we discussed earlier. Or it may be contained implicitly in an
array of different words: "fatherland" and "motherland"; "this
island" and "*grandeur*"; "our sons" and "our soil." Respect for the
key symbol may, indeed, be expressed in postures and gestures that
are word-equivalents requiring no vocabulary at all: standing to
attention, saluting the flag, raising "goose pimples" when the symbolism is vividly exposed.[2]

When a key symbolism accumulates a rich and resonant the-
saurus of equivalents, and when these are codified into a lexicon
widely employed in exposition of the rationality and morality of a
polity's behavior, then it constitutes an ideology.[3] Such an ideology,
which dominated European ways of thinking and talking for cen-

turies, is nationalism. The history and exegesis of meanings that have clustered around the key symbol NATION is perhaps the most voluminous corpus of writing in modern political analysis.[4]

While nationalism was evolving as the supreme ideology of modern Europe — we recall that the national integration of Germany and Italy continued into the late nineteenth century — competing symbols were already seeking to displace NATION. As exploration of the globe led to the great conflicts of colonization, wars among the colonizers, and coercion of the colonized, European thinkers began to speculate about possible scenarios in which European nation-based wars over the world's lands and seas could be avoided to the greater good of all concerned. By the seventeenth century, the creation of Utopias had become a major enterprise for thinkers concerned about the disruptive world effects of national policies that led recurrently to collision courses.[5] The eighteenth century, more secular and this-worldly, stirred some intellectual innovators, led by the French *philosophes,* to move from Utopias to the projection of ideologies based on putative universals of human nature.[6]

Only in the nineteenth century, however, did these trends of intellectual concern with humankind as the reference group — the vision of a world commonwealth of human dignity which still animates forward policy thinking today — coalesce around a symbolism capable of giving NATION a good run for its money. This was the symbolism of CLASS, which clustered with such terms as working class, proletariat, the poor, and underprivileged (and latterly underdeveloped) to codify the universal ideology of the have-nots called socialism. Karl Marx formulated the monumental code of "scientific socialism" which articulated the rising expectations of the new urban industrial population that had gained mobility and transformed their lifeways in the great transition from fields to factories, from farms to flats. The intellectual power of Marxian ideology derived from a rudimentary developmental construct, formulated as prophetic dogma rather than historical probability — namely, that the trends and conditions of industrial society were such that the means of production (source of modern wealth) must ultimately pass from proprietors to producers.

Upon this construct were based the socialist parties which for about one hundred years, roughly from mid-nineteenth to mid-twentieth century, came to represent the major counterelite formation in virtually every country of Europe. The socialist promise to the have-nots of modernizing society was comprehensive and global. Their key slogan ran: "Workers of the world, unite! You have nothing to lose but your chains!" Its appeal to the world's poor was exceeded only by its appeal to the world's intelligentsia — an appeal that remains ideologically compelling among scientists and other intellectuals today. (See Annex Three, which compares the political attitudes of European scientists at CERN with the national elite panels of TEEPS.)

Paralleling the global diffusion of nationalism by empires, the ideological code of socialism was diffused globally via transnational institutions of political action — from the First International to the Fourth International, which expired with the death of Trotsky. Whatever the merits or debits of their institutions, and the ideology upon which they were based, they infused their members in every country with an intense and lasting sentiment that a world commonwealth of human dignity under the key symbol of CLASS was historical destiny.[7] Perhaps their most durable accomplishment in Europe was to consolidate, and partially incorporate, the great tradition of Christian socialism and its variants in each modern country — a range symbolized by the "Red Dean" of Canterbury in Britain, by the Fulda Bishops in Germany, and most vividly by the "worker-priests" in wartime and postwar France.[8]

2. The Routinization of Political Life

As the competing symbolisms of NATION and CLASS were codified into the ideologies of nationalism and socialism, they built rivalrous institutions of political action designed to mobilize adherents and direct their behavior. These took the form of voluntary associations and civic movements, sometimes global in scope such as Britain's Society for the Propagation of the Gospel and France's League for the Rights of Man. Others were primarily designed as sociopolitical watchdogs of the domestic scene, usually in opposition to the regime in power, such as the pre-World War I Fabian Society in Britain, the interwar Freiherr Korps in Germany, the Club Jean Moulin in post-World War II France.

The main institutional form was, of course, the political party designed to win elections and gain the seats of power. This objective required "party discipline" — whether by persuasion (via the party press which increased rapidly over the past century) or by coercion (via various forms of political penance culminating in expulsion from the party in opposition, imprisonment by the party in power, or execution by either). Through the party institution, acting in terms of the rationale and morale codified in its ideology, evolved the routinization of political life characteristic of Europe over the past century. Through its symbols and icons, its rituals of devotion and penance, the political party absorbed and adapted the successful methods of the church.*

The routinization of political life, as of religious life, was the outcome. Party members routinely obeyed political dogma as church communicants obeyed religious dogma. In France, few Radical Socialists would support government subsidy of parochial schools any more than Christian Democrats (or indeed Christian Socialists) would oppose it. Even matters that are now regarded as technical issues to be resolved in the public interest by professional specialists were then dealt with strictly along party lines. Thus, in Britain, few Tories would support wage increases as a matter of public policy and few Labourites would oppose it.

The larger effect of ideology as institutionalized by parties was to routinize imagery, posture, strategy, and action within the political arena. This effect is most readily discernible in France, always the most ideological of European countries. It was in France that the image of politics as a Left-Right continuum was most fully routinized. So far was this image elaborated that seating in the parliamentary hemicycle of the Palais Bourbon had to be in strict Left-Right order. As the sentiment of *gauchisme* grew in force and favor among the French electorate, some of the most heated controversies were over which party should be seated to the Left of which others.

The codified imagery shaped, indeed rigidified, the posture of each party. Maintenance of its image required that it codify its "positions" (including the classic French position of "abstention") according to the ideology — indeed, to the ideological variant most appropriate to its regional base.[9] As party postures rigidified, so did party strategies — particularly the formation of party coalitions to gain a workable parliamentary majority.[10] The incapacity to form

---

* André Siegfried once summarized the differences between the American two-party and French multi-party systems in an apt sentence: "Each American party is a cathedral with many chapels observing different rites; each French party is a chapel trying to act as if it were a cathedral."

durable working majorities plagued the postwar Fourth Republic as it had the prewar Third Republic with its notorious "instability." Extremist coalitions of the Left or Right, seeking to pursue some definite forward policy, were rapidly blocked. Centrist coalitions tended to be immobilized by their *ad hoc* commitment not to rock the boat — a phenomenon to which postwar Frenchmen attached the pejorative label *"l'immobilisme."*

The conspicuous incompetence of such a political system became intolerable to large and growing segments of the elite and electorate in postwar France. This was part of the larger revulsion against the traditional ideologies of nationalism and socialism that spread through the debilitated lands of postwar Europe, whose peoples were eager for new paths to a life better than that represented by recurrent wars of reciprocal devastation.

3. The Postwar Revulsion Against Ideology

The postwar revulsion among Europeans was directed against the traditional ideologies because they were widely associated with the two world wars. If it was the inflated ambition of nationalism that provoked World War I, it was the pusillanimous voting of war credits by German socialists that activated it, just as the ideological blinders of French socialists under the "popular front" of Léon Blum left Western Europe unprepared against the aggressive nationalism of Nazi Germany. And if it was Hitler's version of National Socialism — or for that matter Stalin's version — that represented the fusion of the two traditional ideologies, then most Europeans wanted no part of it in their future. All but the most routinized socialists were revolted by Stalinism.[11] The complex of postwar European sentiments can be simplified, in summary fashion, under three heads: "propaganditis," anticolonialism, Euramericanism.

"Propaganditis" affected Europe in the aftermath of World War I, as some crucial campaigns of Allied propaganda — such as the notorious "Belgian atrocities" with their mutilated babies and raped nuns in particular — were demonstrated to be false.[12] It acted as an antitoxin that fortified Europeans, who were widely exposed to such antiwar and antipropaganda films as *La Grande Illusion*, with a strong dosage of skepticism about politically motivated messages of

---

* The label *"l'immobilisme"* was first attached to the government of Joseph Laniel, which lasted fourteen months and thereby became the most durable ministry of the Fourth Republic.

all sorts. As a result, in the Allied psychological warfare campaigns of World War II conducted in the ETO (European Theater of Operations), "credibility" was a major constraint. This time around, many Nazi atrocities that actually occurred were *not* reported or utilized lest they be dismissed by Europeans on the Allied side as "mere propaganda."[13] The Nazi-Soviet pact was the booster shot that set the antitoxins of "propaganditis" coursing vigorously through the European body politic once again. But this time it was "socialism in one country" (the Stalinist fusion of NATION and CLASS) that lost face and faith.

Anticolonialism developed as a sentiment of great force in postwar Europe. The seeds had been planted by earlier generations of antinationalist intellectuals, adherents of virtually every variety of socialism, who believed that imperialist extension of the national domain to other lands was antithetical to the projected world commonwealth of human dignity. Anticolonialism had spread as well among returned soldiers, now voters, who had done wartime service in former imperial domains. Some of these veterans were not only the electors but the elected: The new M.P.'s chosen in the Labour sweep of the first postwar British election of 1945 were ideologically anti-imperialist with a strong commitment to decolonization.[14] Not only was their moral position clear but, in Britain at least, their rationale as well — Britain no longer could afford an empire. While official French policy on decolonization ceded the empire more slowly and violently, the anticolonial sentiment also weighed heavily upon leftist intellectuals, in and out of uniform, and through them the literate segment of ordinary *poilus* (GI's) and their officers.[15]

Euramericanism in postwar Europe took many forms, including some with a large component of anti-Americanism. As in many Euramerican interactions in the postwar decades, the paradox here is more apparent than real. The Euramerican syndrome among such people was aptly expressed in a quip popular with British soldiers during the war: "The trouble with the Yanks is they're overpaid and overfed — and what's more, they're over here."[16] Many postwar Europeans who disliked having large quantities of Americans among them did not at all dislike having large quantities of American goods — and learning how to make these Good Things for themselves. It was precisely this identification of American "haves" with European "wants" — a spectrum ranging from chewing gum through refrigerators and bathrooms to motor cars — that subverted the traditional codes and led to the reconstruction of political ideology.[17]

B. RECONSTRUCTING IDEOLOGY: FROM IDEA TO PRAGMA

The codes of nationalism and socialism were hanged together, as well as separately, by the rising tide of expectations among postwar Europeans. For it soon became clear that neither NATION nor CLASS, as key symbols, pointed in the direction they wished to move. Neither was likely to provide the "gets" needed to satisfy their new "wants." What they wanted was freedom from fear — of war and threats of war that nationalism had generated between the nations of Europe. Also freedom from want — a fair share of the necessities and even the amenities of the good life that socialism offered only through violent depredation against the "haves" by the "have-nots" (one of Hitler's key symbols). Recognition spread that the good life was not likely to be attained by grabbing for oneself, by virtue of one's membership in a particular class or nation, a bigger slice of the old pie. The good things of life were more likely to be attained — and this was perhaps the deepest lesson taught by the American model with its focus on "productivity" — by baking bigger and better pies from which all could get larger slices without depriving others.

The notion of a bigger pie appeared at first to involve merely the application of new technological solutions to old social problems. As "productivity" took command, however, it became clear that a whole way of life was involved in meeting the conditions of this new symbolism. The new lifeways transformed routinized practices, via geographic and occupational mobility, as well as habitual perspectives. The new test of an idea was not loyalty but efficacy, not whether one pledged allegiance to an ideology but whether it produced the results that were sought. It was in this sense that Europeans went about reconstructing their ideological heritage. The direction was: *from* idea *to* pragma.

1. The Passing of Nationalism and Socialism

We do not speak of an "end of ideology." Many Europeans still identify strongly with the traditional codes of the Left and the Right. Other Europeans, who have been won to the new pragmatic ways, often invest them with ideological elements. Nor do we speak of an "end of nationalism." The polities of Europe are still constituted as nation-states. Moreover, as we have seen, many Europeans who have accepted the new transnationalism as a way of life continue to judge transnational policies, in some measure, in terms of national interest.

We speak rather of the "passing" of nationalism and socialism as a developing process that remains to be completed. The plain fact is that postwar Europeans have renounced the traditional *ideology* of nationalism. A solid majority of our panelists in each country declare that the nation-state as a political form is obsolete, and even larger majorities believe that its obsolescence is (or would be) a good thing. Two questions were put to the panels in 1961 and 1965: "Do you think that present trends are making the nation-state obsolete as a political form? Do you consider this to be a good thing?" The percentages answering yes are given in Table 8.1.

TABLE 8.1. OBSOLESCENCE OF THE NATION-STATE

	Britain		France		Germany	
	1961	1965	1961	1965	1961	1965
Nation-State Is Obsolete	57%	55%	57%	64%	92%	73%
This Is a Good Thing	75	67	69	62	92	78

We note a decline among the German panel from near-unanimity in 1961 to three out of four in 1965 (a matter we shall annotate in Chapter Ten). Still the German panel recorded the largest majority feeling the nation-state is obsolete. The French panelists, even at the acme of the Gaullist period, affirmed also that the exclusive nation-state is no longer effective. The pattern of response here is similar to that reported in the last chapter: While most French panelists felt that Gaullist policies had "weakened" the Atlantic alliance and American leadership, few felt the damage was serious.

The disavowal of nationalism and the traditional trappings of sovereignty commanded stable, and generally increasing, majorities among all panelists. We asked the elites in 1956 and 1959 to what extent they would approve the limitation of national sovereignty "in favor of a common policy." The options were: "only in so far as it promotes the present alliance"; or beyond alliance to "confederation" (defined as common policy by majority rule) or to "a supra-national institution" (defined as a single common decision-making body). Table 8.2 shows the distribution of ballots between these two options.

TABLE 8.2.   TO WHAT DEGREE SHOULD NATIONAL
SOVEREIGNTY BE LIMITED?

	Britain	France		Germany	
	1959	1956	1959	1956	1959
Only to Promote Present Alliance	41%	31%	24%	21%	25%
To Promote Confederation or Supranational Institution	48	53	68	57	74

Note: Deviations from 100 per cent are due mainly to DK responses.

Increasing support for supranational structures is clear in the case of France and Germany. Although Britain showed greater reluctance here, her concern for the broader issues of supranationalism is clear from her response to another question asked in 1959. We asked whether limitation of sovereignty should be confined to short-term issues on an alliance basis; be enlarged to fundamental issues on a supranational basis; or have no limitation at all. Table 8.3 gives the responses.

TABLE 8.3.   HOW MUCH LIMITATION OF SOVEREIGNTY? (1959)

	Britain	France	Germany
Confined to Short-Term Issues on Alliance Basis	4%	8%	15%
Enlarged to Fundamental Issues at Supranational Level	85	70	83
No Limitation/DK	11	22	2

That Britain is strongly interested in resolving issues now blocking supranational institutions is clear from Table 8.3. In the 1961 survey, we posed this question: "The postwar trend has been toward international associations which limit each participant's national sovereignty to some extent. To what degree would you favor

Britain [France, Germany] moving in this direction: wholeheartedly, only cautiously, or not at all?" Table 8.4 details the answers.

It is quite striking that the consensus here wholeheartedly ap-
proves of limitation of national sovereignty in principle. Better

TABLE 8.4.   SHOULD YOUR NATION MOVE TOWARD INTERNATIONAL
COOPERATION POSITIVELY OR CAUTIOUSLY? (1961)

	Britain	France	Germany
Wholeheartedly	77%	77%	76%
Only Cautiously	20	16	21
Not at All/DK	3	7	3

than three out of four respondents in all panels share this picture
of the future.

To see how this affected the Common Market members in 1961,
the year when De Gaulle's campaign for a *Europe des patries* got
under way in earnest, we asked the French and German panels:
"Which of the following two political concepts do you consider the
more effective in the long run: a confederation of sovereign states
[*Europe des patries*] or a 'United States of Europe' (a common
government and citizenship)?" Table 8.5 shows the 1961 vote. Despite the Gaullist campaign for a Europe of sovereign states under

TABLE 8.5.   CONFEDERATION OR UNITED STATES OF EUROPE? (1961)

	France	Germany
Confederation of Sovereign States	31%	45%
United States of Europe	52	51
Other/DK	17	4

the banner of national *grandeur* and despite its alleged "weakening" of the transnational trends of the postwar years, a clear majority of French — even more than German — panelists opted for not
only the transnational but indeed the supranational system of
political life as "more effective in the long run."

Another 1961 question was designed to see how the panelists applied these general preferences and projections to current controversies. We focused on protection, since hot debate had arisen on
the issue of control of a Polaris missile system. The question was
phrased: "The key problem of Polaris control appears to force a
choice between adopting the most effective system of collective de-

fense now available, or maintaining intact the historic institutions of national sovereignty. Should Britain [France, Germany] in this situation give priority to collective defense or national sovereignty?" The responses to this question are given in Table 8.6.

TABLE 8.6.   COLLECTIVE DEFENSE OR NATIONAL SOVEREIGNTY? (1961)

	Britain	France	Germany
Collective Defense	84%	55%	95%
National Sovereignty	7	10	0
DK	9	35	5

The outcome is clear. When protection appears to be at stake, few panelists give a fig for national sovereignty. Not a single German, and a mere handful of British and French respondents, took the sovereignty option.

We returned to this issue in the 1965 survey. This time we did not pose the question sharply as between sovereignty and efficient defense, but rather phrased it in this manner: "In your judgment, should Britain [France, Germany] give priority to its own Polaris fleet, to a multinational Polaris fleet, or some other approach?" Table 8.7 shows how the elites answered the question.

TABLE 8.7.   NATIONAL OR MULTINATIONAL POLARIS? (1965)

	Britain	France	Germany
National	27%	20%	4%
Multinational	41	58	93
Other/DK	32	22	3

De Gaulle's policies concerning both the MLF and the ANF, as we described in Chapter Four, blocked the preferred judgment on this issue. Here we note only that, in the reshaping of ideology and identity among the European elites, *traditional* nationalism was dead as the dodo.

A similar process had led to the "passing" of socialism as a codified ideology that shapes the political perspectives and behavior of many Europeans, systematically dividing those on the Left from those on the Right across the full range of issues in public policy. On the major issues that have faced postwar Europe, moderates of the Left and Right often have been closer to each other than to extremists of their own party or political tendency. There has been an "interpenetration of old and new values" as we shall see in the next section. Internationalism is no longer a defining characteristic of socialism, for the data just presented show that in Europe today nearly everybody is an internationalist in some sense. Nor is pacifism a defining characteristic, for we have seen that Europe today is strongly committed to collective security — a commitment accepted by the socialists equally, if not more so, with the nationalists. Nor is social welfare a defining characteristic, for the old socialist ideas subsumed under such labels as "social security" and even "profit sharing" now are widely accepted among capitalists and other rightists.

In losing these defining characteristics, socialism lost its distinctive role in the polities of Europe. The political spectrum of postwar Europe has moved leftward. In the process, much that was distinctively Left in prewar Europe is now in the center and equally "available" to partisans, especially moderate partisans, on either side of the spectrum. The process seems analogous to the leftward shift of prewar American politics under the New Deal which, according to Norman Thomas, restricted American socialism by partially incorporating its distinctive policies. The interpenetration of ideologies in Europe today has been summarized succinctly by André Malraux: "The Left is no longer on the left, the Right is no longer on the right, and the Center is no longer in the middle."

Before we turn to this, it is relevant to annotate what has happened to one unique feature of historical socialism — its role as an *international* political movement (the French socialist party is still called SFIO, which stands for French Section of the Workers' International). The history of the Socialist Internationals has been competently recounted elsewhere.[18] Here we note only that, since the Bolshevik Revolution of 1918, international socialism had been strongly tied to Russia through the Third International (Communist). This tie had created great confusion between democratic socialism and pro-Soviet policies in the prewar years of the Popular Front (when, even in America, the key slogan proclaimed that "Communism is 20th century Jeffersonianism"). The confusion lasted well into the first postwar decade.[19]

However, the air had cleared considerably by the start of the TEEPS decade. Throughout most of the survey we repeated one question: "What would you do in a Communist Britain [France,

Germany]?" The open-ended answers were fully recorded and sub-sequently recoded. To summarize a rather complex set of data, we have regrouped all responses into three categories: (1) *antagonism*, which includes those who said they would engage in active resistance, emigrate, be killed, made to suffer, have no job, as well as those who found this projective situation "inconceivable"; (2) *passivity*, which includes those who said they would cooperate, withdraw, or privatize, as well as those who foresaw "no change" in the projective situation; and (3) *other/DK.* Table 8.8 shows how these categories of response were distributed over the years.

Although there is not strict comparability, a consistent majority or substantial plurality voiced antagonism in all panels in all years. This is a matter of historical interest in view of the concerns often expressed during the first postwar decade that the nations of Western Europe might "go Communist" by internal political action. The data show that this danger was remote, at least in the second postwar decade. In addition, the convergence of percentages in the three categories of antagonism, passivity, and DK (with the notable exception of Germany) shows a decline of intensity of interest in the issue. The two factors are of considerable analytical importance in their indication that the Europeans no longer are associating European socialism with Soviet communism, that European socialism has been liberated from an obsolete bondage, or at least linkage, to the Soviet Union and a codified ideology.

2. *The Interpenetration of Old and New Values*

The passing of nationalism and socialism as codified ideologies did not bring their influence to a full stop. Residues of both ideas remained influential, and continue so today in the political thinking of postwar Europeans. But their residual influence is strong where they represent concerns that were always compatible and have now become common, and weak where the concerns always were and still remain conflicted. Thus, there is no shared interest in the "victory of the proletariat," but there is a strong common interest in the "welfare of the poor." What has come to be called "the welfare state" in postwar parlance is an example of the residual influence of socialist ideas. The idea of a "mixed economy," in which public and private ownership of the means of production and control over the means of distribution coexist, is another such residual. Prosperity, in short, has become a common concern rather than a sectarian shibboleth in the postwar policy of European nations.

positive) use illustrates the transformation of political modes that we have been discussing. The "technocrats" are those who deal with issues of public policy in the manner of social scientists rather than political ideologues. They identify the values to be maximized, estimate the probability of success for the available policy alternatives, and weigh the ratio of costs to benefits of each alternative. This is, of course, a simplified version of a complex process. The theory and technique of scientific decision-making are in an early stage of development and the procedures they use are still quite rudimentary.[21] But they are developing rapidly and are spreading throughout Europe at a rate exceeded only in the United States, as is shown in recent studies of this process at work.[22]

The transformation of policy thinking among Europeans has brought into the foreground of political life new men with new ideas — what has aptly been called, in Britain, "the meritocracy."[23] These are men whose main political capital is their knowledge and their capacity to apply it to the solution of current problems. Sometimes they rise to the summit of political power: Chancellor Erhard was a professor of economics, Prime Minister Wilson a professional statistician. Where they do not rise to such official heights, they are the policy advisors now considered indispensable by top decision makers in every advanced society — particularly with respect to the values of prosperity. In postwar America, their role is exemplified by the Council of Economic Advisors and the National Security Council, as well as the Policy Planning Board in the Department of State and the "consultants" associated with virtually every major agency of the executive branch of government.

In Europe, perhaps the most interesting example of a meritocracy — those men with professional skills who bring to current policy issues an anti-ideological, problem-solving mode of thought — is Gaullist France. Behind the grandiose (and sometimes grand) oratory of the General is arrayed a high civil service which is generally regarded as the best on the continent. Most of them in *les grands corps de l'Etat* (the major departments of government) are graduates of *les grandes écoles*, the excellent graduate schools of France. The younger generation has been trained in the *Ecole Nationale d'Administration* (ENA), a unique higher academy for civil servants founded early in the postwar period by De Gaulle's first Prime Minister and close advisor Michel Debré.

The ascent of the technocrats to top levels among the elites —

their designation as a meritocracy based on skill by contrast with an aristocracy of birth or a plutocracy of wealth — represents the new pragmatism at work among the peoples of postwar Europe. Unbound from faith in secular ideologies, as generations earlier they had been unbound from faith in sacred theologies, European technocrats have reshaped the ways of thinking among their peoples to fit better their transformed ways of living in the postwar world. (A fuller discussion of those who have become "Eurocrats" is given in Chapter Eleven.)

A basic change in personal style — in that deep part of personality which has come to be called "identity" — was required. Personal judgments on public issues could no longer be drawn, more or less automatically, from the available stock of responses codified by one's preferred ideology. In the postwar world of the technocrats, each issue had to be judged anew on its merits and each decision had to be reached afresh as the outcome of a policy-thinking process. A new mix of identifications, expectations, and demands was in the making.

C. RESHAPING IDENTITY: THE NEW PRAGMATISM AT WORK

We have seen the new pragmatism at work among the European elites on the key issues of public policy. Economic ideas about prosperity once uniquely confined to socialists are now "available" to persons of all parties or none — as are strategic ideas about protection once uniquely confined to nationalists. The interpenetration of old and new ideas has provided a common fund of policy alternatives that each person can judge on its merits in each case. This is the new intellectual pragmatism that is replacing the old ideological dogmatism once expressed in the "party line." Its operation in the public opinions of the European elites has been made abundantly clear in the TEEPS data already presented. Even the ambivalence and inconsistency we have often stressed are an exhibit of the new pragmatism at work: ambivalence because pragmatic persons often cannot rationally decide issues of this gravity with the partial information available to them, inconsistency because pragmatic persons often cross "party lines" to choose the option that seems to them more effective or desirable regardless of its ideological label.

When a person incorporates a new political style, he simultaneously evolves a new personal style as well. According to the Lasswellian formula, political behavior is private affect displaced onto public objects and rationalized in terms of the public interest.[24] On this understanding, the patterning of political attitudes is a public manifestation of one's personality, although the relationship often must be discerned dialectically (rather than directly), owing to the intervening mechanisms of displacement and rationalization. In various years and countries over the TEEPS decade, we asked questions designed to test personality variables directly and dialectically. We focused particularly on those components of "private affect" that reshape identity in ways bearing upon political evaluations and expectations.

1. "We Live in a New World"

Thus in 1961 we posed a set of three questions asking each panelist to characterize his own personality in a general way. These were the questions:

(1) A person's particular views tend to express a more general outlook. Would you consider yourself, in general, to be rather an optimist or a pessimist?

(2) And, again in general, would you consider yourself to be rather an idealist or a pragmatist?

(3) One rule of political life states that "politics is the art of the possible." Another holds that a statesman should "never compromise his principles for the sake of expediency." Which more nearly suits your own view of proper political conduct?

The responses of the 1961 panelists are shown in Table 8.9.

TABLE 8.9.   WHAT SORT OF PERSON ARE YOU? (1961)

	Britain	France	Germany
(1) Optimist	80%	70%	86%
Pessimist	15	14	11
(2) Idealist	47	43	55
Pragmatist	42	31	37
(3) Art of the possible	66	64	71
Never compromise principles	27	18	11

Note: Deviations from 100 per cent in totals are due to DK.

An overwhelming majority of panelists in all countries consider themselves to be optimists rather than pessimists. The split is much closer on the second question, although a clear plurality consider themselves to be idealists rather than pragmatists. Were we to stop with these direct questions on personality and draw inferences to probable political attitudes, we should be seriously misled. A corrective is supplied by the third question, which adds a dialectical dimension. In projecting their personal values into political life, better than two out of every three panelists across the board believe that politics is the pragmatic "art of the possible" whereas only a fraction take the idealistic view that a statesman should "never compromise principles." This showing indicates that if our panelists are "optimists" they are very realistic optimists, and if they are "idealists" they are very pragmatic idealists. Such a collective self-portrait is highly congruent with the attitudinal profile that has emerged from their responses to political issues throughout the TEEPS decade.

To say that one is a pragmatic idealist is not to minimize the quality of his idealism; it is rather to add the dimension that he takes his ideals seriously enough to want to make them work. To see how our panelists evaluated the functioning of idealism in the contemporary political arena, we asked them another set of three questions in 1961. These were:

(1) Is idealism, in your judgment, an important element of political power?
(2) Do you consider that the Western world, in general, lacks idealism?
(3) Do you believe that the Communist world is, in general, more idealistic than the West?

The proportion saying yes to each question is shown in Table 8.10.

TABLE 8.10.   IDEALISM IN POLITICS (1961)

	Britain	France	Germany
(1) Idealism Is an Important Element in Power	78%	77%	86%
(2) West Lacks Idealism	45	52	66
(3) Communists Are More Idealistic	42	54	57

This set of responses appears to account for much of the stress and strain, ambivalence and ambiguity, that appear in the attitudes of our elite panels on key issues, particularly when they are projecting these issues into the future. There is a strong consensus in all panels that idealism *is* an important element of political power. Thereafter, small but significant differences appear. The British, traditionally unimpressed with ideological formulations, alone deny that the West lacks idealism and that the Communist world is more idealistic. This view is reversed by slight majorities among the continental panels. The French and Germans affirm *both* that the West lacks idealism and that the Communist world is more idealistic. It seems reasonable to hypothesize that these views derive from their recent shift away from ideology to pragmatism, which occurred within the lifetime of virtually all these panelists and during the mature years of most of them. During the immediate prewar years, the French and German panelists lived within a political culture that regarded ideology as scriptural. And ideology, with its pervasive tendency to rationalize all private affect in terms of the public interest, schooled its acolytes in "pure" rather than "applied" idealism. Indeed, the coercive ideological movements of interwar Europe taught its adherents to profess idealism even while they were applying themselves to atrocities such as the Communist Russian massacres and the Nazi German genocides of the 1930–1945 period.

Having lived through the prewar and wartime holocaust, the European elites underwent postwar conversion to pragmatism with a strong sense that the deepest need was to make their idealism operational. There was a positive sense of purpose and responsibility in their conversion, as well as a feeling that the experiences they had lived through gave their generation a special competence to put the psychopolitical life of Europe on a new basis. This is indicated by the rather uncanny absence of morbidity about the horrors they had witnessed. In 1959 we asked: "Which do you think the best generation to live in — your parents', your own, or the next generation?" Table 8.11 records their responses. Clearly there is neither nostalgia for the recent past — despite heavy sentimentalization of the Edwardian era and *la belle époque* — nor envy of the proximate future. Instead there is a very strong sense of identity with one's own time. This was expressed by an eminent French

TABLE 8.11. WHICH IS THE BEST GENERATION? (1959)

	Britain	France	Germany
Parents' Generation	12%	12%	10%
Own Generation	51	65	75
Next Generation	28	18	9
DK	9	5	6

respondent, who considered Europe today the most opportune time and place to be alive because it was full of alternatives and options hitherto unknown. Said he: "We live in a new world."

2. From Empathy to Expathy

There exists no comprehensive theory of political personality, and none is offered here. We seek rather to clarify the psychological structure of private identification with political life in postwar Europe. How people relate to public affairs varies widely in time and place. These variations range from utter withdrawal to vigorous participation in political activity. A major psychological mechanism that mobilizes individuals for "political behavor" is *empathy,* the capacity to identify oneself with rules and situations "outside" of one's own life situation. Empathy thus includes a capacity to perceive alternative modes of behavior, to evaluate them in terms of probable "payoff" to one's own values, to choose one's own preferred option among the available alternatives, and to adapt one's own behavior so as to maximize one's chances of attaining the preferred option.

Empathy, so conceived, is a cognitive as well as a perceptual mechanism. It starts with a percept of alternatives that represent new "wants"; it eventuates in a concept of how to act in order to "get" what one wants most. Empathy is thus the primary mode of personal interaction with one's environment. It activates the "Want: Get Ratio," the ratio between what one wants and what one gets from the environment, which is the core of political participation and an essential component of the political process as a whole. Since politics deeply affects what people get by its control over the distribution of all values, and empathy is the mechanism that enables people to identify what they want, their interaction in the Want: Get Ratio is the central process whereby individuals relate to their environment.

As we view the comparative history of psychopolitical development, it appears that all peoples organized as polities pass through a phase of empathic transformation as they go to meet their future.

This is not to propose a theory of history as "stages," according to which every society goes through the same ordered sequence of phases in roughly the same intervals of time. Our theory is neither so general nor so deterministic. It asserts, much more modestly, that every society on the way to "self-sustaining growth" (which is the objective of political and economic development everywhere) must undergo an empathic transformation in *some* way and at *some* point in its history. Otherwise, if people do not learn to identify what they want and seek to get it, social change is undifferentiated and growth does not occur.

The transformation occurs in many different ways at different times and places. Without devaluing the diversity of the process, we suggest that there are also certain uniformities worth attention. On the simplest and most parsimonious level, some empathic transformations succeed in increasing participation and equilibrating the Want:Get Ratio at rising levels of self-sustaining growth, while others fail to do so. We have schematized these two societal paths in terms of the psychopolitical modes of identification that predominate in their successive phases. Figure 8.1 shows the scheme.

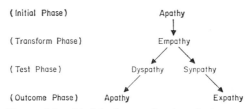

Figure 8.1. Modal phases of political identity.

As many of these terms are neologisms coined for expository convenience, it will be useful to clarify the meanings assigned to them here. Apathy is the initial phase from which development typically starts, for predeveloped societies usually are nonparticipant in the sense that the vast majority of their members are and always have been isolated from political life. The growth process typically involves a transform phase in which empathy, the acquisition of new wants, becomes widely diffused through a significant segment of the population. Once the diffusion of Wants is sufficiently widespread, the question of Gets comes to the focus of public attention. With the emergence of the Want:Get Ratio as a criterion of societal success, the developing society enters into a critical test phase.

The test phase is critical because the society's performance during this period tends to determine the direction that the modal psychopolitical structure will take during the outcome phase. If the performance is inadequate and the Want:Get Ratio becomes intolerably imbalanced — if the significant segments of the population come to want more than they can possibly hope to get — then empathy turns into dyspathy, which is a neologism for dysfunctional empathy. Dyspathy arises when the aspirations discovered by empathy are frustrated beyond hope, when the new level of Wants is not even approached by an acceptable new level of Gets. Continuous frustration typically leads to a regression to apathy in the outcome phase.

This may occur after a period of extreme reaction to frustration by aggression; and in some cases, as in Bolshevik Russia, aggression can be sufficiently well articulated and activated to produce a successful revolution. In such cases, all bets are off and a new sequence of psychopolitical structures comes into operation. But successful revolution is a relatively rare phenomenon and may be regarded here as a special case. The more typical outcome of prevailing dyspathy in the test phase is regression to apathy. The significance of apathy is that the generation of people who live through the test phase of dyspathy and regress — because their new aspirations have been hopelessly frustrated — are unlikely to undergo another empathic transform in their own lifetime. This enterprise will be left to a later generation. Such, indeed, has been the outcome in many societies of the underdeveloped world that sought to achieve self-sustaining growth in the postwar period.

Their frustrated outcome throws into relief the more satisfying experience of postwar Europe. In suggesting a comparison, we must promptly recall that Europe went through the empathic transformation many centuries ago, beginning with the Age of Exploration in the fifteenth century and continuing through the Renaissance in the sixteenth. Europe then passed through a series of test phases — the Reformation in the seventeenth, the Industrial Revolution in the eighteenth, and the consolidation of nations in the nineteenth century — with relatively successful (even if costly and painful) outcomes.

At the end of World War II, then, Europe was readier than most of the world to deal with the new test phase of self-sustaining growth. Its past successes had accumulated a reserve of material human resources without parallel outside of the superpowers, and in terms of skilled human resources probably exceeding Russia, which had come through the test phase of dyspathy by the special route of revolution.

In concluding this discussion of the reshaping of identity in post-war Europe, we wish to focus attention not on the economic value of its human resources but on the modal psychopolitical structure of the politically significant segment of its peoples. Since their acquisition of empathy many centuries earlier, Europeans had become habituated to successful encounters with test phases of the crucial sort we have mentioned: Exploration, Renaissance, Industrial Revolution. Thus they developed a sense of synpathy, which is a neologism for synchronous empathy; they were attuned to the tempo and balance of social change and could readily adapt their private affect, notably their wants, to the capacity of the environment. The habits of synpathy, passed on through successive generations by upbringing and education, enabled each generation to maintain a tolerable if not ideal Want:Get Ratio in its own time.

Unlike those less developed peoples who allowed excessive aspiration to produce excessive frustration, and through continuous dyspathy regressed to apathy, the Europeans were able to maintain a dynamic equilibrium with their environment. Thus, while the regressed apathetics tend to withdraw from the public arena, the Europeans stand their own ground and take adversity as a transitory setback that is to be regained the next time around.

This is the deeper meaning of the attitudes toward their own historical and political identity expressed by the TEEPS panelists. As we have reported, they identify their own as the best time to have lived in — better than their parents' or their children's. They have little wistful sentiment about the past, including their own life history, and most would not significantly change their lives if they had them to live over again. These are the indices of synpathy that reveal a strong sense of identity with time and place in one's own person.

The outcome of synpathy in the test phase — in Europe a succession of crucial test phases — is expathy, our neologism for expressed or explicit empathy. Whereas the initial empathic transformation is mainly an intaking of new percepts and concepts into the personality, almost literally an "incorporation" of public affairs within the domain of private affect, expathy is the application of the transformed person to the rational (or rationalized) solution of public issues. Whereas empathy internalizes a new view of the environment, expathy externalizes what empathy has taught in a positive value-oriented effort to rearrange the environment.

The positivist attitude toward public affairs clearly is the modal psychopolitical style among our TEEPS panelists. They identify themselves as optimists and as idealists. They make clear that their optimism is realistic and their idealism is pragmatic. They view politics as the "art of the possible." They are concerned that the next generation should learn to think about political life with the same strength of identity as themselves, and in the same perspectives of realistic optimism and pragmatic idealism.

CHAPTER NINE

Postures and Processes: The Nations in Transition

EUROPEAN leaders brought to the common crisis of postwar Europe a diversity of national traditions. The common crisis was the loss of European hegemony over the rest of the world. The great nations of postwar Europe could no longer master the globe; decolonization was the order of the day. Nor could they completely master themselves; the dynasties had fallen, and interdependence was more essential than sovereignty.

Even the two historical requisites of national sovereignty — the protection and prosperity of their own people on their own land — appeared to be beyond purely national reach, with a consequent decline in national prestige. As contrasted with the superpowers represented by Washington and Moscow, the great nations of Europe suddenly appeared to be small potatoes. France, Germany, even Britain, were themselves dependencies. Dependencies of whom: the superpowers? each other? the United Nations? After much turmoil about neutralist, bridge-building, and third-force ideas in the first postwar decade, the nations of Europe settled down to a serious consideration of their real options. By the second postwar decade, these had been identified as Europa and Atlantica.

To the conception and construction of these new key relationships, each of the big three nations of Europe brought a different set of historical involvements and contemporary commitments. Britain's ties to North America, via Canada and the "special connection" to the United States developed during World War II, led inevitably to a widespread acceptance of Atlantica. This was, moreover, the key relationship most readily compatible with Britain's

215

interests in a Commonwealth whose dimensions were still global.

France, deprived of its former imperial interests beyond Africa and lacking Britain's close ties to North America, saw the reshaping of its key relationships in a somewhat different context. The watershed, as France passed into the second postwar decade, was the defeat of EDC. This rejected, in effect, the idea of a continental "region" to be subsumed under a NATO led by the Anglo-Americans. It turned France in the direction of a continental "system" capable of acting independently of Atlantica and preferably under French leadership. This conception of Europe as a key relationship, based on Franco-German cooperation under French primacy, has been articulated with gusto since De Gaulle returned to power in 1958. It has become the Euronational version of Europa.

Germany has faced a somewhat different set of preoccupations since World War II and developed, during the second postwar decade, its own particular set of perceptions and preferences. Involved in no area outside of Europe by old imperial ties, but deeply involved in Europe by reason of its postwar division and by the need to rebuild relations with its former victims on the continent, it was natural that Germany should consider Europa as a key relationship. All of Adenauer's statecraft was directed to this purpose. At the same time, Germany's prosperity and security — its present viability and future prospects — were uniquely dependent upon the American guarantee embodied in the NATO framework. It was equally natural, therefore, that Germany should perceive Atlantica as a key relationship. Underlying German ambivalence between Europa and Atlantica was the fundamental reliance upon the Euramerican system of postwar relationships.

Our task in this chapter will be to articulate and illustrate the different perspectives which the three main European powers brought to their common concern for the formation of powerful and durable institutions of collaboration. As we shall be stressing distinctions and differences, it is important to bear in mind that these have arisen out of common concerns. It is essential to remember, for example, that "nationalism" is virtually dead among all these panelists in the traditional sense of reliance upon the nation-state as guarantor of peace and prosperity. On these common concerns, the European leaders are virtually all "internationalists" in one sense or another. Further, their internationalism is favorable toward *both* Europa and Atlantica in *both* the Euramerican and

Euratlantic modes. Few in any panel exhibit systematic hostility toward these key relationships for their country.

The differences are those of conception and emphasis, of preference and priority. Even these differences emerged clearly only when we obliged our panelists to make forced choices. Only then did Britain emerge as the *Atlantic* nation, France as the *European* nation, Germany as the *ambivalent* nation. Where choices were not forced, panelists in all countries tended to favor both modes of international collaboration. There may be a lesson to be drawn by De Gaulle; and perhaps a lesson for Washington. We defer consideration of these possibilities. Our interest here is to alert the reader to the common concerns and even common convictions out of which have grown, during the second postwar decade, the attitudes we shall report in this chapter. We change here to the present tense to underscore our conviction that these attitudes are durable for the next period of time.

A. BRITAIN: THE ATLANTIC NATION

Throughout the years of TEEPS surveying, Britain has remained an Atlantic nation. This characterization is appropriate because the British panel, when faced with a broad array of choices, has consistently given the Atlantic form priority in the various arenas of international cooperation. Whether questions have been asked in general terms or with specific references, the British panel has made clear its preferred commitment to Atlantica. The stability and intensity of the British attachment to Atlantica has only recently, in the 1965 survey, begun to show signs of change. The new direction, which includes a heightened sensitivity to the continent, is what we call Euratlantic.

The priority which the British panel attaches to the Atlantic commitment can be demonstrated in a variety of contexts. The responses reported here include selections from all years of the TEEPS survey, and illustrate questions which pose choices for or against Atlantica as well as choices for Atlantica as one among other relevant relationships. Table 9.1 reports the findings of a probe in the last three surveys which asked the panel to choose the single most important relationship for Britain.

There are several important dimensions in this table. Of primary interest here is the consistently large choice for an Atlantic relation-

TABLE 9.1. BRITAIN'S SINGLE MOST IMPORTANT RELATIONSHIP

	1959	1961	1965
Commonwealth	33%	33%	10%
European Community	7	9	27
Atlantic Alliance	13	10	20
Anglo-American Connection	28	19	20
United Nations	8	10	13
DK	11	19	10

ship, either in the bilateral form of the "Anglo-American connection" or in the Atlantic alliance. These two options jointly draw the greatest number of respondents in both 1959 and 1965. Only in 1961 does its chief competitor, the Commonwealth, temporarily draw slightly more respondents and the DK category temporarily swell. Even in the 1956 survey, though the question is worded differently and therefore not presented here, the Atlantic priority is chosen.

By 1965, the Commonwealth had lost its attraction for a goodly number of respondents. As subsequent tests show, these panelists have tended to choose either Atlantica or Europa as the most important single relationship for Britain. In terms of Atlantic priority, it is significant that the gains for Europe were not losses for the Atlantic commitment. Instead the ranks of *both* groups swelled, a subject that will be pursued in more detail. At this point, we report two other tests of priority among British leaders.

Questions that force a choice between the Atlantic and European options are difficult for panelists in all countries. Such forced choices are especially difficult for the British, who would prefer to believe that the two options are compatible. Nonetheless, we persisted in probing this area of choice, which became painfully vivid at the time of De Gaulle's first rejection of Britain's application for membership in the Common Market — in part at least, as a result of the Atlantic choice made by Britain in the Nassau Agreements. That British leaders now recognize the existence of some forced choices between De Gaulle's version of Europa and their own version of Atlantica is clear from Prime Minister Wilson's statements prior to entering a second round of exploratory talks on British entry in 1967.

One example of earlier British difficulty in responding to the forced choice is the large DK on a question which asked: "Which

European organization, in its own way, is more valuable for Britain than NATO?" The distribution of responses is shown in Table 9.2.

TABLE 9.2. EUROPEAN ORGANIZATION MORE IMPORTANT
TO BRITAIN THAN NATO

	1959	1961	1965
Common Market	6%	1%	14%
Council of Europe	5	1	2
OEEC (OECD after 1961)	35	8	2
None	28	49	44
Other	11	8	1
DK	15	33	37

A large group of panelists in 1959 chose OEEC, which had an Atlantic base. This conformed to the avowed British interest in broadening the Atlantic Community beyond its military base in NATO, expressed at that time in the public discussion about Article 2 of the NATO treaty. In later years, after the British effort to expand the economic and political functions of Atlantica had lapsed, a clear plurality of the panel was able to sort through the complexities of the question and decide that no European organization was more important to Britain than NATO. This is further testimony to the strength of the Atlantic commitment when measured directly against alternatives.

The panels were then asked to choose among alternative regional frameworks in still another sensitive context, namely, the integration of armies. Table 9.3 demonstrates the development of the Atlantic priority as the British elite was asked if they would prefer European, Atlantic, or UN auspices for integrating the British army.

Tables 9.1–9.3 have one major common factor: When forced to choose among their several key relationships, all the British panels have given the Atlantic relationship priority. In addition to this comparative data over time, there also exists a corpus of materials on British evaluation of the Atlantic relationship in the context of the functions it is supposed to perform. The basic function of the Atlantic relationship for Britain is the guarantee of military security in Europe. Fully 89 per cent of the panel in 1961 and 80 per cent in 1965 responded in the affirmative to questions asking if the United

TABLE 9.3. REGIONAL PREFERENCE FOR INTEGRATING BRITISH
ARMY

	1959	1961	1965
European	26%	32%	10%
Atlantic	47	61	47
UN	57	48	36

Note: In 1965, the regional option was "filtered" to include only those who first agreed to integration in principle. The 1965 column adds to only 93 per cent because 7 per cent of the panel did not agree to integration in principle and therefore was filtered out. The columns for 1959 and 1961 add to over 100 per cent because respondents were allowed to choose more than one option. On this basis, the 1965 distribution would be: European 14 per cent, Atlantic 70 per cent, UN 11 percent, DK 5 percent. This indicates even more strongly the British commitment to Atlantica on military issues.

States were prepared to guarantee the military security of Western Europe "even as the North American Continent becomes vulnerable to direct attack by new weapons."

In addition to testing British feelings about the general American commitment to the military security of Europe, we probed to see if the panels believed that NATO, the institutional framework for the American guarantee, would be strong enough to *deter* the Russians "over the next five years." In both the 1961 and 1965 surveys, when this question was asked, two thirds of the panels each time responded with a positive evaluation of NATO's deterrent capability. The level of affirmative response was not nearly so high when NATO's capacity to *defend* was examined. In 1961, only 31 per cent of the panel thought NATO could adequately defend Europe against the Russians. However, by 1965, this number had increased to 44 per cent, with only 25 per cent of the panel believing that NATO could not *defend* against the Russians. Since NATO has never been designed and implemented to "defend" Europe, this response indicates the large measure of positive feeling that the British panel assigns to the security value of Atlantica. The measure is even more striking when we note that 19 per cent of the panel refused to answer on the grounds that the question was not relevant for the current situation. This means that a majority of the panelists who accepted the question and evaluated NATO as a defensive organization responded in the affirmative.

A similar trend in support for NATO, over the last three surveys, is shown by British responses to the forced choice of maintaining a divided West Germany armed in NATO or promoting a neutral and reunified Germany outside of NATO. The history of the second postwar decade has been marked by continued British doubt about the role of Germany; British sensitivity to the question of West Germany as an ally has never been completely erased from the public pronouncements of its spokesmen. However, the British panel has undergone a change of mind on the subject of Germany's role in NATO. From their sharply divided response in 1959 (40 per cent Germany in NATO and 46 per cent neutral), they have moved toward a clear consensus that West Germany should remain in NATO (69 per cent in 1961 and 70 per cent in 1965). Not only did over two thirds of the British panel affirm this view in the two latest surveys, but also, by 1965, there was no longer any coherent opposition to this consensus. The opposition, having dwindled from 46 per cent to 27 per cent to 11 per cent over the years, had either joined the West Germany-in-NATO consensus or diffused itself into the DK category. The trend of British elite opinion is shown in Table 9.4.

TABLE 9.4. BRITISH PREFERENCES ON A DIVIDED GERMANY INSIDE NATO OR A REUNIFIED GERMANY OUTSIDE NATO

	1959	1961	1965
Divided Germany in NATO	40%	69%	70%
Reunified Neutral Germany Outside NATO	46	27	11
DK	14	4	19

By 1965, therefore, the distribution of responses in the British panel indicates that the Atlantic security structure had been overwhelmingly accepted. British leaders had virtually given up any serious opposition to American policy on the "German solution" via NATO. In addition, they had given up almost completely on the likelihood of a "general agreement" on international disarmament, another submission to Atlantic harmony under American leadership. In the 1959 survey, 39 per cent of the British panel expressed its belief in the likelihood of a general agreement covering conventional and nuclear weapons and 50 per cent expressed their disbelief. By 1965, the disbelievers' ranks swelled to 80 per cent and the believers fell to 10 per cent. Thus, all of our evidence, as of 1965, indicates that a firm Atlantic commitment had been made by the British panel.

Furthermore, the increase in the estimation of American power, which we documented in Chapter Six, also applies to the West as a whole. Table 9.5 records British responses to comparable questions asking for estimates of relative strength of the East and West blocs. Though there is some change in question wording, the decline of the East and relative gain of the West is impressive.

TABLE 9.5.   BRITISH ESTIMATE OF EAST AND WEST
INFLUENCE IN WORLD AFFAIRS

1961   So long as the situation of mutual deterrence limits military action in disputed areas by both camps, which side is more likely to make greater gains of power and influence in world affairs?

1965   Is the West as a whole likely to maintain or improve its position relative to the Communist countries under these conditions or is the Western position likely to decline?

	1961		*1965*
East	57%	Maintain	33%
West	23	Improve	21
Other	4	Decline	26
DK	16	DK	20

This evidence makes it clear that the British elites are in great measure oriented to Atlantica. Whether we measure the commitment in terms of a forced choice between Atlantica and alternative key relations or whether we focus on positive evaluation of particular elements in the Atlantic framework, a great deal of positive sentiment is expressed by all British panels over the years. The dominant feeling, by far, is that the Atlantic orientation is central to British interests. This preference does not, however, exclude other considerations.

British spokesmen have traditionally seen Britain as a balancer of power, or as a bridge between divided nations, or as a mediator in disputes. The British response to international differences has often been to seek a position in which Britain can play a positive role on both sides of the division. Thus, while Britain may be an Atlantic nation, one would expect the British panel to see this commitment as compatible with other desires. Indeed, much evidence can be amassed to show that, while the Atlantic commitment takes priority, it does not do so to the exclusion of other options. The British panel has shown an increasing interest in a European tie for economic and other reasons.

In search of prosperity, three quarters of the British panels in the last two surveys believed that Britain could not afford to be excluded from the Common Market. This has affected British thinking about their political ties: Over half of the British panel in the last two surveys believed that Britain should sacrifice its Commonwealth ties to promote its European interests. Even the security linkage with Europa has been involved: Half or more of the British panel in the last four surveys believed that Britain should join a European Defense Community. (It is noteworthy that in 1965 DK increased sufficiently to lower the positive response.) Thus, in each of these major areas, the British panel has shown an abiding interest in joining forces with continental countries in the Europa format.

It should be clear, however, that the British interest in European relations is not located in a non-Atlantic framework. The British panels express an eclectic approach which places high value on both attachments. One does not exclude the other. The Atlantic priority includes a European purpose. As evidence, Table 9.6 shows the

TABLE 9.6.   BRITISH EVALUATION OF EUROPEAN COMMUNITY

1961   Turning to the European Community, do you consider the idea valuable in itself?

Will it produce a political counterpoise to Soviet Russia?

Will it produce a counterpoise to the United States?

1965   Turning to the Common Market, do you consider the idea valuable in itself?

In the next five years, is the Common Market likely to produce a political counterpoise to Russia, to the United States?

	1961	*1965*
Valuable Idea:		
Yes	90%	93%
No	9	5
DK	1	2
Counterpoise to the US:		
Yes	38	16
No	56	79
DK	6	5

results of measuring British sentiment in a question giving the panel an opportunity to say whether they see Europa as a counterpoise to the United States. It is clear that while Europa is valued, it is not valued as a counterpoise to the Atlantic leader. Nor is it valued as a counterweight between the two superpowers. Apparently Europa is favored, mainly on economic grounds, as a viable and valuable adjunct to Atlantica in a Euratlantic framework.

The British panel's assent to Europa was explored in Chapter Five, where we traced the development of this interest among panelists who have been interviewed over time. In this chapter, the major point to be noted is that the British panel now is dominantly Euratlantica, not to the exclusion of some form of Europa, but as a matter of priority over all other relevant "key relations." This Atlantic orientation is all the more pronounced when contrasted with the preferences of the French panel over the decade of the TEEPS survey.

B. FRANCE: THE EUROPEAN NATION

The French priorities are as stable as the British, but in a different direction. Instead of the Atlantic option, when forced to choose among alternatives, the French panels consistently chose the European option. This choice has been repeated from one survey to another and in all functional areas of protection and prosperity. The European priority therefore antedates De Gaulle and is likely to be a long-term characteristic of French elite preferences. We measure its scope and intensity by selecting a battery of questions which asked the French panels to express their preferences as to "key relationships."

The earliest form of inquiry asked the panelists to choose the most effective international community. In 1955, 1956, and 1959, over half the French panelists chose the European Community. Less than one quarter in 1956, and one quarter in the 1959 survey, chose the Atlantic community. The question was posed somewhat differently in later surveys, when the panels were asked to choose the single most important relationship for France. Table 9.7 records the high, and rising, orientation toward Europa among the French panel.

Not only does Table 9.7 indicate a European priority, but it shows a recent movement away from uncertainty (expressed by DK) and

TABLE 9.7. FRENCH CHOICES OF THE SINGLE MOST IMPORTANT
RELATIONSHIP FOR FRANCE

	1961	*1965*
French Community	16%	7%
European Community	31	58
Atlantic Alliance	11	9
United Nations	7	1
German–French Alliance	16	13
DK	19	12

toward a European Community. If we combine the choice of a bilateral Franco-German relationship with the broader European Community choice, we get an overwhelming orientation toward Europa by the French panel.

The European response is also strong in a number of dimensions related to French security. When the 1965 panel was asked where it would like to place priority for a nuclear force, the European option was relatively the most favored: European Force (39 per cent); Atlantic Force (19 per cent); *force de frappe* (20 per cent); DK (13 per cent); None (9 per cent).

The results were substantially the same when the questioning moved to integrating French troops in these various international frameworks. From 1959 to 1965, the French panelists choosing a European Command for the integration of French troops into a supranational army grew from a plurality to a majority of 54 per cent. Those choosing the Atlantic option fell from one half in 1959 to 29 per cent by 1965.

The growth of interest in a European army is manifest in both the absolute increase over the previous years and in the relative increase over the NATO option. A further indication of absolute increase can be found in the responses to a question asking for support of the European Defense Community. Repeatedly since 1956, the EDC has had a bare majority of support in the French panels. By 1965, the supporters had grown to 70 per cent of the panel. Whether the question of a European orientation is placed in a framework competitive with an Atlantic option, or whether it is judged on its own, the French panel's priority for Europa is evident.

The same preference applies to the development of atomic energy for peaceful purposes. The results of our questioning in this area are reported in Table 9.8. This question is at the heart of what will likely be one of the next major Atlantic issues: technological development. We have, in the sphere of atomic development, a clue to likely priorities that may be expressed in other fields such as electronics and computers and aeronautics. Table 9.8 is reported here in full because the predominance of the European priority over the Atlantic alternative could be a harbinger of future competitiveness in French attitudes toward a broader range of activities than atomic energy. Since 1961, the French panel's Atlantic minority has remained stable, but the interest in the United Nations has dropped considerably, to the benefit of Europa. The attitudinal predispositions reported in Table 9.8 are part of the larger pattern of Europeanism in French thought.

TABLE 9.8.   FRENCH VIEWS ON THE FUTURE DEVELOPMENT OF
ATOMIC ENERGY

1961   How about the future development of atomic energy for peaceful purposes, do you think this should be controlled by an international organization or not?

Would you prefer such international control to be European, Atlantic, or United Nations?

1965   Do you prefer that the development of peaceful atomic energy should be placed under national, European, Atlantic, or UN auspices?

	1961	*1965*
European Control	13%	48%
Atlantic Control	11	13
UN Control	41	19
National Control	27	16
DK	8	4

On most of our questions, the French panels demonstrated a consistent priority for European solutions that is in marked contrast to the British preference for Atlantic options. Perhaps of equal significance is that a good number of French panelists perceive the European priority as competitive with the United States. While few British panelists think that Europa will produce a counterpoise to the United States, many Frenchmen do think of Europa as a counterpoise to Euramerica and Euratlantica. This reached its high point in 1961, when 60 per cent of the French panel affirmed that "the European Community will produce a political counterpoise to the United States." By 1965, perhaps as a reaction to extreme Gaullist promotion of the "counterpoise" idea, its affirmation by the French panel declined to 41 per cent.

For while the questions reviewed thus far show a clear French priority to Europa, there is still widespread recognition that the Atlantic resource is important. For example, as we saw in Chapter Four, the French panels register a positive evaluation of Atlantic security functions. In spite of debate and strategic argumentation in support of the *force de frappe*, the French panels remain convinced that the American guarantee of European security is not impaired by American vulnerability to new weapons. In 1961, 68 per cent of the panel thought America would honor her guarantee. In 1965, after years of open questioning and criticism at the highest levels of French public life, a fulsome 73 per cent of the panel still positively endorses the validity and necessity of the American guarantee.

Even more striking changes in a positive direction have taken place in the French panel's evaluation of NATO. Table 9.9 shows a striking increase of confidence in the efficacy of NATO to deter the Russians over the next five years. Whether this increase results from an improved view of NATO or from a sense of the diminishing nature of the Russian threat cannot be inferred from these data. We do know that the perception of the Soviet threat is reduced. But we also know from cross-tabulational analysis that this reduction does not correlate strongly with attitudes toward NATO and

TABLE 9.9. FRENCH EVALUATION OF STRENGTH OF NATO

1961 Is NATO, as now constituted, strong enough to deter the Russians over the next five years?

1965 If the Russians should attack in the next five years would NATO, as now constituted, be strong enough to defend the West?

	1961	*1965*
Deter USSR:		
Yes	45%	64%
No	33	19
DK	22	17
Defend the West:		
Yes	11	47
No	53	31
DK	36	22

other Atlantic matters. Whatever may be the source of the increase in the evaluation of NATO's capacity to carry out its functions, it remains the case that the French panel believes NATO can do the job for which it was designed. A surprising number even believe that it can not only deter the Russians but defend the West as well.

The favorable evaluation given to NATO by the French panelists should not be interpreted as an insignificant assent to an organization that is otherwise seen as unnecessary. When we asked the 1965 panel if they thought France should withdraw from NATO, only 5 per cent said yes. The predominant sentiment is for reorganization (50 per cent), but a sizable minority (34 per cent) wish to stay in NATO even with little organizational change. Such favorable responses to NATO may well be analogous to the increasingly favorable British views toward Europe. Both sides appear to be converging in recent years toward a Euratlantic consensus based on confidence in the Euramerican system of relations.

The British give more assent to Atlantic institutions when compared to European, but they also give assent to European institutions by themselves. The French give more assent to European institutions when compared to Atlantic, but they also assent to Atlantic institutions by themselves. In this sense, there appears to be a parallelism in convergent directions between the two panels. The parallelism is not precise, however. The British panel tends to stress compatibilities between the European and Atlantic modes of cooperation while a larger group of French panelists sees the two modes in somewhat more competitive perspective.

One consequence of this parallelism may be the evident French alienation from present government leadership. It is obvious that there are important differences between the French elite panel and government policy under the De Gaulle regime. These differences have been investigated, and the findings are reported in the Annexes. At this point, we note that the panel and De Gaulle share a European orientation, despite important differences on the degree of transnational control over French actions that the panel and their President will tolerate. There are also differences in elite and presidential attitudes toward the United States. However these variations may affect French policy in the future, on two matters of central concern the TEEPS survey data are clear: The positive French orientation toward Europa antedates the Fifth Republic and has attitudinal roots that are likely to survive its present leader;

the same may be said of the positive French attitude toward the American guarantee and the Euramerican system.

C. WEST GERMANY: THE DILEMMA OF DOUBLE EXPOSURE

The German elite panels have, since the first survey, consistently reflected their nation's profoundly ambivalent position in international affairs. On the one side, as a prime target of a hostile and powerful USSR, Germany requires allies and allegiance in the Atlantic security framework. On the other side, Germany is in the magnetic field of attraction of European integration, which requires allies and allegiance in the European Community context. That this double exposure has not developed into a unified picture is the basic problem — along with their continuing division between two separate states — underlying German attitudes toward the world arena in the second postwar decade.

At times, during the postwar period, the European and Atlantic visions have seemed compatible and complementary to the German elite. It was not necessary at these times for a German to choose between the two scenarios unless a social scientist forced one's choice in an attitude survey. However, there have been other times when it was quite clear to German leaders that a choice had to be made. In the early years of our survey (1955–1959), the choice between a Europe of Six and a Big Europe (as in the Euratlantic framework of the OEEC) could readily be harmonized by allocating appropriate functions to each. By the end of the TEEPS decade, conflict between De Gaulle and the United States was tending to force German choices between Europa and Atlantica — perceived, at least under the regime of De Gaulle, as a choice *between* Paris and Washington. Official German policy has tried to avoid the choice and insist on the mutual compatibility of good relations with both of its indispensable allies. Whether or not these choices are compatible in the long run, there are always a number of short-run decisions to be made; and the TEEPS surveys often have focused on these choices as a recurrent theme in postwar German political life.

Questions similar to those used to measure attitudes among the British and French panels were asked in Germany as well. In the sense that we have epitomized Britain as an Atlantic nation and

France as a European nation, Germany appears as an ambivalent nation — which opts clearly for the Atlantic priority only under conditions of forced choice. However, we must promptly add that the German panels, while their forced choice is clearly Atlantic, exhibit a degree of Europeanism that is often much stronger than the sentiments expressed by the British and even French panels.

The German elite's attraction to Europe and supranationalism has been so profound that priorities are much more difficult to establish. The German panels have, throughout the decade, consistently been ardent supporters of supranational European institutions. Consistently, as well, they have chosen to subordinate strictly national objectives far more widely and deeply than any other panels. While the French have declared themselves for Europa with equal frequency, there is an important nuance: Europeanism for the French panels has never meant quite as much subordination to a higher common purpose, for it was assumed that a United Europe would be led by France. It is possible for a Frenchman to transpose his national perspective onto the European framework in a way that is not realistic for a West German panelist.

Because of this special German commitment to Europe, the strongly pro-Atlantic aspect of the distributions reported in Tables 9.10–9.12 looks like British Atlanticism but differs in some important ways. In one sense, for example, it might be said that the Atlanticism is even stronger in Germany, where it is competing against a much stronger alternative than in Britain. On the other hand, the stability of the commitment may be under greater stress than in the British case. We shall see the stress when reviewing our TEEPS findings for the later years. But thus far, under forced choice, the stress has not succeeded in altering the basic priority given to the Atlantic commitment by the German elite.

Over the years, the German panels have been asked to express their priorities in a number of different forms. It is therefore difficult to measure the change over time exactly. In each year the change in question wording could account for some differences, and the amount of bias interjected is sometimes difficult to assess. However, no matter how the questions were asked in any given year, their aggregate weight lay on the side of Atlantica as the predominant commitment. But the picture is not uniform: On some occasions, the stress between the Atlantic and European orientations results in an ambivalent attitude and a divided panel. Yet, as the data to be presented indicate, the Atlantic position is the strongest overall.

In 1956, the German panel opted for the Atlantic form of Europeanism as well as choosing two other categories with an Atlantic base. Their choices among forms of international cooperation are given in Table 9.10. The distribution in the table shows clearly that the German panel preferred a broad Atlantic rather than a narrow European base for international cooperation. The Big Europe (OEEC–OECD) option is essentially Euratlantic since it includes Britain and North America; the Free World option is clearly Euramerican. Adding these three options together shows a majority of 63 percent for the broader system of Euratlantica.

TABLE 9.10. GERMAN PREFERENCES ON MOST DESIRABLE FORM
OF INTERNATIONAL COMMUNITY (1956)

Little Europe (the Six)	23%
Big Europe (OEEC–OECD)	30
Atlantic	12
Free World	21
World	12
DK	2

This pattern repeated itself in 1959 and 1961, when a question was asked which probed for the most effective form of international community. Table 9.11 illustrates the predominance once again of the Atlantic orientation among the German panel in these years.

TABLE 9.11. GERMAN OPINION ON MOST EFFECTIVE FORM
OF INTERNATIONAL COMMUNITY

	1959	1961
European	22%	17%
Atlantic	36	55
Free World	9	11
UN	26	14
World	3	3
DK	4	0

The stable history of Atlantica operated on relevant indicators throughout the years. In 1965, when we asked the panel to choose the single most important of Germany's key relations, 69 per cent made the Atlantic choice (and 62 per cent of these specified the

"German-American connection"). Of the remaining respondents, 20 per cent were ambivalent, only 9 per cent clearly opted for Europa, and the UN option dwindled to 2 per cent. When we formulated the issue in more specific ways, the pro-Atlantic priority of the German panel was shown even more clearly. For example, when we asked for a choice of key relationships in the context of military security, NATO garnered the support of nearly three quarters of the panel and the German-American relation almost two thirds. By contrast, neither the German-French nor the national solution to the need for protection gathered more than 10 per cent.

We then asked the panel to evaluate the preferred NATO connection against existing European organizations. Their response is indicative of the same Atlantic message. Two thirds say no European organization is more valuable than NATO, while only one fifth make any European choice. Once again, the priority is evident. When the German panel evaluates its key relations, and is forced to do so in a closed choice, it chooses the Atlantic option.

As a last comparative measure, we present one that does not arise from a forced choice. Table 9.12 presents the results of questions asking how important each key relation is to Germany; it shows the proportion saying "very important" to each.

TABLE 9.12. GERMAN CHOICES OF THE "VERY IMPORTANT"
AMONG GERMANY'S KEY RELATIONS (1965)

Germany's international position is based on her membership in different institutions and on her relations to different countries and organizations. How important do you think the following institutions or relations are: German-American relations, German-French relations, membership in the EC, membership in NATO, relations to the UN?

German–American Relations	86%
German–French Relations	34
Membership in EC	53
Membership in NATO	51
Relations to UN	14

Since the choice is not forced, each panelist can evaluate more than one relation as "very important." Hence the results bear close investigation. The chief link in the preferred Atlantic connection is the bilateral German-American relation; it is rated higher by even more panelists than the NATO membership. The parallel European link for the Germans is in German-French relations, but this is rated far lower than the American nexus and is lower than membership in the European Community itself. Thus, the web of interconnections in the Atlantic framework centered on America clearly is more highly valued by the German panel than the European relationship centered on France.

Though the American relation is by far the most important, one should not overlook the similarity of response to both the European Community and NATO when they are not evaluated in competition with each other. This suggests that the bilateral relation with America is responsible for tipping an otherwise delicate balance in the German panel's evaluation of its international relations.

It is possible to adduce further evidence of support for the Atlantic system of international relations which protects West Germany. Such evidence includes the nearly unanimous faith in the American guarantee exhibited in the last German surveys. The record shows, further, that better than three quarters of the German panel believe NATO can deter the Russians. More than half believe NATO can defend Europe and the West. Such evidence of positive Atlantic sentiment is abundant in any selection of German data from the past years of TEEPS surveying.

However, as a counterpoint, it is also possible to show the panel's assent to certain European solutions for security problems. For example, about three quarters in the last two surveys continue to favor EDC. One also finds evidence of pro-European attitudes on problems other than security. These have been discussed in previous chapters in the context of the widespread rejection of nationalism by the German panels. However, as has been shown, the European interest is subordinated to the Atlantic interest when the panel is forced to choose. This pattern is so pronounced throughout the years that it would be quite easy to conclude that this German panel is an Atlantic panel. Yet, as we have been at pains to show, any such conclusion would be oversimplified, and possibly misleading, if it failed to take adequate account of continuing German ambivalence. The clear preference is for Euratlantic institutions based squarely on the Euramerican system of relationships.

Table 9.13 reports recent developments on another matter of tension that is of special concern to the German panel. The dilemma of double exposure to East and West intensifies a division in the panel on the question of German reunification. In the 1959 and 1961 surveys, the pendulum of opinion oscillated rather markedly from a bare majority for reunification to a bare majority for NATO. In 1965, when the question was slightly rephrased to make the option for reunification explicitly exclude NATO membership, the panel divided sharply into two nearly equal groups — with no majority for either option.

TABLE 9.13. GERMAN PREFERENCES ON A DIVIDED GERMANY INSIDE NATO OR A REUNIFIED GERMANY OUTSIDE NATO

1959) Is it better to keep Western Germany in NATO or to have a neu-
1961) tral united Germany?

1965 Do you prefer a divided Germany inside NATO or a reunified Germany outside NATO?

	1959	1961	1965
West Germany in NATO	37%	53%	41%
Reunified Neutral Germany Outside NATO	50	34	46
DK	13	13	13

The tension caused by this unresolved issue indicates that German Atlanticism is to be viewed somewhat differently from the consistent British commitment to NATO. While the British have no enunciated goals which are incompatible with the Atlantic connection, the West Germans are not in the same situation. This does not mean that the German panel is prepared to resolve the issue of reunification in either direction at present. When asked if too little or too much stress is put on reunification, the panel replied: too little, 36 per cent; enough, 46 per cent; too much, 13 per cent; DK, 5 per cent. Though only a minority of 36 per cent would like to push the reunification issue further at the present time, the existence of this group bears mention as one of the qualifiers in the Atlantic commitment of the German panel.

Still another qualifier, which appears for the first time in the most recent survey, is the perception of Germany's European ties as a possible counterpoise to its dependence on the United States. Recalling the British data, Europa did not have any significant support as a political device to deal with the Americans. Until 1965, there was no trace of this in the German data either. However, there has been a growth in the feeling that one key relationship can be used to reduce undesirable elements in the other. In 1961, only 23 per cent thought Europa a counterpoise to the United States. By 1965, the German panel was evenly divided (40–40 per cent) on the use of its European connections vis-à-vis the Atlantic relationship. While this is a complex issue, which may have more bearing on Franco-German than on Euramerican relations, it is a recent shift that may be indicative of future tendencies.

Thus, we find that two persistent German interests — reunification and the European Community — appear in 1965, for the first time, to be operating upon the otherwise highly stable and pronounced Atlantic orientation of the German panel. No conclusions should be reached on the basis of a few indicators when the great bulk of evidence still suggests that West Germany is, in the last analysis, a Euratlantic nation. We stress only that the German situation is more complex than the British; their Atlanticism must be viewed as a commitment embedded in the context of Germany's double exposure.

Some possible implications of the three major European nations having three divergent orientations may be suggested. If the French alone give Europa top priority and the Euratlantic panels in Britain and Germany do not follow the French lead, then especially in the context of Franco-American competition, the rapid progress of European integration in the near future becomes problematical. Two important factors, however, do weigh heavily in favor of continued European integration. First, none of the three big nations is in any sense opposed to Europa; underlying their divergent emphases and priorities is a very substantial area of consensus. Second, there now exists at Brussels an institutional apparatus with considerable power to act transnationally in the economic field and with a demonstrated capacity to mobilize political support by member-nations when needed. In the next two chapters, we deal with these factors in turn.

Part D: Perspectives

Introduction

Here we arrive at our interpretations and conclusions from the TEEPS data previously presented. We conclude that the European elites still face attitudinal problems imposed upon them by the world in which they live as described in Part A. They have not yet, as shown in Part B, reached complete agreement on the questions of protection, prosperity, and prestige which they perceive as their own key issues. Yet, as Part C reveals, they are increasingly dominated by common constraints and pluralist perspectives.

The perspectives we see as governing the attitudinal history of the TEEPS decade are those that have produced the transition from ideology to pragmatism. Much of this, which we interpret in Chapter Ten, is brought into sharp focus in Chapter Eleven. There we introduce the special version of pragmatic and pluralistic thinking that is characteristic of those transnational elites at Brussels whom we call the "Eurocrats." Though they have, as yet, only limited power over the nations, it is our conclusion that their commitment to Europa — and perforce to Euratlantica — will prevail.

This leads to our presentation of the "Euratlantic prospects" in Chapter Twelve. We are convinced that the majority of TEEPS elites, including many of the Gaullists, now believe that intimate interaction between Europa and America is necessary for their own welfare — hence that the Euramerican system is inevitable. Only on this basis, if the convergent consensus of our panelists over the TEEPS decade is a reliable guide, can there be built the widely desired institutions of Euratlantica.

239

CHAPTER TEN

The New Pragmatism:
Consensus in Diversity

WE have surveyed ten years of attitudinal history. The decade began in the context of Europe's loss of its dominant position in world power and the decline of European nations from primacy to dependency — on America and on each other. It ended in the context of a resurgent Europe, strong and prosperous, but in which nations were still linked to transnational institutions for their protection and prosperity. During the decade, the elites were called upon to make choices involving collective rather than national approaches to problem solving. With surprising willingness, they consistently opted for transnational solutions.

Indeed, there has been a convergent consensus in Europe over the last decade that national options are not viable and that transnational choices are the only realistic alternatives. We have witnessed the passing of nationalism in the form familiar to previous generations and even to the early years of the generations now in charge. In the major areas of investigation — protection, prosperity, and prestige — we have found the elites ready to subordinate (or subsume) national alternatives in favor of collective initiatives and institutions.

A closely related process is shown in our data as the passing of traditional ideologies, socialist as well as nationalist. We do not assert that the basic ideas of nationalism and socialism are dead. We assert, rather, the more interesting and complex idea that they have "interpenetrated" each other. In so doing, they have undermined their coherence as separate and hostile ideologies. The effect on living Europeans has been to divide the partisan cohorts, Left

241

and Right, that traditionally were formed around these cohesive ideologies. As we have seen, much of the Right now accepts the basic commitment to collective social welfare and much of the Left now accepts the commitment to collective military security. Under these conditions, it makes little sense — or much less sense than in earlier times — to speak of Left *versus* Right, Socialist *versus* Nationalist, at all. The process of "restriction by partial incorporation" has subverted the traditional commitments of the ideological partisans and has obliged them to seek a new pragmatic consensus.

These are the themes of this book, and as we enter into this concluding set of chapters, the first thing we want to explore and explain is the deep transformation of thoughtways among the European elites: from *idea* to *pragma*. The collapse of traditional ideologies has made the European elites into pragmatists. They have tried to face the realities of their postwar situation in ways that work. This new pragmatic perspective has made the European elites more pluralist as well: They can now work more effectively with each other on problems of common interest even when they do not share a common ideology that tells them how to talk about these problems.

This is what we call "the new pragmatism." Wedded to pluralism, it represents a fundamental transformation of thoughtways among the European elites. It is this fundamental transformation of thoughtways — what we are calling the shift from idea to pragma — that explains their convergent consensus on the key issues. A special feature of the consensus, beyond its great numerical strength, is its impact upon those who deviate from it. There are relatively few in any panel who are systematically opposed to the basic ideas of Europa or Atlantica. Deviation tends to take the form of sporadic and erratic dissent on particular points rather than consistent and consecutive opposition. Although the dissidents appear to be relatively ideological in their views, they have not been able to unify their opposition around one or more polar ideas.

Accordingly, the pragmatic consensus prevails not only by its own numerical strength but also by the quantitative and qualitative weakness of its opponents. That the consensus is organized in pragmatic rather than ideological terms thus appears to add strength to its operation upon the attitudes of the European elites. The underlying sentiment is that European integration/Euratlantic cooperation based on the Euramerican system of relations are historically "right" — in the sense that they represent the most rational options open to Europeans in the historical conditions of the postwar world. Under these conditions, ideologizing is irrelevant and moralizing may even be harmful. The pragmatic idea is to recognize what must be done, once such basic values as protection, prosperity, and prestige are assumed, and then do it.

This pragmatic transformation of postwar thinking among the European elites shows itself in two important findings of our decade-long study. One finding is that pragmatism has supplanted ideology as the way of organizing attitudes and opinions. Instead of relying upon an ideologically codified set of propositions about the "nature" of the historical process and the deviation of opinions from this image of "historical necessity," the European elites now tend to proceed in a pragmatic way: analyze the historical conditions, project the policy alternatives, and choose the option best calculated to maximize one's values. The pragmatic transformation has had a liberating effect on the European elites by removing the ideological blinders they have worn at least since the French Revolution.

The other closely related finding is that the new pragmatism has enabled our TEEPS panels to differentiate between what is "feasible" and what is "desirable." Ideological thoughtways focus almost exclusively on what is "desirable"; pragmatic thoughtways, which assume that the collective values of a developed modern society are established, focus on what is "feasible" — what can be done to maximize those values. Throughout the TEEPS decade, we asked many questions about what was desirable and what was feasible for contemporary Europe. The panels responded, increasingly, in the pragmatic mode.

Their responses turned our attention to protection, prosperity, and prestige as the key issues that emerged from their analysis of the historical conditions that confronted them. Their responses revealed that Europa and Atlantica contained the preferred solutions to their common problems. Their responses showed that their conceptions of the "desirable" were nearly unanimous — that their societal values could be taken for granted — and that the outcome for Europe hung upon their decisions about what was "feasible."

Errors were made: (1) The same French parliament that rejected EDC on August 31, 1954, ratified WEU in a long New Year's Eve session on December 31, 1954. Thereby France failed and Germany won. As a member of NATO, Germany became a strong participant in Atlantica and the Euramerican system. (2) General De Gaulle sought to reclaim from Europa and Atlantica (in short, from the Euramerican system) the key issue of prestige by asserting a *national* base for protection (via the *force de frappe*) and for prosperity (via the gold-based attack on the dollar), a heroic individual quest which has failed. (3) President Kennedy said that participants in the Euratlantic and Euramerican systems were "equal partners," another heroic individual quest, in response to De Gaulle, which failed the moment France turned down both MLF and ANF. (4) The British have been rejected twice by De Gaulle from membership in EC. This error, related to the General's ideological position on *national* posture, will not survive De Gaulle.

What we are saying, in short, is that De Gaulle and the "Gaullists" in all of our countries have failed. They have failed because they tried to turn the overwhelming tide of converging consensus among the European elites who believe Europa and Atlantica to be their best option — and, moreover, believe that the Euratlantic institutions must be based on a "feasible" Euramerican system of relations. They do not believe that they are "equal partners" or "national powers" because they recognize that they need America even more than America needs them.

Pragmatic beliefs such as these tend to be pluralist as well. They incorporate dissidents as well as adherents. The prevailing consensus in our panels led us to the interpretation that the European elites have become pragmatic pluralists. The evidence already presented documents this conclusion: In technical jargon, "marginals dominate partials." What this means in plain language is that the prevailing consensus is so strong that few can rally against it. The consensual distribution of responses for every panel is so strong that cross-tabulational analysis only emphasizes, with minor deviations, the few and feeble voices that are raised against it. We turn now, mindful of these dissident voices, to the stronger consensual views.

Though national patterns vary, one belief all elites have held in common is that they cannot protect themselves by themselves. There has been a dominant consensus within and among countries in favor of collective action via Atlantica, which has not been seriously challenged by any alternative plan for protection. European defense systems such as EDC have achieved much favor, and national capacities have some acceptance in Britain and France. But such ideas of national, regional, or collective world security through the United Nations have usually not been construed as competitive with the Atlantic alliance based on the American guarantee. While these other forms may be desirable, none are so feasible as NATO; accordingly, the pragmatic European elites converge on the Euratlantic solution.

In the areas of prosperity, a similar picture emerges. There is a consensus that the European nation-state can guarantee neither protection nor prosperity. Throughout the decade, and peaking in 1959, the sentiment for European collective economic institutions has been widespread. Throughout the decade, with measures changing as different issues become salient, the elite responded with positive evaluations to multiple forms of transnational behavior. Ultimate solutions did not stand in the path of interior measures. The desire for, and the circumstances of, prosperity were seen to require collective action. Regional preferences varied. While Atlantic forms at the end of the decade were fully competitive with European options in the protection area, they were not so well established in the area of prosperity. Only the Germans express a strong consensual desire to extend the institutions for prosperity and protection together, making the Atlantic alliance an Atlantic Community. While the early years of the decade found this formulation of interest among all panels, in recent years the French largely and the British partially have turned to Europa as the source of future prosperity. Despite these national differences, however, the European consensus steadily has favored transnational forms for economic expansion — and the increasing approval of Europa has not, we have seen, entailed an increasing disapproval of Atlantica. Quite the contrary.

The ranking of the nations by the elites further confirmed that they evaluated their own and neighboring nations as significantly inferior, in power and wealth, to the superpowers now and in the long-term future. Indeed, the long-term future of Europe was diffuse and uncertain for the elites. They found their nations were difficult to place in the hierarchy of world powers. Even among those who did offer a ranking, no European nation achieved a place among the top three powers, nor was there any clear consensus on the relative ranks of the European nations on the lower rungs of the ladder.

This downgrading of their nations does not signify the end of nationalism. Nationalism is a much more complicated phenomenon than the ranking of one's own nation relative to others. But these responses do provide additional evidence that nationalism has been transformed among the European elites — and why. Their sense of relative weakness and dependency has led the elites to endorse so much transnational behavior that the compelling power of nationalism in the traditional sense is truly obsolescent among most and obsolete among many. In all countries in all years, our panels so consistently and in so many fields gave priority to transnational activity and responsibility that nationalism itself has been deeply reshaped. The idea of national honor is regarded by many of the elite as a bad joke and the idea of national interest is regarded by most as a collective responsibility.

While some of the elite may still test an idea by the measure of its contribution to national advancement, the test is nearly always made in a context which forces the transposition of national interest into some type of cooperative action with others. What is good for a nation in this decade most often turns out to be some new form of transnational agreement and action. This is a direct consequence, we submit, of the new consensus among Europeans that their own nation cannot "go it alone" on the key issues of national life.

So, while national interest remains for some panelists a test of the worth of international plans, operationally the elite is committed to transnational solutions. Indeed, the most extreme form of nationalism encountered in the decade has been the quest for solutions of national problems designed to fit within the transnational context. British nuclear weapons and the French *force de frappe* were extreme forms of national assertion of this type. Yet, even if these weapons systems were intended to enhance the nation's place in the sun, they clearly were not accepted by the elites as replacing the Euratlantic system of NATO based on the American guarantee. If one recalls the large number of respondents saying yes to the necessity of the American guarantee, then it is certain that national weapons systems are not serious competitors in the minds of the elite. At most, national capacities are seen as part of the new collective security system; they are regarded as compatible, not divisive, in the Euratlantic framework. Those who do see them as divisive in all countries, including France, tend to oppose them.

The converging consensus in Europe, which replaced the nation with the transnational collective as the central force to meet the challenges of the second postwar decade, did not result in uniform priorities throughout the national panels. For while classic nationalism is an outmoded form of thought, which no longer helps leaders choose among alternatives, national differences have not disappeared. But, as we have seen, national differences are not the same as nationalist feelings. The former are negotiable items in a collective bargaining framework; the latter are not subject to bargaining. The panels have consistent and positive attitudes toward the key transnational relations which they must make in a world where collaboration is necessary. All elites agree that they cannot stand alone; they disagree only in their choice of the partners — and their hierarchic relations to each other — with whom they would like to make their common stand.

For the British, there has been a persistent and profound preference for an Atlantic connection. When put to the forced choice — an unpleasant choice which many British, irrespective of De Gaulle, think is a false choice — they respond without ambiguity to a preference for the American and Atlantic connection. The French choice is consistently European. The French want both European and Atlantic options, but they are readily prepared to manifest their European orientation by giving priority to European forms of international institution building. Only the committed Gaullists, however, have carried this to the point of competing with Euratlantica and Euramerica. Most Frenchmen reject the competition by avoiding the Gaullist alternatives and by turning, perhaps transitorily, to the DK position. It seems clear that many French respondents, in respect to their extraordinary leader, prefer to wait for the "post-De Gaulle" period to state their mind.

For the Germans, the choice is indeed difficult. They are largely European in their desires; but when pressed, they make the same Atlantic choice as the British. However, for the Germans to choose the Atlantic option as against the European is especially difficult because the European option is so highly favored in its own right. The ambivalence that characterizes the German panel is cleared up only in the situation of a forced choice. What this reveals, at bottom, is that the Germans give priority to the Euramerican connection for themselves, will go along with the Euratlantic concepts as long as they are backed by the United States, but also want to achieve "normalcy" with France and their other European neighbors.

In sum, we are dealing with a phenomenon that exhibits variations by national panels, but which nonetheless is underlined by a deep consensus on the issues of the decade. All Europeans agree on the necessity of transnational options for the achievement of protection and prosperity. They all agree that the role of America is primary. They all have been willing to accept a continuation of the dominance of Atlantic forms in the security arena; only recently has some weakening of this posture begun to be manifest. But the weakening does not take the form of questioning the principle of collective security. It seeks, rather, a position within the alliance that is more comfortable for the French and Germans. Reform of the arrangements, not a scrapping of the basic consensus which served the elites well for the last two decades, is among their attitudinal alternatives. The French are most serious about challenging the current consensus, but they have not attitudinally gone as far as upsetting their fundamental commitment to Euratlantica based on Euramerica.

This consensus does not play quite the same role in economic affairs as it does in security affairs. Here the alternatives have been perceived in frames much more closely related to European integration. The consensus calling for closer economic ties among the Europeans is stable and shared by all elites. While there are important national differences in what each panel seeks from economic integration, there is strong agreement on the necessity and desirability of such integration. Prosperity can only be assured in a transnational context, according to all of the national elites; and in all of the years of surveying, their responses have attested to the desire to seek prosperity in common. Even here, despite De Gaulle's public pronouncements, there has been only marginal opposition to the Euramerican system — as expressed in anxiety over the "technological gap," which we shall examine more closely in Chapter Twelve. The consensus has remained intact, indeed has strengthened, over the "desirability and feasibility" of such Euratlantic economic institutions as GATT, the Club of Ten, and the use of the international monetary system (IMF *et seq.*) as a stabilizer of economic life.*

* Note: The importance of this pragmatic view was made clear when the Gaullist regime, under the severe attack of the May–June "strikes" of 1968 was obliged to request (and received) aid from the international monetary system.

A. THE NEW EUROPEAN PRAGMATISM AND CONSENSUS

This summary provides only one test of our conclusion that the elites have consistently stated their preferences in compatible and consensual terms. The conclusion asserts that the European elites, in losing their place at the center of world power, also lost their traditional guidelines relevant to making up their minds about policy options that would shape their future. In the place of ideologizing and moralizing, they have turned pragmatic. Like the American Model they now emulate, they want to know, in terms of their human and societal values, "what works." In reaching for this new view of their own human relations in developed modern society, the Europeans have discovered that replacing ideology with pragmatism confers upon them new freedoms. They are free to say yes; and within limits but without wars, no. They are free to take opportunities as they are offered; and within limits but without destructive competition, to reject them. They are no longer obliged to structure their preference systems very rigidly, and they see alternatives as compatible whenever possible. They continue to think of what is desirable as they focus on what is feasible. That so deep a transformation of thoughtways among the European elites has produced occasional oscillation is a natural outcome for elites faced with "too many choices."

Throughout the decade of data gathering, we analyzed the results in search of critical ideas that would make distinctions among the elites. Our effort was directed toward finding the dominant "logic" chosen by major groups of elite members. We sought to delineate a computerized logic tree, whose branches were the key ideas that made distinctions among men. Often we tried sociological distinctions as the source of attitudinal distinctions. The results were not always promising in a homogeneous group such as a European elite, among whom almost everyone had a university background and high media exposure. Sometimes, however, nuances were discovered. None served the purpose of a simple and elegant statement, by generation or occupation or communications behavior, which could make profound and broad coverage of our data. It would be difficult for sociological distinctions to dominate when, for example, we see the results of a special survey of French businessmen. It has been widely claimed that business, heavily protectionist in general and particularly sensitive to disturbances of its main overseas markets in the French Union, was generally opposed to European economic integration. Fear of higher German productivity and of lower Italian prices were alleged to motivate a systematic business opposition to European projects. Our data indicate that among the most influential persons in the business sector, their top corporate spokesmen, this was not the case.

On all questions calling for judgment by the French business elite of the consequences of European unification, the predominant sentiment expressed was pro-European. When asked, "Would the economic integration of Europe be favorable to the French economy?" 417 respondents said yes, 230 said no. Asked "What consequences would European integration have on relations between France and the French Union?" 297 checked favorable, 199 unfavorable. (On this question about one out of three respondents had no opinion.) And the question requesting a net judgment "for" each European institution gathered between 65 per cent and 75 per cent positive responses. This includes the "no opinion" responses.[1]

With such a dominating sense of collectivity, the sociological distinctions based on occupation do not stand much chance of forming logic trees. Attitudinal distinctions were more productive of logic trees. We sought to investigate different types of respondents. We chose distinctions in responses to questions which should have been relevant if our elites were still in the grip of divisive ideologies of Left *versus* Right, or Nationalism *versus* Socialism, or Deterrence *versus* Disarmament. We sought these basic distinctions; and we also broadened these dichotomies into trichotomies, which would divide the elite into groups consisting of opposition or footdraggers to the central consensus. Our analytical job was to try to break the consensus that emerged from our trend report. It proved to be difficult. We searched the data with concepts of great historical importance to the European elite. We tried our hypotheses by free-search techniques reported in the Annexes.* Our data were

---

* The numerical taxonomy given in the Annex demonstrates, with sophisticated methodology, essentially the same conclusions as the analyses we report here: Few respondents separate themselves from the main clusters of consensual ideas in the arena of protection and prosperity.

In all three countries of the 1965 survey, we selected important questions dealing with the key issues. In each of the issue areas, we searched for patterns

shown to have very different structural logic than the alleged history of traditional European political attitudes would lead us to expect. The time-honored political divisions of Left and Right, Nationalist and Socialist, worked as cognitive or evaluative aids for only a very few of our panelists. The new dominant pragmatic consensus pervaded all efforts to defeat it time and time again. The deviants had no ideological, or other, rallying point around which to challenge the pragmatic consensus coherently.

As a result, we define consensus by a pattern in which the marginal distributions dictate the cross-tabulations. Technically this definition is often satisfied when we isolate attitudinal dichotomies. That is, the consensus is so great on how to achieve protection, prosperity, and prestige that even the opponents of the dominant mode do not maintain their opposition systematically. They are usually swept into the force of the consensus at some critical point, and the distinctive character of their opposition is lost.

In fact, the consensus in Europe is so profound on the issues of protection, prosperity, and prestige that supporters for these dominant positions include many strange bedfellows. Under these conditions, where cleavages are neither deep nor lasting, a man can say yes to one idea, accept alternative opportunities when presented, and define different preferences for the interim and ultimate as compatible rather than competing. In a pragmatic attitudinal environment, pluralism is the natural concomitant.

B. FROM PRAGMATISM TO CONSENSUS

As the pragmatic mode of thought spread among the European elites, it built a consensual base of attitudes among them as well. To illustrate the force of the elite consensus in Europe, we examined

---

of agreement by clustering together those respondents who were more like each other than they were like the total group. A new computer program was used to make taxonomies to see how effectively we could classify subgroups on political dimensions such as nationalism, Europeanism, Atlanticism, or other labels. In spite of a weighting procedure which specifically de-emphasized those questions on which there was nearly total agreement, we found very few respondents in very few groups who differentiated themselves significantly from the dominant cluster. In relatively short order, the programmed computer instructions found that agreement among the respondents was greater than disagreement. The consensual ideas, more often than not, attracted the deviants from their cluster of like-minded respondents to the prevailing consensus that we have summarized so far in this chapter.

some major divisions of opinion that might account for deviant attitudinal coalitions on the American guarantee. Traditionally, in Europe, political parties are believed to be the custodians of opinion among their adherents. In the years of our surveying, we have found this to be the case only rarely, and almost never do party divisions account for attitudes on collective security within the Atlantic framework. We find instead that the overall attitudinal consensus is reflected within the various subgroupings. There are occasional variations of the pattern and occasional French contradiction of the pattern. But generally, on the security range of issues, the preference for collective security in the Atlantic framework dominates all distinctions of nation and party.

In Table 10.1, the irrelevance of party identification for attitudes on security matters is manifest. The table gives the results of the 1965 survey, which confirm the findings of earlier years. We have further simplified the table by presenting only the two major parties

TABLE 10.1. PARTY DIVISIONS AND SECURITY CONSENSUS (1965)*

	Britain		France			Germany	
	Labour	Conservative	Left	Center	Right	SPD	CDU
US Guarantee Continues	75%	82%	78%	90%	59%	98%	94%
		(81)†	(74)			(92)	
NATO Deters	71	79	63	70	73	79	82
		(76)	(62)			(77)	
NATO/US Offer Most Security‡	77	84	76	100	77	67	76
		(81)	(81)			(73)	

* The n for party affiliates varies from question to question but remains approximately: Labour 119, Conservative 96; Left 34, Center 10, Right 22; and SPD 75, CDU 121.

† The number in parentheses is the marginal expressed as a percentage of the total panel response to the option and is offered to show that the technical definition of consensus, whereby the parts share the direction of the whole, is met.

‡ In Britain, the question was designed to compare a national option with NATO and the American guarantee. We aggregate the latter two responses as a measure of commitment to an Atlantic-based security system. In France, we also aggregated, but the Frenchmen were offered another alternative, a Franco–German connection. No party affiliates chose that option. In Germany, the question was not asked in a competitive framework. We asked for a measure of how significant NATO was for German security. The strongest option ("decisive") is included here.

in Britain and Germany and an aggregated trichotomy for the multiple French parties.

Party identification thus is not of divisive consequence for the Atlantic-centered consensus on European protection. Our technical definition of consensus is met. The total response (in parentheses) dictates the response of the partials. The basic beliefs on security override party considerations. To be sure, party considerations become relevant as we move further away from these basic consensual beliefs. In the attitudinal periphery we find that French leftists tend to disagree with French rightists on the military significance of the *force de frappe,* although not on its political advantage for France.

We tested the consensus on dimensions other than party with similar results. For example, we traced through the debate, in the middle years of our survey, about whether European security would best be found in armament or disarmament. In Chapter Four, the results of that debate in terms of elite attitudes were reported. Here we report, in Table 10.2, what difference a preference for armament or disarmament means in terms of support for the Atlantic-based security system. We can compare the results only for Britain and France, because the German line of questioning was not parallel on this item.*

These distributions indicate that even those who give priority to disarmament agree to the basic premises of the Atlantic-oriented security system. Only those who seek unilateral disarmament, the most divided group, deviate from this consensual pattern — and then only in Britain where a political movement grew up around the unilateralist idea. On most measures, for most respondents, the collective consensus is firm. It is weaker in France, as is the overall response reported in Chapter Four, but it is nonetheless evident. While the disarmers have a low score on two measures, it reflects a general French low score rather than the divisiveness of the disarmament priority. The pluralities follow the dominant direction. Even differing priorities as profound as fundamental approaches to

* The attitudinal groups are defined by their priority to disarmament over deterrence, and an acceptance or rejection of unilateral nuclear disarmament. The Germans did not have the option to dispose of nuclear weapons unilaterally and therefore were excluded. The small n in Britain and France is due to "filtering" the full panel through a prior battery of test questions to achieve "pure" subgroups.

TABLE 10.2. DISARMAMENT PRIORITY AND SECURITY CONSENSUS
(1961)

	Britain			France		
	Deter	Disarm	Unilateral Nuclear Disarmament	Deter	Disarm	Unilateral Nuclear Disarmament
American Guarantee Will Continue	92%	95%	75%	81%	53%	65%
		(89)*			(68)	
NATO Deterrent Can Deter USSR	79	74	45	55	43	41
		(67)			(45)	
Integrate National Forces with NATO	79	68	32	52	43	47
		(61)			(49)	
Prefer Germany in NATO to Reunited and Neutral Germany	88	67	40	87	53	53
		(69)			(69)	

* See corresponding note to Table 10.1.

dealing with the Soviet Union fail to undermine the consensus that
favors an Atlantic security system.

In both of the preceding tests searching for those who divide the
consensus, it is clear that adherence to NATO is generally regarded
as necessary and desirable for Europe. Neither leftist ideology nor
disarmament predilections change this basic fact. We also note that
this commitment has been least fully accepted by the French.
Special analysis was done to discover if French deviation is based
on systematic nonconsensual strategic thinking or attachment to
pragmatic opportunities. Table 10.3 indicates that the special
French perspective is more clearly related to their acute interest in
pragmatic opportunities they consider compatible with their basic
interest in Atlantic security.

TABLE 10.3. FRENCH OPINION ON THE AMERICAN GUARANTEE AND
ALLIANCE SUPPORT (1965)

	Guarantee Good	Guarantee Doubtful
NATO is now strong enough to deter the Russians for the next 5 years:		
Yes	65%	72%
No	20	17
DK	15	11
France should take an independent position in the US–USSR conflict:		
Yes	29	27
No	60	53
DK	11	20
At expiration of NATO Treaty in 1969, France should:		
Leave NATO	1	—
Stay if Reorganized	57	52
Stay Even if Not Reorganized	38	38
DK	4	10
Support for a larger European share in the costs of Western defense:		
Yes	31	26
No	45	53
DK	24	21

We divided the French panel into two groups: One affirmed the credibility of the American guarantee ($n = 85$), and the other small group ($n = 21$) expressed doubts. Thus, we broke the dominant consensus in two, although the deviationists were necessarily small in number. The curious fact to be reported is that, even when subgroups are constructed on opposite poles, the opposition is not consistent on relevant elements of the consensus. While the groups differ from each other on several issues, they are similar in a rather critical array of measures testing alliance support.

In these four questions, three demonstrating support and the last demonstrating nonsupport, there is no significant difference between the doubters and the believers in the American guarantee. The French panel is prepared to accept the guarantee, but not to weight it heavily against other preferred factors in the strategic equation. Indeed, as the last response indicates, even the believers in the guarantee are no more willing to support it financially than the doubters. Pragmatism is evident in the acceptance of varied opportunities and the rejection of exclusive choices among these opportunities. Thus, neither party, nor priority, nor credibility affects the basic consensus of the Atlantic alliance.

There are many other cases in which the collective consensus in favor of an Atlantic system of protection for Europe dominates the divisions between subgroups on other, even closely related, issues. This can be inferred from the high degree of support for an Atlantic system demonstrated in Chapter Four and can readily be seen in the data presented here. Furthermore, this commitment to collective security and a pragmatic attitude to all key issues pervade elite evaluations of alternative solutions for keeping Europe prosperous. The key issue of prosperity is, indeed, a remarkable indicator of the new pragmatism among the European elites.

Political parties have traditionally disputed their relative capacity to bring prosperity to their citizens. In recent years, the party lines on programs designed to carry out the promise of prosperity have become increasingly blurred. In political behavior, we have witnessed a convergence of programs among holders of power in all advanced countries. In political attitudes, we can now report a similar consensus on defining the international relations of prosperity. Table 10.4 summarizes data from all countries in the 1965 survey on key issues of the new prosperity. Note that the marginals (total distributions) are reflected even within the partials (party divisions).

This pattern, where the dominant groups within parties reflect the national position, meets our technical definition of consensus. Where there are differences of degree, it is even more striking that divisions of opinion within the parties go in the same direction as divisions within the national panels.

If the opposition is only *less for* something than the party in power, rather than against it, we have a significant consensus and the basis of pluralist participation. We see that political parties do not contest the consensus that the nation-state is obsolete or that the growth of European integration cannot be halted, for it has passed the point of no return. Furthermore, the geographic limits of the nations are satisfactory at present for all except the Germans, but there is no division by party in any case. That the route to prosperity is transnational is an uncontested fact by the majority of all parties.

TABLE 10.4. PROSPERITY AND PARTY

	Britain		France			Germany	
	Labour	Con- ser- vative	Left	Center	Right	SPD	CDU
The Nation– State Is Obsolete	66%	47% (55)°	61% (66)	68%	50%	72% (73)	78%
EEC Has Reached Point of No Return	68	61 (66)	75 (67)	78	50	68 (67)	75
Should Not Create Larger Economic Community	48	55 (53)	55 (51)	44	60	21 (28)	32

° The number in parentheses is the marginal expressed as a percentage of the total panel response to the option.

We note, however, that while the French Right goes along with the national patterns it deviates most from the national norms. We therefore present some additional information on French nationalism gathered from the middle years of the survey. This exhibits the severe limits of contemporary nationalism, even among the subgroups of Frenchmen who are clearly more nationalist than the general panel.

In 1961, we identified some of the more nationalistic Frenchmen by taking those thirty-one people who preferred a confederal Europe of sovereign states (Euronationalism) to a federal United States of Europe. Among these thirty-one respondents that chose the weaker form of transnationalism, there was still near-unanimity on the general value of the European idea. Some 90 per cent of them believed that the economic community would effectively develop the economic potential of Europe, and fully 61 per cent were willing to sacrifice French Community (ex-colonial) interests to promote European interests. Thus, even the minimal transnationalists among Frenchmen agree to seek prosperity in the context of European integration.

In 1956–1959 we had made a stronger test of nationalism, using more political issues to identify nationalists. We selected a group of thirty-seven Frenchmen who expressed strong nationalist views on two burning issues: (1) that France should not give up its sovereignty in Algeria; and (2) that France was not an aggressor in the Suez invasion of 1956. These two attitudinal attributes marked off the extreme nationalists from other panel members. When we asked their opinions about European organizations, the distribution of affirmatives was dramatic for such a politically nationalist group. Table 10.5 indicates their support for economic transnationalism;

TABLE 10.5. POLITICAL NATIONALISTS AND THE ACCEPTANCE OF ECONOMIC TRANSNATIONALISM IN FRANCE

	1956	1959
Favor:		
ECSC	70%	80%
OEEC	68	76
Council of Europe	50	81
Common Market	78*	95

* In 1956, the Common Market was discussed as an extension of ECSC to other areas.

it also indicates the growth of economic transnationalism since the 1956 survey when the same respondents were asked the same questions.

Clearly, political nationalism is of little relevance to the evaluation of transnational economic institutions. Indeed, when we asked these respondents if they considered themselves nationalists, internationalists, or supranationalists, it was evident that these words had little distinctive meaning. Those who called themselves "nationalists" nevertheless made choices in all institutional categories, almost equal numbers choosing transnational affiliation and rejecting it. Indeed, those favoring transnational affiliations are in every case a large, and growing, majority.

Perhaps the reason for the failure of these self-identifying labels to discriminate is the fact that 89 per cent of the "Nationalist" group also felt that French participation in Europe would augment French national power. In a pluralist sense, Europe is a "success" for all attitudinal types. Perhaps these Euronational Frenchmen are merely lifting parochialism to a higher level. Whatever the reason, na-

tionalism is now compatible with transnational beliefs and behavior. The divisive attitudinal gulf between the nationalist and
supranationalist has been crossed so often that Europe's elites no
longer insist on moving in an ideologically determined direction.
They are attitudinally prepared to accept prosperity from whatever
source.

Even followers of De Gaulle, whom we examined in the 1965
survey, did not follow his ideological stance.[2] The pragmatic capacity to accept multiple alternatives of desirable nationalism but
feasible transnationalism, which we see among the self-identified
nationalists, is only part of the general consensus developed by all
elites over the TEEPS decade. This generation of Europe's leaders
want to solve problems, not to create them. If the nation cannot
provide prosperity, then they will accept transnational prosperity
that provides for the nation. If this requires transnational institutions and decision-making authorities, then that too can be accepted. For prosperity, as for protection, the new pragmatic mode
of thinking among Europe's leaders paves the way for a consensus
on collectivity.

In the attitudinal realms of both protection and prosperity we
have thus seen a phenomenon of particular interest to historians of
the second postwar decade in Europe. The elite responded to the
new challenge posed by the postwar world arena by adapting to
"reality" and adopting those alternatives that best promised to solve
its current problems. There was a conspicuous absence of grand
designs and comprehensive ideologies. Instead, the decade has
produced, pragmatically, a collective consensus within which much
variation and attitudinal experimentation was allowed. We have
seen a commitment to some basic ideas of achieving protection and
prosperity in common. While there have been national variations
throughout the decade, the European elites in general have passed
beyond nationalism of the sort which traditionally anchored attitudes to firm foundations and pre-established priorities in handling
their key issues.

Nationalism has transformed itself via transnationalism. Basic
collective formulae for the prosperity and protection of Europe
attract a substantial consensus among Europe's leadership. However, these formulae are not — or at least not yet — a new structured ideology. Thus, while we can report the reshaping of
traditional nationalism, we cannot foresee the final structure of the

new internationalism. Transnational reality is accepted, but it does not yet provide a sufficient attitudinal key for a new systematic set of preferences. We have succeeded only in identifying the diversity of positions subsumed, as of now, under the collective consensus that includes Europa and Atlantica as institutional expressions of the Euramerican nexus in a Euratlantic system.

Beyond the desire to repudiate the nation as a sufficient guarantor of protection and prosperity, there lie differing degrees of desire for European integration and differing degrees of integration that are desired. Ways are still being sought to harmonize varying priorities for Atlantic and European relations. Thus, while we have reported a substantial consensus on the collectivization of some major responsibilities of nationhood, we have also reported national differences showing that this collectivization does not yet restructure all the attitudinal predispositions of the elites. They see many alternatives as compatible. They are eclectic in their thinking. They deny few possibilities.

The attitudinal transformation among Europe's leaders is their new pragmatic capacity to share basic assumptions within a collective consensus. Whereas previous generations of European leaders relied on ideological formulae that created political divisions within national parties and within Europe, the contemporary generation shows a remarkable flexibility to unite with strange bedfellows and overcome ideological divisiveness. The divisions have lost their ideological bitterness, and there is a sufficient pragmatic base for being affirmative to allow these leaders to work with each other.

In the second postwar decade, we have seen that attitudinal pragmatism creates new coalitions where the traditional Left, Right, or Center cannot be located with reasonable accuracy. The new consensus on major issues has reduced ideological radicalism everywhere in Europe. The passing of traditional leftism, and the destruction of most measurable positions on a Left-Right continuum, has been made so clear that it needs no retelling here. Ours is the attitudinal history that occurred during the decade when the SPD in Germany transformed itself into a coalition partner for the SDU; when the Labour Party in Britain took over the implementation of the programs for protection and prosperity that previously had Conservative labels on them; when the French leftists recognized the need to bend to the requirements of Europa and Atlantica. Nor do we imply that the decade saw the diminution only of the Left.

Both poles lost their orientation. Nationalism of the Right was equally diminished by the need to recognize national weakness and appreciate collective strength.

The political history of the decade shares the pragmatic orientation of its attitudinal history. We have witnessed a decade of acceptance of transnational integration. Many different interests have been subsumed under the European consensus. These interests are perceived to be pursued in common, even when they are not common interests. This, too, is a quality of pragmatic leaders. Europe's pragmatism seems complete. Completing Europe is the next task. For this task there is a special group of people, the most pragmatic and pluralist of all, who are entrusted with putting the attitudinal consensus into political practice. These are the high officials of Europe, the Eurocrats, to whom we now turn.

CHAPTER ELEVEN

The View from Brussels

BRUSSELS is the *de facto* capital of Europa. It houses the GHQ of Europa's institutional expression, the three communities EEC, ECSC, and Euratom. The Eurocrats are the high officials of these communities. In 1965, the year we made our survey of the Eurocrats, a decision of principle was taken to merge the three communities under a single executive commission — although its implementation extended to 1967. The integrated Commission presided over an institution styled simply EC — European Community. Accordingly, we refer to the Eurocrats as the EC elite.

A. THE EC ELITE: INTRODUCTION TO THE EUROCRATS

The EC consists of four principal organs — the Commission, the Parliament (EP), the Court of Justice, and the Council of Ministers. Only the last is composed of spokesmen for the national interest of member states. The others are explicitly charged with the initiation, enactment, and adjudication of public law and order on a Community-wide basis. While we interviewed top personnel in all four institutions, this account will be focused on the Commission, the "executive branch" of EC, which is generally considered to be the "motor" of the Community.

In surveying the Commission, we took the top three levels of its officialdom: (1) the Directorate-General, which is responsible for the functioning of the several Departments (*Directions*); (2) the Directors, each of whom supervises the daily operation of a single Department comprising several Divisions; and (3) the heads of important Divisions. By common consent, the officials on these three levels are the "elite" of the Community. We interviewed the Com-

262

missioners themselves but have excluded them from the tables here because they function outside the civil service system of the EC. For the same reason we have excluded the results of our interviews with members of the Council of Ministers, the Court of Justice, and the European Parliament.

Our focus here is on the high officialdom of the Commission, the corps of top civil servants responsible for the functioning of EC. Accordingly, we proceeded by taking a census of all officials on these three levels. We obtained personal interviews or self-administered questionnaires from approximately 200 persons occupying these top posts. This yielded 185 usable responses (divided about equally between interviews and questionnaires), as several responses were discarded because of incompleteness, illegibility, or excessive jocularity. In general, cooperation was good and our census list was very nearly completed. We did not interview the few officials that were absent from Brussels during the survey period; there was only one refusal. Our report, based on these 185 responses, can thus be regarded as a fair approximation of a census of the EC elite.

The EC elite, unlike the TEEPS national panels, is composed entirely of public officials — persons appointed on merit to a salaried post in the high civil service of the Community. Only the Commissioners themselves, excluded from our tabulations, are exempt from typical civil service procedures of selection and promotion. All others, in principle, hold their posts by virtue of a career sequence that includes competitive examinations (written and oral), prior experience, and past performance as evaluated by superiors. They are in a very real sense a "meritocracy."

Many of the Eurocrats are professional civil servants. Among our EC elite, indeed, many have made their careers in the service of the Community, starting from the European Coal and Steel Community (ECSC) in 1952. The majority of the others are professionally qualified and certified lawyers, economists, engineers, statisticians, teachers, and college professors of various disciplines. As compared with the TEEPS panels, the EC elite is distinctive in its occupational specialization to public service, its higher average education, its lower average age, and its multinational composition.

What unifies the EC elite is precisely its professional character as a higher civil service plus an impressive *esprit de corps*. The professional quality of their attitudes exhibits many of the traits attributed by Max Weber to all "bureaucratic-rational" institutions. The extra ingredient in their *esprit de corps* is the pervasive sense that they are *the* public service of the Community and that the Community is *the* builder of Europa. In our year of living with the Eurocrats, we were impressed by their deep sense of identification with the Community. When EC suffered a setback they were irritable or depressed; when EC scored a success they were jubilant.

Their sense of European identity shows consistently in their answers to our questions. We asked: "Do you consider the EC valuable for the West as a whole?" Everybody answered: 96 per cent yes, 2 per cent no, 2 per cent DK. For the Eurocrats, as contrasted with the TEEPS panels, EC value to the West derives from its own strength. Thus they had little difficulty with our forced choices between Europa and Atlantica. To our question whether "EC is more important or less important for Europe than NATO," the responses were 84 per cent more, 8 per cent less, 8 per cent DK.

Not only is EC more important than NATO but, to the Eurocrats, its importance has already been underwritten by history. With the achievement of a common agricultural price policy in 1965, after protracted resistance by the French (principal EC exporters of agricultural products), two of every three Eurocrats affirmed that European integration had reached the "point of no return." Moreover, only 15 per cent believed "that further European integration can still be stopped or seriously delayed." History, as we shall now see, was clearly on the side of *their* Community.

B. EUROPA: PRESENT AND FUTURE

The Eurocrat image of their preferred Europa, present and future, is clear and consensual. We asked them, as we had asked the TEEPS panels, "which idea of political unification is closer to your own preference": only 5 per cent chose "*Europe des patries*" (Gaullist scenario) as compared with a fulsome 93 per cent who opted for "*Etats-Unis d'Europe*" (Monnet scenario). Among the vast majority preferring a united Europe, there was in 1965 considerable discussion of the relative merits of a looser confederal form as against a tighter federal form. Accordingly, we asked: "Which form of political organization would you personally favor for a united Europe?" Better than two of every three Eurocrats opted for federation.

While their preferences are made quite distinct, the EC elite do not turn their wishes into horses as they project the present into the future. Instead, they relate their evaluations to their expectations in the classic "bureaucratic-rational" style. Their projections to the future are made issue by issue and on the weight of the available evidence, and they have access to more comprehensive evidence on most issues than the TEEPS panel. For example, we asked: "Do you believe that the EC will form some sort of political union in the next five years?" A solid majority of 58 per cent said no, despite their overwhelming preference for the most tightly integrated form of political union and their belief that it would be built eventually.

Because their projections are carefully weighed, we note with special interest their reversal of judgment on a pair of questions dealing with future relations between Europa and America. The first asked: "Is the EC likely to produce an independent political counterpoise to the US in the next five years?" A majority of 58 per cent said no. A switch occurred on the second question, however, and a majority of 55 per cent said yes when asked: "Is the EC likely to increase European influence, vis-à-vis the US, in Latin America during the next five years?"

That these are answers weighted to the evidence on the specific issues, rather than any sort of anti-American bias, will become clear as we continue to present the data. It is indicated, as a start, by comparison of EC responses on the same pair of questions relative to the Russians. There was an even split on the likelihood of EC producing "an independent political counterpoise to the USSR" in the next five years: 47 per cent yes, 49 per cent no. But the balance shifts decisively on the second question: "Is the EC likely to increase European influence, vis-à-vis the USSR, in Eastern Europe during the next five years?" Here the response is 73 per cent yes, 23 per cent no.

It is a matter of considerable consequence, which we shall discuss more fully, to comprehend that these projections derive from deep preferences — but that these preferences have been disciplined by empirical evaluations and pragmatic expectations. If the Eurocrats forecast an increase of European influence in Latin America and Eastern Europe, it is not because they envy or emulate the superpowers. On the contrary, they count on the superpowers to maintain the international system in which EC strength has increased and is likely to continue to increase. They are cognizant of the continuous flood of Latin Americans coming to seek closer relations with EC; they are aware that EC has opened two central offices in Latin America; they know the figures that show steadily increasing trade between these continents. By the approved method of policy scientists, their future constructs are derived from careful analysis of past trends and present conditions.

We are therefore impressed when a majority of 73 per cent answers yes to the question: "Would you say that, in general, Western Europe is more influential in world affairs today than it was five years ago?" And we are even more impressed when a majority of 75 per cent answers yes to the follow-up question: "Do you expect Western Europe's influence in world affairs to be greater five years hence than it is today?" The sense that Europe's influence has increased as EC strength increased — and that this process will continue in the proximate future — is not mere parochialism and self-centered pride. It is the core of Eurocrat commitment to the Euramerican system of relations and the basis for their conviction, which we have seen to be 96 per cent affirmative, that EC is "valuable for the West as a whole."

Evidence for this interpretation of the preceding data is given by the EC elite's response to another set of questions earlier in the interview: "Do you foresee any important changes over the next five years in Western Europe's relation with Eastern Europe? with the USSR? with the US?" The proportions saying yes to each of these are given in Table 11.1.

TABLE 11.1.   EUROCRATS' OPINIONS ON DIRECTION OF EUROPA'S FOREIGN RELATIONS (1965)

Increase with Eastern Europe	71%
Increase with the USSR	55
Increase with the US	28

This confirms independently what was suggested by the data just reported. Europa's expectation — based on personal contacts, official negotiations, trade relations, and other evidence — is that its relations with the Eastern countries, already undergoing important changes, are sure to deepen and broaden in the next five years. Associated with this, in the majority view of 55 per cent, as Table 11.1 shows, is the expectation that these changes will become operative in the relations between Europa and Russia itself.

No such association is made between the projected increase of

European influence in Latin America, vis-à-vis the United States, and any change in Europa-America relations. The EC elite perceive the Euramerican system to be built on firmer foundations than its relations with any other nation or region of the world. This will become evident as, in the sections that follow, we review each of Europa's key relations.

1. Europa and America

The Euramerican system reposes, in the first instance, upon the American guarantee to protect Europe. The EC elite are confident that this guarantee is reliable and durable, in significantly larger proportions than the TEEPS panels. For example, 85 per cent affirm that "the US will continue to guarantee the military security of Western Europe" despite its own increasing vulnerability to "direct attack by the new weapons." A majority of 71 per cent deny that "the American guarantee of Europe has become less reliable since the death of President Kennedy." The importance of these evaluations is attested by the belief of 87 per cent that it would be "dangerous for the security of Europe . . . if the American guarantee ceased to operate."

The EC elite's allegiance to the Euramerican system goes well beyond protection to embrace prosperity. Indeed, their principal concern as Europa's high civil service is with economic rather than military matters. Among their proudest accomplishments in this respect was their authorization to negotiate for the Community as a whole in the Kennedy round of tariff reductions at GATT. This was their major access to a participant role in the Euramerican system with regard to the shaping of economic policy. A parochial civil service would tend to safeguard rather jealously such an increment of its prerogatives — which would entail keeping America at a distance so that EC's role as the Community negotiator might be enhanced. In this context, it is all the more striking that the Eurocrats have done no such thing. On the contrary, they show a greater concern with American economic problems, as well as a greater readiness for Euramerican economic integration, than do the TEEPS panels.

The evidence emerges from comparison of EC with TEEPS attitudes to the American "dollar problem." In 1965, a Eurocrat majority of 75 per cent affirmed "that Europe should try to help solve the American dollar problem (deficit payment balances with Europe)." Their more sympathetic and more sophisticated judgment on this issue is shown in their response to the follow-up question: "Which of the following actions designed to solve the American dollar problem do you approve?" Table 11.2 gives their answers.

TABLE 11.2.   EUROCRATS' RESPONSES ON HELPING SOLVE THE AMERICAN DOLLAR PROBLEM (1965)

Reduce US Military Costs in Europe	28%
Reduce US Purchases in Europe	12
Reduce US Investment in Europe	56
Reduce US Tourism in Europe	11
Increase European Purchases in US	55
Increase European Investment in US	60
Increase European Tourism in US	65
Abandon Dollar in Favor of Gold Standard	22

Several features are noteworthy in this distribution, especially by comparison with the TEEPS responses. In general, the Eurocrats prefer to see European expenditures in America increased rather than American expenditures reduced — in line with recent economic doctrine that increasing the volume of exchanges is more efficacious, for prosperity, than decreasing the volume. They do not, for example, share the readiness of TEEPS panelists to reduce American tourism in Europe. In this sense they take a more analytical as well as a more humane view of Euramerican relations. They would rather increase European tourism in the United States, thereby expanding the volume of human as well as economic exchanges.

The only area in which a majority of Eurocrats approve reducing American outlays on their continent is investment, and this is counterbalanced by even greater approval of increasing European investment in America. Unfortunately, the question of increasing European contributions to the cost of Western defense was inadvertently omitted from the EC questionnaire, so that no direct comparison with TEEPS is possible on this point (although we may record our impression from data presented later in this chapter that EC approval would have been significantly higher). Clearly there is little approval of the Gaullist campaign to abandon the dollar in favor of the gold standard. In addition to the economic analysis underlying this judgment, we shall see later that pervasive lack of confidence in De Gaulle and his policies is an important component.

This high degree of informed interest in Euramerican economic relations, within the general Euramerican system, leads the EC elite to give a strikingly positive response to the idea of economic integration. Our question asked: "Would you favor the formation of an Atlantic economic community that would include the EC, other European countries and the US?" A majority of 57 per cent said yes.

2. *Europa and Britain*

In the response just reported, the question of "other European countries" includes, notably, Britain. The majority approval would seem to include Britain in any project of forming an Atlantic economic community. Indeed, the Eurocrats do approve the inclusion of Britain, but with a differentiated and judicious view of the issues.

Our first pair of questions began by asking: "Do you think the EC can maintain a durable and prosperous growth over the long term without Britain?" A majority of 68 per cent said yes. However, a substantially larger majority of 79 per cent reversed the field and said yes again when the follow-up question asked: "Do you think Britain's membership would be beneficial even if not indispensable?" This extremely strong endorsement of British membership may have its origin in sentiment, but it is buttressed by a relatively high evaluation of Britain's present and future place in the world. As we shall see, EC and TEEPS agree that the ranking nations at the end of the century will be United States first, Russia second, China third. But a significantly higher ballot in EC than in TEEPS (notably France) assigns the fourth place to Britain. The view from Brussels exhibits three components: (1) Britain is ranked higher by the Eurocrats than by the French; (2) Britain is ranked higher than France by the Eurocrats; (3) France is ranked lower by the Eurocrats than by the French panel.

This set of relationships acquires special poignancy in the light of our second pair of questions, which began: "The rejection of British membership in EC was due to French action. Which country would you say was mainly responsible for the failure to agree?" A majority of 55 per cent assigned responsibility to France. But

the picture took on another dimension in the response to our follow-up question: "Which is likely to suffer more by a continuation
of British nonmembership — Britain or EC?" An overwhelming majority of 87 per cent said Britain.

This response bespeaks primarily the strong identification and
sense of confidence in their Community that pervades the Eurocrats. They are appreciative of Britain's potential value to the
Community and they judge that British membership in the EC
would be beneficial to both. But, if the choice were forced, they
believe that the Community can get along without Britain more
easily than Britain can get along without the Community. So the
inference is drawn that if the British want in, they will just have
to reorder their priorities and make the necessary arrangements.
The Community has problems enough of its own with Gaullist
France, a set of issues on which most Eurocrats have very pronounced views.

3. Europa and Gaullist France

We title this section out of deference to the Eurocrats' strong
distinction between *la France éternelle* and its current management under President De Gaulle. Their strong positive affect for
France was shown when the EC elite was asked: "If you had to
live in another country, which would you choose?" France led the
field by a huge plurality of 23 per cent — its nearest competitors
being Switzerland with 14 per cent and the United States with
10 per cent.

But Eurocrat affect toward De Gaulle is considerably less
positive, in consequence of which respondents make a sharp distinction between the country and its present leader. Our initial
question asked: "Do you think that De Gaulle's public statements
represent the sentiments of most Frenchmen?" A majority of 57
per cent said no.

Eurocrat disaffection from De Gaulle, apart from his personal
style, centered upon distrust of his basic policies toward Europa,
Atlantica, and the Euramerican system. Table 11.3 gives the responses to our question concerning the fundamental objective of
De Gaulle.

Thus, two of every three Eurocrats think that De Gaulle aims
to create a separate and independent third force under French
leadership. The troops for such a force could only be European,

TABLE 11.3. EUROCRATS' DEFINITION OF DE GAULLE'S
FUNDAMENTAL OBJECTIVE (1965)

To make a separate "third force" in the world, under French leadership, and *independent* of the East and West blocs?	64%
To make a "third place" for France, equal to that of the US and Britain, *inside* the Western bloc?	22
Other	14

and there is no great disposition among the EC panel to see European strength used in this way. Indeed, the view from Brussels is diametrically opposite. In a later part of our questionnaire, we asked: "*Should* Europe take a 'third force' position? Is Europe *likely* to take a 'third force' position?" Majorities of 61 per cent and 66 per cent — roughly two of every three Eurocrats — said no to these questions. Clearly De Gaulle's fundamental objective, as they understand it, is on a collision course with European objectives.

Not only is De Gaulle's policy undesirable, but also it is unattainable. We asked: "Do you think De Gaulle will achieve his objectives?" A consensual 70 per cent said no (with only 24 per cent saying yes and 6 per cent DK). In the bureaucratic perspective, it is folly to pursue an undesirable objective; to pursue an undesirable objective that is also unattainable is downright inefficient. Among the Eurocrats, there is a widespread feeling that the inefficiency of Gaullist policies fails to build his objectives and succeeds only in hampering the attainment of Community objectives with respect to Atlantica as well as Europa.

The position on Atlantica emerges from the same pair of questions that were put to the TEEPS panels in 1965. Among the Eurocrats, 52 per cent believe "that De Gaulle's policies have weakened American leadership of the alliance." And a larger majority of 61 per cent believe that "the alliance itself has been weakened."

That De Gaulle's policies have entrained France on a course which is nationally "wasteful" (among the nastiest words in the bureaucratic-rational lexicon) is indicated by the responses to an additional pair of questions. A majority of 51 per cent believes "that, after De Gaulle, France will continue to develop the *force de frappe* despite its cost." This will happen, according to a huge 71 per cent of the Eurocrats, even though it will *not* "be worthwhile for France to do this."

During our survey in Brussels, the view was occasionally expressed that De Gaulle had, despite his preferences and policies, produced some effects that were ultimately beneficial to the Community. A current instance was the agreement on common agricultural prices obtained after one of the famous "marathon" meetings between the Commission and the Council of Ministers. The interpretation was that, while De Gaulle insisted on an agreement only to serve French national interests, the effect of his pressure was to speed an agreement that benefited the Community as a whole.

To see how widespread was this view of De Gaulle as a Community benefactor *malgré lui*, we asked: "Would you say that De Gaulle's role, on balance, has been beneficial for Europe — or the contrary?" Evidently the dialectical reasoning had not spread very far: 33 per cent said beneficial, 60 per cent said the contrary. It is equally evident that many of the dialecticians had not fully convinced themselves. We asked: "Would you vote for or against De Gaulle [to be] the first president of Europe?" Results of this straw vote: 17 per cent for; 76 per cent against.

It is appropriate to conclude with a reminder of the positive affect among Eurocrats for *la France éternelle*. Our final question asked: "Do you think that France, after De Gaulle, will be more European or less European?" Only 7 per cent said less European; a whopping 85 per cent said more European.

4. *Europa and the Communist World*

In projecting the future world environment, the EC elite were most widely convinced that the important changes in Europa's external relations over the years ahead would be with the Communist countries of Eastern Europe (71 per cent) and that these would entrain changing relations with the USSR as well (55 per cent).

Another situation in the current world arena, the Sino-Soviet rift, seemed likely to affect Europa-Soviet relations. Accordingly, we asked a series of questions designed to elicit Eurocrat attitudes to this situation. We began: "In your view, is Russia or China more responsible for the present conflict in Sino-Soviet relations?" The responses distributed thus: China, 49 per cent; Russia, 14 per cent;

both, 28 per cent; DK, 9 per cent. China is clearly the guilty party and Russia is relatively innocent except, as suggested by the higher ballot for "both," of inefficient management. (This cardinal sin, in the bureaucratic-rational perspective, is akin to the EC judgment that France was the responsible party vis-à-vis Britain but that it is up to Britain to better manage its affairs.)

We then asked a set of questions to determine the view from Brussels on the character and probable outcome of the conflict. The first question asked: "Do you think the Sino-Soviet conflict is a struggle for leadership of the world Communist movement?" The answer: 74 per cent yes. We next asked: "Do you think the Sino-Soviet conflict will continue until one country clearly wins world leadership, or will a compromise be reached that divides the Communist world between two leaders?" Only a minority of 24 per cent believed that one side would continue the conflict until victory; the majority of 62 per cent estimated that a compromise would divide the Communist world between the two giants. This estimate was related in good bureaucratic-rational fashion to the judgment that continued conflict would not "pay," because neither side would win. This appeared in response to the last question in the set: "If the Sino-Soviet struggle were to continue, who do you think would win world leadership?" The Eurocrats divided evenly: 38 per cent said Russia, 39 per cent said China.

A final pair of questions solicited EC expectations about the Sino-Soviet impact on the rest of the world. We asked: "In any division of the Communist world, do you foresee a tendency for the Communist leadership in colored countries to align with China, and in white countries to align with Russia?" Whereas TEEPS panelists shied away from this question, a fulsome 70 per cent of the Eurocrats said yes. An equal majority said yes to our final question: "Do you think such a tendency would be dangerous for the rest of the world?" As the Eurocrats agree that the Communist giants are this century's ranking nations — Russia second, China third — such a tendency would indeed have potent implications for the international order, particularly for the system of East-West relations.

5. Europa Between East and West

We have seen that a clear majority of Eurocrats turn their face against the idea of a "third force," — two of every three affirming that Europe neither *should* nor *will* follow any such policy. This does not mean acceptance of vassalage to America. On the contrary, an even larger majority of 74 per cent — three of every four Eurocrats — think that "Europe should take a *more independent position within* the alliance." While rejecting neutralist or third force ideas, they approve more independent policy thinking in Europe, so long as it is kept *within* the Euramerican framework.

It is important to note this nuance because it is associated with a somewhat less sanguine view of East-West relations than was exhibited by the TEEPS panels. For example, 58 per cent of the Eurocrats are still sensitive to "the Russian danger to Europe today" — and 39 per cent of these consider it "a long-term problem with which Europe must reckon for many years." An even larger majority of 89 per cent consider China a "danger to Europe today," of whom 85 per cent say it is a long-term danger. As Russia and China are this century's second and third powers in the EC rankings, their importance as sources of long-term danger for Europa is not to be taken lightly.

The Eurocrats take it seriously indeed, as shown by their judgment on where "the most important political problems facing the Western world are most likely to come from." By contrast with the TEEPS panelists, of whom a plurality expected the main problems to come from *within* the West, a clear majority of 51 per cent among the Eurocrats identify the Sino-Soviet bloc as the future source of main problems for the West.

The emphasis is on the Chinese because the Eurocrats believe, with their accustomed rationality, that continued conflict with the West is not a "paying proposition" for the Russians. They see it as a no-gain policy for both sides in the long run. This is shown by their projective response to the question whether "the world balance of power will favor the Communist side or the Western side . . . as the end of the century is approached." Again the Eurocrats split down the middle: 41 per cent said Communist side; 43 per cent said Western side.

The view that continuing the Cold War promises no payoffs to either side runs consistently through the Eurocrat responses. Unlike the TEEPS panelists, they believe that mutual deterrents benefit neither the Communists nor the Atlantic states. The only substantial plurality (better than one of every three) believes that the

nonaligned countries of Afro-Asia will make the greatest gains under these conditions.

The Eurocrats divided evenly on the import of mutual deterrence
upon the Western position in world force; 44 per cent believe that
the Western position will be maintained (of whom 16 per cent say
"improved"); 42 per cent say it will be weakened. Any gains that
might be made by either side are more than counterbalanced, under mutual deterrence, by the risks of escalating a limited conflict.
Better than half of the Eurocrats believe that this is a serious risk
for both sides and also "the most likely way in which a global war
might develop."

There is no animus against the superpowers underlying these
views. On the contrary, the Eurocrats give both superpowers high
marks for their professionalism throughout the postwar decades.
A majority of 51 per cent say "that Soviet leadership of the Eastern
bloc since 1945 has been, on balance, successful"; an equal number approve of Khrushchev's leadership. The United States scores
even higher. A majority of 62 per cent consider "that American
leadership of the Western bloc since 1945 has been, on balance,
successful." No less than 77 per cent of the Eurocrats express approval of Kennedy's leadership.

Eurocrat attitudes toward the East-West conflict may be summarized as follows. They take a relatively benevolent attitude
toward both superpowers, while considering Europe to be firmly
located *within* the Western system. They consider it important
that, within this system, Europa acquire a more independent position than it has had heretofore. They recognize the difficulties
involved in achieving such an objective and take a realistic view
of the problems modern weapons pose for collective security. This
emerges from their views on the relations between Europa and
Atlantica, to which we now turn.

6. *Europa and Atlantica*

Eurocrats are relatively confident in the capacity of NATO to
fulfill its commitments, now and in the visible future. A plurality
of 41 per cent believe "that NATO, as now constituted, is strong
enough to *deter* the Russians over the next five years." (Only 16
per cent reject this view.) A majority of 53 per cent think "that
an Atlantic nuclear force based on Polaris would substantially im-

prove the military security of Europe." If such a force were created, 77 per cent would want it to be organized as "a supranational force under a single command" (only 9 per cent choosing
the alternative of "national components under separate command").
Again, two of every three Eurocrats would agree, if a supranational
force were created, "that its commanding officer be American."
They are, however, skeptical "that an Atlantic nuclear force of
some type will come into being over the next five years." Only
32 per cent are optimistic on this projection; 50 per cent consider
it unlikely.

Under these conditions, the Eurocrats show increasing interest in
the possibility of creating a European force of some type. Their
general commitment to the transnational principle is very clear. No
less than 95 per cent "approve the integration of the major part
of your own country's armed forces into a permanent supranational
force." A plurality of 47 per cent would prefer such a force to be
under European auspices, as compared with 34 per cent who approve NATO auspices. This is in no sense anti-NATO. It reflects,
rather, the projection just reported that the creation of an Atlantic
force now seems unlikely to the Eurocrats. It reflects as well their
long-standing commitment to the idea of an integrated European
defense community. A fulsome 82 per cent of the Eurocrats were
for the EDC when it was under discussion in 1954, and 84 per
cent would in principle be *for* an equivalent of the EDC today.

The problem they foresee centers primarily around the high cost
and low effectiveness of present and prospective nuclear weapons
in Europe. They are keenly aware of this problem in relation to
the existing British and French nuclear weapons systems. While a
majority of 56 per cent believe that the British nuclear force has
political advantages, a larger majority of 64 per cent believe that
it has no military significance. An even sharper distinction is made
with reference to the French *force de frappe*. Again some 52 per
cent assume that it may have political advantages for France, but
affirm that it has no military significance for anybody.

These views appear to derive from a strong consensus that national
nuclear forces are not a paying proposition in Europe. Payoffs
would come, if at all, only as a result of collective European effort.
We asked, "Do you favor possession or manufacture of thermonuclear weapons by your own country?" Possession was rejected by

72 per cent of the Eurocrats and manufacture by their own country was rejected by 81 per cent. The development of nuclear weapons in Europe was favored only in connection with the possible formation of "a future European military force." Even in this connection, the Eurocrats had apparently learned, from Britain's experience with Blue Streak and similar efforts elsewhere which wasted economic resources, that the cost of manufacture was likely to be disproportionate to the benefits of possession. Never inclined to place prestige above the rational calculus of costs and benefits, the Eurocrats therefore tended to prefer that the cost of nuclear weapons should be reduced by purchasing weapons manufactured elsewhere.

Only if nuclear weapons were to be put in the transnational service of "a future European force" would a majority (61 per cent) of Eurocrats favor the higher cost of their manufacture in Europe. Even under this hypothesis, however, many of them took the view that Europe had other, more important, ways of using its economic resources. Among these was the development of a genuinely European policy of economic aid to underdeveloped countries.

7. *Europa and the Developing World*

The Eurocrats are deeply committed, in strong contrast with the TEEPS panels, to the expansion of European economic aid to underdeveloped countries. About three of every four respondents (74 per cent) affirmed that the Community should make a substantial increase in its long-term commitment of economic aid. Since these are not men who spend money lightly, it is all the more impressive that they responded (Table 11.4) in rather grand terms to our question, "How much greater? Which order of magnitude is closer to your idea?"

TABLE 11.4. EUROCRATS' OPINIONS ON INCREASE IN
EUROPEAN FOREIGN AID (1965)

Favor Increase of:	
about 10 per cent	12%
about 50 per cent	25
about 100 per cent	19
more than 100 per cent	11
DK	33

The three middle figures sum to 55 per cent, indicating that a majority of Eurocrats favored *very* substantial increases of European economic aid to underdeveloped countries. This is confirmed by their response to the question, "What should be the European countries' contribution by comparison with the US?" Some 40 per cent of the Eurocrats said the European community's contribution should be about 50 per cent of the US contribution; another 23 per cent said that the contribution should be "equal" to the US; 2 per cent even said that it should be "larger" than the US.

As might be expected, the Eurocrats expect a fair return on their money. A majority of 68 per cent are unwilling to accept the idea "that economic aid be supplied in terms of dominant spheres — Africa by the European, Latin America by the American, and Asia by agreement." Nor do they accept the idea that "economic aid should be administered bilaterally." Only 13 per cent of the Eurocrats accept this as compared with 78 per cent who prefer multilateral aid. On the question of preferred auspices under which a multilateral aid agency should be established, they divide it as follows: European 27 per cent, Atlantic 27 per cent, United Nations 34 per cent. A final indicator of the seriousness with which Eurocrats regard the objective of aiding underdeveloped countries is their apparent willingness to give away something for nothing. Impressive majorities affirm that they "favor preferential treatment for selected imports from underdeveloped countries and for selected exports to them": 60 per cent prefer on exports and 69 per cent on imports. While this attitude is generous, it should not be construed as a giveaway dictated by sentiment. The Eurocrats, for all their devotion to rational calculus, are quite capable of taking the long view and calibrating economic costs to themselves with socioeconomic benefits to the larger world community.

C. THE EUROCRATS AS VANGUARD OF EUROPA

The Eurocrats are, first of all, Europeans. They have lived through the same phases of history as their compatriots and have experienced the same acceleration of history in the postwar decades. Like most of the European elites represented in our TEEPS panels, they had some direct experience of World War I, then passed through the interwar agony of the totalitarian movements and regimes into the devastating World War II which laid their continent low. Like most of the TEEPS panelists they developed the allergy called "propaganditis" and a high output of antitoxin toward ideology.

As postwar Europe moved from ideology to pragmatism, from nationalism to transnationalism, from socialism (in the Marxian vision of one historically chosen CLASS) to pluralism — as these separate but interactive tendencies evolved, the Eurocrats were among the vanguard. Not for them an image of the future based on the victory of the proletariat (or any other CLASS) or on the hegemony of France (or any other NATION). Not for them a polity based on contending ideologies which simplify and even falsify issues in order to gain votes for a sponsoring political party. Their vision of a desirable and effective polity centered upon the application of intelligence to evidence in order to move as far and fast as possible along the most likely routes to their preferred social goals.

As the TEEPS panelists concurred that politics should be regarded as "the art of the possible," so the Eurocrats went beyond this primitive pragmatism to a more sophisticated level of pragmatic pluralism. For them the "art" of politics included the continuous exploration of alternatives and invention of initiatives that would extend the limits of "the possible." It was this turn of political thinking, this quest for frontiers wider than the constraints of national geography, which led these men from their homelands to Brussels. The sequence of psychopolitical events that made them Eurocrats, we believe, in turn made their Eurocracy the vanguard of Europa.

For the Eurocrats are, as we have seen, distinctive among the European elites in several important ways. As compared with the national panels of TEEPS, they are relatively younger and better educated persons. They are men of high professional qualifications who have attained their present positions mainly by the test of merit. They are also men of deep commitment to public service — and particularly to the public service of Europe — since none is where he is against his will and virtually all are convinced that EC is the most important place to be in Europe today. Their identification with EC is profound, pervasive, personal. The Eurocrats regard themselves as the present builders of the Community which represents the best — most desirable *and* most feasible — future for Europa.

To depict them as a bureaucracy with distinctive characteristics is not to assume, according to an obsolescent and largely irrelevant stereotype, that the Eurocrats are apolitical. This is rarely true of the highest officials of any civil service, who are obliged to deal with politicians at all levels. It is conspicuously inapplicable to the Eurocrats and especially to the Commissioners, who have been excluded from this report mainly because their office is political and semiministerial rather than bureaucratic and administrative. It is worth noting that those at the apex of the EC Commission in 1965 — President Walter Hallstein, Vice Presidents Robert Marjolin and Sicco Mansholt — show a record of political involvement in their respective national polities that is manifold and continuous. Hallstein, as a close collaborator of Adenauer in the Christian Democrat regime that governed Germany over the two postwar decades, had developed a basic rule of German foreign policy that came to be called the "Hallstein Doctrine."[1] Mansholt had been, and continued to be, a leading figure in the high councils of the Dutch Socialist Party. Marjolin twice received the nomination as *député* to the *Assemblée Nationale* from the French Socialist Party (SFIO) and, though he failed to win the elections, remained a valued advisor on international — and especially Euramerican — relations to his own party and to other political movements.[2]

Political awareness was more rather than less characteristic of the Eurocrats from the Commissioners down to the Directors. Their acute sense of political reality was exhibited pervasively by their operating style at Brussels. Some of their procedures, such as the "marathon" sessions with the Council of Ministers, were masterpieces of political timing. On other and more profound levels, such as the technique of "package proposals," they brought the ancient political art of "logrolling" to a new height of refinement. They developed great skill in spotting the causes of logjams — and even foreseeing them in advance of their "marathons" with the representatives of the member-nations. Their "packages" contained solvents that usually freed logjams in the nick of time. In each "package" there were proposals put forward, or held in reserve, that proved irresistible to the guardians of national interest from the six member-nations foregathered in the Council. In behalf of their bold new objectives, the Eurocrats played the wary old games of political negotiation with vigor and with wit.

That the Eurocrats should become pragmatic pluralists in the vanguard of those reshaping political analysis and behavior among the European elites seems natural in the light of their personal backgrounds and their political perspectives. Since they are professionally trained civil servants committed to bureaucratic-rational norms, they naturally tend to think in pragmatic terms: That is, any policy is only as good as its achievement and gets no "brownie points" for its aspiration. For the Eurocrats, too, politics is the art of the possible. Their distinctive aim, however, is to make many things "possible" that previously were not thought to be so. All their techniques of "package proposals" delivered at "marathons" are means designed to serve these ends in the EC political arena. Their success in establishing new Community policies and practices is the valid measure of Eurocrat effectiveness as political pragmatists.

The Eurocrat commitment to political pluralism derives in a fundamental way from the structure of EC itself. The Community is composed of six member-nations, plus an increasing number of associated nations, each seeking to promote (or at least protect) its own national interest through the EC. The separate national interests are powerfully represented by the Council of Ministers, who are authorized by the Treaty of Rome to accept or reject all initiatives proposed to them by the Commission. The principal countervailing power to these national spokesmen is lodged in the Commission, to which the Treaty of Rome granted the exclusive prerogative of initiating the policies and programs that the Council may accept or reject. (The Court only adjudicates EC regulations after they have been initiated by the Commission and ratified by the Council; the Parliament has yet to grow teeth.) It is by the astute political use of its legal monopoly of the initiative that the Commission has become by general agreement the "motor" of the Community.

To do this, the pragmatic Eurocrats *had* to operate as pluralists. Converging the interests of six member-nations with often divergent aims, and winning their consent to regulations equally binding upon all, made pluralism an indispensable *modus operandi*.

The pluralism of economic options worked into Eurocrat "package proposals" was delicate enough, but the margin of political options was often invisible until the Eurocrats invented it. For the nations of Europe, though greatly diminished in the world arena, carry a big stick within "their own" Community. Without the consent of their national representatives in the Council of Ministers, Eurocrat initiatives must come to naught. Accordingly, it is wise for the Commission to initiate only proposals that will carry the greatest benefits for the Community as a whole at the lowest cost to each and all of the member-nations.

This involves the complex strategy, articulated mathematically by the theory of "games and decisions," which has become known as *minimax strategy* — minimizing risks (potential costs) while maximizing payoffs (expected benefits). Moreover, the Eurocrats cannot work with the simplest strategy of game theory, the two-person zero-sum game in which winner takes all and loser gets nothing. Any such procedure would alienate all losers and rapidly disrupt the Community. Eurocrat initiatives must proceed along the most complex lines of strategy, procedures so complicated that game theory has not yet been able to formulate their canonical rules. The Eurocrat "package proposals" must be addressed to an n-person (in this case six national leaders) in a non-zero-sum situation. That is, there must be something satisfactory to each and acceptable to all in every package. This is why the pragmatic Eurocrats are also pluralists; and they are the vanguard of political pluralism because they alone are obliged to think and act in terms of the global interests of Europa rather than the parochial interests of its constituent nations.

The process is exemplified by two alternate strategies that the Eurocrats have domesticated for Community purposes. The first is "harmonization," the reshaping of divergent national policies now in force so that they will converge toward a common policy during some longer-term period. This strategy is applied on issues where a common policy is not urgent and indeed may not be feasible, in the judgment of these pragmatic pluralists, over the short run. An instance is their slow but steady progress toward the harmonization of six highly diversified national programs of social security into a single unified social security system for Europa. As matters stood, when EC was created in 1958, each member-nation followed a different practice — and even a different fundamental concept — of social security. France stressed family benefits, while Germany stressed unemployment insurance, Italy stressed old-age pensions, and the Benelux nations stressed other components of the cradle-to-grave sequence. A ranking Eurocrat charged with "harmonizing" these diverse procedures told us that to *merge* them into a single system (by adding them together) would cost several times the present total income of the EC. As pragmatists, the Eurocrats saw little benefit in bankrupting their treasury; as pluralists, they saw little risk in moving with less speed and cost toward a single social security system.

But pragmatic pluralism is not always permissive. Where the Eurocrats have judged an issue to require rapid transnational solution *now,* lest permissiveness diminish the benefits and augment the costs later, they have acted with foresight and vigor. As compared with "harmonization," the accommodation of diverse national practices until a common policy can be evolved, this is the strategy of "integration" — the strategy that national preferences be subjugated to a single unified regulation *now.* On issues of basic principle, where they saw the present and future of their Community to be involved, the Eurocrats have refused to compromise essentials to gain transient triumphs. Most of the great "marathons" have been run under these circumstances, and most of the indispensable victories the Eurocrats have won. Instances, in the period of our 1965 survey, were the common agricultural price policy (binding on all members) and the agreement that the EC Commission would alone make the European offers (binding on all members) in the Kennedy Round of negotiations at GATT.

This is pragmatic pluralism at its best. By its judicious application, the Eurocrats have shown the way to a new mode of political thinking and acting for the national elites of Europe. Already the word "technocrat," only ten years ago a pejorative label, has become a standard and respected symbol in the European vocabulary. Increasingly the national governments, including notably Gaullist France, are calling upon these Eurocrats because they best understand the Euramerican system. The Eurocrats, trained to analyze problems in terms of the costs and benefits for all participants, have already begun to build the foundations of the Euramerican system among Europeans. Where the Eurocrat vanguard has led, we believe, because their path moves in directions favored by the convergent consensus of the national elites as revealed by our TEEPS studies, Europa will go.

The "view from Brussels" is well expressed in a statement by Walter Hallstein, former President of EC, entitled "Europe Between Yesterday and Tomorrow."[3] The title is indicative of the pragmatic pluralist orientation toward "today" — a point in time between a constraining "yesterday" and a promising "tomorrow." Hallstein, reviewing his long years of contest with De Gaulle (and others), starts from a fundamental premise: "The Six have invested so much in the Common Market that none of them could leave it without causing irreparable damage to their own economies."

The thrust of Hallstein's argument is that nationalism in Europe, as traditionally understood, is finished; that there is, in fact, no viable alternative to transnationalism available to Europe and its leaders. He affirms: "This is true despite the other, mysterious observation that before our eyes, in the midst of this new world, the outdated concept of Europe based on national philosophies has been renewed." Hallstein rejects Gaullism because he believes: "History has shown that nationalism is an unsuitable basis for a European order that is to last into the next century."

Hallstein's description of trends leads him to an analysis of conditions. In particular, he elucidates the importance of protection and prestige now that Europe has achieved prosperity: "Confidence has waned in Europe's ability to unite owing to the stalemate in noneconomic spheres." He stresses that Europa and Atlantica are interactive, not antipolar, concepts. Thus he insists that "the starting point must be the belief that British membership is inevitable." And thus he states that "America is more than an Atlantic power. . . . In large measure it is up to us to reassert America's complete trust in Europe. . . . Why, for example, have no European proposals for a reform of NATO been made in the meantime?"

His analysis of past trends and present conditions leads Hallstein to some expectations about the future. These are predicated upon three European conditions: (1) recognition of American leadership in a durable Euramerican system of partnership; (2) reassurance of Russian leaders "that a united Europe would indeed be damaging its own interests if it were hostile to the Soviet Union"; (3) resolute conviction that "one aspect is indispensable: the representation of common European interests through an independent organ set up for this purpose."

This is the language of pragmatic pluralism. The interests of all concerned are considered and evaluated in reaching a net conclusion about the future course of policy. The rational optimism of the Eurocrats is simply expressed in the final sentence of their former President: "Nothing has detained us, and nothing will."

CHAPTER TWELVE

Euratlantic Retrospects and Prospects

THE modern mind began to take shape, historians tell us, when men started to reflect on the meaning of their past as related to their present. From the Renaissance forward, historical thinking replaced, or at least supplemented, philosophical speculation as a mode of ordering reality. History became a source of policy thinking as well as cautionary tales, and historiography became a disciplined field of scholarship. The historical mode predominated from the Age of Exploration in the late fifteenth century through the Enlightenment in the late eighteenth century.[1]

It was in the nineteenth century, with the advent of ideology, that history as the reading of human experience from the past to the present came under sharp challenge. The ideologues, most conspicuously Karl Marx, were also historiographers, but with a significant difference. Their object was to interpret the past so as to formulate guidance for the future. The ideologues were not content with reporting past trends. They were more interested in interpreting the "discontinuities" of history, those critical turning points at which an existing trend was arrested and replaced by historical movement in a different direction. Such discontinuities were particularly precious to the ideologues because, in revealing the transition points of social change in the past, they conveyed useful lessons on how to manage and even accelerate social change in the future. For the ideologues were not merely historians; they were also activists and agitators. They codified the lessons of history in order to shape policies leading toward a more desirable future.[2]

Orientation toward the future increasingly became an acceptable style of intellectual effort over the past century. From Karl Marx to Harold D. Lasswell, analysis focused on the creation of developmental constructs: projections to the future based on description of past trends and evaluation of the conditions under which these trends occurred. Indeed, in the decades since World War II, "futurism" has become a serious discipline among scholars and something of a cult among the literate public in Europe as well as America.[3] This orientation toward the future is the intellectual background of the many psychopolitical changes that have occurred in postwar Europe.

A. FROM CONFLICT TO COOPERATION

Among the most fundamental changes in European thinking has been the new view that conflict does not pay. Since Europe had been the most warlike of all continents over the centuries of modern history, this view represents a deep change in their attitudes. We have already presented substantial evidence of this change among the TEEPS panels and the Eurocrats. The changing mentality of European thinkers since Karl Marx was accelerated by the experience of World Wars I and II among living generations. We have seen the reaction-formation of "propaganditis" following World War I. World War II, with its powerful emphasis on the global and total character of the stakes, produced conspicuous reaction-formations in its aftermath as well.[4] We turn to a brief review of these elements in current European thinking.

1. From Propaganditis to Pragmatism

The "propaganditis" that developed after World War I was a sort of antitoxin formed to defend the body politic against the toxic effect of wartime propaganda — with the subsequent exposure that much of it had been exaggerated or false. Since the propaganda of those years was largely ideological, the reaction-formation included ideologies as well as their articulation by propaganda designed to shape public opinion. The revulsion against ideology was deepened and widened during the interwar years by the abusive policies and practices of the "coercive ideological movements" such as the Bolsheviks, Fascists, Nazis, Falangists, and others.[5]

The passing of ideology as a guide to policy thinking opened the way for the new pragmatism which we have seen to be pervasively at work among the European elites. Our panelists no longer decided whether an idea was acceptable because it came from the Left or from the Right. The merit of an idea now was tested by how well it "worked" — that is, how effectively it produced the results sought by policies. This was a new intellectual orientation for European thinkers long habituated to providing historical justification or ideological sanction for their ideas. Under the new pragmatic dispensation, history and ideas validated themselves only in the measure that they inspired policies that were *both* "desirable and feasible." And where they could not have both, our elites regularly opted for the feasible.

Postwar Europe thus laid to rest the two major ideological codes — nationalism and socialism — which had shaped political thinking among its leaders for several centuries past. Our earlier chapters have amply documented the passing of socialism as well as the reshaping of nationalism among the TEEPS and EC panels. We have been at pains to make clear that the passing of socialism did not spell the end of social idealism. On the contrary, it left a strong residue of social welfare values which postwar Europeans took more seriously in the sense that now they intended to make these ideas "work." Similarly, the reshaping of nationalism has not meant that end of patriotism or pride of place. The very term "transnationalism" suggests that some qualities of private affect associated with nationalism were transferred to a higher level of organization. People discovered that they could develop strong emotional commitments to Europe or the Community without ceasing to be Frenchmen, Germans, or Italians. It may well be that this degree of emotional elevation — which one skeptical French Deputy described as "parochialism raised to the next higher level" — will not be adequate to meet the future needs of a European Community. Nonetheless, it represents a significant transition in the psychopolitical structure of European thinking and, as our data abundantly suggest, it provides a visible staging level for the further evolution of political percepts and concepts. The "interpenetration" of Left-Right ideas as between nationalists and socialists — the pragmatic focus on what is "feasible"—has led the European elites from their ideological perspective on globalism to their pragmatic commitment to regionalism.

2. From Globalism to Pluralist Regionalism

The ideal of a "peaceful world" has been with mankind for a long time. In the nineteenth century, the philosopher Kant brought this ideal to the summit of modern expression in his book *Universal Peace*.[6] While the ideal remains as desirable today as it ever was, the new pragmatism is more concerned with making it "work" in practice than it is with restating the ideal in lofty prose. The diagnosis of conditions under which war occurs has been pushed further by contemporary students than ever before in recorded history. While we are not much nearer than William James to finding intellectual substitutes for war, and rather doubt that the causes of war are primarily intellectual in their etiology, we have developed frameworks for analysis of the "international system" which provide types of "distant early warning" that were never before available to political actors and analysts. Contemporary systems analysis of the world political arena alerts us, with a degree of foresight that is new, when two or more nations adopt policies that may lead to a "collision course." This has been accomplished not by inspirational rhetoric about the desirability of peace, but rather by taking the ideal of peace for granted and diagnosing dangers to the peace system which are likely to transform international relations into a war system. It may well be that the cause of world peace and comity is better served by this pragmatic, even if occasionally hard-nosed, mode of political analysis.

A fundamental feature of the new intellectual mode is to perceive the globe as pluralistic — a world in which a diversity of trends and countertrends is occurring among nations at more or less developed phases of social organization. People everywhere were deeply touched when Wendell Willkie, during World War II, produced his moving book *One World*. These were the hopeful days when many people, and perhaps Americans more than others, felt that victory would bring with it a peaceful world community. When this did not happen, popular opinion reacted with either excessive frustration or antipathy to the maneuvers of international politics.

Those whose task it is to understand and act in the international political system turned their attention to discovering why the peaceful world desired by all did not "happen" when World War II ended. They were quick to perceive that the "One World" of Wendell Willkie had in fact divided itself into at least three different worlds — East, West, and the rest. The Western world, led by Washington, was the most modern, rich, and powerful region on earth, with a continuing high growth potential. The Eastern world, led by Moscow, was less advanced in many ways than the West; but it possessed nuclear weapons as well as an organizational dynamism that promised accelerated modernization. The rest of the world, as World War II ended, was still mainly subjugated to the imperial dominion of European governments. Their main task, in the two postwar decades, was to secure their political independence and "emerge" as new nations.[7] Once independence was achieved, they then faced the longer and harder task of modernization — becoming more like the Western world, or even the more advanced countries of the Eastern world, by overcoming poverty, illiteracy, apathy, and the pestilence that had made chronic sickness and early death their accustomed way of life.[8]

These are the three worlds with which the new postwar international system had to deal. We turn to a consideration of these elements among the postwar ABCD's.

B. RESHAPING THE WORLD ARENA: THE POSTWAR ABCD's

Four fundamental factors have shaped the international system in the postwar period: (1) the splitting of the *atom* and the development of thermonuclear weapons; (2) the *bipolarization* of the world arena as between the two atomic superpowers; (3) the *containment* of each other by the two coalitions organized around the superpowers; and (4) the *development* of former colonies and other backward areas of the world into independent and modernizing nations. We consider each of these four elements briefly as they have influenced the political thinking of the postwar Europeans.

1. Atomics

The atomic age began before World War II when scientists, mainly in Europe, discovered that the atom could be split under experimental conditions. It took a new turn technologically when wartime scientists and engineers, mainly in America, discovered how to use the explosive power generated by atomic fission and fusion to produce weapons of unprecedented force. These weapons, collectively designated as "the ultimate weapon" in the early post-war years, rapidly shaped a new system of international power relations.

It was inevitable that the atom, as a new source of power, should entail a new system of power. Protection, as we have seen, has always been a primary requirement of nationhood. No nation could long remain sovereign without being able to guarantee its own military security. During the first postwar decade only the United States, with its nuclear monopoly, was in this sovereign position. (The British nuclear capability was a lesser, and increasingly dependent, force.) By 1952, on the eve of our TEEPS decade, the Soviet had achieved control of the atom for military purposes and thereby moved into the world arena as a superpower in its own right.[9]

With the world divided between the two continental and nuclearized giants, it was essential to develop a new system of international relations that could bring a measure of order into a rapidly accelerating and highly disorderly phase of historical growth. This was the system, which came to be known as Bipolarity, that reshaped thinking among the European elites in the two postwar decades — and, most emphatically, in the second postwar decade of our TEEPS study.

2. Bipolarity

The bipolar system evolved on a zigzag course, by fits and starts, with many trials and errors. During the immediate postwar years of American nuclear monopoly, there occurred the Great Debate over the idea that the United States should "take out" Russia by means of a pre-emptive nuclear strike. Happily for the peace of the world, this idea was rejected as an element of American world policy. In the years following Soviet acquisition of a nuclear capability, and particularly during the Khrushchev years, Moscow engaged in a sequence of threats that were given the label "atomic blackmail."[10] These threats occurred at the moments of most intense crisis in the postwar period — at Berlin, at Suez, and at Cuba — and brought the Cold War to a fever pitch that risked disintegrating the entire world system based on bipolarity. In these crises, happily, the United States kept its nerve and responded firmly but without pressing the panic button. Happily, too, the Soviets kept their heads and did not push their risky initiatives beyond the point of no return. No atoms fell at Berlin or Suez. At Cuba, with the withdrawal from Soviet installations during the missile crisis, the critical phase of intensified Cold War receded.

Thereafter the bipolar system operated in a lower key. The tactics of "atomic blackmail" were put aside by both superpowers. Instead they moved to the more stable and peaceable alternatives of bipolarity which the Russians have called "competitive coexistence" and the Americans have called "containment." Many factors entered into the calculus of the superpowers as they moved toward this more pacific posture. In the Communist camp, the Sino-Soviet rift established China as a contender for leadership of world communism, particularly among the colored peoples of the world. Khrushchev's policy of destalinization rapidly led to the development of "polycentrism" among the European members of the Communist bloc. This process was well under way when the Budapest uprising occurred in 1956, at the same moment when Britain and France were making their first postwar effort at Suez to operate in the world arena independently of American advice and consent. While the Suez initiative failed, it was to be followed only two years later by the advent of the Fifth Republic under De Gaulle. French Gaullism was to become the counterpart, in the Western world, of Eastern "polycentrism."

In addition to the loosening of central control within the respective blocs, both America and Russia began to take account of the high costs imposed upon them by centralized responsibility for the protection of their allies. The maintenance of large conventional forces in Europe was a heavy drain upon the budgetary resources of each superpower. Some military leaders tended to the view that these funds could be spent more effectively in the further development of nuclear weapons, a view which has been largely responsible for the sequence of bipolar "arms races" in recent years. Perhaps most important, both superpowers felt obliged to turn to the grave internal problems that had emerged within their own societies. The Russians, long habituated to denying their own people significant improvement in private consumption and welfare for the sake of increasing national power, decided that the time had come to move their economy in the direction of higher mass consumption. The Americans, after decades of neglect, decided that their blighted cities had to be renewed and their degenerate race relations had to be elevated to a level consonant with the "American dream."

During the TEEPS decade, therefore, internal as well as external constraints led the superpowers to a broader conception of bipolarity as a "system regulator" for the world arena. Clearly, it was possible for America and Russia to adjust the level of their confrontations in such ways as to heighten or lower the degree of tension in the world system. By the same token, changes elsewhere in the world system could act as constraints upon the superpowers. The strategy of "containment" became not only a strategy of conflict but a mode of conflict resolution.[11]

3. Containment

The principal meaning of containment as a strategy in the bipolar system is that the superpowers contained each other. This is the strategy of "mutual deterrence," which has sometimes been more dramatically labeled "the balance of terror."[12] While it is true that containment has produced agonizing moments within the superpowers and in the rest of the world — as in the Cuban missile crisis — it has nevertheless functioned as a system regulator with considerable effectiveness. As its major outcome, there has been no engagement of nuclear weapons anywhere in the world during the postwar period. Even the threats of war labeled "atomic blackmail" have greatly diminished and are likely, as the bipolar détente is prolonged and deepened, to reappear less frequently (although perhaps, as a corollary, more dangerously when they do reappear).

The superpowers, in addition to deterring each other from nuclear aggression and even from direct military confrontation, have also been contained (or at least constrained) to abide by their responsibilities as leaders of world-wide coalitions and alliances. American withdrawal of its cherished proposal to create an Atlantic multilateral nuclear force (MLF) is a case in point. Russian restraint — in the face of opposition by Yugoslavia, China, Albania, and Rumania — is another case in point.*

If bipolarity as a system regulator often has contained the superpowers, its constraining effects upon the lesser members of each

---

* See the series of studies on the "Sino-Soviet Conflict" edited by William Griffith and published by The M.I.T. Press.

global coalition have been even more profound. This is notably the case in Europe, which has been the center of bipolar contest from the start. Despite expressions of resistance and even revolt in East Germany, Czechoslovakia, Hungary, Poland, and Rumania, none of these Comecon and Warsaw Pact members has adopted an independent policy in its military or economic relations — the key issues of protection and prosperity. Similarly, the resistance of Gaullist France to some aspects of American leadership, and even the displacement of NATO from Paris to Brussels, has not led France to adopt policies indifferent to the Euramerican and Euratlantic system as a whole. Just as the nations of Eastern Europe have been tied to Moscow, so with less coercion and more consensus the nations of Western Europe have been "contained" by their dependence on Washington for protection and their interdependence for prosperity.

Where the European nations have been capable, if not compelled, to develop relatively independent policies and programs is the postwar issue of development. As the seat of empires which formerly ruled most of the rest of the world, Europe has been obliged to move from decolonization to the provision of economic and human resources needed for the development of the "emerging nations." This has been a genuinely *new* element in the world system, started by the superpowers as global contestants, but followed by the diminished nation-empires of Europe, having regained their own protection and prosperity, as they sought to "repay their way" in the world.

4. Development

The postwar issue of development has been handled in ways tangential to the key issues of protection, prosperity, and prestige. This has been possible because the key issues were "contained" within the bipolar system of international relations based on an East-West division of the globe. Development, as a new element in the world system, was organized on a North-South basis following the natural contours of the global distribution of the world's wealth — the relatively prosperous northern half of the world being capable of, and committed to, the development of the relatively impoverished southern half of the world.

The ultimate goal of development efforts has been "modernization." For most of the underdeveloped world this has meant emulating the western quadrant of the northern half of the world. The Western model has provided those images of modernity which were incorporated by the backward new nations. Urbanization and industrialization, education and literacy, public health and welfare, political and social participation — all these have been the characteristics of modernity which the rest of the world has sought, and is seeking, to acquire.

Modernity, however, is a moving target. While the former dominions of Britain often look to London for guidance, and the former colonies of France look to Paris, the nations of Europe have themselves looked to America for the image of their own future. Thus, while the rest of the world has been seeking a "takeoff," in the sense of Walt Rostow, Western Europe has been moving in the direction of "affluence" on the American model.[13] In the emerging nations of Afro-Asia, the process of modernization is still in the early phases of transition from highly traditional, and often rigidly routinized, social orders. In Western Europe, the modern social process of self-sustaining growth which supports "affluence" has become a secular religion. In its quest for the American version of modernity, Europe has become increasingly and inextricably involved in the successful development of the Euramerican system of relationships.

C. SHAPING THE EURAMERICAN SYSTEM

The Euramerican system was initiated in the years immediately following World War II, by the fundamental commitment to Europe made by the US. American initiatives in the Marshall Plan (1948) and in the formation of NATO (1949) were the cornerstone of the system. Other American initiatives, usually taken at the request of the European nations, contributed to the welding of the Euramerican system. Such an initiative was the Truman Doctrine, which relieved Britain of responsibility for the military security and political stability of Greece and Turkey; the Eisenhower Doctrine performed the same function, less effectively, with respect to the Eastern Mediterranean, particularly Lebanon and Jordan. The cumulative effect of all these initiatives, usually requested and approved by the European governments, was the new Euramerican system of transnational relations. Among its consequences was the limitation of historic sovereignty of the European nations as well as the imposition of significant constraints upon America's capacity for unilateral action. As a counterpoint, the Euramerican system offered to the European nations greatly enlarged possibilities for growth — possibilities virtually unlimited by comparison with the severe limitations imposed upon each European nation separately by its particular circumstances. Both aspects of the system merit brief review in this concluding chapter.

1. Europa Limited

Postwar Europe was limited in its potential for growth by its ecology as well as its history. When perceived as "a peninsula at the wrong end of the Eurasian land mass," Western Europe is geographically small and geopolitically disadvantaged. It is only by transatlantic linkage to the American continent that Europe's geopolitical deficits can be balanced and even converted into assets. In two world wars, America has been the strategic reserve of human resources and the logistical reserve of material resources that balanced, and indeed overbalanced, the conflicting forces on the old continent.

European dependence on America for protection is likely to be a permanent component of the Euramerican system. Thomas Schelling has pointed out that any future war in Europe — whether small, conventional, or nuclear — will always be affected by the huge nuclear forces of America.[14] The consequence is that Europe must remain committed to, and in some measure dependent on, American power. By the same token, if the American guarantee of European security is to continue, then its leaders must accept, as most of our TEEPS and Eurocrat respondents do, a high degree of American control over NATO strategy and transatlantic policy. It is quite clear that European leaders cannot reasonably claim "independence" from, or even parity with, American policy leadership while basing their essential national and collective security on American military power.

As Europe remains dependent upon America for its protection, and will long continue to do so, it is worth noting that a greater measure of interdependence has entered the system with respect to European prosperity. After the spectacular European recovery during the Marshall Plan years (1948–1952) the old continent went on to produce the celebrated "European miracle." In the period 1955–1960 one after another of the European nations showed that they could overtake and even surpass the growth rate of the American economy. The next period 1960–1965 showed that Europe could maintain high growth rates over the long run. Europe today is prosperous beyond all historical precedent and confident that it can maintain its prosperity over the years ahead. Most responsible leaders are aware, however, that this can be sustained more readily within the Euramerican system — and possibly not at all without it.

The workings of economic interdependence have been illustrated in a variety of ways throughout the TEEPS decade. A conspicuous example that has been inadequately noticed is the treaty between Euratom and the United States, whereby American leadership in the technology of peaceful uses of atomic energy is contributing to the development of the atom-based industrial domain of Europe. Another instance is the Kennedy Round of tariff negotiations at GATT. This negotiation, in which the EC represents all the member nations of the Common Market, is likely to free a greater volume of world trade than any previous "bilateral" negotiation in modern history.

A third and final example is the Group of Ten. This informal and *ad hoc* group is composed of the central banks representing the principal financial powers in the non-Communist world. Their decisions and actions designed to correct the American "dollar problem" (arising from continuing deficits in the American balance of international payments) are impressive testimony to the sharp sense of economic interdependence which animates European thinking at the highest levels. Their contributions during the "gold crisis" of 1968 maintained the stability of the American dollar and showed that interdependence within the transatlantic monetary system had become as indispensable as is the transatlantic economic system for the healthy functioning of the Euramerican system as a whole.

The most publicized issues confronting the Euramerican system during the TEEPS decade were those associated with prestige. These confrontations were provoked almost uniquely by Gaullist France. For a brief period some leaders of resurgent Europe, now prosperous and highly self-confident, followed the Gaullist lead. There were some "German Gaullists" at Bonn and some "British Gaullists" in London. But this resurgence of national pride was quickly spent and now seems to have lost its force. It is clear that De Gaulle's quest for *grandeur* in France is not likely to be desirable *or* effective. In any case, the national *grandeur* of France would add little or nothing to the prestige of other European nations. The findings of our 1965 survey indicate quite strongly that the Gaullist afflatus has lost its breath and is nearing collapse.*

2. Euratlantica Unlimited?

Throughout the TEEPS decade, our surveys revealed that the European elites largely and increasingly believed that the US was now the world's first power and that it would continue to be so at the end of this century. The second and third ranks went to the Communist giants, respectively Russia and China. The nations of Europe hardly figured in any coherent way among the ranking nations of the world today and at the end of the century.

This image of the present and future underlies their commitment to the Euramerican system. For their protection they are dependent upon it. For their prosperity they are, and must remain, interdependent within it. The new pragmatism which shapes their views of prestige is less concerned with the traditional symbols that denoted national honor than with the substantive building of a transnational system that works. It is upon the benefits conveyed by a stable system of protection and a self-sustaining system of prosperity that the European elites now rely for their prestige. And for this they appear to have reached a convergent consensus that their best bet is the transnational system that some have called "Euratlantica Unlimited."

This conclusion must be evaluated along with informed judgments that Europe is now "prosperous, parochial, confident, its stock of gratitude toward the U.S. exhausted."[15] This characterization of Europe today seems to us plausible but partial. The missing link is what European leaders think they can do about their situation, other than put pressure upon Washington for a larger role in the Euramerican system. This has little nowadays to do with gratitude to the United States but much to do with the new recognition that Europe may not be able to manage without, and in any case will manage better with, close cooperation with America.

It is this recognition that has led European elites and governments to repudiate Gaullism as a philosophy of political action. The 1965 survey foreshadowed the isolation on the key issues — the three P's — that overtook Gaullist France in 1967–1968. When De

---

* This passage was written in January 1968. The massive anti-Gaullist demonstrations occurred in April–May 1968.

Gaulle occasioned the displacement of the NATO headquarters from Paris to Brussels, the other NATO members quickly rallied around this major military institution to express their confidence in Euratlantic solidarity. As reported in a lead article in *The New York Times*, fourteen of the fifteen NATO members (only France did not participate) drew up "a blueprint to alter the basic nature" of NATO and "reform the Alliance to face new diplomatic tasks foreseen for the 1970's."[16]

This was mainly a symbol of fealty to the Euratlantic system on the key issue of protection, since many of the NATO allies, notably the US, are in fact uncertain that NATO could or should be given a political role to perform "new diplomatic tasks." More than symbolism was involved, however, when Gaullist France attacked the Euratlantic system on the key issue of prosperity. When the European run on gold threatened the stability of the American dollar early in 1968, the Club of Ten (major monetary and economic participants in the Euratlantic system) promptly isolated Gaullist France. As reported in another *New York Times* lead article:

Nine Western nations defied France today and went ahead without her to agree to plans to reform the world monetary system by eventually creating new reserve assets, popularly called paper gold. . . . The French now find themselves isolated from world opinion, particularly from their five European Common Market partners, which supported the US-backed proposal.[17]

The isolation of Gaullist France by its European partners indicates that the findings of our surveys among the TEEPS and Eurocrat elites are accurate and even predictive. Nationalism is no longer an acceptable "philosophy" among European opinion leaders as they face the constraints of a transnational system in which Europa must be linked to Euramerica and Euratlantica in its own best interests. What the Europeans did in facing the "dollar crisis" of 1968 had already been rehearsed in their facing of the "sterling crisis" several months earlier, when the Club of Ten acted to "save sterling" by putting their money where their mouth was. As described by John Brooks:

Nothing of the kind had ever been asked of the Continent before. In the centuries since central banking had arisen, along with industrial capitalism, the usual attitude of central banks toward each other had been *sauve qui peut*, when it had not been beggar-my-neighbor; international monetary cooperation had come into formal existence only in

1944, and a system of emergency credits, known among central bankers as the "swap network," for use in situations like this one, had existed only since 1961.[18]

These testimonials to the compelling force of the Euratlantic system, with regard to both protection and prosperity, witness as well the key issue of prestige. De Gaulle's orations and actions have been perceived by most of our elite panelists as endangering protection and prosperity without enhancing prestige. The *grandeur* of France, loved by many but trusted by few among the elites who take a larger transnational view of Europe's future, has appeared as a vivid posture rather than a viable policy. The endless discussions about "after De Gaulle," in which this remarkable individual himself has shared with a certain levity, have reached the level of political action. The European elites have had enough of their tragicomic "hero" at the center of the stage; they now want to move, without awaiting too long his retreat into the wings, on the issues ahead.

D. ISSUES AHEAD

Some of the principal issues that lie ahead are those connected with the notorious "gaps" that have bedeviled comparisons of Europe with America in recent years. Starting with the "technological gap," this discussion has been diffused over the full range of societal activity and has identified a half-dozen or more separate but interactive "gaps": management, innovational, financial, institutional, educational, cultural, and political.[19]

The central idea of a "gap" between Europe and America is meaningful; it refers to observable phenomena. Indeed, many of these phenomena have been astutely observed, by Tocqueville among others, for over a century. The recent alarm over the "gap" among Europeans arises from their new postwar concern with prosperity, protection, and prestige — probably with prestige as the major animus. Current discussions of R & D, auto financing, and corporate size tend to narrow the issues ahead by focusing attention on one or another technical issue rather than facing the contextual concern over the different "lifeways" that have evolved in Europe and America over the past century.[20]

The whole set of gaps may be summarized, in this perspective, as an "ecological" gap, a gap that originates not in European inferior-ity of human resources and skills but in American superiority of physical size and scale. From these origins have developed American institutions and practices appropriate for rapid growth in a large-scale society. So conceived, the gap becomes manipulable and even manageable. For the pragmatic leaders of Europe today, the environment is no longer a sacrosanct constant "given" by nature but an independent variable produced by history and subject to deliberate rearrangement on short notice. Rearranging the environment is part of the new pragmatic process by which decision makers evaluate their alternatives and choose their options.[21]

One obvious way to close the ecological gap is to enlarge the size and scale of European activity in a measure nearer to the American size and scale. The indicated technique for enlarging Europe is "integrating" its diverse command posts under a single GHQ. European integration, which is clearly the preferred option of our panelists throughout the TEEPS decade, is in fact well advanced already. By common consent, it has passed the point of no return and further movement toward European integration can no longer be seriously delayed.

By common consent, too, the panelists favor expanding European purchases, tourism, and investment in America rather than reducing American activities of these sorts in Europe. As shown earlier, there is a strong convergent consensus that close Euramerican economic interaction is desirable and feasible. The only reservation of consequence was the widespread conviction that it would be well to reduce the rate of American investment in Europe. As is well known, American investment in Europe has risen steeply over the present decade. It now stands at over 20 billion dollars, as a result of which Western Europe has for the first time displaced Canada as the area with the highest proportion of American foreign investment. Small wonder that many Europeans consider that reduction of the rate of increase may well be in order.

There is in this view relatively little petulance about American economic superpower, but rather a clear-sighted determination to move along the main routes indicated by the American model to expand the size and scale of European economic activity. These routes are: expansion of productive resources *within* countries by mergers and pools; expansion of distributive resources *between* countries by common price and marketing arrangements under the

European Community. As these larger arrangements become institutions binding both continents, Euramerica moves toward Euratlantica.

The acceptance of American superpower as unique in some ways, but as a valuable model for European emulation in other ways, permeates our TEEPS data — and more clearly in 1965 than in earlier years. It is understood as well by the Left as by the Right, by nationalists as by transnationalists, by Frenchmen as by Germans. Thus the leftist weekly *Le Nouvel Observateur* concluded a review of American press comment on "the European miracle" of economic growth with a feature article on "the American miracle." Its headline read: "The U.S. grows by half of all France [*une demie-France*] every year." The theme of the article was that, when measured by American dimensions, the nations of Europe are "almost underdeveloped" and it concluded that America had attained a state of superpower with regard to all competitors including Russia.[22]

Such evaluations have become commonplace in European discussions since 1965. Thus the influential *Die Zeit*, late in 1967, summarized the impact and import of the American model for Germany and Europe in terms of the need for rapid national and transnational expansion. The argument stressed size of firm as a key lesson:

American industry has long since taken up positions for the race to beat all competitors for Europe's business. . . . Most EEC governments are helping to arrange mergers and encouraging companies to pool their economic resources. . . . Although this country is the most powerful industrial nation in Europe, [its] firms are not among the giants. . . . As a result of the Montecatini-Edison merger, Bayer, the country's largest chemical concern, has dropped to third place behind [Britain's] ICI and the new Italian mammoth firm. Only Volkswagen is still among Europe's leaders. For years pro-merger groups in this country were suspected of being anticompetition. Attitudes are now beginning to change under [Schiller's] "new cartel policy". . . . Monopolies, of course, will not be tolerated. But no such danger lurks on the European market for the foreseeable future. Even if Federal Republic auto manufacturers decided, without exception, to join forces, they would still be in no position to dominate the EEC market. With a turnover of 16 billion Marks [about 4 billion dollars], they would be about a fifth as strong as General Motors.

The conclusion reached by this German analysis was strongly transnational, for it was based on the proposition that "competition in most industrial sectors no longer functions on a purely national basis." The lesson for Europe is that national resources must be pooled and even merged transnationally because "only those countries will defend their positions on the European and world markets of the seventies which have large-scale industries, backed by sufficient capital and possessing adequate research facilities." For this the EEC is Europe's best hope, and the article concludes: "Europe's great day is fast approaching. On 1 July 1968 the remaining customs duties in the Common Market will be abolished. The European Economic Community will then be a homogeneous market for industrial and agricultural products, after America the second largest in the world. It will also be the world's most keenly contested market."[23]

The Europeans thus have taken the American superpower not as a defeat or degradation, but rather as a measure and model for their own future. As expressed in the title and contents of Servan-Schreiber's book on the American model — a book which appears to have broken all records as a European best-seller on public affairs present and prospective — "the American challenge" has provided Europe with that "image of its own future" which over past centuries Europe provided to the rest of the world. The stimulant administered by the American presence in postwar Europe, from the Marshall Men forward, has carried the ailing old continent through the toxic stage into the tonic phase. The American model is now regarded by European leaders as the self-administered medicine that will lead them to self-sustaining growth, which is the health of a modern body economic.

So pervasive is the new pragmatism and pluralism among the European elites that the issues ahead are likely to be reduced, in short order, to operational dimensions. This means that traditional orientations to ideology and identity are likely to cut no ice — or only very thin shavings of ice — in the shaping of opinions and making of decisions on the issues ahead. The conspicuous failure of Gaullism to alter existing trends in the economic sector (as expressed in continuing American investment and in the Kennedy Round at GATT) is evidence that the convergent consensus shaped among our TEEPS elites is likely to prevail in the long run — as it has in fact prevailed, despite De Gaulle, on most of the short-run issues of which accelerated history is made in our time.

One of the more striking examples since 1965 is the prevalence of European and Euramerican defenses in the face of Gaullist offensives against the transnational monetary system based on the dollar:gold ratio. While the fiscal intricacies of this system surpass our capacity for concise exposition, the policy meaning of recent decisions by the Europeans is clear. When the "gold rush" abetted by Gaullist France threatened the American dollar as a world reserve currency, the potent Club of Ten elected to create a new "paper gold" technically known as SDR ("Special Drawing Rights"). In so doing, the central bankers of Europe put their fiscal resources squarely behind the dollar:gold ratio that guarantees the dollar's utility in the world's money markets.

That this puts certain constraints upon the dollar as a unique medium of global exchange — unique because the British pound has now, by devaluating, effectively reduced its role in the system — is well understood by all participants. In this sense the Europeans, with their new affluence, have put a set of constraints upon US fiscal policy that are equally well understood and accepted among the relevant American elites. This is the set of constraints which require the United States to balance its international payments so that the dollar:gold ratio can be maintained as the basis of the world monetary system *sans* crises of confidence. In making these arrangements for "paper gold," the Club of Ten reaffirmed its confidence in the Euratlantic system even though this obliged them to acknowledge the isolation of Gaullist France as the sole abstainer.[24]

We have seen that Gaullist France isolated itself as well in the military field when it ordered the NATO headquarters out of Paris. The account of a meeting of fourteen NATO allies which "drew up a positive blueprint" to help the alliance face "new diplomatic tasks foreseen for the 1970's" was headlined "Only France Abstains."[25] This bespoke the deliberate isolation of Gaullism from the dedicated Europeanists and Atlanticists who have committed their political lives to the Euratlantic system.

The issues ahead are likely to involve controversies over detail and techniques, for the basic commitments of principle and policy have been made. Even the decision to loosen Washington's reins and let the Europeans have their head (as in the withdrawal of MLF) testifies to the great strength of the Euratlantic system. As the Swiss analyst Curt Gasteyger has put it, "The American-European nexus is now so strong that the U.S. can afford to let Europe shape itself."[26] The British analyst Alistair Buchan has taken this view a step further: "The American aspiration to have a strong West European partner is more likely to be realized if the nature of the process is argued out in Europe rather than in Washington."[27] And the French analyst Jacques Mornand has added a word that virtually all Europeans, in their newly won autonomy within the Euratlantic system, would accept: "The question now posed is what the U.S. will do with its superpower."[28] An American may add as a postscript: What will Europe do with it? Much hinges on the attitudinal predisposition to action among the European elites.

E. PROSPECTS AND PROJECTIONS

We believe that the new pragmatism will be central to the shaping of future European policies and prospects. It is not merely that the European elites are less ideological and less nationalistic than they once were believed to be — although this is an important outcome of the TEEPS study — it is that their perspectives on political life have been transformed by the new pragmatism.

Fundamental to their new view is the conviction that conflict is an inefficient mode of social relations. This is a radical revision of the role that conflict has played in European life over past centuries. Conflict between classes has been practiced steadily for two hundred years; under socialist parties it became the principle of political organization and under Marxian ideology it was glorified as the essential condition of historical progress. Conflict between nations has been practiced in Europe even more steadily over even more centuries.

The new view that conflict does not pay — or, more pragmatically, that its payoffs are low relative to its costs — has already reshaped traditional thinking in most dimensions of social life among the European elites. This transformation, which we call expathy, is most fully documented in TEEPS with respect to political issues and public affairs. Here we may refer to the connection between pragmatism as a personal style, pluralism as a political mode, and expathy. We see the new pragmatism as a new way of thinking about all issues, and its extension into pluralism as a new way of thinking about political issues. Expathy is the coordinator of these private and public modes; it "monitors" them in an expathic person for consistency and coherence.

Construed psychologically, pragmatism is the personality variable whereby a person perceives and manages his own values in cost:benefit terms. Its extension to public affairs guides the person in evaluating his system of values relative to the environment and in estimating the chances that his preferred events will occur. Pragmatism is usually associated with pluralism in that the capacity to perceive and estimate one's own values in a relatively detached and objective manner enhances the capacity to treat the values of others in the same way. Pragmatically based pluralism, considered as expathy, is thus associated with the political modes of tolerance, negotiation, compromise, and consensus (as contrasted with dogmatism, intransigence, conflict, and coercion).

Because expathy disclaims codified ideologies and downgrades one's personal preferences as the "principled test" of public policy, it appears to some as lacking idealism. We consider this to be a basic though transitory error in the appreciation of expathy, which is the uniquely modern recognition that developed societies now have at their disposal more humane and reasonable techniques for handling social conflicts than the mode of coercive ideology which so long has despoiled Europe's prosperity and disrupted its polity.

But expathic evaluation and estimation is a harder (because newer) mode of dealing with *la chose publique* than empathic identification and demand. Whereas empathy requires only an appreciation of oneself, expathy requires a further evaluation of oneself in terms of one's environment — including the manifold identifications and demands that environment presents. Empathy requires direct personal action; expathy additionally requires detached impersonal adjudication. It is hard to be impersonal and adjudicative when one is young and full of beans. Our speculation is that the young protesters, demonstrators, rioters in Europe (as in America) will become expathic. In doing so, they will forge the Euratlantic system on an even stronger expathic basis than their elders have been able to do as they groped their way toward more humane and reasonable ways of dealing with the deep problems of developed modern societies. They will learn, in a phrase, to put their heads where their hearts now are.

This speculation is beyond the power of our TEEPS data to document. Yet we have some evidence worth considering. Our 1956 survey of the *grandes écoles* of France, those unique graduate schools which are producing the next elites, strongly indicates that these youngsters will become adults with idealism but without ideology. The new expathic tradition seems to pervade even this sample of the younger generation now living in Europe. Not only did the students at the *grandes écoles* give majority assent to Europa and Atlantica as pragmatic necessities and pluralistic desiderata for their own country, but they did so without caring whether these ideas are identified as Left or Right. In this sense, they are even more pragmatist than their parents. But it is their parents that TEEPS has been mainly concerned to describe and interpret. Given their age and place, our panelists will be "governing" Europe over the next decade or so. It is their prevailing perspective, therefore, that is our principal concern in this study. That they are pragmatists and pluralists — in the sense of expathy — we have already demonstrated. What these transformations — from ideology to pragmatism, from nationalism to pluralism — mean to the present elites of Europe we have indicated in every chapter of this book. To avoid being tiresome to the careful reader, we shall be concise in spelling out the conclusions we have drawn.

The transition from ideology to pragmatism involves "planning," what Karl Mannheim once called "thought at the level of planning" and "freedom at the level of planning."[29] The transition from nationalism to pluralism involves organization: how the polities can be brought to recognize and approve transnational solution for their national problems. The transition from empathy to expathy involves education: how the politically relevant sectors of society can be brought to a common understanding of their concepts and methods of action.

TEEPS demonstrates, in our view rather conclusively, that the present expathic generation of European elites is both pragmatist and pluralist. Their pragmatism is demonstrated by their readiness to face virtually all issues by intelligent analysis rather than ideological code; we refer here to the findings on the key issues of protection, prosperity, prestige presented in Chapters Four through Nine. Their pluralism is demonstrated throughout the book by their dedication to transnationalism, their conviction that Europe can no longer solve its problems by conflict but only by consensus and cooperation.

General De Gaulle is a superb example of the effort to overturn, or reverse, the newly acquired pragmatism and pluralism of the European elites. Himself a pragmatist, he has sanctioned every measure that promised greater prosperity for France. Himself a pluralist, although with considerable restrictions in this dimension, he has sanctioned only those programs that promise more benefits than costs for France. De Gaulle's example has been followed by only a few panelists in France, by fewer in Britain and Germany, by still fewer among the Eurocrats in Brussels.

This is why Gaullism is not consonant with the empirical findings of our TEEPS survey. The new pragmatism and pluralism of the European elites simply does not jibe with the Gaullist view of their world — their own society, their own continent, their own place in the global system. These we have represented by the ABCD of atomics, bipolarity, containment, and development. To these matters, the European elites have responded with alacrity and excitement and consensus. Their views are clearly transnational. The differences among them as to Europa and Atlantica are minor as compared with their deep commitment to the Euramerican system of relations and its eventual institutionalization in some Euratlantic pattern. It is this deep sense of the Euratlantic system — expathic to those who have faced the fact that American military and economic superiority imposes upon them only the need to incorporate new psychocultural and sociopolitical ways — on which the elites base their expectation of the ultimate failure of Gaullism.[30]

The evidence for this assertion about the future has been reported in our data dealing with the attitudes of the European elites on what they have come to consider their own key issues: protection, prosperity, and as a derivative, prestige. The explication of this evidence has been given in Chapters Seven through Nine, which deal with their expectations, identifications, and demands. Chapters Ten through Twelve summoned further confirmation from our TEEPS and Eurocrat surveys; the annexes demonstrate our points in methodological detail. It remains here only to state clearly our own views of the "prospect" and to summon those witnesses who have made the "projections."

One principal conclusion is that Europa — a more or less integrated, and even unified, set of European nations acting as a single transnational body — is very likely to grow and prosper. The commitment to this goal by the TEEPS elites has been made clear. The pragmatic inference by Walter Hallstein that the member-nations have already committed themselves so much to the common purpose of EC that none could "afford" to withdraw is an inference that we accept. We recall his words: "The Six have invested so much in the Common Market that none of them could leave it without causing irreparable damage to their own economies." More important, our data show that the TEEPS and Eurocrat elites accept this inference: Very substantial majorities believe that European integration has passed the point of no return.

A second principal conclusion is that Euratlantica — at least as a confederated set of nations bound by a common world policy — is very likely to grow and prosper. While NATO has run into serious troubles during recent years, mainly but not solely associated with De Gaulle, the trend of pro-NATO sentiment among the European elites is high and growing. What opposition there is has mainly to do with the new antagonism toward conflict as a mode. The new system of Euratlantica is seen by leading Europeans as a *necessary* transformation of old ideas and institutions that have brought to the Old Continent one disaster after another. Perhaps the most expressive utterance of this view is that of the great French man of letters, Jules Romains, when he parted company with De Gaulle over NATO:

What appears to us absurd and intolerable is that France should withdraw from an institution that was formed primarily to spare France from a repetition of the ordeals she has known in the past.[31]

A final conclusion is that the Euratlantic system is also beyond the point of no return. Even those who have prophesied catastrophe for NATO — meaning, as one reads them carefully, that the British role in the Euratlantic system will be scaled down relative to that of France and Germany — have not brought into serious question Europe's continuing interdependence with America for all its major values.[32] Less excitable and more judicious commentators have perceived that the Euratlantic ties cannot be severed by any European politicians, however strong-willed, or any European policy, however self-directed, without arousing powerful opposition among the European elites. It is upon this attitudinal rock that Euro-nationalist Gaullism foundered.

The supreme issue is protection. A serious student of the Western Alliance has concluded that the Euramerican, and even Euratlantic, system is durable because it is predicated upon European "fear of losing the benefit of immediate and powerful American protection." This motivates "political leaders in Europe . . . to accept unilateral dependence on, and leadership of, the United States." He then relates the key issues of protection and prosperity in the following way:

> Broadly speaking, the defense budget of each European country varies with its relative national income. But all have one thing very much in common: all are substantially below the level required to maintain an independent national defense policy. This is clearly evident and widely recognized.[33]

The prospects and projections we would make for Europe lie in these directions. The making of Europa is beyond recall in 1969; Atlantica may be revised, but cannot be revoked, in 1970. The Euratlantic system is seen as both desirable and feasible by the European elites. If the leaders of America can evaluate what has been wrought, by the pragmatic and pluralist perspectives that have guided European leaders as well as themselves, then the formation of a genuinely Euratlantic system is likely to occur. If expathy can become the prevailing mode of private and public feeling, in a Europe and America that still harbor "a decent respect for the opinions of mankind," there is a promising prospect that Euratlantic regional institutions will be created that could make accelerated progress toward an eventual world commonwealth of human dignity.

Annexes

Note

In these annexes we seek to provide further illustration and documentation of the data-handling processes used in the TEEPS project. The annexes deal, usually in methodological rather than substantive terms, with the collection, processing, and analysis of the TEEPS data. We have annotated the annexes lightly — just enough, we hope, to help the reader with methodological interests to find his way as far as he wants to go. The annexes are presented as follows:

Annex One: British Questionnaires, 1955 and 1965

Annex Two: Sample Tables of Marginal Distributions

Annex Three: TEEPS and CERN: A Comparative Memo

Annex Four: Elites and Governments: An Evaluative Memo

Annex Five: Personality and Politics: A Memo on Cross-Tabs

Annex Six: Computer Experiments: A Memo on Clusters

Annex Seven: TEEPS and ADMINS: A Memo on Data Management

Annex Eight: Select List of TEEPS Memos, Theses, Publications

Our only point in including Annex One, which follows directly on the next pages, is to show the interested reader which questions we asked at the start (1955) and end (1965) of the TEEPS survey. The British questionnaire was the basic document from which translations (and occasional revisions) were made in the French and German versions. These illustrate, among other things, the transition from open to closed (and precoded) questions.

British Questionnaires, 1955 and 1965

TEEPS QUESTIONNAIRE (1955)

I. What do you think were the most important events during 1954?

    1. What do you see as the main world problems in 1955?

        a) What name do you think best characterises the present period?

        b) This has been called the 'Age of Anxiety.' What do you think of this name?

    2. What major developments do you foresee in world problems from now on?

    3. (If war not mentioned in reply to Q.2) Do you think there will be a third world war?

    (If Yes) What course of events do you imagine will bring it about? How will it end?

    4. What *is* the British Government's policy with regard to war? What *should* Britain's policy be?

        a) Should Britain make a substantial effort to manufacture hydrogen bombs? Why?

        b) Should Britain possess, if not make, such bombs?

    5. If you were responsible for the country's policy what would be the main lines of your policy?

II. There has been much talk about different European federal projects. We should like to have your ideas on these questions.

    6. What does the idea of European unity mean to you? What is your view on European unity?

7. What do you think about each of the following European institutions?

   a) OEEC
   b) NATO
   c) Coal and Steel Community (Luxemburg)
   d) Council of Europe (Strasbourg)
   e) ECE (Geneva)

8. Should the key idea of a common market already applied by the Coal and Steel Community be extended to other fields?

   a) To which fields and why?

   b) To what fields should it *not* be applied and why?

   c) What is your view on the idea of an armaments pool, at present under discussion?

9. a) What do you think of the London and Paris agreements on European defence reached at the end of last year? [WEU]

   b) In your view how did they compare with the original idea of EDC?

10. a) Why do you think EDC was rejected by the French Parliament?

    b) Why do you think the London and Paris agreements were ratified so quickly by the same French assembly that rejected EDC?

11. a) How do you think German-French relations should be settled?

    b) What do you think Britain can do toward helping such a settlement?

12. What part should Britain play in European cooperation?

    a) What effect would close British integration with the Continent have upon the British Commonwealth?

    b) What do you think of this?

III. We should like to have your views on some other international problems that concern the British people:

13. a) What form do you expect East-West relations to take now and in the near future?

    b) To describe the situation would you use the term Coexistence or Cold War or some other expression?

14. What do you think should be the role of Britain in relation to East and West? Can she avoid a choice between the two camps?

15. a) Which nations would you say play a decisive role in world politics today?

    b) Do you expect this to change?

    c) In what way?

16. What do you think of the *general lines* of US policy since the end of the war?

17. What do you think of the *general lines* of Soviet policy since the end of the war?

18. Is it desirable to negotiate with Soviet Russia? For what purpose? Under what conditions?

19. What do you think about the United Nations? How do you see its future?

20. All sorts of happenings are often explained in terms of 'British character'. What are some special British traits? In what respects do they seem to you desirable/undesirable?

21. If you *had to* live in another country, which would you choose? Why? Where has your impression of this country come from?

22. Do you believe any of these people have particularly desirable/undesirable traits? What sort of traits?

    | French | Spaniards | Indians |
    | Italians | Germans | Chinese |
    | Russians | Americans | Turks |

IV. Concerning British domestic policy:

23. What do you think of the current policies on:

    a) Increased productivity

    b) Control of monopolies and trade associations

    c) Lowering of tariffs

24. What do you consider are the most urgent changes needed in the economic field? In the political field?

25. a) Do you think the following groups play an important role in current affairs in Britain?

    i) businessmen
    ii) members of Parliament
    iii) higher civil servants
    iv) intellectuals
    v) lawyers
    vi) leaders of the Church
    vii) trade union leaders

b) How would you describe the role they play?

26. Are there any other groups you consider important in this respect?

27. What kind of image do you think the public has of people in your profession and what, if anything, do you think should be done to correct this?

28. Do you know personally:

   a) your M.P.
   b) other M.P.'s of your own party/of other parties
   c) officials of your professional/business associations
   d) leaders of the trade union in your line of business
   e) government officials
   f) leaders of the church

29. When you have a business or professional problem to whom do you turn? (e.g., legal, financial, public relations)

30. When you run up against a problem that you feel needs governmental action what do you do?

31. Do you discuss with your family the problems that bother you? What are the problems you discuss?

32. Do you have regular contacts with other parts of the country? What kinds of contacts and with what parts?

33. Do you know any foreigners? How do you maintain your contacts with them? Which of their characteristics are most striking to you?

34. Which of these sorts of people are included among your circle of friends?

   a) businessmen
   b) bankers
   c) politicians
   d) journalists
   e) lawyers
   f) doctors
   g) university or school teachers
   h) trade unionists
   i) farmers

35. Have you kept any of your friends from school days/from university? How do you maintain contact?

36. What are the main differences between your parents and you in outlook? Between your children and you?

37. To what social group would you say you belong ?

38. If you could remake your life, what sort of life would you make? Why? (If the same, then) Are there any modifications or small changes you would have wanted?

39. What functions do you think you could fill in a Communist Britain?

Biography No.

1) *Birth* (Year, place, nationality)

2) *Education* (Name and place of schools, years of study, exams; degrees; comments)

   Primary

   Secondary

   Higher

   Others

3) *Present Profession*

   Positions Held (Function, place, reason for change)

4) *Other Professional Activities* (Now and in the past)

5) *Parents* (Place of birth, profession and education)

Father

Mother

Paternal Grandfather

Maternal Grandfather

6) *Brothers and Sisters* (Ranking in the family, place of residence, education, profession; which do you see often?)

7) *Wife* (Education, profession, does she work now? father's profession)

8) *Children* (Age, sex, education, profession, residence)

9) Which of your relations are distinguished either by their activities or by their titles? (Name, relationship, living or dead, why distinguished)

10) Which newspapers or other periodicals do you read regularly? (Titles, are you a subscriber? frequency of reading, value of the publication)

11) How do you maintain contacts abroad? With which countries chiefly? (Newspapers, periodicals, films, discussions and conferences, correspondence, personal contact, comments)

12) *Journeys Abroad* (Countries, year, duration, purpose, impressions)

13) *Foreign Languages* (Languages, degree of competence, how acquired, practice)

14) *Associations, institutions, circles and clubs to which you belong.* (Name, object, mode of action. Type: professional, military, scientific, religious, social, sporting, artistic, etc.)

15) *Military Service* (Date, place, arm of the service, wars served in; comments)

16) *Decorations* (Names, occasions, dates)

17) *Activities outside your profession* (sport, music, personal research, etc.) which you think play an important role in your life

TEEPS QUESTIONNAIRE (1965)

Serial No.

I. CURRENT AFFAIRS

1a) Do you foresee any important developments in British Foreign or Defence policy under the Labour Government?

Yes   1
No   2
Don't know 0

b) IF YES
What are these likely to be?

2a) Specifically, do you foresee any important changes over the next five years in:

	Yes	No	*Don't know*
Anglo-American relations	1	2	0
Anglo-Russian relations	1	2	0
Anglo-Chinese relations	1	2	0

b) ASK ABOUT EACH ANSWERED "YES"

What important changes do you foresee in:
Anglo-American relations?
Anglo-Russian relations?
Anglo-Chinese relations?

3a) Do you foresee any important changes over
the next five years in:

	Yes	No	*Don't* *know*
American-Russian relations	1	2	0
American-Chinese relations	1	2	0

b) ASK ABOUT EACH ANSWERED "YES"

What important changes do you foresee in:
American-Russian relations
American-Chinese relations

II.   EAST-WEST RELATIONS

4.   Taking a somewhat longer view of the West's
relationships with Russia how do you foresee
the development of the Cold War in the
remaining years of this century: Do you
think they

will reach a durable accommodation by peaceful means,	1
will maintain the status quo of recent years,	2
will intensify their conflicts,	3
or will there be a global war?	4
Don't know	0

5a) What do you feel is the most likely way in
which a global war might develop:

by accident?	1
by extension or escalation of a limited conflict?	2
by design?	3
Don't know	0

IF BY DESIGN

b) Whose?

	American	1
	Russian	2
	Chinese	3
	French	4
State _____	Personality	5
State _____	Other	6
	Don't know	0

6. Do you think that as the end of the century is approached, the world balance of power will favour the Communist world or the Western world? Slightly or greatly?

Communist greatly	1
Communist slightly	2
Western slightly	3
Western greatly	4
Will not clearly favour either side	5
Don't know	0

7a) So long as mutual deterrence limits military action in disputed areas, which countries are likely to make the greatest gains in power and influence in world affairs?

b) Is the West, as a whole, likely to maintain or improve its position relative to the Communist countries under these conditions; or is the Western position likely to decline?

Maintain	1
Improve	2
Decline	3
Don't know	0

8. What about Britain's role in the Western alliance:

a) Do you think Britain *should* take a more independent position within the alliance?

Should	1
Should not	2
Don't know	0

b) *Should* Britain go so far as to take a neutral position?

Should	1
Should not	2
Don't know	0

c) Is Britain *likely* to take a more independent position?

Likely	1
Not likely	2
Don't know	0

d) *Likely* to go as far as a neutral position?

Likely	1
Not likely	2
Don't know	0

9a) Are the most important political problems
facing the Western world in the years ahead
most likely to come from the Western system
of alliances, from the Soviet bloc, from the
Chinese Communist bloc, or from other areas?

Western	1
Soviet	2
Chinese	3
State _____ Other	4
Don't know	0

IF "WESTERN" AT Q.9a

b) From which countries?

USA	1
Europe	2
France	3
Germany	4
Britain	5
State _____ Other	6
Don't know	0

IF "OTHER" AT Q.9a

c) From which countries?

Africa	1
Asia	2
Latin America	3
State _____ Other	4
Don't know	0

10. Which of Britain's main allies is most likely,
by its own policies, to hamper the fullest
development of a sound Western policy in
world affairs?

USA	1
France	2
Germany	3
State _____ Other	4
Don't know	0

III.   ARMS CONTROL

11a) Do you consider it likely that other nations
in Europe and elsewhere will develop effective nuclear arms in the next five years?

Yes	1
No	2
Don't know	0

b) Which?

China	1
Germany	2

Egypt	3
India	4
Sweden	5
Switzerland	6
Indonesia	7
State _____ Other	8
Don't know	0

c) Should the present nuclear powers try to prevent the further proliferation of nuclear arms in the world?

Yes	1
No	2
Don't know	0

d) In particular, what do you think should be done about China's nuclear arms?

12. Which method of conducting negotiations on arms control is most likely to produce useful results?

Bilateral negotiations between America and Russia	1
Multilateral negotiations among the nuclear nations	2
Generalised negotiations within the UN	3
State _____ Other	4
None	5
Don't know	0

13. Negotiations for arms control seek two different objectives:

a) to reduce the probability that war will occur;

b) to reduce destructiveness if war should break out.

While both objectives are important, to which would you give priority in the years ahead?

Reduce probability	1
Reduce destructiveness	2
Both essential (no priority possible)	3
State _____ Other	4
Don't know	0

14. As a major objective of future negotiations, would you approve depriving all nations of major nuclear weapons in order to create a nuclear monopoly by a supranational force designed to maintain peace?

Yes	1
No	2
Don't know	0

15. Do you think the Government should take serious steps toward the adoption of unilateral nuclear disarmament as official policy?

Yes	1
No	2
Don't know	0

16a) How about the future development of atomic energy for peaceful purposes, should this be promoted mainly under national, international, or supranational auspices?

National	1
International	2
Supranational	3
Don't know	0

b) If other than strictly national auspices are involved, would you prefer these to be European, Atlantic, UN, or some other?

European	1
Atlantic	2
UN	3
State _____ Other	4
Don't know	0

17. Do you consider it likely that a general agreement on international disarmament, covering both conventional and nuclear weapons, will be reached in the next few years?

Yes	1
No	2
Don't know	0

IV. THE COMMUNIST WORLD

18. Three factors that are having an effect on the Communist world are: the continuing effects of destalinisation in Russia, the Sino-Soviet conflict, and the spread of polycentrism. How would you rank the three factors in order of their importance for the future shape of the Communist world?

	Most	Next	Least
Destalinisation	1	1	1
Sino-Soviet rift	2	2	2
Polycentrism	3	3	3
Don't know	0	0	0

19. In your view is the Sino-Russian rift more attributable to changes in Russia's policy or more attributable to the development of China?

Russia   1
China   2
Both   3
Don't know   0

20. What would you feel to be the most realistic prospect:

changes in Russia's policy to accommodate the Chinese position   1

changes in Chinese policy to accommodate the Russian position   2

continued Sino-Soviet struggle for world leadership   3

a fundamental restructuring in the Communist world   4

little change from the status quo   5

State _____ Other   6

Don't know   0

21. If the Sino-Soviet struggle for world leadership should continue, who in the end will come out on top?

Russia   1
China   2
Neither   3
Don't know   0

22. In any restructuring of the Communist world, do you foresee a tendency for the coloured countries to align with China, and the white countries to align with Russia?

Yes   1
No   2
Don't know   0

23. How important do you think such a tendency would be for the rest of the world?

Very important   1
Fairly important   2
Unimportant   3
Don't know   0

24. As between the elements of race and economic development, which is likely to weigh more heavily in the future alignment of the world's Communist parties?

Race (colour)   1
Economic Development   2
Both (mixed)   3
Neither   4
Don't know   0

V. WESTERN ALLIANCE AND BRITAIN

25a) Britain's international position is a function
of her role in the Commonwealth, the European Community in general, the Atlantic
Alliance, the United Nations and the Anglo-
American relationship.

As I read them again would you say how
important each is to Britain: decisive, fairly
important, or not so important?

b) And which is the most important to Britain
in your view?

		(a)			(b)
	Deci- sive	Fairly impt.	Not so impt.	Don't know	Most impt.
Commonwealth	1	2	3	0	1
European Community	1	2	3	0	2
Atlantic Alliance	1	2	3	0	3
United Nations	1	2	3	0	4
Anglo-American connection	1	2	3	0	5
			Don't know		0

26a) One relevant factor is the future policy of
De Gaulle. Do you believe his intention is:

to make a separate "third force" in the world, independent of East and West under French leadership	1
to achieve a position of equality within the Western Alliance	2
or is it something else? (State) _____	3
Don't know	0

b) Do you think De Gaulle will achieve his
long-term objectives?

Yes	1
No	2
Don't know	0

27a) Do you feel that De Gaulle's policies have
weakened American leadership of the
Western Alliance?

b) Has the alliance itself been weakened?

	(a) US lead- ership	(b) Alli- ance itself
Yes	1	1
No	2	2
Don't know	0	0

IF "YES" TO EITHER
In what way?

a) _____

_____

b) _____

_____

28. On the matter of Britain and the EEC, some
views are that Britain cannot afford to join;
others say that Britain cannot afford *not* to
join. Which, on balance, is closest to your
view?

Cannot afford to join   1
Cannot afford *not* to join   2
Don't know   0

29. What in your view is the value of the Commonwealth: mainly economic, mainly political, mainly as a bridge between the white
and coloured peoples, or has it some other
main value, e.g., a bridge between white
people of British stock in different parts of
the world?

Mainly economic   1
Mainly political   1
Mainly bridge between white and coloured   3
All three   4
No value at all   5
State _____ Some other main value   6
Don't know   0

VI. EEC

30a) Turning to the Common Market, do you
consider the idea valuable in itself?

Yes   1
No   2
Don't know   0

IF YES

b) Is its value mainly:

Economic   1
Political   2
Social   3
Ideological   4
Cultural   5
Military   6
State _____ Other   7
Don't know   0

ASK ALL

c) Would you say its main purpose is:

to defend the common interests of the European nations	1
to enlarge the sphere of European interests and influence	2
to make Europe's voice equal to, or at least independent of, the US and USSR in world affairs	3
or other (State) _____	4
Don't know	0

31a) What are the significant over-all achievements of the EC to date?

b) Which do you consider *the most* significant?

DO NOT READ OUT

	(a) Signif-icant	(b) Most signif-icant
Economic growth of the continent	1	1
Political growth of the continent	2	2
Social benefits to peoples	3	3
Creation of a European identity in peoples' minds	4	4
Other (specify) a) _____	5	
b) _____		5
No significant achievements	6	6
Don't know	0	0

32a) What are the significant over-all failures of the EC to date?

b) Which do you consider *the most* significant?

DO NOT READ OUT

	(a) Signif-icant	(b) Most signif-icant
Rejection of Britain	1	1
Inadequate political unity	2	2
Inadequate military unity	3	3
Agricultural policy	4	4
Fiscal policy	5	5

Other (specify) a) _____ 6

b) _____ 6

No significant failures 7   7
Don't know 0   0

33a) In the next five years, is the Common Market
likely to produce a political counterpoise to:

	Yes	No	Don't know
US	1	2	0
Russia	1	2	0

b) In the next five years, do you believe that
the "Six" will form some form of political
union?

Yes 1
No 2
Don't know 0

IF YES

c) What kind will it be?

34a) With the decision on a common agricultural
price policy and the entry into "Kennedy
Round" negotiations, high officials of the
Common Market believe that European inte-
gration has reached a "point of no return."
Do you agree?

Yes 1
No 2
Don't know 0

b) Do you think that further European integration can still:

be stopped, 1
be seriously delayed, but not stopped, 2
or that it can no longer even be seriously delayed? 3
Don't know 0

35a) Which do you consider to be the most valuable for Britain of the existing European
organisations?

b) And which, in its own way, is more valuable
for Britain than NATO?

	(a) Most valu- able	(b) More than NATO
OECD	1	1
EFTA	2	2
EEC	3	3
Council of Europe	4	4
Other	5	5
Don't know	0	0

State _____

36a) Are the West European countries likely to
increase their political influence vis-à-vis the
US in Latin America during the next five
years?

Yes	1
No	2
Don't know	0

b) And are they likely to increase their political influence vis-à-vis the USSR in Eastern
Europe during the next five years?

Yes	1
No	2
Don't know	0

37a) If it became necessary for Britain to reduce
its Commonwealth ties in order to promote
its European interests, should it be done?

Yes	1
No	2
Don't know	0

b) Do you think this choice will in fact have to
be made?

Yes	1
No	2
Don't know	0

c) Do you think the Common Market can maintain a durable and prosperous growth over
the long term without Britain?

Yes	1
No	2
Don't know	0

d) Do you think Britain's membership would
   be beneficial even if not indispensable?

Yes 1
No 2
Don't know 0

e) What conditions must be met to make British membership feasible?

38a) As the differences over Britain's membership
   of the Common Market seem to be between
   Britain and France, which country would
   you say was mainly responsible for the
   present divided situation?

b) And which country is likely to suffer more
   by a continuation of the differences?

c) Which country should take the lead in seeking a solution?

	(a) Responsible	(b) Suffer more	(c) Take lead
Britain	1	1	1
France	2	2	2
Neither	3	3	3
Both	4	4	4
Other	5	5	5
Don't know	0	0	0

State (a) _____
State (b) _____
State (c) _____

39. Should a larger economic community be
    formed by creating a new Atlantic institu-
    tion that would include the Common Market,
    other European countries, and the United
    States?

Yes 1
No 2
Don't know 0

VII. MILITARY SECURITY AND NATO

40a) Do you favour ownership of thermonuclear
    arms by Britain? And strategic ballistic
    missiles?

	Yes	No	Don't know
Thermonuclear arms	1	2	0
Strategic ballistic missiles	1	2	0

b) FOR EACH YES
Do you favour British manufacture of:

	Yes	No	Don't know
Thermonuclear arms	1	2	0
Strategic ballistic missiles	1	2	0

41a) Do you approve of the integration of a part of the British armed forces into a permanent supranational force?

Yes	1
No	2
Don't know	0

IF YES

b) Under which auspices would you prefer it: European, NATO, or some other?

European	1
NATO	2
State _____ Other	3
Don't know	0

42. Would you favour the creation of a permanent "fire brigade" to prevent eruptions of local violence — as in the Congo — from spreading to wider areas under:

NATO command	1
United Nations command	2
or neither	3
State _____ Other	4
Don't know	0

43. Do you feel that NATO as now constituted is strong enough to deter the Russians over the next five years?

Yes	1
No	2
Deterrence not relevant	3
Don't know	0

44. In the event of a Russian attack in the next five years, would NATO as now constituted be strong enough to defend the non-Communist world?

Yes	1
No	2
Defence not relevant	3
Don't know	0

45a) Do you see the Russian threat today as a
short-term problem that will pass in the years
ahead, or is it a long-term danger with which
the West will have to reckon for many years?

Short-term	1
Long-term	2
Neither	3
Don't know	0

b) Is the danger mainly economic, political, or
military?

Economic	1
Political	2
Military	3
State _____ Other	4
Don't know	0

46. In the long run, what provides the greatest
military security for Britain: strictly national
control, Anglo-American connection, or collective security through NATO? Which is the
most essential, which next most important,
which least important?

	Most essen-tial	Next most im-por-tant	Least im-por-tant
Strictly national control	1	1	1
Anglo-American connection	2	2	2
Collective security through NATO	3	3	3
Don't know	0	0	0

47. What do you consider to be the main role of
British overseas military bases?

48. For the strategic problems to be met in the
next five years, which one of the following
would you rank as *most* effective, which next
most effective, and which least effective?

	Most	Second	Least
Present surface system	1	1	1
Underseas nuclear system	2	2	2
Outer space satellite system	3	3	3
Don't know	0	0	0

49a) Do you think that the multinational Polaris
system would substantially improve the military security of Britain?

Yes	1
No	2
Don't know	0

IF YES

b) Would the main value of a multinational
Polaris system be Britain's deterrence capacity or defensive power?

Deterrence capacity	1
Defensive power	2
Both	3
Neither	4
Don't know	0

50a) In your judgment, should Britain give priority
to its own Polaris fleet, to a multinational
Polaris fleet, or some other approach?

Own Polaris fleet	1
Multinational fleet	2
State _____ Other	3
Don't know	0

IF MULTINATIONAL

b) Which form do you prefer, ANF, MLF, or
some other?

ANF	1
MLF	2
State _____ Other	3
Don't know	0

51a) If a multinational Atlantic nuclear force
is created, would its significance be mainly
political or mainly military? Would you
regard this as a positive or negative
significance?

Military positive	1
Military negative	2
Politically positive	3
Politically negative	4
Neither	5
Don't know	0

b) What, specifically, would the significance
be?

c) Do you consider it likely that such a multi-national force will come into being?

Yes	1
No	2
Don't know	0

52. Britain and France have developed their own weapons:

a) Do you think the British force has military significance?

b) Has the French *"force de frappe"*?

c) Is the British force politically advantageous to Britain?

d) Is the French force politically advantageous to France?

e) Will France maintain its plans for an independent deterrent over the long run?

	Yes	No	Don't know
a) British force significant	1	2	0
b) French force significant	1	2	0
c) British force advantageous	1	2	0
d) French force advantageous	1	2	0
e) French force over long run	1	2	0

53a) At the time when EDC was under discussion were you for or against?

For	1
Against	2
Don't remember	3
Don't know	0

b) Would you, in principle, be for or against an EDC today?

For	1
Against	2
Don't know	0

VIII. THE AMERICAN POSITION

54. As the North American continent becomes more vulnerable to direct attack by the new weapons, do you think the United States will be prepared to continue its guarantee of the military security of Western Europe?

Yes	1
No	2
Don't know	0

55. Do you think the American guarantee of Europe has become more reliable or less reliable during the last year?

More reliable	1
Less reliable	2
No change	3
Don't know	0

56. If the American guarantee ceased to operate, how dangerous would this be for the security of Britain: very, fairly, or not dangerous at all?

Very dangerous	1
Fairly dangerous	2
Not at all	3
Don't know	0

57. It has been said that United States foreign policy tends to be dominated by "The Pentagon" and by "Big Business". Do you think that either or both of these in fact exercise too much influence?

Pentagon	1
Big Business	2
Both	3
Neither	4
Don't know	0

58. Is this situation likely to change under President Johnson?

Yes	1
No	2
Don't know	0

59. Various reports have circulated regarding President Kennedy's assassination over a year ago. Do you think it was the deed of a single man or of a conspiracy?

Single	1
Conspiracy	2
Both are possible	3
Don't know	0

60. In your judgment, what is the most important problem for America today?

SHOW CARD B

61. On the economic side, do you consider the American "dollar problem" (import-export gap) to be a matter for long-term concern to Europe?

Yes	1
No	2
Don't know	0

62. Various steps have been proposed to help solve the American "dollar problem." Would you approve or disapprove of the proposals on this card?

SHOW CARD C

	Ap-prove	Dis-ap-prove	Don't know
A larger European share in the costs of Western defence	1	2	0
A larger European share in economic aid to underdeveloped countries	1	2	0
A restriction on American purchases in Europe	1	2	0
A devaluation of the dollar vis-à-vis European currencies	1	2	0
The use of International Monetary System as a stabiliser	1	2	0

63. Quite apart from the American "dollar problem", do you think the European countries should make a substantial increase in their long-term commitments of economic aid to underdeveloped countries?

Yes	1
No	2
Don't know	0

64a) Would you favour preferential terms for selected imports from underdeveloped countries?

  b) Would you favour preferential terms for selected exports to underdeveloped countries?

Yes	1
No	2
Don't know	0

65a) Would you assess each of the following countries as to whether you feel they are already overextended in terms of aid granted, are supplying a sufficient share, or should make larger contributions?

	Ex-tended	Suffi-cient	In-crease	Don't know
France	1	2	3	0
Germany	1	2	3	0
USA	1	2	3	0
USSR	1	2	3	0
UK	1	2	3	0

b) Should foreign aid be supplied in terms of "dominant spheres" — that is, Africa by the Europeans, Latin America by the Americans, and Asia by agreed divisions of responsibility?

Yes	1
No	2
Don't know	0

IF "NO"

c) What alternative concept would you prefer?

66a) Should British economic aid be administered bilaterally — that is, strictly between Britain and each receiving country — or through a multilateral agency specially designed to administer a large common fund according to a common policy determined by the contributors?

Bilateral	1
Multilateral	2
Both	3
State _____ Other	4
Don't know	0

IF MULTILATERAL

b) Under which auspices would you prefer to see such a multilateral agency established — European, Atlantic, United Nations, or some other?

European	1
Atlantic	2
United Nations	3
State _____ Other	4
Don't know	0

IF NOT MULTILATERAL

c) How do you think the aid programmes of
various countries should be coordinated?

IX. FUTURE PROSPECTS

67a) Which nations would you rank as the five
most powerful in the world today, and what
is the order of their importance?

b) What do you think the position will be by
the end of the century?

	(a) Present					(b) End of Century				
	1st	*2nd*	*3rd*	*4th*	*5th*	*1st*	*2nd*	*3rd*	*4th*	*5th*
US	1	1	1	1	1	1	1	1	1	1
USSR	2	2	2	2	2	2	2	2	2	2
UK	3	3	3	3	3	3	3	3	3	3
France	4	4	4	4	4	4	4	4	4	4
Germany	5	5	5	5	5	5	5	5	5	5
China	6	6	6	6	6	6	6	6	6	6
India	7	7	7	7	7	7	7	7	7	7
_____	8	8	8	8	8	8	8	8	8	8
_____	9	9	9	9	9	9	9	9	9	9
Don't know	0	0	0	0	0	0	0	0	0	0

68. What do you think will happen in France
after De Gaulle?

69a) Do you expect German reunification within
the foreseeable future?

Yes	1
No	2
Don't know	0

b) Are you personally in favour of or against
German reunification?

Favour	1
Against	2
Don't know	0

c) Do you prefer a divided Germany inside
NATO or a reunified Germany outside of
NATO?

Divided inside	1
Reunified outside	2
State _____ Other	3
Don't know	0

70a) Do you think the idea of the nation-state is
      becoming obsolete?

Yes	1
No	2
Don't know	0

UNLESS "DK"

 b) Do you personally think this is a good or
    bad thing?

Good	1
Bad	2
Don't know	0

71a) If you had to live in another country, which
      would you choose?

Germany	1
France	2
Italy	3
Benelux	4
Scandinavia	5
Switzerland	6
USSR	7
US	8
State _____ Other	9
Don't know	0

 b) As between France, Germany, and America,
    if your choice of another place to live were
    limited to these three, what would be your
    order of preference?

	1st	2nd	3rd
France	1	1	1
Germany	2	2	2
US	3	3	3
Don't know	0	0	0

72. The final question apart from classification:
     What would you do if Britain became
     Communist?

     X. INFORMATION SOURCES

73. Which do you regard as your major means of
     keeping abreast of business, economic, and
     political events abroad?

74a) Which daily and Sunday newspapers do you
      read regularly?

b) Which do you find most useful in terms of
information on foreign events?

	Read	Most use- ful
Financial Times	1	1
Daily Mirror	2	2
Daily Express	3	3
Daily Mail	4	4
Daily Sketch	5	5
Daily Telegraph	6	6
The Guardian	7	7
The Sun	8	8
The Times	9	9
Daily Worker	1	1
Le Monde	2	2
The New York Times	3	3
State _____ Other	4	4

	Read	Most use- ful
News of the World	1	1
People	2	2
Sunday Mirror	3	3
Sunday Express	4	4
Sunday Times	5	5
Sunday Telegraph	6	6
Sunday Citizen	7	7
Observer	8	8
State _____ Other	9	9

75a) Which of the British or foreign weeklies do
you read regularly?

b) Which do you find useful in terms of information on foreign events?

c) Which would you judge *most* useful?

	Read	Use- ful	Most Useful
The Economist	1	1	1
Statist	2	2	2
New Statesman	3	3	3
Spectator	4	4	4
New Society	5	5	5
Business Week	6	6	6
L'Espresso	7	7	7
Newsweek	8	8	8
Time Magazine	9	9	9

U.S. News and World Report	1	1	1
The Reporter	2	2	2
Die Zeit	3	3	3
Der Spiegel	4	4	4
Réalités	5	5	5
L'express	6	6	6
Die Weltwoche	7	7	7
State _____ Other	8	8	8

76. When during the week do you do most of your reading of weeklies?

SHOW CARD D

77. Which of the following weeklies would you regard as the best for:

	Econo-mist	States-man	Ob-server	News-week	Time Maga-zine	Sun-day Times	Don't know
a) The British political scene	1	2	3	4	5	6	0
b) The British business scene	1	2	3	4	5	6	0
c) The British economic scene	1	2	3	4	5	6	0
d) American politics and business	1	2	3	4	5	6	0
e) European affairs	1	2	3	4	5	6	0
f) African and Asian affairs	1	2	3	4	5	6	0

IF ECONOMISTS READER (QUESTION 75a)

You said you were a regular reader of *The Economist*:

78a) What are your main reasons for reading it?
  b) What would you regard as its main strengths?
  c) What are its main deficiencies?

d) Do you read regularly in *The Economist*?

	Yes regularly	Yes occasionally	No
Leaders	1	2	3
Commentary	1	2	3
International Report	1	2	3
American Survey	1	2	3
Business (British)	1	2	3
Business (International)	1	2	3
Economic Indicators	1	2	3
Stock Market News	1	2	3
Books	1	2	3
Surveys (of the country, etc.) & Enquiries	1	2	3

XI.   BIOGRAPHICAL INFORMATION

1a) What is the nature of your current occupation?

b) In the past, have you had different occupations?

Yes   1
No   2

c) Which?

2a) Where were you born?

Country: _____

County: _____

b) In what year?   (Last 2 figures)   . .

c) Where did you live for the major part of your childhood — up to 15?

Country: _____

County: _____

3a) Where did you receive your secondary education?

Public   1
Grammar   2
Secondary   3
State _____   Other   4

b) If you attended University, which one?

Oxbridge	1
Other British	2
Foreign	3
Oxbridge/foreign	4
Oxbridge/Other British	5
Other combination	6

c) Did you go beyond a first degree?

Yes	1
No	2

IF "YES"

d) Which degrees do you hold?

4a) Are you single, married, or divorced, or remarried?

Single	1
Married	2
Divorced	3
Remarried	4

b) Do you have children — how many?

Yes: one	1
two	2
three	3
four	4
five	5
six	6
seven	7
eight +	8
No	9

5a) If you have a religion, which one?

No religion	1
Catholic	2
Church of England	3
Church of Science	4
Nonconformist	5
Jewish	6
State _____ Other	7
Yes, but not stated	8

IF RELIGION

b) How often do you attend religious services?

Weekly	1
Monthly	2
Every 2–3 months	3
Once or twice a year	4
Less often	5
Never	6

6a) Do you hold any public offices?

Yes	1
No	2

IF "YES"

b) Which? The three most recent if you have more than 3

a) _____

b) _____

c) _____

IF MARRIED

7a) What was your wife's education?

Public	1
Grammar	2
Secondary	3
Other	4
University	1
Not University	2

b) Where was she born?

Country: _____

County: _____

c) Has she an occupation? _____

d) What is or was your wife's father's occupation?

8. What was:

a) Your father's birthplace?

Country: _____

County: _____

b) His occupation? _____

c) Education? _____

9. What was:

a) Your mother's birthplace?

      Country: _____

      County: _____

b) Occupation? _____

c) Education? _____

10. What are the most important associations, institutions, clubs, circles etc., to which you belong?

Length of time member

	Less than year	1–3	4–6	7+	Don't know
a)	1	2	3	4	0
b)	1	2	3	4	0
c)	1	2	3	4	0
d)	1	2	3	4	0

11. If you did military service, when, what branch, and final rank?

No service 1

When		Branch		Final rank	
State a) _____		State a) _____		Noncommissioned	2
b) _____		b) _____		Lieutenant/Pilot officer	3
1914–18	1	Army	1	Captain	4
1920's	2	Air Force	2	Major	5
1930's	3	Navy	3	Colonel	6
1939–45	4	Marines	4	Brigadier	7
1946+	5			Higher	8

12. Do you know personally:

	Yes	No	Don't know
Your M.P.?	1	2	0
Other M.P.s of your own party?	1	2	0
Officials of professional or business association?	1	2	0
Leaders of trade unions?	1	2	0
Government officials?	1	2	0
Leaders of the Church?	1	2	0
Military leaders?	1	2	0
Journalists?	1	2	0
Scientists?	1	2	0
Academics?	1	2	0
People in the City?	1	2	0
People in the arts?	1	2	0

13a) Do you have a television set ?

Yes	1
No	2

ASK ALL

b) How often, if ever, do you watch television?

Daily or several times a week	1
Weekly	2
Less often	3
Hardly ever	4

14a) Which party comes closest to representing your political views?

Conservative	1
Labour	2
Liberal	3
State _____ Other	4
Information Refused	5

b) Are you a member?

Yes	1
No	2

c) In the past, have you preferred other parties?

Yes	1
No	2

IF "YES"

d) Which?

Conservative	1
Labour	2
Liberal	3
State _____ Other	4

e) Would you describe your politics now as:

f) How about in your early twenties?

	(e) Now	(f) 20's
Extreme left	1	1
Left	2	2
Moderate Left	3	3
Centre	4	4
Moderate Right	5	5
Right	6	6
Extreme Right	7	7
State _____ Other	8	8

Sample Tables of Marginal Distributions

These tables have been selected to illustrate and document points of data collection and data processing that are mentioned, often briefly, in the text.

Table A2.1 illustrates the stability of national responses over the decade in the marginal distributions (totals) on the question of internationalizing the future development of atomic energy for peaceful purposes. Table A2.2 shows stability on the related question of whether the big European nations should own — and, if own, manufacture — their own H bombs and strategic missiles. The answer, by and large, is affirmative. It is only, as we have shown in the text, when this affirmative is confronted with forced choices of less costly and more effective nuclear weapons that the European elites change their minds as in their repeated endorsement of the American guarantee, NATO, and the Euratlantic system. This is most approval on open choice (despite the interesting national differences shown in the table) but NATO wins on forced choice. This is the point underscored by Jules Romains — no militarist he! — when he judged the Gaullist idea that France might leave NATO to be "absurd and intolerable." (See Chapter Twelve.)

The next pair of tables indicate the reconsideration made by the TEEPS panelists on two related issues which some of them hoped to be able to judge separately. Table A2.4 shows some interesting variation of recall and evaluation. More relevant to this annex, it shows that support of EDC has grown over the years since it was defeated in the French Assembly. Most important, it shows that French support "nowadays" has leaped over all others in the transi-

TABLE A2.1. FUTURE OF ATOMIC ENERGY FOR PEACEFUL PURPOSES

How about the future development of atomic energy for peaceful purposes, do you think this should be controlled by an international organization or not?
Would you prefer such international control to be European, Atlantic, or United Nations?

	Britain				France				Germany			
	1956	1959	1961	1965	1956	1959	1961	1965	1956	1959	1961	1965
Controlled by International Organization				*								
Yes	36%	42%	43%	S-N 17%	67%	70%	76%	79%	89%	86%	71%	66%
No	64	51	56	IN 34	24	22	16	17	8	14	26	24
DK		7	1	8	9	8	8	4	1	1	3	10
				N. 38								
				All 3								
IF YES												†
European Control			4	17			13	37	11		6	25
Atlantic Control			3	11			11	3	12		19	16
UN			33	29			41	19	47		49	25
Atlantic and Others								9				
European and Others								12				
Other				10			3		24		1	24
DK			3	32			8					10

* Code: DK — Supranational — International — National — All Three
† National Control or European, Atlantic, UN

TABLE A2.2. H BOMBS AND STRATEGIC BALLISTIC MISSILES

Britain
France   This brings up some difficult questions of military security; do you favor the manufacture of thermonuclear arms by Britain/France?

Strategic ballistic missiles?

Germany   Given a suspension of the present prohibition for Germany to manufacture atomic weapons, would you favor the manufacture of thermonuclear arms?

Strategic ballistic missiles?

| | Britain | | | | | | France | | | | Germany | | | | |
	1955	1956	1959	1961	1965 Own	1965 Mfr. if Own	1956	1959	1961	1965	1956	1959	1961	1965 Own	1965 Mfr. if Own
Manufacture H Bombs															
Yes	65%	58%	63%	57%	54%	85%	49%	50%	46%	53%	24%	9%	9%	18%	24%
No	11	30	33	42	37	14	34	37	43	37	70	88	90	78	62
DK	24	12	4	1	9	1	17	13	11	10	6	3	1	3	14
Manufacture Ballistic Missiles															
Yes				52	54	77		64	54	49			68		
No				46	37	21		21	34	40			29		
DK				2	9	2		15	12	11			4		

TABLE A2.3. MOST VALUABLE EUROPEAN ORGANIZATIONS: MORE
VALUABLE THAN NATO*

Which do you consider to be the *most* valuable of the existing European
organizations?

Which in its own way is *more* valuable for Britain [France, Germany]
than NATO?

	Britain			France		Germany	
	1959	1961	1965	1959	1961	1959	1961
Most Valuable			$n = 319$				
CECA	4%	—	—	11%	13%	3%	2%
Euratom	2	—	—	3	—	3	4
Common Market	35	25%	31%	39	49	58	44
Council of Europe	7	2	5	4	2	9	3
OEEC + OECD	33	25	15	11	8	18	7
EFTA	—	3	31	—	—	—	—
DK	17	37	15	31	12	9	38
More Valuable than NATO							
CECA	3	—	—	1	1	1	1
Euratom	4	—	—	1	—	—	—
Common Market	6	1	14	20	21	13	14
Council of Europe	5	1	2	2	—	7	—
OEEC	35	8	2	3	1	4	—
EFTA	—	2	7	—	—	—	—
DK	25	38	31	12	41	28	16

* Differences from 100% are due to rounding, filtering, and multiple choice.

tion from earlier years. In reconsidering their action on EDC, the
expathic French leaders have learned a lesson of importance.[1]

The related Table A2.5 shows the choices over the years between
the option of keeping West Germany in NATO (the American
policy) or promoting a neutral reunified Germany outside of NATO.
In addition to the methodologically nice "convergence" — all panels
moving from initially divergent toward laterally convergent consensus — there are some substantive points of interest in this table.

TABLE A2.4. EDC, YESTERDAY AND TODAY

As a final question on Britain's relation to the European Community, at the time when the idea of the "European Defence Community" was defeated in 1954, were you for or against the EDC?

Would you, in principle, be for or against Britain joining a European Defence Community today?

	Britain				France				Germany			
	1956	1959	1961	1965	1956	1959	1961	1965	1956	1959	1961	1965
At the Time:							$n = 144$					
For	—	50%	59%	51%	—	58%	50%	56%	64%	74%	70%	75%
Against	—	16	16	17	—	28	41	33	28	23	23	18
Don't Remember	—	21	20	20	—	14	5	4	—	2	4	4
DK	—	13	5	12	—	—	4	7	8	1	3	3
Today:							$n = 142$					
For	70%	50	65	46	51%	—	55	70	—	—	73	72
Against	12	23	31	32	33	—	35	24	—	—	23	21
DK	18	27	4	22	16	—	10	6	—	—	4	7

TABLE A2.5. WEST GERMANY IN NATO OR NEUTRAL REUNIFIED
GERMANY

Britain   Is it better to keep West Germany in NATO or to have a
France   neutral united Germany?

Germany   What would you prefer: a divided Germany whereby West
            Germany is a member of NATO or a reunified Germany out-
            side NATO?

	Britain			France			Germany		
	1959	1961	1965	1959	1961	1965	1959	1961	1965
West Germany in NATO	40%	69%	68%	70%	69%	60%	37%	53%	41%
Reunified Neutral Germany	46	27	23	13	18	14	50	34	46
DK	14	4	17	17	13	41	12	12	12

TABLE A2.6. GENERAL AGREEMENT ON DISARMAMENT

Do you consider it likely that a general agreement on international disarmament, covering both conventional and nuclear weapons, will be
reached in the next few years?

Do you think the British government should consider more seriously
the feasibility of unilateral nuclear disarmament as official policy?

	Britain			France			Germany		
	1959	1961	1965	1959	1961	1965	1959	1961	1965
Likelihood of Such an Agreement:									
Yes	39%	38%	10%	33%	33%	7%	44%	39%	26%
No	50	55	80	45	48	87	41	53	67
DK	11	7	10	22	19	6	15	8	7
Unilateral Disarmament as Official Policy:									
Yes	—	26	19	—	21	—	—	11	—
No	—	70	75	—	66	—	—	87	—
DK	—	4	6	—	13	—	—	2	—

It is noteworthy that the British, given their initial anti-German bias, have moved to the strongest pro-Germany-in-NATO position. The French, who were strongest in the heyday of their idea that Franco-German unity would serve French Interests (1959–1961), dropped to a lower — but still majority — level in 1965. Only the Germans themselves oscillated enough to bring their ballot from a majority to a plurality.

Table A2.6 shows that the general agreement on disarmament reposes upon a downward congruence of optimism. In every panel over the years, significantly fewer respondents believe that a general agreement will be reached. We have stressed the substantive importance of these views in the text. In these annexes, we wish to illustrate mainly their methodological import.

This is why we have included Table A2.7, which shows the need

TABLE A2.7. COMMUNITY OR WESTERN SIDE FAVORED BY END OF CENTURY

How do you foresee the trend of events? Do you think that over the next forty years, that is by the end of this century, the world balance of power will favor the Communist or the Western side? Slightly or greatly?

	Britain			France			Germany		
	1959	1961	1965	1959	1961	1965	1959	1961	1965
Communist Side:									
No Qualifications	2%	—	—	9%	—	—	—	1%	—
Greatly	24	19%	6%	11	15%	9%	8%	10	7%
Slightly	21	23	21	18	18	17	12	4	13
DK	20	14	17	31	39	16	22	15	19
Western Side:									
No Qualifications	1	—	—	4	—	—	—	10	—
Greatly	7	7	5	2	3	10	12	15	11
Slightly	19	19	19	1	8	17	37	18	30
Neither Side Clearly	6	18	32	24	17	32	18	27	20

for context that is provided by cross-tabulation. A rapid reading of Table A2.7 would make it easy to draw faulty inferences from untested marginals. Annexes 5–7, by their emphasis on cross-tabulation, cluster analysis, and list processing will demonstrate the pitfalls of overlooking the clustering of responses, in all countries and all years, around the option "neither side clearly."

We include Table A2.8 in this batch to indicate the sort of data-

TABLE A2.8. ROLE IN COMMUNIST COUNTRY

As a final question: What would you do in a Communist country?

	Britain					France			Germany			
	1955	1956	1959	1961	1965	1956	1959	1961	1956	1959	1961	1965
		n = 102										
Active Resistance	8%	4%	13%	13%	19%	3%	13%	11%	3%	13%	9%	—
Emigration	—	—	15	21	26	4	14	16	—	35	46	41%
Killed, Suffer	42	53	24	11	—	54	20	13	12	20	19	3
Cooperation, Inner Immigration	14	} 33	} 31	20	6	} 9	35	10	—	} 24	10	17
No Change	17	}	}	14	22	}	—	11	13	}	11	—
Other	—	—	3	14	4	—	—	28	—	—	—	14
No Job	14	—	—	—	—	—	—	—	—	—	—	—
Inconceivable	—	—	—	—	16	—	—	—	—	—	—	8
Multiple Answers	—	—	—	—	—	—	—	—	—	—	—	3
DK	5	10	14	7	17	30	18	11	23	8	5	14

processing problem we faced with an open-ended question asked in most countries over most years of the TEEPS survey. Before useful cross-tabulation could be done on these responses, it was necessary to reduce them to a smaller number of "responsive" categories. How this was done is illustrated by the handling of this table in Chapter Eight.

TEEPS and CERN:
A Comparative Memo

A. INTERNATIONAL SCIENTISTS

WITHIN the past two decades, under pressure from the needs of so-called big science, Europe has seen the development of a number of large-scale joint research facilities, where international collaboration in scientific work has become a continuing, institutionalized activity. In the particular fields of high-energy physics, space, and nuclear research, where advanced experimentation requires allocation of financial and skilled human resources on a scale viable only for the superpowers, Western European scientists and engineers have found unique opportunities for technical activities in international laboratories.

One of the oldest (established in 1954) and perhaps the most successful is CERN.[1] This is the thirteen-nation European Center for Nuclear Research located in Geneva. Here one of the world's largest subnuclear particle accelerators (a 28 GeV proton synchrotron) has been constructed under the auspices of the member-states. Scientists and engineers from these and other nations work together in the execution of experiments which none of these nations could afford to do alone without great strain, if at all.[2] The budget — more than 40 million dollars for the basic program in 1967 — is covered by contributions from the governments of the member nations in proportion to their national incomes. CERN employs a permanent staff of about twenty-three hundred people; it also plays

* This report, and the analysis on which it is based, is mainly the work of Albert H. Teich, Ph.D. candidate in Political Science at M.I.T.

host to an average of four hundred fellows and visiting scientists at all times. In addition, teams of researchers from Europe's national universities and laboratories bring experiments to CERN and carry them through at the unique facilities CERN provides.

The professional staff of such centers as CERN is drawn from an elite segment of European society — that segment often called *les technocrates*, which includes scientists as well as engineers and divers technologists. This group is growing more important in the formation of government policy, or at least in its influence among those other elite segments that see technology shaping the future of polity and society.

B. THE SAMPLE

In order to compare the views of these international scientists with those of other elites, many of the same questions asked of the TEEPS leaders were posed, via a self-administered questionnaire, to a panel of approximately one hundred scientists and engineers at CERN in 1965. In addition, some seventy CERN scientists and engineers were interviewed in a loosely structured manner concerning their experiences at and impressions of CERN.[3]

The CERN questionnaire responses were cross-tabulated by nationality. Although the total sample contained all thirteen nationalities, the majority of respondents came from Britain, France, and Germany. Thus it proved possible to generate adequate groupings at CERN which corresponded, in terms of nationality, to the TEEPS panels. All comparable items from the questionnaires were selected and processed. Tables comparing the TEEPS marginals (British, French, and German panels) with those of the corresponding CERN group were produced. The latter portion of this annex is devoted to an analysis of the comparisons that were produced in this manner.

The loosely structured interviews were treated in a more qualitative manner. Transcripts of these interviews (which had been tape recorded with the subjects' knowledge) were carefully read, and relevant material was extracted. The purpose of this analysis was to determine the general framework within which the CERN scientists structure their views on specific political issues. To this end, a descriptive model of the attitude structure was developed.

C. INTEREST AND EMOTIONAL DEVELOPMENT IN POLITICS

The over-all impression is that CERN scientists generally maintain a strong interest in political affairs. Politics is a significant element in the world picture of these individuals. In the words of one German senior engineer, who was asked if scientists were not interested in politics: "Not interested? Of course they are! They are full of opinions."

Even among the relatively few respondents who claimed that they were not interested in politics, there is reason to believe that the answer would have been positive had the question referred to "international developments," "world affairs," "social problems," or other such references to the larger political domain. It appears that the word "politics" alone carries, for some respondents, connotations of local party activities, campaigning, banner waving, and personal bargaining — activities which are not appealing to men whose basic operational mode is problem solving. In contradistinction, such terms as "international developments" and "world affairs" represent aspects of life with which an intelligent person cannot help being concerned.

The CERN scientists are a highly cosmopolitan group, and the focus of their political interests does not lie in the realm of local or even national issues, but rather in the international system — those larger issues which concern at least several countries and often the entire world. One German physicist said:

You see, the kind of politics which interest me, and which interest at least the physicists I know here, is not so much the national politics of their own country. It is not Swiss politics at all. It is international politics — large developments like the European Common Market, EFTA, NATO, the United Nations, and surely the armaments question.

To the CERN scientists, local and even most national issues seem trivial in comparison to the implications of international issues. Furthermore, to most of these individuals, participation in the routine activities of politics on the local level — attending party meetings and rallies, campaigning, fund raising, etc. — holds little attraction.

The scientists' strong interest in international politics, while matched by a relatively high level of information, is not usually accompanied by an equally high emotional investment. There seem to be two basic reasons for this at CERN. First, for many individuals, opportunities to participate in the political issues that interest them are severely limited. Most are not living in their native land; and legal requirements make it quite bothersome, if not impossible, to vote in their own country. (Of course they cannot vote in the country where they happen to be living.) Beyond voting, the fact that the scientists' interests lie in international affairs, rather than national or local politics, makes direct participation for all except the most eminent still more difficult. Within CERN itself, organizational rules wisely prohibit political activity.[4] Second, scientists, as several psychological studies have pointed out, invest a great deal of their emotional energy in science itself.[5] Physics, clearly, is more than a "nine-to-five job" for these individuals. Most respondents are too deeply committed to their work to be able to involve themselves in politics — an outside activity which is neither related to their family life nor recreational. As a Swiss physicist noted simply: "I am interested in politics, but I have never been very active, because you cannot be active in so many things."

One by-product of the scientists' low emotional investment in political affairs is their feeling that their informational level is also quite low, although in fact it compares reasonably well with other elites. Because of their scientific training, they hesitate to draw inferences and to state firm conclusions on some questions. Due to this "expert syndrome," many of the scientists resisted answering questions which they perceived as requiring specialized knowledge outside of their own field. Questions dealing with economics, for example, which were confidently answered by the nonscientific elites, were often rejected by the scientists with such comments as: "I'm not an economist." As they are accustomed to speaking with authority within their own field, they are unwilling to give "amateurish" opinions in areas where they feel less knowledgeable.

D. LEFT-RIGHT ORIENTATION

Within this framework of detached interest in politics, primarily international politics, several common threads emerge. A very clear tendency toward the Left is evident in the scientists' self-identification on the conventional Left-Right political spectrum. Virtually all of the respondents declared that their views, while not necessarily conforming to those of a particular political party, did tend toward the Left rather than the Right.[6] At the same time, many echoed (apparently accurately) the opinion of one Frenchman that "all of the people who work in science are more or less on the Left side."

While agreeing on this general dictum, the respondents frequently objected to being placed in simple categories. It appears that the scientists' notion of the Left does not indicate adherence to something that could rightly be called an ideology, in the sense of a codified doctrine associated with a particular party or political movement. It is rather a shared set of values that produces a common political sentiment of leftism. This is what the French, long habituated to such nuances, call *gauchisme* — and the scientists tend to be *gauchisants* (leftist-oriented) rather than *gauchistes* (Left-affiliated).[7]

From this orientation derive two sets of distinctive, though diffuse, images associated with the Left and the Right. The image of the Right is strongly negative: Its properties are self-interest, power, militarism, traditionalism, and pessimism. In contrast, those properties associated with "leftism" tend to be idealism, generosity, objectivity, and optimism — adding up to a much more positive picture. The degree to which these images are common to scientists of different nationalities and with different degrees of interest in politics is striking.

It should be noted that these generalized sentiments create a broad transnational consensus that enables European scientists of diverse origins to feel "at home" with each other in facing the world political arena. It is not a "party line" in any narrow sense. It is rather a sharing of values and assumptions, style of thought, and tone of voice. A few excerpts from the interviews will convey the flavor of these images. No direct question was asked here; all of these responses are spontaneous, usually by way of explanation of each respondent's classification of his own political orientation. Here, then, are the words of four physicists of different nationalities.

If a person is on the Right, he has some interests. If he is on the Left, he has some ideals. . . . In other words, he is capable of an objective evaluation of the world's social problems without taking his own particular interests into account.

Italian physicist

. . . Right people are fundamentally for themselves, for their own particular group . . . . Whereas the Left — they think of the maximum good for the maximum number.

British physicist

. . . Rightists (in Germany) are very much for good old tradition; they are very much for good old allegiance; they are very much for good old soldiers and so on. I don't like it so much.

German physicist

We can define two kinds of people. Those from the Left think that generosity to other people is the main thing. On the other hand, the people from the Right think that power is the main thing. . . . What I call a Left man is a little bit optimistic about the possibility . . . for man to do better — not in a trivial way, you see, but to a better knowledge of nature and man. On the other hand, a pessimistic view of life is held by the man from the Right.

Swiss physicist

It is important to emphasize again that the prevalence of leftist sentiments is the result of a preferred general orientation toward social problems and not the choice of one political party line or economic ideology over another. The notion of ideology — with its implication of rigidly codified "positions" on a wide range of issues — was roundly rejected by most of these scientists. Although they generally classify themselves as leftists, the CERN scientists strongly reject any effort to impose a fixed pattern or structure on their views. They prefer compromise, problem solving and what seems to be a generally pragmatic approach to the political problems of the world.

E. OPINIONS ON SPECIFIC CURRENT ISSUES

The application of this general orientation among CERN scientists to opinion formation on specific current issues can be seen by examination of their responses to our questionnaire. As described earlier, subsamples were extracted by nationality from the completed CERN questionnaires. These groups were then compared (on common questionnaire items) to their national counterpart panels from the TEEPS study. The discussion that follows is concerned with the analysis of these comparisons. The tables distributed throughout the text give percentage breakdowns based on the n of 230 British, 200 French, and 350 German for the TEEPS panels, unless otherwise noted.[8]

1. European Integration

Some interesting divergences between CERN and the national elite panels become apparent in the questions concerning European integration. The prospects for political unity in the European Community, evaluated quite similarly by the French, German, and British TEEPS panels, are viewed with considerably more skepticism by all the CERN respondents. Tables A3.1 and A3.2 show this

TABLE A3.1.   THE EC AND POLITICAL UNION*

In the next five years, do you believe that the European Community (EC) will form some sort of political union?

	Britain		France		Germany	
	TEEPS	CERN	TEEPS	CERN	TEEPS	CERN
Yes	38%	20%	35%	0%	45%	0%
No	51	70	46	70	47	100
DK	12	9	19	30	8	0

* Due to rounding, totals may vary from 100 per cent by one percentage point in all tables of the annex.

TABLE A3.2.   IS EUROPEAN INTEGRATION NOW INEVITABLE?

With the achievement of a common agricultural price policy, some people believe that European integration has reached a "point of no return." Do you agree?

	Britain		France		Germany	
	TEEPS	CERN	TEEPS	CERN	TEEPS	CERN
Yes	66%	13%	67%	0%	67%	18%
No	20	70	28	80	26	68
DK	14	17	5	20	7	14

skepticism, consistent in all the CERN groups, and strongest (unanimous, in fact) among the Germans. The German TEEPS panel, it should be noted, is evenly divided on the expectation that a political union is near, while their compatriots at CERN completely reject this belief. Whereas a consistent two thirds of the TEEPS panels replied in the affirmative, at least two thirds of the CERN panel replied with equal consistency in the *negative*.

This is a very interesting result, which is only an apparent paradox. One can state with some certainty, from other evidence internal to our survey, that the CERN respondents are at least as favorable to the concept of European integration as the TEEPS panelists. Their responses, however, show a markedly greater skepticism about the efforts of the Six to achieve this goal. To what may this be attributed? A useful clue lies among the comments volunteered by the respondents.[9] On questions relating to the EC, there appear a substantial number of remarks of the following nature:

The E.C. itself is only a "half" solution without, for instance, the EFTA countries.

By "European integration" I understand *all* European countries, not only the six EC countries. A true integration effort must still be made.

EC is not the whole of Europe.

In other words, skepticism about the future integrative prospects of the EC may be seen in part as a reflection of their vision of "Europe" as more than a bloc of six nations dedicated mainly to the enhancement of their own prosperity. They prefer integration on a larger scale, including other West European nations as well as — eventually — East European and non-European nations. The scientists at CERN have no particular ties to a Europe of Six. CERN itself, we recall, is comprised of thirteen member-nations throughout Europe, from England to Greece and from Norway to Spain.

The most immediate prospect for larger integration beyond the Six, at the time of the inquiry, was the entry of Britain into the Common Market. Table A3.3 shows how the CERN scientists, as

TABLE A3.3. BRITAIN AND THE COMMON MARKET

Do you think Britain's membership (in the EC) would be beneficial even if not indispensable?

	Britain		France		Germany	
	TEEPS	CERN	TEEPS	CERN	TEEPS	CERN
Yes	88%	100%	77%	80%	87%	96%
No	4	0	11	10	7	0
DK	8	0	12	10	6	4

compared with the TEEPS panels, responded to this issue. The results, not surprisingly, were strongly positive in all the panels. It was not to be expected, however, that the response would be even *more* positive among the CERN panelists. In fact, only one individual in the entire CERN panel (a single Frenchman) replied in the negative. The CERN respondents' inclination toward wider integration is at work here.

It is difficult to judge the nuanced quality of this feeling from the question posed in Table A3.3 because it does not divide the panel at all — consensus is very nearly unanimous. A finer discrimination is provided by responses to the first part of the same question, presented in Table A3.4. While substantial majorities in all TEEPS

TABLE A3.4. DOES THE EC NEED BRITAIN?

Do you think the EC can maintain a durable and prosperous growth over the long term without Britain?

	Britain		France		Germany	
	TEEPS	CERN	TEEPS	CERN	TEEPS	CERN
Yes	74%	56%	79%	50%	68%	45%
No	19	44	16	40	30	50
DK	7	0	5	10	1	4

panels believe that EC can maintain its growth without Britain, this judgment is significantly diminished among the CERN panels. Nearly half think British membership is indispensable as well as desirable.

2. Atlantica

The CERN scientists, then, distinguish themselves from their fellow countrymen by their stronger commitment to a Europe larger than the Six. How wide does this vision extend? Does it cross the Atlantic? Table A3.5 gives their answers. At this point, differences between the nationalities begin to appear within the CERN subgroups. The Germans are most consistent, about two thirds lining

TABLE A3.5. AN ATLANTIC ECONOMIC COMMUNITY

Would you favor the formation of an Atlantic economic community that would include the EC, other European countries, and the United States?

	Britain		France		Germany	
	TEEPS	CERN	TEEPS	CERN	TEEPS	CERN
Yes	41%	52%	34%	10%	66%	68%
No	53	30	49	50	28	22
Other	0	14	10	30	0	10
DK	6	4	7	10	6	0

up in favor of an Atlantic Economic Community in both the TEEPS and CERN panels. On the other hand, the greater weight of both French panels is opposed. The British panels divide on this issue — TEEPS coming up slightly opposed and CERN slightly in favor.

In view of their commitment to a larger European entity, one is curious why the CERN panelists are not more enthusiastic about this idea. In collating these with other results, it appears that the explanation lies in the greater desire for "independence" from America at CERN (a matter we shall discuss later) than is found among most TEEPS panelists. Had the question spoken of extension of the EC only to other European countries, excluding the United States, it is clear that the CERN response would have been much more strongly positive. The question drew a substantial number of voluntary comments such as: "Yes, but without US" or "EC and other European countries — yes; United States — no."

It is reasonable to conclude that many, if not most, of the negative responses were directed at the notion of joining the United States to an integrated community, but that there is considerable sentiment for an enlarged *European* community. However, some sentiment for an Atlantic Community is also present, as can be seen in the table — most strong among the Germans, least strong among the French. This desire for ties with America is apparently stronger with regard to economic than political relationships. Other aspects of these Atlantic ties are discussed later, in connection with CERN views on East-West relations.

3. CERN Consensus versus National Perspectives

In many of the questions just discussed, indeed in most questions examined in this study, one observes the interesting phenomenon of convergent consensus among the scientific panels. In other words, the CERN subgroups from Britain, France, and Germany resemble each other more closely than they resemble their national counterparts. The degree of attitudinal agreement on many issues is greater between the scientists of different nations than it is between scientists and nonscientists of the same nation. This is a finding of particular interest because in recent years no parallel was found by comparing the many professions studied in the TEEPS panels — government and politics, business and labor, communications and pressure groups, the church and the military. TEEPS analysis showed that, in each country, respondents in all sectors tended to resemble their own compatriots rather than their professional peers of different nationality.[10] The uniquely contrary findings of the CERN study are a valuable indication that science may well produce transnational ways of thinking about extrascientific as well as scientific matters — or, more narrowly, at least that CERN scientists resemble their professional peers on the range of political issues in our questionnaire more closely than they do their nonscientist compatriots.

This is not to say, of course, that there are no controversial issues on which CERN respondents conform quite closely to their national counterparts. The British-French disagreement on the issue of British entry into the European Community is a case in point. As shown in Table A3.6, a clear majority of the British, both in TEEPS

TABLE A3.6. BRITAIN, FRANCE, AND EC

The rejection of British membership in the EC was due to French action.

Which country would you say was mainly responsible for the failure to agree?

	Britain		France		Germany	
	TEEPS	*CERN*	*TEEPS*	*CERN*	*TEEPS*	*CERN*
Britain	10%	13%	49%	50%	14%	0%
France	64	56	8	20	55	46
Both	19	30	28	10	24	46
Neither	2	0	3	10	0	0
DK	5	1	12	10	7	8

and CERN, blame France for the failure to agree; and a clear majority of the French in both panels blame England. In a direct confrontation between their two countries on issues of high national policy, the factors that orient the scientists toward a common point of view on other issues do not appear to operate with the same vigor.

4. East-West Relations

Disagreement among the scientists with regard to the British-French controversy gives way, however, to a strong agreement — as compared with the TEEPS panels — when it comes to larger issues facing the Western Alliance. The panels' views on the place of Europe in the Western Alliance are recorded in Table A3.7. The

TABLE A3.7. EUROPE'S ROLE IN THE WESTERN ALLIANCE

Do you think Europe (TEEPS: replace "Europe" by Britain, France, and Germany respectively) *should* take a more independent position within the Alliance?

	Britain		France		Germany	
	TEEPS	CERN	TEEPS	CERN	TEEPS	CERN
Yes	36%	83%	36%	80%	48%	73%
No	60	4	57	0	45	5
DK	4	13	7	20	7	22

Should Europe (TEEPS: Britain, France, Germany) go so far as to take a "third-force" (TEEPS: neutral) position?

Yes	7	60	15	60	19	64
No	90	22	74	10	73	9
DK	3	18	11	30	8	27

Is Europe (TEEPS: Britain, France, Germany) *likely* to take a "third-force" (TEEPS: neutral) position?

Yes	1	44	26	60	11	32
No	94	39	60	10	81	27
Other	0	4	0	10	0	23
DK	5	13	14	20	8	18

degree of divergence between the CERN and TEEPS panels is undoubtedly accentuated by the difference in question wording — since "third force" is a much stronger posture of independence than neutrality, and independence is a more tenable position for Europe as a whole than for Britain, France, or Germany alone. However, the evident trend is that the TEEPS panelists do not favor independence whereas the CERN panelists do — probably owing to their stronger desire for European autonomy from the United States which has already been indicated.

The two sets of panels are remarkably consistent across nations on this issue. A substantial majority of all three CERN national groups (83 per cent, 80 per cent, and 64 per cent) are even willing to see Europe take a "third force" position between the two superpowers. (The French group at CERN is the only one, however, that seems to believe that Europe is *likely* to do so.) The TEEPS panels, on the other hand, do *not favor* greater independence (with the exception of Germany, where the split is about even) and all three are quite strongly *against* a neutral position. Why this great divergence?

One factor which may account for it, at least in part, is the CERN panelists' evaluation of the military threat to Europe, presented in Table A3.8. The differences between the TEEPS and CERN panels indicate that the scientists are clearly much less concerned with a military threat to Europe than are the TEEPS panelists. Although the numbers vary somewhat, the trend is consistent across all three nationalities. Looking at the military situation this way, the scien-

TABLE A3.8. IMPORTANCE OF AMERICAN MILITARY GUARANTEE

If the American guarantee ceased to operate, how dangerous would this be for the security of Europe?

	Britain		France		Germany	
	TEEPS	CERN	TEEPS	CERN	TEEPS	CERN
Very Dangerous	48%	4%	0%	20%	68%	9%
Fairly Dangerous	28	39	79	10	23	40
Not Dangerous at All	16	52	14	30	5	18
DK	8	5	7	40	4	33

tists can certainly afford to seek greater independence for Europe.

In addition, the CERN scientists approach the whole problem of East-West relations in a significantly different way than do the TEEPS panelists. There is a tendency for CERN respondents to try to choose options that counteract, or at least minimize, the perpetuation of strong blocs of powers on either side. One German physicist's comment on the question of forming an Atlantic economic community (see Table A3.5) typified this attitude:

No, because the U.S.A. would dominate it and would therefore deepen the division of the world between the "Good West" and the "Evil East."

The tendency is also reflected in the responses given in Table A3.9, regarding a supranational force.

Here the CERN tendency to choose options that oppose regional formations — whether European or Atlantic — is clearly expressed. In the TEEPS survey, nearly three fourths of the British and German panels and more than a third of the French panel agreed to NATO auspices. At CERN, none of the British, none of the French,

TABLE A3.9. A SUPRANATIONAL FORCE

Would you approve the integration of the major part of your own country's armed forces into a permanent supranational force?

	Britain		France		Germany	
	TEEPS	CERN	TEEPS	CERN	TEEPS	CERN
Yes	58%	96%	67%	90%	38%	91%
No	36	0	17	0	59	0
DK	6	4	16	10	3	9

If such integration was agreed to by your government, would you prefer it to be under European, NATO, or UN auspices?

European	14	8	66	30	14	4
NATO	70	0	38	0	74	18
UN	0	78	—	30	0	59
Other†	11	13	13	30	9	14
DK	5	1	*	10	3	5

* Per cent in favor, asked individually yes or no.
† European and UN combined, chiefly.

and less than one fifth of the Germans preferred the NATO option. Some (especially among the French) chose the European option, but more favored the United Nations. Evidently, this is a much different type of military force than that envisioned by the TEEPS panelists. In view of the limited likelihood that such a UN force could come into being, and the severe constraints on its possible uses, one can interpret this idealistic response as expressing the desire of CERN panelists to impede further consolidation of the bipolar blocs or indeed to facilitate their decomposition.

A manifestation of this same orientation is evidenced in Table A3.10 in the choice of auspices for a rather different function — a multilateral agency to administer economic aid.

While there is wide variation among the TEEPS panels, CERN demonstrates a consistent preference for the UN option on this very different sort of issue. There is a very deep and widespread commitment at CERN to avoid hard East-West choices and to promote a maximum of opportunity for a larger world community.

5. Supranationalism or Transnationalism on Nuclear Weapons

This orientation bespeaks a type of *supranationalism* at CERN that goes beyond the *transnationalism* evidenced by the TEEPS

TABLE A3.10. WHICH MULTILATERAL AGENCY SHOULD ADMINISTER
ECONOMIC AID?

If such a multilateral agency were established, which auspices would
you prefer — European, Atlantic, or United Nations?

	Britain		France		Germany	
	TEEPS	CERN	TEEPS	CERN	TEEPS	CERN
European	4%	0%	31%	0%	13%	9%
Atlantic	4	0	14	0	36	0
UN	79	91	47	80	35	82
Other	9	4	0	10	7	4
DK	4	5	8	10	9	5

respondents. It involves more than acceptance of transnational solutions in fields of collective interest where it is politic to do so. The question of nuclear weapons is one on which many scientists, and in particular physicists, have been known to take strong stands.[11] At CERN the question of nuclear weapons served to point up another facet of the scientists' supranationalism. In Table A3.11, the CERN and TEEPS panels give their evaluations of the military and political significance of the British and French nuclear forces.

The British and French responses are worthy of close examination here. As compared with TEEPS, the CERN panelists of these nationalities are less likely to feel that these national nuclear forces are militarily significant and more likely to feel that they have political advantages. Of the British CERN panelists, in fact, 70 per cent feel that the British force has political advantages, while 80 per cent of the French CERN panelists ascribe political advantages to their nation's nuclear force.

Having recognized the political value of their national nuclear forces, the scientists at CERN then proceed to express, in Table A3.12, a willingness to surrender this advantage unilaterally.

The British TEEPS panel strongly rejected unilateral nuclear disarmament, three quarters replying negatively. But at CERN — even though 70 per cent of the British respondents felt that their force had political advantages (and 44 per cent felt it had military significance) — an overwhelming majority of 87 per cent favored giving it up unilaterally. In France, where 80 per cent of the scientists felt the force de frappe had political advantages, only 10 per cent opposed unilaterally abandoning it, whereas 30 per cent favored

TABLE A3.11.   MILITARY AND POLITICAL SIGNIFICANCE OF BRITISH
AND FRENCH NUCLEAR FORCES

Britain and France have developed their own nuclear weapons: Do you
think the British force has military significance? Political advantages?
Has the French *force de frappe* military significance? Political advantages?

	Britain		France		Germany	
	TEEPS	*CERN*	*TEEPS*	*CERN*	*TEEPS*	*CERN*
A. British force: military significance?						
Yes	60%	44%	39%	30%	25%	36%
No	28	52	37	50	57	50
DK	12	4	24	20	18	14
B. British force: political advantages?						
Yes	62	70	57	80	60	96
No	28	30	29	10	28	4
DK	10	0	14	10	12	0
C. French force: military significance?						
Yes	34	30	33	10	16	27
No	52	65	50	70	70	59
DK	14	5	17	20	14	14
D. French force: political advantages?						
Yes	59	74	59	80	63	91
No	32	26	28	10	28	9
DK	9	0	13	10	9	0

TABLE A3.12.   UNILATERAL NUCLEAR DISARMAMENT

Do you think your own national government should take serious steps
toward the adoption of unilateral nuclear disarmament as official policy?

	Britain		France		Germany	
	TEEPS	*CERN*	*TEEPS*	*CERN*	*TEEPS*	*CERN**
Yes	19%	87%	21%	30%	11%	46%
No	75	9	66	10	87	9
DK	6	4	13	60	2	45

* Not really applicable nationally (owing to German laws on ABC weapons).
British and German figures are 1961.

unilateral disarmament. It is perhaps a tribute to De Gaulle's promotion of the *force de frappe* that 60 per cent of the CERN Frenchmen fell into the Don't Know category. This may be an interesting example of a strong "cross-pressure" between the scientists' own views and a government policy. In any case, the fact that some 60 per cent are ambivalent on unilateral disarmament is significant for the deviance of the French contingent at CERN.

F. SUMMARY AND CONCLUSIONS

From the interview and questionnaire responses of these CERN scientists, we have attempted to bring out some of the salient features of their world view. Bearing in mind the general *caveats* which must accompany any interpretive analysis of this sort and the additional qualifications that stem from the restricted size of the CERN panel, we found that several nascent themes nevertheless emerge from the data.

The strong interest in politics which the scientists professed in the interviews was evidenced in their willingness to complete the lengthy political questionnaire and in their generally thorough and knowledgeable treatment of it. The broad scope of the TEEPS project and the fact that the questions were posed to individuals of several different nationalities at CERN necessitated that the subject matter deal with political issues at the international level. Thus the scientists, who indicated that their political interests were focused on the international rather than the national or local level, were conveniently accommodated. The scientists' low emotional involvement in politics — as contrasted with their high level of analytical interest and relatively high level of information — was manifested through the "expert syndrome." This was exhibited by their hesitancy to give "amateurish" opinions in areas which they felt required expert knowledge outside of their own competence.

The general tendency for the scientists to be Left-oriented (as distinct from Left-affiliated) was illustrated in the interviews. Their broad consensus *qua* scientists on values, assumptions, and styles of thought — deriving from the association of "leftism" with such qualities as idealism, generosity, objectivity, and optimism — showed in the substantial tendency of the CERN scientists to agree with each other on specific issues more often than they agreed with their nonscientist compatriots.

CERN scientists from Britain, France, and Germany disagreed with their compatriot TEEPS panelists in their prognosis for the integrative efforts of the European Community. This, apparently, reflected their vision and hopes for European integration on a wider scale. The fact that the notion of an Atlantic Community did not generate great enthusiasm among the scientists was related, together with their expressed desire for greater independence for Europe, to the scientists' consistent preference for United Nations options. On balance, this was seen as part of an underlying commitment among the scientists to avoid hard East-West (Cold War) choices and look toward a wider world community. Finally, the sort of supranationalism among the scientists which developed in these questions was dramatically illustrated in their willingness to surrender unilaterally (apparently for the perceived good of mankind as a whole) the actual and potential advantages which they recognized in their national nuclear forces.

The outcome of the disarmament question, while not conclusive in itself, suggests a tentative analytic scheme that can be used to relate many opinions on specific issues into the general framework outlined at the beginning of this annex. We recall that one major conclusion of the TEEPS study concerned the transformation of nationalism. The British, French, and German panels over the decade 1955–1965 approved of and gave priority to so many different forms of transnational activity that nationalism itself has been transformed.

While the test of "goodness" for some of the TEEPS elites is still how well an idea contributes to national advancement, the European environment today tends to encourage the reshaping of TEEPS transnational values into supranational form among the scientists and "technocrats" of CERN. It is suggested, along these lines, that one may distinguish the supranationalism shown by the CERN respondents by the fact that they do *not* judge the "goodness" of international activities (and even some national activities, like unilateral disarmament) by their contribution to national advancement. The scientists' interest in world affairs — shaped by an image of a world community in which idealism, generosity, and objectivity guide the public affairs of all peoples — manifests itself in many of the views just described. The frame of reference within which they evaluate national and world problems and policies is certainly much larger than their own national origins and loyalties.

It is evident that the number of scientists and technocrats, represented in our study by the CERN panel, is increasing in Europe today. It is also likely that their influence upon the other elites, represented by TEEPS, is increasing. What remains to be seen is the tempo and balance of historical acceleration by TEEPS, under the influence of CERN among others, in the direction of a world commonwealth of human dignity.

Elites and Governments: An Evaluative Memo*

THIS experiment was designed to find some of the limits of the evidence and inference in the TEEPS materials. The first problem posed is the "eliteness" of the panels. While a great deal of thought and theory went into the design of the panels, there is no readily acceptable and operational definition of elite that can establish, without controversy, that the TEEPS panels are truly the elites of the countries under investigation.

The definition of elite varies with different assumptions, purposes, criteria, and specifications of elite status. Without a narrow and limited set of specifications, there always will be some doubt about eliteness. We cannot provide a definitive answer to this question.

However, linked to the question of the definition of elite is still another question of the impact of the elite on the future of the countries' policies. We cannot simply extrapolate our elite marginals to determine the policies of the governments on the issues in the interviews. Between the statement of elite attitudes and the formulation of government policy lies the intervention of a political system with its multiple causal factors which mediate between desire and performance. Clearly the analyst would do well to provide some limits of inference which would establish at least the lower limits of certainty regarding the inferences about the applicability of TEEPS data to government policy in the countries under investigation.

The question of the definition of elite and the inference about the

* Adapted from a working paper by John Child, Jr.

379

elite survey results are linked questions because one criterion of eliteness might require that elite people are those whose preferences create government policy. If people are important for policy, then their preferences should matter. The link between these questions is the inference that if elite opinions are causal, then their preferences must be congruent with government policy. We cannot answer the causal question here, but a measure of congruence between elite preferences and government policy might be part of the certification of elite status, though congruence is neither a necessary nor sufficient test of eliteness.

We have designed a measure of congruence, but before presenting the results an important limit on the test must be made. The purpose of the TEEPS program was not simply to measure the attitudes of the men in power. Other techniques would have been more efficient for that. The definition of elite used in panel selection is not bounded by decision-making capacity; rather it is more broadly drawn to see how leading men in Europe responded to the challenge of the new era following World War II. Leading men in various sectors do not necessarily add up to government performance. We wanted to interview the "outs" as well as the "ins." Therefore, the test of congruence is used in this context to help explore the limits of inference from TEEPS data to government policy. In sum, the TEEPS data cannot be used like an opinion poll before an election. It is not designed to predict the winner. Its purposes are broader. However, the temptation to use it to predict likely policy is understandable, and after examination of the results of the experiment, it will be shown to be partially possible.

The test for congruence between government policy and elite preferences consisted of coding government policy in the same codebook used to produce marginals on the computer. We then matched the marginals against the government "answers." We selected approximately twenty questions each from the 1961 and 1965 surveys in Britain, France, and Germany. Questions were selected for which there was a clear government policy enunciated. Where the judges, Dr. Lerner, Dr. Gorden, and Mr. Child, could not agree what government policy was at the time of the interview, the question was struck from the list of indicators. Examples of congruence, dissonance, and question rejection will serve to illustrate the methodology.

One example of elite-government congruence can be found in

the question concerning British entry into the Common Market. In 1965, in Britain and West Germany, there was a congruence between government policy to encourage British entry, and the elite marginals in the two countries. In France, however, the same question is an example of dissonance, because the marginals showed the French elite clearly favored entry but the government did not.

An illustration of the type of question rejected because of ambiguity in classification can be found in the questionnaire item asking for a preference between foreign aid administered bilaterally or multilaterally. Government preference is difficult to determine since both forms of aid are practiced, and there is no easily agreed upon criterion for establishing government preference. Therefore, the judges excluded the question from consideration.

The results of the coding suggest three separate findings. There are patterns by nation, by time, and by degree of elite consensus. The national difference is marked between France and the other two nations. The West German and British elites both have a high rate of congruence with government policies compared to the French, as is illustrated in Table A4.1.

TABLE A4.1.   ELITE — GOVERNMENT-POLICY CONGRUENCE

	Britain		France		Germany	
	1961	1965	1961	1965	1961	1965
	$n = 19$	$n = 19$	$n = 24$	$n = 21$	$n = 23$	$n = 18$
Degree of Congruence	79%	89%	61%	48%	83%	82%

The table shows the marked national patterns. We cannot say if the French dissonance is to be explained by panel selection or by a schism between the French government and the French elite. However, there is much more other evidence to suggest that foreign policy, which makes up the bulk of the questioning, is not formulated by a large number of Frenchmen. If we want to know the determining force of French foreign policy in the Fifth Republic, relatively few, and perhaps one, interview would do.

The patterns over time are also subject to national differences. A stable relationship between the West German government and its elite is evident. The British panel shows a gain, but the n is small and the questions are not exactly the same. Overinterpretation must be avoided. The decline in French congruence is only slightly more marked. However, the change is in the direction of maintaining national patterns with a congruence between the British and West German elites and their respective governments and a divorce between the French elite and government.

All the available surveys were not used in this experiment; so the findings can be expanded in the future. One last finding must especially await confirmation. With the high percentage of congruence, the n for dissonance is too small to verify patterning. However, in the British and West German cases, it appears that a unified elite is always congruent with government policy. The cases of dissonance occur only on the questions where the elite itself is divided.

For example, in both years treated there is only one case of dissonance in Britain on a question for which the elite marginals were 75 per cent or more in favor of a position. All the rest of the dissonance occurs below the 75 per cent agreement level. In West Germany, in both years, there is not a single case of dissonance above a 70 per cent level of agreement. Thus, a unified elite is a strong indicator of government position in the two countries where elite and government positions are congruent. In France the lack of any strong relation between elite preferences and government policy precludes any such pattern based on a unified elite. Even when the elite is unified, there is no marked tendency for congruence.

Annex Four has shown that in two countries, the elite panels' preferences are congruent with government policy. The elite preferences were poor guides to government policy in the French case. From this exercise, we cannot conclude that the elites cause government policy. We do not know whether they influenced policy or were influenced by it. We do, however, have some sense of the limits of inference that may be drawn from our marginals. Clearly the elite relationship is not one-to-one; but in two of the three cases. we do have a congruence encouraging consideration of elites as a factor in the formulation of government policy.

Personality and Politics:
A Memo on Cross-Tabs

MUCH emphasis in this book has been placed on the distribution of responses in each TEEPS panel as a whole, because a significant record of the transformation of the European elite was depicted by the year-to-year trends in these marginals. In this annex, we will report results from cross-tabulation analysis that illustrate some of the useful qualifiers obtained by this finer-grained mode of testing marginal distributions. A major purpose of cross-tabulation is to highlight the frequency and significance of differences *within* panels. Differences among TEEPS respondents often failed to reveal consistent and stable lines of division; on many key issues, "deviant cases" in the cross-tabs comprised minorities of 10 per cent or less of the total panel. Such cross-tabs reconfirmed the widespread consensus shown by the marginal distributions. However, some cross-tabs did produce more interesting qualifiers on marginal results.

One suggestive set of results was found when we cross-tabulated French responses on a variety of questions by a few basic personality variables. While this matter did not receive primary emphasis in the survey design, a few questions regarding the fundamental personal predispositions of our panelists were placed in several surveys. Thus, they were asked questions requiring the projection of themselves into hypothetical situations. They were asked where they would like to live if they could no longer live in their native country. They were asked what they would do if their country became a Communist nation. They were asked which generation — their own, their parents', or their children's — was the best one in which to live. They were asked: "What would you do if you had your life to live over again?" From this array of projective questions, an attempt was made to find those who were hypothesized to be more closed-minded and traditionalist, less able to project into unknown situations, and generally narrower in their perspective of "what is possible."

It was expected that these people could be contrasted against the more open-minded who sought new ways to solve problems; who could envisage themselves in unknown situations; who could imagine the world to be other than it is. The basic distinction between open- and closed-mindedness succeeded only partially in explaining some of the attitudinal differences among our respondents. These several projective questions were combined in various arrays to see if a consistent pattern among them would allow a differentiation of personality types on the principle of open- or closed-mindedness. While results of limited significance were obtained in a few instances, we soon discovered that consistent and stable groups could not easily be built on the indexes formed by these questions.

An example of the limited results obtained is the question asking French respondents where they would like to live if they could not live in France. The respondents were separated into four groups according to the degree of "wandering" they would be willing to do. The group that chose a culture and a distance farthest away from France was contrasted with other groups choosing to stay closer, in miles and in language. Thus, a respondent who chose Belgium was ranked as someone who preferred to stay near "home" as opposed to another who chose America or Brazil, and still another who chose some non-French-speaking Asian or African country.

It was hypothesized that those who are willing to travel farthest from home would also be those most willing to accept new ideas. This hypothesis proved correct only in a limited number of cases. For example, those wishing to wander farthest away identified themselves as least nationalistic of all respondents. They were also most willing to accept supranational organizations, even those that would restrict France's foreign policy.

A similar attempt was made to separate those who approved of modern art from those who did not, but the results again yielded no clear-cut correspondence with political attitudes on Europa and Atlantica. These results were not so much negative as inconclusive. This is due largely to the strong consensus on these key issues that we have reported throughout the book. The panels did not divide *enough* on these issues to support *any* cross-tabular explanation of differences among individual respondents. Europa and Atlantica were, in this sense, "beyond personality."

On a few issues, however, there was some evidence that attitudes toward international relations are linked to personality variables. For example, we found that respondents who supported the manufacture of atomic bombs and other military equipment also tended to believe in corporal punishment of their children. This example led us to pursue the relation between child rearing and political choices.

Three groups were established on the basis of the responses to the question: "In your opinion, should one praise a good child before other people?" The yes and the no responses defined relatively coherent groups, while the DK response failed to designate a profile as consistent as the others. Table A5.1 shows consistent differences between the yes and no groups in response to further questions on child rearing such as:

Should one punish a child if he is bad?
Should one reward a good child?

TABLE A5.1. CHILD-REARING PRACTICES

	n	Punish			Reward		
		Yes	*No*	*DK*	*Yes*	*No*	*DK*
Praisers	(43)	28%	72%	0%	69%	7%	24%
Nonpraisers	(40)	44	54	2	60	20	20
DK	(15)	33	60	7	31	9	60

While the differences are not great, they do run consistently in the same direction as between these two equal-sized groups. The 43 praisers are less disposed to punish and more disposed to reward children than the 40 nonpraisers. Pursuing this cross-tab further, we found the praisers to be more exposed to their external environment than the nonpraisers. For example, 20 per cent more of them own a television set. And again, when asked about their travel habits, 20 per cent more of the praisers indicated the highest category (3–4 times a year) than among the nonpraisers. An item of special piquancy is the question: "In your opinion, have the social sciences reached a point where they can significantly modify man?" The affirmative response to this was 72 per cent among praisers as compared with 51 per cent among nonpraisers.

As this response may contain ambiguous elements which we did not test, we suggest only that it may indicate among the praisers a greater sense of optimism about human perfectibility — or at least human improvement. A similar interpretation is suggested by comparing their responses to the question: "Of the three basic concepts — Liberty, Equality, Fraternity — which responds best to present needs?" A full 55 per cent of the praisers chose Fraternity, while the nonpraisers scattered their ballots or were nonresponsive. It seems reasonable to infer that the praisers are more "open" personalities, if only in the sense that they expose themselves more widely and frequently to the external world and take a more optimistic view of its possibilities.

The optimism of the praisers is exhibited rather consistently in a series of questions about current world politics. When asked whether "your generation will see a third world war" two thirds of the praisers said no as compared with one third of the nonpraisers. On the success of summit talks in Geneva, the praisers were almost evenly divided, while the nays outnumbered the yeas by over two to one among the nonpraisers. Again, the praisers were considerably more optimistic that the Cold War was yielding to coexistence in the world arena — and would continue to do so in the years ahead. They were, indeed, even more optimistic about France's current economic position and about the prospects that it would improve "over the long run." Table A5.2 gives some of the cross-tabulations on which the foregoing summary is based.

A final set of cross-tabulations relates more directly to the central concerns of this book and raises some interesting questions. We have noted the predominant consensus that favors both Europa and Atlantica throughout the TEEPS surveys. The consensus reappeared, of course, in these cross-tabs, but they produced a small though consistent deviation that seems noteworthy. With respect to all existing European and Atlantic institutions, the praisers were consistently less positive than the nonpraisers. The former gave substantial majorities of yea-sayers to The Six, OEEC, and NATO, but these majorities were regularly smaller than those among the nonpraisers — and smaller by as much as 16 per cent!

This seemed rather surprising until we noted how differently the two groups responded to the question: "In your opinion, will the

TABLE A5.2.   OPTIMISM OF PRAISERS

| | World War III? | | | Geneva Summit Success? | | | Cold War/ Coexistence? | | | France's Position? | | |
	Yes	No	DK	Yes	No	DK	C.W.	Coex	DK	Good	Bad	DK
Praisers	23%	60%	17%	40%	47%	13%	19%	40%	41%	40%	43%	17%
Nonpraisers	42	35	23	30	64	6	26	30	44	32	56	12

French make good Europeans?" Here the cross-tab was as shown in Table A5.3.

This lower appraisal of their compatriots' Europeanism appeared to be inconsistent with the more optimistic views expressed by the praisers on most issues. A clue was provided by one French respondent — a declared transnationalist — who disdained the existing institutions of Europa and Atlantica because they "merely raise parochialism to an international level." For this individual,

TABLE A5.3. FRENCH MAKE GOOD EUROPEANS?

	Yes	No	DK
Praisers	47%	24%	29%
Nonpraisers	62	9	30

otherwise an optimistic praiser, the Europe of Six was little more than a foreclosure of more open and adventurous experiments in rearranging the environment of the postwar world. The praisers in our cross-tab appear, in like manner, to reserve their enthusiasm for what they regard as larger enterprises.

So, the nonpraisers, with their relatively lower expectations of the future, come down more firmly in support of the existing institutions. They perceive the Europe of Six, in particular, to be invested with that closed structure of relationships which they consistently prefer in other fields as well — from child raising to world politics. The praisers, on the other hand, are rather less keen about those existing structures, particularly the Europe of Six, which seem to them closed rather than open and rigid rather than adaptive to new experience. Of the existing European institutions, only the Council of Europe (the largest and least effective, but certainly most "open") draws from them a larger margin of support than it draws from the nonpraisers.

Even more striking is the support drawn from the praisers by the United Nations. Even before De Gaulle snubbed it as *ce machin-là*, many Frenchmen tended to regard as *pas sérieux* an organization in which Gabon could have a vote of equal weight with the vote of France. The studies of Marguerite Nusslé-Kramer (listed in Annex Eight), along with other findings reported in this book, amply document the relatively low esteem for the UN among our French panel (relative, for example, to the evaluations expressed by our British and German panels). All the more surprising, in this context, is the finding turned up by our cross-tab on the UN. The question asked simply: "Do you think the UN will be able to play an important role in the future?" Table A5.4 reports the results.

Is this significant? In the statistical sense, the answer is affirmative. In the sociological sense, since we are dealing with a "reasonable sample" of the French elite, the answer is again affirmative. In the political — or policy science — sense, the significance can

TABLE A5.4. IMPORTANT UN ROLE IN FUTURE?

	Yes	*No*	*DK*
Praisers	62%	32%	6%
Nonpraisers	42	51	7

only be inferred, intuitively, from the data. Perhaps this is as much service as attitude research can render to policy thinking at present. But it is surely useful to know that, even among the "hard-headed" French elite, there exists a small hard core of people who, without rejecting Europa or Atlantica, still look beyond these existing institutions toward a larger and more inclusive framework for organizing the world political system. How the leads given by these cross-tabs may be followed up methodologically is indicated in the following annexes.

Computer Experiments: A Memo on Clusters*

SURVEY research often introduces a deliberate bias into its own procedures. In the design of a survey instrument, for example, one often makes a conscious decision to deal with choices of political significance rather than arrays of personal wishes. The TEEPS data are the outcome of many such decisions. Throughout our study we have formed groups of respondents by *a priori* defining a characteristic or set of characteristics and clustering respondents who shared these attributes. Although the ADMINS system described in Annex Seven was designed to allow for more flexibility in the search for empirically derived attitudinal patterns, we still sought an experimental technique that would allow us to rely less on preselection and make a more open search for patterns in the data. The present experiment is unique in that it borrowed a taxonomic program originally designed for botanical classification and adapted it to aid the identification of attitudinal coalitions.

A. ALTERNATIVE APPROACHES IN PATTERN ANALYSIS

1. Factor Analysis

Data classification has received attention from systematists in many disciplines. One of the original attempts at a systematic overview of variation among attributes was factor analysis of psychological data, which we first used to help reduce the attributes of

* This annex is based mainly on work done by Bruce Jacobs, then an undergraduate majoring in Political Science at M.I.T., and Richard A. Barnes of Barss, Reitzel, and Associates, Inc., Cambridge, Massachusetts.

personality to major independent "factors." The research approach was soon restructured to enable selection of individuals into independent personality types. Actually, each individual personality was seen as a linear function of independent personality components or factors. The "input data" were usually ordered quantitatively (e.g., as scores on tests), or dichotomously (e.g., male or female). The data were thus amenable to simple correlation analysis for the calculation of similarities between individuals.

2. Agreement Analysis

One output that early factor analyses failed to provide was a list of attributes held in common across the membership of a personality type. Instead, the personality type was listed as a set of linear numerical coefficients. Louis McQuitty attempted to overcome this problem.[1] Called *agreement analysis,* the McQuitty method first calculated "agreement scores" between individuals. It then clustered the individuals so as to satisfy the following criteria:

1. There were a set of attributes which were held in common by *every* member of the type; and
2. Any attribute that did not fulfill the first criterion was termed "irrelevant."

Relevant attributes could then be listed. The descriptive weakness in factor analysis was thus overcome.

McQuitty's criteria for the relevant attributes deserve close scrutiny, for they are importantly differentiated from factor analysis. In the latter method, the factor coefficient indicates the degree to which the set of attributes obtaining for an individual holds to a component type. This probabilistic property of a factorial typology may be called "polythetic." On the other hand, the criteria for clustering in agreement analysis impose "monothetic" requirements, for an individual's attributes must be those commonly held by all members of a cluster in order to qualify for membership in that cluster.

3. Numerical Taxonomy

A quite different discipline attacking the classification problem has supplied a further step in the development of pattern analytic methods. As in McQuitty's analysis, biology's numerical taxonomy must classify units according to similarity in both unordered and ordered data. Moreover, numerical taxonomy must face the problem of "level of explanation" in its classification of biological species. A unit could, for example, be classified as an "animal" with certain attributes common to all animals. Alternatively, it could be classed as a "mammal," with specific attributes distinguishing it from other animal classes. Each classification is correct; each provides a different set of information. Thus, the level of explanation is seen to be dependent on the purpose of the study.

The approaches just outlined have been described according to three characteristics:

1. The nature of the measurement of similarity;
2. The monothetic versus the polythetic criterion for membership in a cluster; and
3. The level of explanation required for the classification.

By relating these issues to our TEEPS data, we were able to identify a single approach as most applicable to the task of quickly identifying empirically derived attitudinal patterns.

B. PATTERN ANALYSIS OF POLITICAL ATTITUDE DATA

The data in The European Elite Panel Survey are, for the most part, neither ordinal nor dichotomous. As they are not readily amenable to correlational analysis, the data of this project do not satisfy the criteria originally set down by factor analysts. Although some of these criteria have recently been relaxed as the factor analytic process has become more sophisticated, its application to our form of attitude data is still subject to some difficulty.[2]

Comparing agreement analysis and numerical taxonomy, the related issues of level of explanation and monothetic-polythetic criteria come into focus. In performing an agreement analysis, an unanswered question might remove an individual from a cluster even though he would qualify as a member if he had answered the question.

It is easy to see that the greater the number of responses which *must* be given by *all* members of a cluster the less will be the membership of the cluster. If data also happen to be "sketchy," the clusters will further decrease their memberships. The number of clusters can become quite large by such a process, with the result that the attitudinal patterns become meaningless and without operational utility.

Choice of a classification technique is similarly affected by the level of explanation at which one wants to work. It was noted earlier that in every pattern analytic method, the greater the number of respondents in a cluster, the fewer the attributes held in common by all members of the cluster. If strictly adhered to, the agreement analysis approach might produce a type which would be reduced to two or three common responses in order to meet the monothetic criterion.

Numerical taxonomy solves the *reductio ad absurdum* problem. It allows an acceptable number of attributes to be included in the attitudinal pattern by using the polythetic criterion. Moreover, it systematically provides information on respondents clustering at different levels of explanation. This enables the analyst to balance the dichotomy between the number of attributes defining a type and the number of respondents adhering to that type. Finally, numerical taxonomy allows for the correction of similarity scores by keeping missing information from artificially lowering the similarity measure between two respondents.

Theoretical and operational imperatives thus combined to suggest that numerical taxonomy be chosen for use in the research.

C. THE ROGERS GRAPH THEORY METHOD

A method for clustering into botanic types was developed by Professor David J. Rogers of Colorado State University and the University of Colorado. The original program was written by Dr. Rogers and Mr. Robert C. Brill for use on an IBM-7044 computer. It has been improved and revised by Mr. Richard A. Barnes of Barss, Reitzel, and Associates, Inc. for use on an IBM 360/75 computer.

In order to utilize the taxonomic program, the analyst must first specify those questions upon which the similarity coefficients will be based. This group of variables will thus serve as an agenda for clustering respondents. It is also possible at this point to set up simulated respondents by outlining response patterns for the questions and including these patterns in the respondent data base. The simulated respondent will act as a "tracer" and help identify the clusters that form around him.

The first task of the taxonomic program is to calculate for each respondent a coefficient of similarity with every other respondent. These similarity ratios are computed as follows:

1. The computer considers each combination of two respondents individually. The program identifies which of the specified questions have been answered by both respondents.

2. The analyst can specify one of two modes of comparison for these questions. The first of these is the *unweighted mode.* Here, the program simply takes that percentage of answers which the respondents agree on in the preselected data base and stores this percentage as the similarity ratio. Questions that either of the respondents have not answered are not included in this percentage calculation.[3] The second alternative for the calculation of similarity ratios is the *weighted mode.* Here, each question answered by both respondents and specified in the input is handled separately. For each question, the computer first calculates the marginal percentage of each response for the entire sample of respondents. The program then assigns the complement of this percentage as the value of agreement on this response. To make this clearer, consider a question with the following marginals:

Response	Percentage
Yes	65
No	25
DK	10

If the two respondents have different answers to this question, their value of agreement on this question is 0. If they both answered yes to the question, their similarity value for this question is $1.00 - .65 = .35$. If they both answered "don't know," the value would be $1.00 - .10 = .90$. This value is calculated for each question that both respondents have answered. The mean of these similarity values then becomes the similarity ratio between the respondents.

3. The procedure for the calculation of similarity ratios is carried out for each combination of two respondents.

These steps produce a square matrix of similarity ratios among all respondents. This ends phase one of the program.

Phase two of the taxonomic program sorts this similarity matrix in order of the similarity ratios. Hence, the first value in this new set will represent the highest similarity ratio. This then identifies that pair of respondents with most agreement on the survey questions.

Phase three in the program accomplishes the process of clustering respondents according to their similarity.[4] Most of the work in this section of the program involves scanning the sorted similarity matrix produced in the second phase. This search mechanism actually consists of two scanning processes. One of these searches for all respondents which have a minimum similarity with any of the respondents in a cluster. The other scan is a "look-ahead" search for that similarity value which is closest to this minimum but still less than it.

The process then begins with the most similar pair forming the first cluster. The first scan searches for all respondents that either have a similarity ratio equal to this between themselves or with one member of the cluster. If the requirement is met with a member of the original cluster, the respondent joins the cluster. If the similarity is between two respondents not in the cluster, they begin another cluster. This process continues until the similarity matrix contains no more similarity ratios as high as the first (i.e., highest) ratio. Thus, the first "level of explanation" is complete. The most highly similar clusters have been formed. Note, however, that these clusters contain the least respondents.

The look-ahead scan has identified the next highest similarity value and has "gathered" those respondents which will either join existing clusters or form new ones at this lower level of similarity. Each respondent joins that cluster which contains the respondent to whom he is most similar. If, at a level of similarity, respondents in two clusters meet that level of similarity required for cluster formation, the clusters will collapse into one. The process continues until there is one cluster containing all respondents.

At each level, all clusters are printed out. The similarity ratio that was the basis for that cluster formation is specified. The degree to which these cluster members agree to this ratio is also pointed out. This figure gives a measure of the internal consistency of the cluster. Thus, the program identifies attitudinal patterns among respondents on the basis of similarities among them. The taxonomy gives us attitudinally defined coalitions for analysis.

D. SUMMARY OF RESULTS

We made three types of tests with the taxonomic program on the British 1965 security questions. The first was a broad search for clusters with equally weighted questions and one simulated "nationalist" as a tracer. The second included three tracers, adding an internationalist and a supranationalist, but with questions weighted to give the controversial and divisive issues more weight than those on which there was general agreement. The third included all the features of the second but divided the respondents into those expressing a preference for the Conservative Party and those for the Labour Party. In all of these tests, we did an analysis to determine: (1) the characteristics of a group in a cluster and (2) the critical point at which different clusters merged and lost their unique identity. We thus were in a position to define coalitions and the attitudinal requirements for coalition growth. From this information we also were given further support for the conclusion in Chapter Ten that a consensus in security matters has had great impact within the British elite. A summary of each test will indicate the potential of the program.

The salient characteristics of the *first test* (which used the unweighted similarity ratio) were the identification of numerous small clusters of less than ten respondents, one cluster including our simulated nationalist. At one point, a jump in size of the main cluster brought it to 52 people, where we found 96 per cent agreement on 3 questions out of 49, but 65 per cent agreement on 30 out of 49. The analytic feature of interest here is that we do not have to define our cluster as having or not having particular characteristics. We can have a measure of degree so that the defining characteristic is not as rigidly defined *a priori* as in other data-handling systems. The marginals for the cluster can be used to differentiate it from the total panel sample. At the lower level of agreement for admission to the cluster, there was little to distinguish it from the total panel. We therefore turned to weighted marginals to see if a more distinctive group would form.

In *test two* the marginals weighted by the described algorithm netted more distinctive groups. Twenty nationalists clustered around our simulated tracer with the results shown in Table A6.1. It is not our purpose in this annex to describe the substantive findings; it is interesting to note that we identified a multivariate cluster much more quickly than with previous data-handling systems. We also found results we may not have searched for; i.e., that nationalists in security matters in Britain include leftists and pacifists as well as rightists and aggressive respondents.

There are other tables from this run which we have not included here. For example, we identified the consistent internationalists and watched their cluster grow from 13 to 32 members to include the supranationalists as well at a lower level of agreement.

There is one characteristic of this run which is worthy of special mention, for it reinforces the conclusions drawn in Chapter Ten that the Atlantic security consensus in Britain is shared by many different types that are readily aggregated into the consensus. The relatively pure clusters of one or another "ist" were small in number, illustrating the failure of ideological principles of nationalism or transnationalism. Furthermore, by the time the cluster grew to 76 out of 316 respondents, it had already aggregated our extremist tracers, and the cluster marginals were virtually indistinguishable for the total panel. The lowest common denominator was readily found in the Atlantic consensus.

The *third test* limited our respondent list to supporters of the Conservative Party ($n = 103$) and a separate list of Labour Party supporters ($n = 124$). We wanted to compare the clusters within each party to the results of the previous tests. Similar results were obtained — not surprising in the light of the conclusions in Chapter Ten, which showed the weakness of party influence on attitude formation. There were few extremists clustering around our tracers in the Conservative list, 7 nationalists and 23 internationalists and supranationalists. By the time 44 respondents had joined a cluster, it included all our tracers and a very close approximation of the total party distribution. The Labour list was similar with 13 nationalists and 32 supranationalists, and it only took 44 members to approximate the total.

Subsequent tests in all three countries in 1965, with questions selected to investigate the issues of protection and prosperity dealt with in Chapters Four and Five, netted similar results. That is, small clusters of like-minded respondents formed around expected "isms," but the clusters were few in number and quickly collapsed into the larger consensus on the issues, as described in the foregoing chapters.

We conclude that this experiment with taxonomic programing of

TABLE A6.1. NATIONALIST CLUSTER

	Question*	Response	Total Panel	Nationalists
1	cold war trend	1 accom	67%	71%
2	start of war	2 xelte	61	62
3	pwr bal trend	2 comm	21	24
		3 west	18	10
		5 nethr	32	33
4	indep role	2 no	60	76
5	nutrl role	2 no	90	67
6	indep role likely	2 no	73	62
7	nutrl role likely	2 no	93	86
8	xpct problm from	2 france	58	24
9	fav supra nukforc	2 no	47	76
10	fav unil disarm	2 no	75	48
11	fut ae devel br	1 nat	38	43
		2 intnat	34	48
12	fut ae devel	1 eur	32	0
		3 un	28	38
13	dgaul wekn us lead	1 yes	58	57
14	dgaul wekn allianc	1 yes	58	48
15	br afford eec	2 cntnot	74	29
16	union of 6 likly	1 yes	36	19
		2 no	51	71
17	br reduce cw ties	1 yes	58	14
18	eec prosper we br	1 yes	74	86
19	respons 4 eec div	2 france	65	52
20	lgr econ commun	1 yes	41	19
		2 no	52	67
21	own nukes	1 yes	54	57
22	manufacture nukes	1 yes	46	52
23	ntegrat supraforc	1 yes	58	19
24	auspcs 4 supraforc	1 eur	5	0
		2 nato	26	0
25	nato deter suffice	1 yes	67	43
26	nato def suffice	1 yes	43	10
27	rus threat shrtrm	1 yes	36	14
		2 no	37	29
28	rus threat	1 econ	9	14
		2 pol	29	10
		3 mil	16	5
29	mst security br	3 nato	55	24
30	nxt security br	2 am-con	53	33
31	1st security br	1 nat	67	38
32	own fleet br	2 mnf	41	38
33	br nuke signif	1 yes	60	52

Question*	Response	Total Panel	Nationalists
34 fr nuke signif	1 yes	34	38
	2 no	52	48
35 br nuke pol adv	1 yes	62	52
36 fr nuke pol adv	1 yes	59	43
37 fr maintain nukes	1 yes	44	57
	2 no	32	19
38 for edc today	1 yes	46	14
39 am guarnte continu	1 yes	81	48
40 dnger nd us guarnte	1 very	48	19
41 ncrs eur shre def	1 yes	46	19
42 ncrs eur shre aid	1 yes	60	43
43 restrct am invest	2 no	55	43
44 for germ unif	1 yes	43	19
	2 no	39	62
45 germ unif v nato	1 nato	63	38
46 nation state obsol	1 yes	55	29
47 good natstat obsol	1 yes	67	57
48 eec at pt no rtrn	1 yes	66	38
49 further eec integ	2 delayed	48	48
50 party affil	1 conser	32	30
	2 labour	39	35
	3 liberal	15	10
51 political orient	1 xlft	2	10
	2 left	9	20
	3 modlft	29	15
	4 centre	24	5
	5 modrt	20	25
	6 right	3	5
	7 xrt	1	

* See questionnaire in Annex One for full text of questions.

social science data has been highly successful. We have rapidly and empirically determined clusters of attributes and respondents which have reliably identified insights for attitudinal coalition potentials in our data. We have also found general measures of structure within a body of data as we watch clusters develop. The highly automated technique did a rapid and open search with findings consistent with more laborious and time-consuming methods.

TEEPS and ADMINS: A Memo on Data Management

OVER the years of the TEEPS survey, several different data-processing methods have been employed as new capabilities have become available. The most useful current capability is the ADMINS system — an on-line system for the treatment of social science data, implemented on the M.I.T. time-shared computer facilities. As ADMINS has been described adequately elsewhere, only a brief description will be given here.[1] Rather, the major portion of this annex will be devoted to illustrating the improved capability ADMINS has given us (1) to search for logic trees in the structure of attitudes and (2) to analyze logic trees with respondents who participated in more than one survey (i.e., repeaters).

ADMINS is designed to permit the social scientist who is not himself a skilled programmer, working at the console, to start with the rawest of data and to end up with an analysis.[2] The philosophy of the ADMINS systems is based on the premise that the relationship between the social scientist and the computer should be *interactive*. This means that the social scientist should be able to put a question about his data to the computer as he thinks of it; receive an answer in seconds; choose his next question on the basis of the answer he has just received; put his next question to the computer and receive a prompt answer; and so proceed step by step.

This approach to data analysis conforms to the basic conceptual form of data handling used by social scientists. Until recently, however, most social science data was handled by "batch processing" at a central computation facility, where it took hours and often days to receive results. Under these conditions, the analyst tended to ask a great many questions simultaneously to avoid the long delays required by serial questioning. By circumventing this problem of "turn-around time," ADMINS is designed to make analysis a more natural and efficient process by enabling the sequence of questions to grow out of previous answers.

ADMINS was conceived broadly as a data-management system for all types of information files that are in relatively "structured" form (e.g., library catalogues, census statistics, personnel files, etc.). We have used it here only to produce analyses of our TEEPS survey data. That is, we have taken an ensemble of 15 codebooks (5 years, 3 countries per year) and 15 data sets, one corresponding to each codebook, and through ADMINS we have performed various operations both within each survey (codebook and corresponding data set) and across several surveys (cross-file analysis).

Previously, much manual labor was necessary to generate tables that compared distributions from multiple surveys. ADMINS makes these procedures much more feasible. Not all problems have been solved, of course. We shall report some negative results which are due to difficulties in the data base itself. Some of these problems (such as small n) no data management system, however efficient it is, can solve.

A. EXPERIMENT 1: BRITAIN AND EUROPE

As a first example, we shall see how logic trees were constructed from the data by grouping respondents on empirically generated indexes and then comparing the distributions of attitudes expressed by those respondents on a variety of other options presented to them by the survey. This particular analysis sought to find the dominant positions which the British respondents took vis-à-vis British relations to Europe.[3] As we review the findings, an interesting feature, aside from the substantive results, is the capacity of ADMINS to interrogate the TEEPS data base for particular purposes rapidly and efficiently, once the large initial investment of forming data files has been made.

The ADMINS system was used to trace the various attitudes of the British elite towards the problem of Common Market entry. The British panelists, we know, are largely committed to seek transnational arrangements for their economic and military requirements. Atlantic and European institutions vie for consideration; other options, such as the Commonwealth and the United Nations, are also available. In the economic sphere, the Common Market appears to be the most desired option. The present members of the Common Market ask Britain for some sort of commitment; De Gaulle appears to demand that Britain reorient her entire foreign policy; the moderates expect that Britain will make at least those adjustments required by the Treaty of Rome. How, then, does the British elite deal with the various options and conditions of choice?

In the economic sphere, we asked the 1965 British panel these two questions:

> On the matter of the EEC some views are that Britain cannot afford to join; others say that Britain cannot afford *not* to join. Which, on balance, is closer to your view?
> Should the conflict between the Outer Seven and the Inner Six be resolved by the formation of a larger economic community which would include the United States and the countries of Western Europe?

On the EEC, 74 per cent replied positively, whereas only 40 per cent gave a positive reply to the idea of a larger (Atlantic) community. The two questions were cross-tabulated and the following four groups were created to explore the logic of each position:

Euratlanticists: those who favor *both* the EEC and the Atlantic Community $(n = 9)$.
Europeans: those who favor the EEC *only* $(n = 138)$.
Atlanticists: those who favor the Atlantic community *only* $(n = 34)$.
Independents: those who favor *neither* $(n = 47)$.

As a further step in the direction of building a logic tree, the panelists' positions in the economic sphere were compared with their positions in the military sphere. Close interaction between the two spheres was expected: for example, that Atlanticists in the military sphere would fear that a strong economic commitment to Europe might undermine Atlantic ties; conversely, that Europeans in the economic sphere would feel that strong Atlantic ties might impede their entry into the Common Market. We used the following questions to test this hypothesis:

> Would you approve of an EDC today?
> If a multinational Atlantic nuclear force is created, would its significance be mainly political or mainly military? Would you regard this as positive or negative?

The first question is an indicator of opinion on military integration under European auspices and the second of integration under Atlantic auspices. Responses to the two questions were cross-tabulated on ADMINS so that a set of military indexes similar to the economic indexes could be defined.

The two sets of indexes were then cross-tabulated against each other. The results showed that Europeans in the economic sphere are the most likely to favor *both* European and Atlantic auspices for military integration, whereas the Uncommitted in the economic sphere are slightly more inclined to prefer Atlantic auspices *only*. The following three new groups emerged from the cross-tabulation:

Uncommitted: those who are uncommitted to Europe in the economic sphere $(n = 94)$.
Partially Committed: those who are committed to Europe in the economic sphere and uncommitted in the military sphere $(n = 49)$.
Enthusiasts: those who are committed to Europe in both the economic and the military spheres $(n = 27)$.

The three groups are of interest as representing three different basic responses to the demands of the EEC. The Uncommitted have not expressed a commitment to Europe in either sphere; the Partially Committed have made a commitment in the economic sphere but are still concerned about maintaining their Atlantic military ties; the Enthusiasts are for Europe without qualification.

These indexes were tested against a variety of other questions. One, for example, asked whether Britain should take a more independent role between East and West. This cross-tabulation was done to see whether the most Europe-oriented British panelists follow the Gaullist dictates for British membership. We found that the Partially Committed were the most opposed to taking an independent position and the Uncommitted were also relatively opposed. The Enthusiasts for Europe were relatively less opposed, though in absolute terms they adhered to the dominant consensus against independence. Here, then, is another example of the consensual character of the postwar elites, reflecting a finding we have stressed throughout the book.

The relative differences within the consensus, however, provided a useful clue. To follow this lead, we ran the indexes against a question which asked whether the EEC would form a political counterpoise to the US, a sharp and specific test of "independence." The Partially Committed, *relatively* speaking, were more likely to say yes; the others rejected the possibility. This result is quite striking, for the Partially Committed, who were most interested in maintaining their Atlantic and European ties, also were most likely to perceive the possibility of conflict between the two commitments. ADMINS pointed to the need for a new group, which we called the Coordinators, composed of those Partially Committed panelists who rejected the independent role but thought that the EEC would form a political counterpoise to the US. It was hypothesized that the Coordinators were the most concerned with maintaining their Atlantic military ties while making a strong commitment to the EEC, hence that they would attempt to coordinate Common Market policy with policy towards the Atlantic alliance. The Enthusiasts, on the other hand, hoped to deal with the EEC issue as a separate matter on its own terms. The Coordinators would thus be impressed with the possibility of conflict while the Enthusiasts tried to avoid that possibility.

To see how the various groups stood in relation to future negotiations for British entry into EEC, two questions were assessed through the ADMINS system:

As the differences over Britain's membership in the Common Market seem to lie between Britain and France, which country would you say was mainly responsible for the present divided situation?
Which country should take the lead in seeking the solution?

The two questions were cross-tabulated and the following indexes were defined:

Those who thought that Britain is responsible *and* that Britain should take the lead ($n = 23$).
Those who thought that France is responsible *but* that Britain should take the lead ($n = 110$).
Those who thought that France is responsible *but* that some country *other* than Britain should take the lead ($n = 51$).

These indexes were cross-tabulated with the economic-military indexes developed previously. (Two other groups had been added to the economic-military indexes so that their position could be examined, but they turned out to be comparatively uninterested in pushing negotiations and they were dropped.) The largest group, which said that Britain was responsible and that she should take the lead, was recruited from the Enthusiasts. The Uncommitted and the Coordinators fell into the intermediate position.

We used ADMINS in this way to test whether the indexes we

built were tapping relevant dimensions of attitude formation among the British elite. In this case, we found that British enthusiasts for Europe ($n = 27$), while maintaining a consensual relationship with the rest of the panel, were relatively more prone to assign a European priority without perceiving a conflict of interests. This position contrasted with a smaller group of Coordinators ($n = 13$), who saw a conflict between European and Atlantic commitments as very important. It contrasted, on the other dimension, with a larger group of respondents Partially Committed to Europe, who did not stress the need for coordination of the two commitments ($n = 49$). There remained still a larger group ($n = 94$) completely uncommitted to Europe. Let us follow each group just a bit further through its own logic tree to illustrate the detailed patterning of response that can be detected by the ADMINS system even when the n is small.

We can understand something of the logic of each group when we examine its assessment of Britain's position in the ranking of nations. We asked panelists to name the top five nations of the world in rank order. Virtually all of them named the United States and the Soviet Union for the top two slots. Therefore we took the third position as a test of whether respondents accorded to Britain greater or lesser importance in the world arena. It was clear that this option should be related to each group's position on British entry into the Common Market. It was not entirely clear, however, just what this relationship should be. Would pro-Europeanism represent mainly a conviction of British strength or of relative British weakening?

The answer turned out to be a highly interesting qualification of this simple relationship. The linkage between pro-Europeanism and a sense of British decline appeared as expected. But there also appeared a linkage less obvious in terms of prior analysis — namely, that one group of panelists with a dominant sense of continuing British strength should express great interest in the Common Market as an additional (not alternative) way of sustaining that strength. This group comprised individuals we had, much earlier in the analysis, labeled as the Partially Committed.

While the Partially Committed group was far from unanimous in evaluating Britain as the third power in the world today, this tendency was *relatively* the strongest among all groups. Only the Enthusiasts indicated a strong sense that Britain's day as the third power was done. The Coordinators were almost evenly split. Thus, a sense of British decline certainly figured in the motivation of the Enthusiasts' support for Europe. However, a sense of decline was not enough to create Europeanism among the Uncommitted group, which also tends to place Britain lower than third. Those who are only *partially committed* to Europe still have the greatest sense of national efficacy, which they choose to exercise by a dual attachment — to Europa as to Atlantica. These results are presented in Table A7.1.

TABLE A7.1. CROSS-TABULATION OF EEC EVALUATION
AND BRITAIN'S RANK (1965)

| Britain's Rank | Evaluation of EEC | | | |
	Uncom-mitted	Partially Committed	Coordi-nators	Enthu-siasts
Third	34*	27	6	9
	0.00	0.99	0.61	0.00
Less than Third	60	22	7	18
	0.70	0.00	0.00	0.16

* Top number is whole number (*n*) of respondents. Lower number is the significance of each cell as computed by the Fisher exact test. This test was used in all ADMINS procedures.

We may speculate further on why the two groups of Europeans, the Uncommitted and the Enthusiasts, should evaluate Britain's prestige differently. We suggested earlier that the Partially Committed are more prone to evaluate the EEC in terms of its effects on Britain's position in the world arena whereas the Enthusiasts are more prone to evaluate the issue separately. The tendency of the Partially Committed to evaluate the EEC issue in terms of prestige undoubtedly derives from a conviction that Britain is still a major power and that efforts must be made to maintain her influence. The Enthusiasts' lack of concern for Britain's position, then, derives from a feeling that there is no position left to protect. The British panel tends to see Britain as less and less prestigious every time. In 1961, a 55 per cent majority of the sample thought that Britain held the third rank, whereas in 1965 only 35 per cent ranked Britain as third.

Concurrent with this perception of declining national prestige, the panel has developed new criteria for the evaluation of the EEC. We cross-tabulated each respondent's evaluation of various European organizations with his willingness to sacrifice Commonwealth ties in order to strengthen European ties. Here we deal with British panels for several years. An interesting change occurs over time. In 1965, those willing to sacrifice Commonwealth ties were far more likely than the others to favor EEC, whereas in earlier years of the survey (1959 and 1961) no such relationship was discernible. In 1965, then, the British evaluated the EEC in terms of whether they wished to participate in the EEC *themselves*. Earlier they appeared to be more concerned with leading the continentals in the right direction; that is, exercising their responsibilities as a world power without putting much attention on whether Britain itself should join. Finally, there was in 1965 a sharp decline in the percentage of these who think that the Common Market will form a political counterpoise to the United States — giving additional evidence that the evaluation of the EEC is being taken out of the world power context and being reconceived as a separate issue for Britain.

Identification of particular qualities that differentiate groups of TEEPS respondents, as we have outlined it, was done via the ADMINS system. Finding the Enthusiasts and searching the data base to build indexes of their logic were accomplished with much greater speed and fidelity to respondent characteristics than on previous data-management systems. The basic cross-tab operation, which is greatly facilitated by ADMINS, allows us to distinguish different groups of respondents who share positions on different branches of the tree, as illustrated by this experiment on British groups formed in response to the challenge of European integration. We were able to identify like-minded respondents and group them together. We were later able to separate the same groups, on different branches, when shared characteristics were outweighted by critical differences. Painful as this often is, as in forcing us to reject favored hypotheses like "British weakness and European strength go together" (where "go together" implies direct monotonic statistical relationship), it is a valuable way to check hunches that formerly were allowed to ride the freeway of untestability. As further illustration of the use of ADMINS, let us examine a few more results from this analysis.

One of the important issues related to the Common Market question has been the degree of sovereignty that member states must give up. Britain has always feared that the Common Market would take away too much of her sovereignty, and this has always been cited as a major argument against joining the Market. In order to compare the various groups that were prepared to give up a large measure of sovereignty, if necessary, in order to join EEC, we cross-tabulated this opinion with a question which asked whether the Six were likely to form a political union. Those who thought that a political union was likely, on our hypothesis, would probably be more prepared to accept large demands on Britain's sovereignty. The Coordinators and the Enthusiasts both were relatively inclined to think that the Six *will* form a political union, the Enthusiasts being somewhat stronger than the Coordinators. The Uncommitted were relatively unlikely to think that a political union will be formed.

Another vital question concerns how to deal with De Gaulle: Should Britain be prepared to enter the Common Market under the conditions that he might impose, or is there a possibility that better conditions might become available after his death? The 1965 British panel was asked, "Do you think that De Gaulle will achieve his long-term objectives?" Those who answered yes to this question would probably be willing to enter the market under more stringent conditions and would have to consider the consequences of entering under those conditions on Britain's world role. Those who answered no could logically hope to dodge the stringent Gaullist conditions and thus avoid considering their implications. This question was cross-tabulated with the indexes in Table A7.2. The Coordinators and the Partially Committed were the most likely to think that De

TABLE A7.2.   CROSS-TABULATIONS OF EEC EVALUATION
AND DE GAULLE'S OBJECTIVES

De Gaulle's Objectives	Evaluation of EEC			
	Uncommitted	Partially Committed	Coordinators	Enthusiasts
Yes	17*	17	6	5
	0.00	0.98	0.96	0.00
No	71	30	6	26
	1.00	0.00	0.00	0.81

* See note on Table A7.1.

Gaulle would achieve his long-term objectives, while the Enthusiasts and the Uncommitted tended to think that he would not.

We then cross-tabulated the indexes with a question asking which
would be the best auspices for the international control of the
peaceful development of atomic energy. The Uncommitted were
most likely to take the Atlantic option. The Partially Committed
were most likely to prefer the European option. The Enthusiasts,
on the other hand, prefer the UN option. In the case of atomic
energy, then, the Coordinators tend to relate other aspects of policy
with the immediate problem of the Common Market; the Enthusiasts deal with these issues separately. Here, as we saw earlier, the
Coordinators see Britain's membership in Europe as a base for later
policy, for the exercise of influence. In order to achieve that base all
aspects of policy must be directed toward the goal. For the Enthusiasts, membership in the EEC is a goal in itself, to be pursued on
an equal basis with other goals.

The location of the groups we have been discussing in the party
structure is shown in Table A7.3. Those who rejected the Common
Market, defined earlier as the Uncommitted and the Atlanticists,
were most likely to come from the Labour Party. This was reflected
by the Labour Party's coldness to Britain's Common Market bid
under a Conservative government in 1963. In 1967, however, both
parties supported the new bid under a Labour government. This
reflected a relative weakening of opposition and strengthening of
support for British entry *within* the Labour Party. Indeed, it suggests that a fruitful line of future research would be to compare the
relative positions of the different groups, over the years ahead,
within each party. The Coordinators and the Partially Committed
have been strongest in the Conservative Party, while the Coordinators are completely absent from the Labour Party. Leadership
of the Labour Party has been more strongly influenced by the Uncommitted and the Enthusiasts. This statement is borne out when
the actual positions of the two parties are compared over past years,
but there may be a redistribution of attitudes as between the parties
in the next few years.

B. EXPERIMENT 2: THE DON'T KNOWS (DK)

The DK rate was an important indicator of the size, shape, and
strength of the elite consensus in each country throughout the years

TABLE A7.3. CROSS-TABULATION OF EEC EVALUATION AND PARTY AFFILIATION

Party	n	Evaluation of EEC					
		Uncommitted	Partially Committed	Coordinators	Enthusiasts	Atlanticists	Independents
Conservative	100	32*	18	7	10	7	9
		0.65	0.73	0.92	0.65	0.00	0.00
Labour	122	38	14	0	8	21	25
		0.58	0.00	0.00	0.00	1.00	0.98
Liberal	47	16	7	3	7	5	2
		0.69	0.36	0.69	0.91	0.39	0.98

* See note on Table A7.1. Figure for n includes DK respondents in each party.

of the TEEPS survey. A noteworthy feature of the decade, as noted several times in this book, had been the low British DK. In 1965, this situation changed rather radically. Here the British DK was high compared both to its own performance in previous years and to the 1965 performance of the other national panels. As this was a matter of both substantive and methodological interest, we performed an ADMINS analysis of the DK data. We briefly review some of the findings.

In Britain, the sharp increase of DK in 1965 is visible on nearly all the questions. In France and Germany, on the contrary, there was a continuing decline of DK. To trace this over the last three survey years (1959, 1961, 1965), we selected fourteen questions covering various plans for integration of military forces, evaluation of independent deterrents, and aspects of the disarmament question. For each country a count was made to show which and how many of the fourteen questions drew the DK response. The results are shown in Table A7.4.

TABLE A7.4. DK: NUMBER OF RESPONDENTS BY NUMBER
OF QUESTIONS

	Number of Questions (Total = 14)				
	0	1	2–3	4–9	10–14
Britain 1965	90*	84	86	30	23
(n = 313)	29%	27%	26%	10%	8%
France 1965	60	45	49	26	0
(n = 180)	33%	25%	27%	14%	

* The upper cell indicates the number of respondents in the Britain 1965 panel that gave DK. The lower is the percentage of n in each case.

Ninety out of 313 respondents in Britain gave no DK. In the same British panel, however, a significant group of 23 respondents give the DK response on 10 or more of the 14 questions; no such group exists in France, which produced the highest DK rate in prior surveys. (The German panel, we note in passing, exhibited a relatively low and stable DK rate over the years.)

DK was tested against various biographic questions for Britain and Germany. In both countries, those who had university education tended to give more DK responses. In Germany, almost none in the youngest age group gave more than four DK responses, indicating that in Germany a high propensity toward DK is a trait of the old and may be passing from the scene. In Britain, there was no such relationship; if anything, those prone to DK tended to come from the younger group, though not very strongly. In Britain, DK also tended to come from academics and officials of the pressure groups; in Germany, occupation did not produce much variance in DK propensity.

Major changes in the Cold War and Britain's relation to it may best explain the rise in DK in 1965. Earlier the world scene had been dominated by the bipolar split. The two main "fronts" of the Cold War both encouraged the Anglo-American "special relationship." The first was Europe, where the Anglo-American leadership responded with the collective security apparatus of NATO. The second was the underdeveloped world, where postwar Britain's experience with decolonization was an indispensable asset to American development programs. Earlier Britain had been able to respond on both fronts in terms of how she might best influence the course of events as a responsible world power. Britain, for example, often encouraged various movements toward European unity while refusing to participate herself. Now, after two decades of postwar effort, Britain's evaluation of her own power and prestige had diminished significantly. By 1965, the British panel seemed to be thinking more in terms of what must be done to salvage, rather than to extend, Britain's declining influence in Europe and Atlantica.

Those prone to DK in Britain seem to be still thinking in the earlier terms of Britain's global position. Regarding Europe as secure, they have turned their attention to the underdeveloped world. Questions concerning collective security, when framed in the newer terms of concern for Britain's position in Europe, appear to them irrelevant. Those prone to DK think, to a greater extent than the others, that the main world problems will come from the underdeveloped areas. They are not enthusiastic about European membership as they do not think that Europe is Britain's most important key relationship; nor do they feel that the Common Market will form a political union or a counterpoise to the United States. They think that Europe should increase its share of aid to underdeveloped countries and that the administration of aid should be multilateral. They think that no European organization is more important than NATO and that De Gaulle has *not* weakened American leadership of the Western Alliance or the Alliance itself. They are not very concerned with De Gaulle's influence on the course of events in Europe. They view the contest in the underdeveloped world in traditional terms, thinking that Russia eventually will win the Sino-Soviet conflict and that the Communist parties of colored countries will not line up with China. They emphasize the importance of economic development, rejecting race as a major factor in the alignment of the world's Communist parties. Those prone to DK in 1965 Britain are thinking along lines that no longer receive the dominant attention of government policy.

C. EXPERIMENT 3: THE REPEATERS

The 1959–1961 repeaters' files were used to investigate the sources of attitudinal stability and change. Within the ADMINS system, those individuals interviewed in 1959 and reinterviewed in 1961 were identified, and a single file was constructed using these individuals and a list of comparable questions asked of them in both years.

The results are tentative because of the small sample size ($n = 67$), but the analysis demonstrates a useful methodological approach and leads to some very interesting findings. Of the comparable questions, 11 were selected because they had been asked in both years with similar question wording and with the same three response levels: usually yes, no, and DK. For any given question, a respondent was considered to give a "stable" response if he gave the yes response or the no response in both years. (DK has been reported in the preceding section.) For each individual, we counted the number of questions (of the 11 selected) on which he gave the stable response.

The panelists were generally stable on 6 of the 11 questions. This indicates considerable stability mixed with substantial indecisiveness and instability. Three groups were defined: those who were stable on 8 or more questions ($n = 22$); those who were stable on 6 or 7 questions ($n = 21$); those who were stable on 5 or less ($n = 24$).

These groups revealed interesting differences in their responses to some subsets of our questions. The most stable group thought that the balance of power would be held by the East at the end of the century and completely avoided the "neither" option — neither East nor West — on this question. Members of the least stable group were the most likely to pick the "neither" option. Since they cannot make a choice on this basic Cold War issue, they have less of a base for attitudinal stability than the others. The most stable group seems to see the Cold War as a struggle that will eventually be won by one of the contestants. The least stable sees the Cold War as a situation that will require accommodation, but not as a struggle that can be won by either side.

The most stable group concentrates its attention on the enemy; the organization of the West is important insofar as it facilitates the Western response to the Cold War. The least stable group, however, concentrates its attention on adjusting the Western position to the problematics of the Cold War — rolling with the punch rather than scoring a victory. It attends more to the organizational details of the various arrangements for Western cooperation. Along these lines, the most stable group thinks that the most serious international problems of the future will come from the East, whereas the least stable group is more likely to name the West. Furthermore, the least stable group is most likely to think that the United States and Britain, the postwar leaders of the Western Alliance, will cause the most trouble within the Alliance. The most stable, by contrast, picked France as the most troublesome ally. As early as 1961, France had acquired a reputation for raising objections to plans proposed by the Anglo-American leadership for dealing with their common problems. French objections to German rearmament provide an example.

We compared our groups on their attachment to Europa and Atlantica. On most indicators, in Britain, the least stable group was the most closely attached to *both*. The middle group was the least attached; and the most stable group fell in the center of this subset of indicators. The following questions were used as further tests of attachment to Europa and Atlantica: conviction that Britain's Atlantic and European ties were "decisive"; willingness to "sacrifice Commonwealth ties" in order to promote close European ties; and rejection of a "more independent role" for Britain in world affairs.

The most stable group, then, has a clearly defined perspective that helps them make up their minds. Members of the least stable group are the most concerned with the future development of European and Atlantic ties. They are still seeking to work their way through the intricacies of transition from nationalism to transnationalism and from European to Atlantic regionalism. The least stable group appears as more congruent with the decision-making process. Between 1959 and 1961, Britain underwent a major revaluation of her relations with Europe and the Atlantic Alliance, leading to the decision to seek membership in the Common Market. The least stable appear to reflect the attitudinal basis for this revaluation. Our results suggest, tentatively, a two-step decision process. The first phase develops a new approach to a problem; highly structured attitudes on key issues have not yet been articulated, and attitudes on related problems are likely to be highly unstable. As attitudes on key issues become more firmly structured, greater stability and decisiveness develops on other issues as well.

D. POSTSCRIPT

With substantially greater investment of time and effort, the experiments just described could theoretically have been carried out through data-handling systems other than ADMINS. The mechanical and clerical operations codified by ADMINS are based on the mathematics of set theory and the statistics of cross-tabulation. In previous work with surveys, indeed during most of the TEEPS decade, a patient analyst with decks of punched cards and a counter-sorter was expected to perform these manipulations. We note, however, that few persons with that degree of patience exist among the ranks of social science analysts, and as a result, many of the operations theoretically possible on a complex data base never got done.

ADMINS permitted each TEEPS analyst to proceed through the forest of decision trees in a matter of minutes or hours rather than days or weeks. Thus, with his hunches fresh in his mind, he was able to select those findings worthy of following in a sequential and orderly way — by framing each new question in terms of a prompt response to his earlier questions, all the while having before him a typed record of the analytical context of his inquiries. We have included this report of TEEPS and ADMINS to illustrate modestly some ways in which computerized processing may aid social scientists in their difficult quest to understand and improve the complex multiplicity of events with which they must deal.

Select List of TEEPS Memos, Theses, Publications

MUCH of the collection, processing, and preliminary analysis of TEEPS data has not been reported in this book and its annexes. We therefore include a select list of memos, theses, and publications that may be useful to the reader who wishes to trace the evolution of this study.

Publications, because they are public, are obliged to speak for themselves. Theses, because they are academic exchanges between students and their professors, are under no such obligation. We have included four doctoral dissertations written at M.I.T. because they remain valuable contributions to the TEEPS story: the dissertations of Morton Gorden, Marguerite Nusslé-Kramer, Catherine McArdle-Kelleher, and Howard Rosenthal. We have also included one Master's thesis, which has since been published, by Mrs. Susanne Bodenheimer. We have excluded European theses because they are generally unavailable to American scholars, but we signal the existence at the Sorbonne of theses by Geneviève Auclair, Jacqueline Palmade, and Josette Zarka.

A final word must be said about our "memos." These were produced in response to immediate needs of collecting, processing, and analyzing the TEEPS data. Some of these memo writers are now distinguished scholars and would not wish to see these interoffice memos used for other than their original purpose of helping to organize, test, and reshape TEEPS.

416

A. *M.I.T. DISSERTATIONS IN POLITICAL SCIENCE*

Bodenheimer, Susanne J. "Political Union: A Microcosm of European Politics." M.S., June 1966.

Gorden, Morton. "European Security: British and French Elite Perspectives." Ph.D., September 1963.

McArdle-Kelleher, Catherine. "German Nuclear Dilemmas 1955–1965." Ph.D., September 1967.

Nusslé-Kramer, Marguerite. "The Passing of Nationalism in Western Europe: A Study of Internationalism, Regionalism and Supranationalism, Based on French, British and German Elite Panel Surveys 1955–1961." Ph.D., June 1963.

Rosenthal, Howard. "Contemporary French Politics and Sub-strata Analysis." Ph.D., September 1964.

B. *PUBLICATIONS AND UNPUBLISHED MEMOS*

Britain

1955

Bailyn, Lotte. "Notes on the British View of European Union" (1958).

1956

Bailyn, Lotte. "Report on Attitude of British Elite to Existing European Institutions" (1957).

1961

Gorden, Morton. Chapter II, "Britain 1961," from "European Security: British and French Elite Perspectives," M.I.T. Ph.D. dissertation, Department of Political Science, 1963.

Lerner, Daniel. "As Britain Faces the Continent: How Its Leaders Weigh Their Choices," *Virginia Quarterly Review*, Vol. 39, No. 1 (Winter 1963).

———. "The British Political Mood" (1964).

1965

Lerner, Daniel, and Morton Gorden. "Technical Report on the British Elite Attitude Survey of 1965: Changes and Stability" (1965).

France

1955

Lerner, Daniel. "The Sense of Boundaries and French Social Perception" (1955).

————. "Interim Report on the French Project" (1955).

1956

Bailyn, Lotte. "Appendix: France — Coding Reliability" (1956).

Davidson, Judith. "Analysis of Attitudes Toward the Idea of International Cooperation in Europe" (1957).

————. "Analysis of Political Attitudes of French Elite Sample, Based on Selected Cross-Tabulations" (1957).

————. "Analysis of Political Opinion According to Age" (1957).

————. "Attitudes of the French Elite Toward Existing European Institutions and the Idea of European Integration: Preliminary Analysis by Profession" (1957).

————. "Attitudes Toward a Political Community of Atlantic Nations" (1958).

————. "Comparison of French Extreme Gauchists, Moderate Gauchists, and the Elite Opinions: Selected Tables" (1958).

————. "Gauchists: Introductory Notes" (1958).

Gorden, Morton. "Character Sketches Paris Elite 1956" (1959).

Kramer, Marguerite. "Progress Report: Supranationality Among the Paris 1956 Elite" (1958).

————. "How Frenchmen Look at United Nations" (1958).

————. "On the Relationship Between Attitudes on UN and Supranationality in France" (1959).

Lerner, Daniel. "French Business Leaders Look at EDC: A Preliminary Report," *Public Opinion Quarterly*, Vol. 20, No. 1 (Spring 1956).

————. "The 'Hard-Headed' Frenchman," *Encounter*, Vol. 42 (March 1957).

————. "Interviewing Frenchmen," *American Journal of Sociology*, Vol. 62, No. 2 (September 1956).

————. "The Meaning of Opposition to the UN" (1958).

————, and Morton Gorden. "Child-Rearing, Politics, and Personality."

1959

Gorden, Morton. "War, Weapons, and Sovereignty in France" (1956, 1958, 1959).

1961

Lerner, Daniel, and Marguerite Kramer. "French Elite Perspectives on the United Nations," *International Organization*, Vol. 17, No. 1 (1963).

1965

Gorden, Morton. "A Cost/Benefit Analysis of French Elite Attitudinal Response to American Active and Passive Defense Systems."

Lerner, Daniel, and Morton Gorden. "Technical Report on the French Elite Attitude Survey of 1965: Changes and Stability" (1966).

Teich, Albert H., "Analysis of Repeat Interviews: France 1959 and 1965" (1965).

Germany

1956

Bergson, Judith. "German Business Sector" (1965).

Keller, Suzanne. "Attitudes Toward European Integration of the German Elite" (1957).

———. "Attitudes of the German Elite Toward European Unity in Relation to Other Attitudes on Political and Social Issues" (1957).

———. "The German Generals: Attitudes and Opinions About European Organizations and World Cooperation" (1958).

———. "Pro and Anti European Unity: A Comparison, Germany 1956" (1958).

Lerner, Daniel. "Bonn and the Bomb" (1957).

1959

Kramer, Marguerite. "Some Comments on the German Marginals of 1959" (1959).

1965

Lerner, Daniel, and Morton Gorden. "Technical Report on the German Elite Attitude Survey of 1965: Changes and Stability" (1965).

All Countries

1955

Lerner, Daniel. "Elite Perspectives in Europe: Interim Note on a Cross-National Survey" (1955).

———. "Latent Consistency in Political Opinions: The Case of 'Europe'" (1956).

1956

Bailyn, Lotte. "Attitudes Toward NATO as Compared to OEEC and ECSE" (1957).

———. "Notes on Intellectuals" (1958).

———, and Ingrid Hoffmann. "Comparative Analysis: 1 — Weapons and War" (1958).

————. "Comparative Analysis: 2 — Neutralism" (1958).

Keller, Suzanne. "Attitudes of the French, German, and British Business Elite: A Qualitative Analysis of Selected Attitudes" (1958).

Lerner, Daniel, and Suzanne Keller. "Empathy in Cross-National and Occupational Perspectives" (1957).

1959

Lerner, Daniel, and Morton Gorden. "European Leaders Look at World Security," Center for International Studies Document No. C/60–7, 1960.

1961

Bergson, Judith. "Cross-National Analysis of Professions: A Digest" (1964).

Gorden, Morton. "The Coin of the Alliance" (1963).

Lerner, Daniel. "Will European Union Bring About Merged National Goals," *The Annals of the American Academy of Political and Social Science,* Vol. 348 (July 1963).

————, and Morton Gorden. "Elite Attitudes and the Atlantic Security System" (1964).

————. "European Community and Atlantic Security in the World Arena," M.I.T. Center for International Studies Document No. C/61–38, 1961.

1965

Lerner, Daniel. "Interviewing European Elites," *Polls,* Fall 1966.

————. "Ranking the Nations" (1967).

————, and Morton Gorden. "The Setting for European Arms Control: Political and Strategic Choices of European Elites," *Journal of Conflict Resolution,* Vol. 9, No. 4 (December 1965).

Other

Bodenheimer, Susanne J. *Political Union: A Microcosm of European Politics 1960–1966* (Leiden: A. W. Sijhoff, 1967).

Lerner, Daniel. "TEEPS: The European Elite Panel Survey: A Provisional Statement" (1966).

————. "Interview with Alistair Buchan" (London, March 1964).

————. "Interview with General Gallois" (Paris, April 1964).

————. "Interview with Kenneth Younger" (London, March 1864).

————. "TEEPS and Computers" (1965).

————, and Albert H. Teich. "International Scientists Face World Politics: A Survey at CERN," M.I.T. Center for International Studies Document No. C/68–2, 1968.

Notes

Notes

GENERAL INTRODUCTION

[1] "French Business Leaders Look at EDC," *Public Opinion Quarterly*, Vol. 20, No. 1 (Spring 1956), pp. 212–221.

CHAPTER 1

[1] André Siegfried, *America's Coming of Age* (New York: Harcourt, Brace and Company, 1927).

[2] Daniel Bell, "The Year 2000 — The Trajectory of an Idea," *Daedalus*, Vol. 96, No. 3 (Summer 1967), pp. 639–651.

[3] Daniel Lerner, "America's Vocation in Europe and Europe's American Vocation," in *America Interprets Itself*. Published in German as *Amerika deutet sich selbst*, Peter Coulmas, ed. (Hamburg: Hoffmann und Campe, 1965), pp. 83–102.

[4] A discussion of the Want:Get Ratio is given in Daniel Lerner, "Toward a Communication Theory of Modernization," in L. W. Pye, ed., *Communications and Political Development* (Princeton, N. J.: Princeton University Press, 1963), pp. 327–350.

[5] A. N. Whitehead, *Adventures of Ideas* (New York: The Macmillan Company, 1933).

[6] See the volumes by such publicists as Vance Packard, Sloan Wilson, A. C. Spectorsky; such studies as *Crestwood Heights, The Waist-High Culture, The Tastemakers, Mass Culture, Mass Society;* others are cited in Daniel Lerner, "Comfort and Fun: Morality in a Nice Society," *The American Scholar*, Vol. 27, No. 2 (Spring 1958), pp. 153-165.

[7] For a bravura exhibition and overstatement of the great shift from print to audiovisual media, see Marshall McLuhan and Quentin Fiore, *The Medium is the Massage* (New York: Bantam Books, 1967).

[8] See Daniel Lerner, "Comfort and Fun: Morality in a Nice Society," *op. cit.* (note 6).

[9] See M. F. Millikan and D. L. M. Blackmer, eds., *The Emerging Nations: Their Growth and United States Policy* (Boston: Little, Brown and Company, 1961).

[10] Quoted in Marshall McLuhan and Quentin Fiore, *op. cit.* (note 7), p. 131, from *Variety*, Vol. 203, No. 1 (June 6, 1956), pp. 1, 61.

[11] Daniel Lerner, *The Passing of Traditional Society: Modernizing the Middle East* (paperback edition, New York: The Free Press, 1964), p. 214.

[12] See Harold D. Lasswell and Daniel Lerner, eds., *World Revolutionary Elites: Studies in Coercive Ideological Movements* (paperback edition, Cambridge, Mass.: The M.I.T. Press, 1966).

423

13 Laurence W. Wylie, *Village in the Vaucluse* (rev. ed., paperback, New York: Harper & Row, 1964), (2nd ed., Cambridge, Mass.: Harvard University Press, 1964).

14 In addition to Laurence W. Wylie's *Chanzeaux* (Cambridge, Mass.: Harvard University Press, 1966), see C. Bettelheim and S. Frère, *Auxerre en 1950* (Paris: A. Colin, 1950) and L. Bernot and R. Blancard, *Nouville: un village français* (Paris: Institut d'Ethnologie, 1953).

15 J. F. Gravier, *Paris et le desert français* (Paris: Impressions Modernes, 1947).

16 Daniel Lerner and Raymond Aron, *France Defeats EDC* (New York: Frederick A. Praeger, 1957), pp. 201–208. Also published in Paris as *La Querelle de la CED* (1956).

17 Daniel Lerner, Morton Gorden, and Howard Rosenthal, "Static and Dynamic France," M.I.T. Center for International Studies, May 1964, No. C/64–16.

18 Henri Mendras, *La Fin des paysans* (Paris: Société d'Editions d'Enseignement Supérieur, 1968). The American edition, translated by Jean Lerner, is scheduled for publication by The M.I.T. Press in 1969. See also the national surveys reported in "Les Agriculteurs Français," special issue of *Sondages* (1966), and the valuable regional study *Les agriculteurs du sud-est face au progrès technique* by M. Delenne *et al.* (1966).

19 Quoted in Daniel Bell, *Work and Its Discontents* (Boston: Beacon Press, 1956), p. 43.

20 David Binder, "European Youth Is Found Mutinous Against the Establishment," *The New York Times*, December 24, 1968, pp. 1, 42.

21 *Ibid.*

22 The readily available résumé of this transformation of European attitudes is J. J. Servan-Schreiber, *Le Défi Américain* (Paris: Denoël, 1967). Translated by Ronald Steel, *The American Challenge* (New York: Atheneum, 1968).

23 Edward A. McCreary, *The Americanization of Europe* (Garden City, N. Y.: Doubleday & Company, 1964), pp. ix–x.

24 Daniel Lerner and Raymond Aron, *op. cit.* (note 16), p. 212.

25 *Ibid.*, p. 201.

26 A. H. Teich, "Comparative Study of International Scientific Laboratories," unpublished paper presented before the Congress of the World Association for Public Opinion Research (WAPOR), Vienna, August 22, 1967. (To be incorporated in a Ph.D. dissertation in Political Science at M.I.T., in preparation.)

27 See Philip Rahv, ed., *The Discovery of Europe* (Boston: Houghton Mifflin Company, 1947).

28 See H. S. Commager, ed., *America in Perspective* (New York: Random House, 1947).

29 See A. B. Barach, *The New Europe and Its Economic Future* (New York: The Macmillan Company, 1964).

30 Edward A. McCreary, *op. cit.* (note 23), pp. 283–284.

31 W. W. Rostow, *The Stages of Economic Growth* (New York: Cambridge University Press, 1960).

32 Daniel Lerner and Raymond Aron, *op. cit.* (note 16), p. 201.

33 Stein Rokkan and Henry Valen, "Mobilization of Periphery: Data on Turn-Out Membership and Candidate Recruitment in Norway," in Stein Rokkan, ed., *Approaches to the Study of Political Participation* (Bergen: The Chr. Michelsen Institute Publication No. 210, 1962), pp. 111–158; see also Karl W. Deutsch,

"Social Mobilization and Political Development," *American Political Science Review*, Vol. 55, No. 3 (September 1961), pp. 493–515.

[34] Quoted from *The German Tribune*, December 2, 1967, No. 295.

[35] *Süddentsche Zeitung*, October 3, 1967.

[36] *Hannoversche Presse*, October 3, 1967.

[37] *Lübecker Nachrichten*, November 10, 1967.

[38] Peregrine Worsthorne, "Anti-Americanism is Now Non-U," *The New York Times Magazine*, April 1967, pp. 34–35.

[39] Morton Gorden and Daniel Lerner, "The Setting for European Arms Controls: Political and Strategic Choices of European Elites," *The Journal of Conflict Resolution*, Vol. 9, No. 4 (December 1965), pp. 419–433.

[40] *The New York Times*, October 17, 1967, p. 1.

CHAPTER 2

[1] R. K. Merton and A. S. Kitt, "Contributions to the Theory of Reference Group Behavior," in R. K. Merton and P. F. Lazarsfeld, eds., *Continuities in Social Research* (Glencoe, Ill.: The Free Press, 1950), pp. 40–105.

[2] Daniel Lerner, *The Passing of Traditional Society: Modernizing the Middle East* (paperback edition, New York: The Free Press, 1964), Chapter 2.

[3] P. A. Samuelson, quoted from the *Boston Globe*, February 26, 1967.

[4] A. B. Barach, *The New Europe and Its Economic Future* (New York: The Macmillan Company, 1964), p. 3. See also "Income and Growth in Non-Communist Countries, 1955–65," an unpublished manuscript by E. E. Hagen and Ole Hawrylyshyu, M.I.T. Center for International Studies, 1968.

[5] George Lichtheim, "The British Way of Life — and the Common Market," *Commentary*, Vol. 32, No. 4 (October 1961), p. 333. See also his later book, *The New Europe* (New York: Frederick A. Praeger, 1963).

[6] L. de Sainte Lorette, *L'idée d'union fédérale européenne* (Paris: A. Colin, 1955).

[7] Edmond Taylor, *Fall of the Dynasties* (Garden City, N. Y.: Doubleday & Company, 1963).

[8] H. D. Lasswell and Daniel Lerner, *World Revolutionary Elites: Studies in Coercive Ideological Movements* (paperback edition, Cambridge, Mass.: The M.I.T. Press, 1966).

[9] For history relevant to the milestones in the development of Europe over this period, see U. W. Kitzinger, *The Politics and Economics of European Integration* (New York: Frederick A. Praeger, 1963) and Michael Curtis, *Western European Integration* (New York: Harper & Row, Publishers, 1965).

[10] The classic exposition of this framework, a prophetic essay in the policy sciences, is H. D. Lasswell, *World Politics Faces Economics* (New York: McGraw-Hill Book Company, 1945).

[11] *Ibid.*, pp. 20–31.

[12] Daniel Lerner, "Britain Faces the Continent," *Virginia Quarterly Review*, Vol. 39, No. 1 (Winter 1963), pp. 12–25.

[13] K. W. Deutsch, *Nationalism and Social Communication* (paperback edition, Cambridge, Mass.: The M.I.T. Press, 1953).

[14] John K. Galbraith, *Economics and the Art of Controversy* (paperback edition, New York: Vintage Books, 1959), Chapter 6.

[15] Robert Lekachman, *The Age of Keynes* (New York: Random House, 1966).

[16] On the Franco-Dutch opposition in EEC, see Suzanne Bodenheimer,

Political Union: A Microcosm of European Politics 1960–1966 (Leiden: A. W. Sijhoff, 1967).

[17] H. S. Truman, *Memoirs*, Volume One: *Year of Decisions;* Volume Two: *Years of Trial and Hope 1946–1952* (Garden City, N. Y.: Doubleday & Company, 1956).

[18] Walter Lippman, *U. S. Foreign Policy: Shield of the Republic* (Boston: Little, Brown and Company, 1943).

[19] Daniel Lerner and Raymond Aron, *France Defeats EDC* (New York: Frederick A. Praeger, 1957). Also published in Paris as *La Querelle de la CED* (1956).

[20] EEC Information Memorandum, pp. 61–65, European Development Fund, August 1965.

[21] See Catherine McArdle Kelleher, "German Nuclear Dilemmas 1955–1965," Ph.D. dissertation, M.I.T., 1967.

[22] "French Will Give Bicycles to Hanoi," *The New York Times*, January 17, 1968.

[23] *The New York Times*, January 17, 1968, lead article.

[24] Henry Giniger, "Five Ministers Quit De Gaulle Regime in Rift on Europe," *The New York Times*, May 17, 1962, p. 1.

[25] See note 3, Chapter One.

CHAPTER 3

[1] Note, however, that the pioneers of policy-related survey research worked on an even larger canvas. Frederic LePlay spent some forty years studying the urban industrial workers of Europe, Charles Booth some twenty years studying "the people of London." A fuller discussion of these origins is given in Daniel Lerner, ed., *The Human Meaning of the Social Sciences* (paperback edition, New York: World Publishing Company, 1959), Chapter 1.

[2] See Daniel Lerner and H. D. Lasswell, eds., *The Policy Sciences* (paperback edition, Stanford, Calif.: Stanford University Press, 1965).

[3] This section is adapted from Daniel Lerner, "Interviewing Frenchmen," *American Journal of Sociology*, Vol. 62, No. 2 (September 1956), pp. 187–194. Subsequent expansions, as our experience grew over the decade, appeared as: "The Hard-Headed Frenchman," *Encounter*, Vol. 8, No. 3 (March 1957), pp. 27–32; and "An American Researcher in Paris," in Bert Kaplan, ed., *Studying Personality Cross-Culturally* (Evanston, Ill.: Row, Peterson, 1961).

[4] See Daniel Lerner, *The Passing of Traditional Society: Modernizing the Middle East* (paperback edition, New York: The Free Press, 1964).

[5] Daniel Lerner, "French Business Leaders Look at EDC," *Public Opinion Quarterly*, Vol. 20, No. 1 (Spring 1956), pp. 212–221.

CHAPTER 4

[1] For the history of the security problems of this period, see Alistair Buchan, *NATO in the 1960s: The Implications of Interdependence* (New York: Frederick A. Praeger, 1960); Frederick Mulley, *The Politics of Western Defense* (New York: Frederick A. Praeger, 1962); and Robert Osgood, *NATO: The Entangling Alliance* (Chicago: University of Chicago Press, 1962).

CHAPTER 5

[1] For the history of the growth of economic and political institutions which are often credited with the change, see Ernst Haas, *The Uniting of Europe:*

Political, Social, and Economic Forces 1950–1957 (Stanford, Calif.: Stanford University Press, 1958); and Leon Lindberg, *The Political Dynamics of European Economic Integration* (Stanford, Calif.: Stanford University Press, 1963).

2 For a history of the problems of British entry, see Miriam Camps, *Britain and the European Community 1955–1963* (Princeton, N. J.: Princeton University Press, 1964).

CHAPTER 8

1 For the continuing impact of European ideologies upon their former colonial domains, see Daniel Lerner, ed., "Attitude Research in Modernizing Areas," special issue of *Public Opinion Quarterly*, Vol. 22, No. 3 (Fall 1958).

2 The ideas set forth in this paragraph are theoretically articulated in H. D. Lasswell, *World Politics and Personal Insecurity* (New York: McGraw-Hill Book Company, 1935) and operationally demonstrated in H. D. Lasswell, Nathan Leites, and Associates, *Language of Politics* (Cambridge, Mass.: The M.I.T. Press, 1965).

3 See, for illustrative discussion of the ideology based on DEMOCRACY as a key symbol, Ithiel de Sola Pool, *Symbols of Democracy* (Stanford, Calif.: Stanford University Press, 1952).

4 See Karl W. Deutsch, *Interdisciplinary Bibliography on Nationalism* (Cambridge, Mass.: The M.I.T. Press, 1956).

5 See Lewis Mumford, *The Story of Utopias* (New York: Boni, 1922). Also, C. M. Andrews, ed., *Famous Utopias* (New York: Tudor Publishing Co., 1901) and for the later period, G. Negley and J. M. Patrick, eds., *The Quest for Utopia* (New York: Schuman, 1952).

6 On the philosophers, see Carl Becker, *The Heavenly City of Eighteenth Century Philosophers* (New Haven, Conn.: Yale University Press, 1932) and Peter Gay, *The Enlightenment* (New York: Alfred A. Knopf, 1966). On the longer-term movement of European ideas from medievalism to modernism, see J. H. Randall, *The Making of the Modern Mind* (Boston: Houghton Mifflin Company, 1926).

7 For the impact of international socialism in contemporary America, see H. D. Lasswell and D. Blumenstock, *World Revolutionary Propaganda: A Chicago Study* (New York: Alfred A. Knopf, 1939). The earlier background is given in Charles Nordhoff, *The Communist Societies of the United States* (New York: Dover Publishing Company, 1966).

8 John Cogley, "The Priest-Worker Returns in France," *The New York Times*, November 7, 1965, p. 6E.

9 The classic study is André Siegfried, *Tableau Politique de la France de l'Ouest* (Paris: A. Colin, 1913; 2nd ed. 1964). See also the more recent works of François Goguel.

10 See Howard Rosenthal, "Political Coalitions: Elements of a Model and the Study of French Legislative Elections," in *Proceedings of the International Symposium on Mathematical and Computational Methods in The Social Sciences* (Paris: Presses Universitaires de France, 1968). Also: Duncan MacRae, Jr., *Parliament, Parties and Society in France 1946–1958* (New York: St. Martin's Press, 1967).

11 See the moving accounts of this personal revulsion among postwar European intellectuals in R. H. S. Crossman, ed., *The God That Failed* (New York: Harper Bros., 1949).

12 See Ernest Kris and Nathan Leites, "Trends in Twentieth Century Propaganda," in Daniel Lerner, ed., *Propaganda in War and Crisis* (New York:

George W. Stewart, 1951). The classic study is H. D. Lasswell, *Propaganda Technique in the World War* (New York: P. Smith, 1938).

13 See D. Lerner, *SYKEWAR: Psychological Warfare Against Germany, D-Day to VE-Day* (New York: George W. Stewart, 1948).

14 See R. B. McCallum and A. Readman, *British General Election of 1945* (New York: Humanities Press, 1947). See also David E. Butler, *The British General Election of 1951* (1955, 1959, 1964, and 1966 in subsequent volumes).

15 See the candid memoir of this period in Britain by Woodrow Wyatt, *Into the Dangerous World* (London: Weidenfield and Nicolson, 1952). A French equivalent, by the man who has now become the symbol of Euramerican relations, is J. J. Servan-Schreiber, *Lieutenant en Algérie* (Paris: R. Juillard, 1957); this book was translated into English by Ronald Matthews (New York: Alfred A. Knopf, 1957).

16 See Margaret Mead, *And Keep Your Powder Dry: An Anthropologist Looks at America* (New York: William Morrow & Co., 1942).

17 See Edward McCreary, *The Americanization of Europe* (Garden City, N.Y.: Doubleday & Company, 1964).

18 See Julius Braunthal, *History of the International,* translated by Henry Collins and Kenneth Mitchell (New York: Frederick A. Praeger, 1966).

19 The writings of Sidney Hook over the past thirty years are a major contribution to clarifying this confused issue. See especially, *From Hegel to Marx: Studies in the Intellectual Development of Karl Marx* (Ann Arbor, Mich.: University of Michigan Press, 1962) and *Reason, Social Myths, and Democracy* (New York: Harper & Row, 1966).

20 See Albert Memmi, *Portrait du colonisateur* and *Portrait du colonisé* (Corrêa: Buchet/Chastel, 1957). Also J. J. Servan-Schreiber, *Lieutenant en Algérie, op. cit.* (note 15).

21 See the set of three articles, "PPBS: Its Scope and Limits," in *The Public Interest,* No. 8 (Summer 1967).

22 Merle Armytage, *The Rise of the Technocrats* (London: Routledge and Kegan Paul, 1965).

23 Michael D. Young, *The Rise of the Meritocracy 1870–1933: An Essay on Education and Equality* (Harmondsworth, Eng.: Penguin Books, 1958). See also the references cited in Chapter Twelve on the "gaps."

24 H. D. Lasswell, *Psychopathology and Politics* (Chicago, Ill.: University of Chicago Press, 1935), pp. 261–262.

CHAPTER 10

1 Daniel Lerner, "French Business Leaders Look at EDC: A Preliminary Report," *Public Opinion Quarterly,* Vol. 20, No. 1 (Spring 1956), pp. 212–221.

2 Michael R. Leavitt, "Gaullism in Europe," Undergraduate thesis, M.I.T., 1966. The thesis shows the compatibility of Gaullist identification and positive attitudes toward transnational institutions and ideas among the French elites.

CHAPTER 11

1 See Hans Speier, *Force and Folly* (Cambridge, Mass.: The M.I.T. Press, 1969), Chapter 7.

2 Career sketches of the Commission are given in M. T. Loch, *Die Neun von Brussels* (Stuttgart: Europa Verlag, 1963). See also A. Spinelli, *The Eurocrats* (Baltimore, Md.: The Johns Hopkins Press, 1966).

³ *Europa Archiv,* No. 21 (1967). The translation of Hallstein's statement is from *The German Tribune,* February 17, 1968. All the quotes of Hallstein that follow are from this article.

CHAPTER 12

¹ J. H. Randall, *The Making of the Modern Mind* (Boston: Hougton Mifflin Company, 1926).

² Karl Marx, *The Poverty of Philosophy* (1847), this edition (Moscow: Foreign Language Publishing House, 1956). Also Nikolai Lenin, *Materialism and Empiro-Criticism: Critical Comments on Reactionary Philosophy* (New York: International Publishers, 1927).

³ Daniel Bell, ed., "Toward the Year 2000," *Daedalus,* Vol. 96, No. 3 (Summer 1967), pp. 639–651.

⁴ The term "propaganditis" and its conceptual extensions are elucidated in Ernst Kris and Nathan Leites, "Trends in 20th Century Propaganda," in Géza Roheim, ed., *Psychoanalysis and the Social Sciences,* Vol. I (New York: International Universities Press, 1947).

⁵ H. D. Lasswell and Daniel Lerner, eds., *World Revolutionary Elites* (paperback, Cambridge, Mass.: The M.I.T. Press, 1966).

⁶ Ernst Cassirer, ed., *Werke,* 10 vols. (Berlin: 1912–1922).

⁷ M. F. Millikan and D. L. M. Blackmer, eds., *The Emerging Nations: Their Growth and United States Policy* (Boston: Little, Brown and Company, 1961).

⁸ See L. W. Pye, ed., *Communications and Political Development* (Princeton, N.J.: Princeton University Press, 1963).

⁹ See W. T. R. Fox, *The Superpowers* (New York: Harcourt, Brace & World, 1944).

¹⁰ See Hans Speier, *Force and Folly* (Cambridge, Mass.: The M.I.T. Press, 1969).

¹¹ Morton Gorden and Daniel Lerner, "The Setting for European Arms Control: Political and Strategic Choices of European Elites," *Journal of Conflict Resolution,* Vol. 9, No. 4 (1965), pp. 419–433.

¹² Pierre Gallois, *The Balance of Terror* (Boston: Houghton Mifflin Company, 1961).

¹³ W. W. Rostow, *The Stages of Economic Growth* (New York: Cambridge University Press, 1960).

¹⁴ T. C. Schelling, *Arms and Influence* (New Haven, Conn.: Yale University Press, 1966).

¹⁵ Alistair Buchan, "What's Ahead and Behind," *The New York Times Book Review,* October 31, 1965, p. 34.

¹⁶ Peter Grose, *The New York Times,* October 17, 1967, p. 1.

¹⁷ John M. Lee, *The New York Times,* March 31, 1968, p. 1.

¹⁸ John Brooks, "Annals of Finance," *The New Yorker,* March 30, 1968, p. 44.

¹⁹ This classification was introduced by Professor E. B. Skolnikoff in a lecture at M.I.T.

²⁰ R. R. Nelson, *The Technology Gap: Analysis and Appraisal* (Santa Monica, Calif.: The RAND Corporation Document P-3694-1, December 1967). See also the RAND papers by Arnold Kramish.

²¹ J. J. Servan-Schreiber, *Le Défi Américain* (Paris: Denoël, 1967). Translated by Ronald Steel, *The American Challenge* (New York: Atheneum, 1968).

²² Jacques Mornand in *Le Nouvel Observateur,* November 24, 1965.

²³ Dieter Stolze in *Die Zeit,* September 22, 1967.

24 The *New York Times,* March 31, 1968, p. 1.

25 *The New York Times,* October 16, 1967, p. 1.

26 Curt Gasteyger, *Europe in the Seventies,* Adelphi Papers 37 (June 1967), p. 2.

27 *Ibid.*

28 Jacques Mornand, *loc. cit.* (note 22).

29 Karl Mannheim, *Man and Society* (London: Routledge and Kegan Paul, 1946), Parts IV and VI.

30 See John Pender, *Europe Against De Gaulle* (New York: Frederick A. Praeger, 1963).

31 Jules Romains, *L'Aurore,* December 18, 1967; reprinted in *Atlantic Community Quarterly,* Spring 1968.

32 Ronald Steel, *The End of Alliance* (New York: The Viking Press, Inc., 1964). Also R. J. Barnet and M. G. Raskin, *After 20 Years: The Decline of NATO and The Search For a New Policy in Europe* (New York: Alfred A. Knopf, Vintage Books, 1966).

33 Edgar S. Furniss, Jr., ed., *The Western Alliance: Its Status and Prospects* (Columbus, Ohio: Ohio State University Press, 1965), p. 73.

ANNEX TWO

1 See Daniel Lerner and Raymond Aron, *France Defeats EDC* (New York: Frederick A. Praeger, 1957).

ANNEX THREE

1 The acronym "CERN" is derived from the initials of the original French name of the organization: *Conseil européen pour la recherche nucléaire.* Other European organizations such as EURATOM, ESRO (the European Space Research Organization), and ELDO (the European Launcher Development Organization), for various reasons, have not shared the success of CERN.

2 The contributing states are Austria, Belgium, Denmark, France, Germany, Greece, Italy, Netherlands, Norway, Spain, Sweden, Switzerland, and Britain. Poland, Turkey, and Yugoslavia are listed as observer states.

3 This work was carried out, with permission of the CERN administration, by Dr. Vidya Joshi, a research assistant on the TEEPS staff at the M.I.T. Center for International Studies.

4 Some activity relating to political affairs does go on at CERN, however. Evening lectures sponsored by the staff association, which feature speakers on current public issues, are well attended, and the Geneva antiapartheid movement, open to everyone in the Geneva area, contains a substantial number of CERN personnel.

5 See, for example, Anne Roe, *The Making of a Scientist* (New York: Dodd, Mead and Company, 1952), p. 58, and Bernice Eiduson, *Scientists: Their Psychological World* (New York: Basic Books, 1962), pp. 89, 94, 95. Eiduson also proposes that a "disinclination of some scientists for having to respond to personalized considerations and for taking responsibility for others" affects their participation in public issues (p. 228).

6 This finding parallels that of Anne Roe, who states, with respect to her sample of American scientists, that "their political views ranged from rather rightist to very leftish, with the bulk of them definitely liberal." *Op. cit.,* p. 228 (note 5 above).

⁷ See Chapter Three.

⁸ The *n* in each of the CERN groups, especially the French, is rather small, but the consistency of differences which came to light in the analysis justifies their serious discussion. Care should be taken, of course, not to carry the implications too far.

⁹ Space was provided beneath each question for the respondent to expand his multiple-choice answer. Many respondents made little or no use of this space, but some individuals unburdened themselves of comments ranging from wisecracks to philosophical treatises.

¹⁰ See Chapter Ten.

¹¹ Witness, for example, the Pugwash Movement, the Vienna Declaration, the Arms Control seminars, and other formal and informal activities in which many prominent physicists have participated.

ANNEX SIX

¹ Louis J. McQuitty, "Agreement Analysis: Classifying Persons by Predominant Patterns of Response," *The British Journal of Statistical Psychology*, Vol. IX, Part I (May 1956).

² We, in fact, did perform an experiment utilizing factor analysis on our 1965 British data. Employing Goodman and Kruskal's symmetrical lambda (see Les A. Goodman and William H. Kruskal, "Measures of Association for Cross-Classification," *Journal of the American Statistical Association*, Vol. 49 [December 1954]) as a measure of association between our variables, we constructed a lambda matrix which was then factor analyzed. The experiment succeeded in identifying a group of respondents who possessed a cluster of "nationalist attitudes." Our interest in factor analysis, however, waned as the taxonomic program we discuss here became available.

³ It is possible to specify a minimum number of questions which must be answered by both respondents in order to calculate a similarity ratio. This will prevent misleading similarity ratios based on insufficient information. The program will not include these cases in the clustering process.

⁴ The clustering algorithm used in this program is called the "single-linkage" method. This description is derived from the fact that clusters are formed and expanded on the basis of simple pairwise similarities. In contrast with this algorithm, the "average-linkage" method requires a new cluster member to have a minimum average similarity with the entire cluster membership. We feel that the "average-linkage" method will eventually lead to clusters with higher internal validity. For a complete discussion on clustering algorithms see Robert R. Sokal and Peter H. A. Sneath, *Principles of Numerical Taxonomy* (San Francisco: W. H. Freeman and Company, 1963).

ANNEX SEVEN

¹ The reader is referred to the following papers, all by Stuart McIntosh and David Griffel: "ADMINS for Computer-Based Library Management," M.I.T. Center for International Studies Document No. C/67–28; "The ADMINS Primer," M.I.T. Center for International Studies Document No. C/67–30; "The Current ADMINS System for Non-Textual Data," M.I.T. Center for International Studies Document No. C/67–26; "The Language of ADMINS," M.I.T. Center for International Studies Document No. C/67–27.

² A "console" is a device similar to a teletype machine, located at a point

remote from the actual computer (often in the user's own office), by means of which a user on a time-shared system can perform rapid question-answer operations on the computer at times of his own choosing.

[3] The work discussed here is that of Judson Benjamin, who was an undergraduate in Political Science at the time he performed the experiment.

Index